The Law and Theory of Income Tax

James Kirkbride
and
Professor Abimbola A. Olowofoyeku

Liverpool Academic Press

© James Kirkbride and Professor Abimbola A. Olowofoyeku 2001

First published in Great Britain by Liverpool Academic Press

A CIP catalogue for this book is available from the British Library

ISBN: 1-903499-00-3

The right of James Kirkbride and Professor Abimbola A. Olowofoyeku to be identified as the authors of this work has been asserted by them in accordance with the Copyright, Designs and Patents Act 1988.

Typeset by Bitter & Twisted. bitter@cybase.co.uk.

Printed and bound in Great Britain by
Athenaeum Press Ltd, Newcastle upon Tyne

Preface

According to an old Chinese saying, 'may you live in interesting times!'. Tax lawyers are currently living in such times. The advent of a New Labour Government in 1997 ushered in an era of sustained change in the UK tax system. Many of the changes are subtle, but their effect is often far reaching. Income tax is one area which has witnessed such change. Out is the old 'cash basis', and in are two new rates of tax. Schedule A has all but disappeared. Tax avoidance has also attracted the attention of the Chancellor of the Exchequer, and the prospect of a general anti-avoidance rule for the UK looms ever closer. Not to be outdone by the Chancellor, the courts have also been very busy, sometimes intruding into areas where Parliament has feared to tread. The Chancellor may not need to introduce a general anti-avoidance rule because the House of Lords may have done this for him already (witness *IRC v McGuckian*). The question of what constitutes 'plant' keeps recurring, and issues relating to the taxation of compensation payments once again occupy their Lordships.

What, apart from an up-to-date analysis, does a book like this have to offer in these interesting times? What we offer is a different approach. This book seeks to present the reader with a critical analysis of the theories and principles relating to the taxation of income in the UK. In so doing, we undertake detailed analysis of the case law and tackle some of the underlying assumptions thereof. The emphasis is on theory and legal principles rather than the mechanics of implementation. We seek to raise questions and issues to generate debate, rather than to provide prescriptive opinion. However, we also provide a thorough analysis of the law as it is, endeavouring in the process to identify broad themes and general principles. While much of the discussion is academic in nature, we are convinced that students, practitioners and decision-makers would benefit as much as scholars from the analysis and the issues raised for debate. We hope that this book will be a valuable resource, providing reference material for scholars and practitioners alike, and providing instruction for students of taxation.

contents

Chapters and Statistics

chapter one
Tax - History, Functions and Systems

Although the majority of this book is devoted to an examination of the principles and policy surrounding the direct taxes of income, capital gains, and inheritance tax, it is important to develop an awareness of the history of taxation and the declared or presumed functions of tax. It is also of interest to be aware of the *ad hoc* nature of the UK tax system and opportunities and choices for reform. It is suggested that the sections on 'functions' and on 'systems' ought to be revisited once you have acquired and developed a working knowledge of the principles and operation of some of the direct taxes. Your ability to constructively analyse suggested reforms will be enhanced by your understanding of some of the substantive taxes.

The final part of this chapter considers some of the implications for revenue law of our membership of the European Communities.

History and Functions

Income tax was introduced in this country by Pitt in 1799.[1] Its purpose was to finance the cost of the war against France. It was charged on the world-wide income of British residents and the British income of non-residents. This 'temporary' measure was repealed in 1802 (a temporary peace in the war with France) but reintroduced by Addington in 1803. Addington made a number of adjustments and reforms to Pitt's system. In particular, Addington introduced a schedular system of taxation and assessment - a system that remains today![2] Peace in 1815 resulted in the expiration of the 1803 Act. A tax-free period was then enjoyed until 1842 when Peel re-imposed taxes broadly on the previous lines. Once again, it was believed to be a 'temporary' measure but was periodically re-imposed and remains today. The development of tax law and taxation has extended from pure income tax on individuals to encompass taxes on the income of companies

---

[1]   Although it should be noted that taxes and their influences might have been felt at an earlier time. For example, King John's demand for 'scrutage' contributed to the crisis of 1215 and the subsequent submission and the issue of Magna Carta. It should be appreciated that 'tax' has proved difficult to define. The OECD's definition is, 'the term taxes is confined to compulsory, unrequited payments to general government'. This is perhaps the most useful working definition of tax.

[2]   The details of today's Schedules are presented in later discussion.

(corporation tax) and taxes on the capital receipts and gains of individuals and companies through the introduction of capital gains tax, inheritance tax and corporation tax. As we shall see later, the various taxes and their methods of introduction and application have created many opportunities for tax planning and avoidance.

Apart from the above direct taxes introduced on the capital and income of individuals and companies, a number of indirect taxes have been introduced into the United Kingdom. Generally, indirect taxes do not apply directly to our income but are paid indirectly through our expenditure. For example, they are often found to be included in the final price we might pay for goods. Value added tax (VAT) is the more well-known and apparent indirect tax. It is also the tax that is causing concern at European level and is subject to reform.

Finally, it is interesting to note that although income tax in the United Kingdom reflected the development of many overseas systems of taxation - they also commenced life in response to the need to raise finances for periods of war and developed into a complex system imposing tax on most low income individuals - it has been suggested that the British tax system differs from its overseas equivalents in two ways.[3] First, it raises taxes under a system of schedules[4]. Second, its system of collection at source is widespread and sophisticated. The PAYE system is a familiar example of the latter. A further example of collection at source and an indication of the system's expansion is apparent in the 'net' interest payments received on ordinary building society and bank saving accounts. Collection at source necessarily results in a hidden cost. For example, one only needs to reflect on the administration costs to the employer of 'agreeing' to act as tax collector through the imposition of the PAYE system.

Functions and Principles of Taxation

It has been suggested that the tax system has become the 'maid of all work'.[5] This description emphasises the range of functions that taxes and the tax system might perform or be asked to perform. These functions often include a combination of a management function, a redistributive function and a general need to raise revenue. We saw the need to raise revenue in the introduction of income tax to finance warfare. Today, that need might still be one of maintaining the armed forces along with a wider range of

---

[3]   See S. James and C. Nobes, *The Economics of Taxation*, at Chapter 8.
[4]   See later discussion of the Schedular system.
[5]   In the Budget of March 1993, the then Chancellor of the Exchequer announced that in looking for extra revenue he had to be guided by three principles: '... that where possible money should be raised in a way that will not damage the working of the economy'; '... this means reducing the value of allowances and broadening the tax base ... and ...';'.. that taxation should support social, health and environmental objectives'.

services such as law and order and education. But today the raising of revenue is not the sole function of tax - this was strikingly illustrated in the suggestion that a slight increase in income tax rates would compensate for any lost revenue that might ensue if we agreed the removal of capital gains tax and inheritance tax. Of course, the removal of capital gains tax and inheritance tax is unlikely. They exist for their own reasons and support other general objectives and functions of our tax system. In particular, they might make a contribution to the objective of affecting a redistribution of wealth.

The redistributive function will find differing degrees of support reflecting political persuasions and pressures. The progressive tax rates are often perceived as a reflection of the equitable imposition of higher rates of tax upon those who enjoy the greatest ability to pay those rates. Similarly, one could refer to the introduction of capital gains tax as an example of imposing tax on these who were fortunate enough to enjoy their 'wealth' in a form other than as income. An interesting redistributive proposal was the suggestion that a number of tax deductions ought to be replaced by a system of tax credits. It was believed that tax credits would be much more useful to low income families[6] - particularly because the absence of taxable income removed the usefulness of a tax deduction.

Contribution to the management of the economy is a widely accepted function of taxation. Examples of this can be found in the way in which tax rules and allowances are used to control expenditure and inflation; and in the way in which we are encouraged to invest in the UK economy through tax exempt or advantageous savings schemes. For example, Personal Equity Plans (PEPs) have proliferated in the UK since their introduction in the late 1980s. They provide an opportunity to invest in stocks and shares with the advantages of tax-free profits. A similar proliferation can be seen through the introduction of ISAs.

In introducing a 'Saver's Budget' in 1986 the then Chancellor of the Exchequer increased the annual limit on a PEP investment to £6,000 and limited the requirement that the monies must be invested in UK equities to 50 per cent of the portfolio. The Chancellor declared his intention of encouraging long-term investment in shareownership. In the same Budget, the Chancellor introduced the 'Tax Exempt Special Savings Budget' (TESSA). The stated intention of the TESSA is to 'introduce a wholly new tax incentive which will reward saving and encourage people to build up a stock of capital'.

---

[6]   This was a recommendation of the Carter Report in respect of taxation in Canada, the Report of the Royal Commission on Taxation, RC Canada (1966).The UK also considered a tax credit system in the 1972 Green Paper, 'Proposals for a Tax Credit System'.

The management of the economy and the use of tax often involves aspects of credit control, customs' duties and to a lesser extent the control of, or influence on, behaviour. The latter is apparent in the investment and savings behaviour of PEPs and TESSAs, but might also include social behaviour such as taxation of alcohol, tobacco and car fuel. This has become more apparent in the March 1999 budget for the 'family, enterprise and the environment'. It should be noted that Individual Savings Accounts are to replace PEPs from April 1999.

The Principles of Taxation

In developing a tax system to facilitate the above functions (or any other functions) it is normal to consider the 'principles' upon which a tax system ought to be based. These principles are often the measure against which one would judge whether a tax system is good or bad. In considering and developing such principles, the accepted starting point is Adam Smith's proposed canons of taxation[7].

1. Equity - people should contribute taxes proportionate to their incomes and wealth.

2. Certainty - taxes should be certain and not arbitrary.

3. Convenience - the timing and manner of payment of taxes must be convenient.

4. Efficiency - the costs of collecting and imposing taxes must be kept a minimum. The costs of collection should represent a small proportion of the revenue collected. The taxes should be efficient in that they do not distort behaviour - the principle of 'neutrality'.

Over the years, these canons of taxation have been reviewed and discussed and have occasionally been presented under similar or revised headings. For example, in 1978 the Meade Committee considered the 'Characteristics of a Good Tax Structure' as representing six heads[8] :

1. Incentives and economic efficiency.

2. Distributional effects.

3. International aspects.

4. Simplicity and costs of administration and compliance.

[7]   Adam Smith, *An Inquiry into the Nature and Causes of the Wealth of Nations* (1776).
[8]   'The Structure and Reform of Direct Taxation' : Report of a Committee chaired by Professor J. E. Meade, The Institute of Fiscal Studies (1978) at Chapter 2.

5. Flexibility and stability.

6. Transitional problems.

The principles proposed by Adam Smith still dictate and influence thinking in this area.[9] We shall consider aspects of those principles together with aspects of the 'characteristics' proposed by the Meade Committee, under four heads :

1. efficiency
2. incentives
3. equity
4. stability considerations.

Our choice of these 'headings' reflects the economic influences on tax system and reform.

Efficiency

The efficiency of the tax system often involves consideration of its economic efficiency and contributions, and its efficiency measured in terms of administration and costs of compliance. The costs of compliance are the easier to appreciate and recognise. Adam Smith expressed concern over the proportional costs of collection. Similar concerns were expressed by the Meade Committee. The Committee emphasised the need to consider the potential costs of administrative complexity and the pure costs of administration. The latter should incorporate official administrative costs and also the (often neglected) tax compliance costs incurred by the private taxpayer. The Meade Committee believed that private compliance costs were often in excess of the official administrative costs - but were often ignored when judging and analysing the operation of the tax system. Examples of the private costs of compliance would include: the costs of the employer in operating as a tax collector under the PAYE system; the costs imposed on a trader in complying with any VAT system; the social costs to the community of the investment of manpower in developing a tax advisory and avoidance industry; and the costs to the public sector in trying to hinder or prevent any process of tax avoidance. The process of tax change also brings with it the costs to the taxpayers and the authorities of adaptation and response.

The actual costs of compliance ('the hidden costs of taxation') are more difficult to calculate than administrative costs, although attempted calculations and estimates do support the Meade Committee's conclusions that compliance costs are 'substantial'.[10] The Meade Committee's conclusions included the advice that we 'tip the balance away from

---

[9]   For a useful introduction, see James and Nobes, *The Economics of Taxation*. See also, Kay and King, *The British Tax System*.

[10]   Sandford, 'Hidden costs led compliance costs to represent 2.5-4.4 per cent of the revenue collected during 1970'.

compliance costs on to official administrative costs' and develop a coherent tax system that is simple and easy to understand with the consequent advantages of acceptability.

Economic efficiency (or contributions) often invites recognition of what is known as the excess burden of taxation. Economists regard 'efficiency' in terms of contributions to the 'optimal allocation of scarce resources'. Such an allocation demands the existence of perfect competition; and that market forces (supply and demand) dictate the price of goods and services and the allocation of scarce resources of factors of production. In the 'real' world perfect competition does not exist and influences on supply or demand can distort allocations and price, with the accompanying inefficient effects on the economy. The imposition and use of tax can distort choices and subsequent allocations. It is that 'distortion' that amounts to the 'excess burden' of tax. The traditional example is the avoidance of window tax in 1747 when many taxpayers bricked up their windows rather than pay tax. This 'cost' resulted in a lack of amenity with no consequent benefit to the Government or the economy, it represented the excess burden of the window tax.

Similarly, the Meade Report refers to the 'substitution effect' whereby taxes contribute to economic inefficiency by interfering with consumer choice. The Meade Report cites examples: 'the wage earner reducing his hours of work in order to substitute untaxed leisure or do-it-yourself activity at home for taxed work'; 'the housewife who may substitute untaxed domestic work for taxed earnings outside the home'; and 'the business executive who refuses promotion and thus substitutes his present occupation for the alternative more productive job, because the low post-tax increases in his earnings do not compensate for the social costs of moving'. These examples, and others, represent the loss or 'costs' (the excess burden) of tax.

Similarly, it was reported in the *Financial Times* (28 November 1986) that compliance costs represented 3.3 per cent of the tax yield for 1983-84.

Two particular examples of 'excess burden' that we will consider in detail in later chapters are the use of fringe benefits, and tax evasion and avoidance.

Fringe benefits represent those benefits in kind that employees receive instead of salary or income. The hope is that the benefits in kind will escape tax. If the 'benefit' had been received as income or as part of the salary it would probably be taxable. We will examine, in later chapters, the detailed rules for the taxation and assessment of benefits in kind, but at this point it is important to appreciate the potential inefficiency of fringe benefits. If, for example, instead of receiving a company car (a fringe benefit) an employee was provided with the cash equivalent, he would then have the choice of how he might spend that money. That freedom of choice would accord with the economist's concept of 'perfect competition' and his choice would better influence the factors of supply and demand and the allocation of scarce resources. For instance, he could choose to buy a cheaper form of transport (a used car) and invest the remainder or spend it on consumer goods of a different kind.

Tax evasion and avoidance is difficult to measure. The 'loss' or 'costs' represents the effort and the monies expended in avoiding or even evading liability. It is estimated that evasion, and thus the 'cost' and 'loss', is widespread. For example, in 1979 the Chairman of the Board of Inland Revenue suggested that it was 'not implausible' that tax evasion monies could amount to 7.5 per cent of the gross domestic product.

Incentives

Many regard the concept and consideration of incentives as an aspect and measure of tax efficiency, and to that extent 'incentives' belong to the principle of efficiency above. Incentives examine the way in which the tax system should or does encourage people to work, save and invest, and accept risks of enterprise and innovation.

We previously mentioned the 'substitution effect' of taxation and the taxpayer's surrender of work and effort in favour of other benefits such as leisure, hobby and do-it-yourself crafts. Similarly, the tax system might contribute to a substitution effect in relation to forms of business organisation. One might choose to operate as an unincorporated association rather than an incorporated business, depending upon the tax regimes and advantages. Alternatively, one might opt for a less profitable but relatively risk free business instead of the development of a risky venture, albeit that such a development would provide wider benefits to the economy and the community (if successful).

In relation to savings and investment, the 'substitution effect' is often discussed in terms of the 'double taxation of savings' : 'savings' often come from earned income that has already been subject to taxation, and those savings and any interest returned will be subject to further tax. One can point to our discussion on PEPs, TESSAs and ISAs as examples of government attempts to encourage savings and investment in a particular direction through the removal of a 'double taxation' principle.

It is widely believed that an expenditure tax would provide a wider incentive to save essentially because it would, like PEPs, TESSAs and ISAs remove any 'double taxation' fear.

In terms of incentive effects, much discussion and emphasis is placed upon comparing the incentive effects of different forms of taxation. For example, it is widely believed that a progressive tax rate has potentially a higher disincentive effect on work effort than a proportional income tax system or a poll tax system. Similarly, it is believed that indirect taxes are more attractive to savers than progressive income tax rates which contribute to 'double taxation'.

The major difficulty in relation to incentives and tax is measurement. It is difficult to measure incentive responses to tax systems and change. For example, although there have been many studies whose conclusions and reports appear to support the widely believed views on incentives, tax rates and work effort, the methodology, precision and accuracy of the studies have caused concern.[11]

Equity

Equity initially demands a consideration of whether a tax is 'fair' and equitable. 'Fairness' involves subjective judgments although some objective acceptance and perception of the 'fairness' of a tax and a tax system is necessary in order to avoid adverse consequences. For example, evasion and taxpayer resistance to taxation can dramatically increase if the system or the tax is perceived to be unfair.

In considering 'fairness' it is normal to recognise the importance of 'horizontal' and 'vertical' equity. 'Horizontal' equity demands that tax systems treat equal people in equal circumstances in an equal way. 'Vertical' equity permits discrimination between taxpayers in order to facilitate a redistribution between rich and poor. The Meade Committee reported that a good tax system should be horizontally equitable, ie should treat like with like, and that 'a modern tax system must be so constructed as to be capable of use for vertical redistribution between rich and poor.'[12]

An example of an equity argument supporting the introduction of a tax is apparent in the case of capital gains tax. During its introduction in 1964, the Chancellor of the Exchequer, stated that :

---

[11]   See Atkinson and Stiglitz, 'Lectures on Public Economies', (1980); Brown, *'Taxation and the Incentive to Work'*, (1983).
[12]   Supra n8, at Chapter 2.

'Capital gains confer much the same kind of benefit on the recipient as taxed earnings more hardly won. Yet earnings pay full tax while capital gains go free. This is unfair to the wage and salary earner.'[13]

The development and promotion of 'equity' of tax incorporates problems of the definition of 'income', 'wealth' and 'ability to pay'. It also invites discussion of the need to consider tax capitalisation; distribution and the incidence of tax; inflation; and tax avoidance and evasion. Tax capitalisation involves tax benefits being incorporated in and reflected in the capital value of an asset. For example, mortgage interest relief has been reflected, over time, in the increased demand and price of housing. Once this has occurred, it becomes difficult and perhaps inequitable to remove the tax concession. In the instance of mortgage interest relief, those who had paid relief-inflated prices would suffer a capital loss.

The distribution and incidence of tax is difficult to measure. It is assumed that a progressive tax rate coupled with the extension of tax beyond pure income tax has reflected a movement towards equality of liability. However, in determining equality of distribution it is important to appreciate the 'incidence' of tax (who really pays for tax changes and increases). The incidence of tax might include the 'economic' incidence in that the economy and the consumer might suffer if a progressive income tax induces more leisure and less work effort. The consumer might also suffer if the 'incidence' is 'shifted' from the producer to the consumer; for example, through the incorporation of tax rises into the market price of the product or service.

Inflation and its effects on 'equity' are apparent in relation to both earned and unearned income. In relation to earned income it is important under a progressive tax rate system to make proportional adjustments to counter the effects of inflation. Thus, the Chancellor might seek to raise personal allowances and rate bands by the amount of inflation in order to seek to avoid any fall in 'real incomes'. In relation to unearned income, we find complex rules to allow an indexation system to apply to capital gains in order that taxpayers pay for 'real' rather than inflationary gains.

Tax avoidance and tax evasion[14] often contribute to the 'hidden costs' of taxation, but more importantly they have an adverse effect on redistribution because of the retention of wealth by those who successfully operate or contribute to avoidance schemes - an unintended distribution! In addition to the redistribution 'inequity', widespread tax avoidance and tax evasion might contribute to the development of a perception of the 'acceptability' of

---

[13]   Hansard, vol 710, col 245.
[14]   See later discussion on the concepts of evasion and avoidance.

avoidance (or worse still, evasion!) which might find further wasteful avoidance and evasion. It is necessary for the legislature and the courts to respond appropriately to artificial avoidance schemes in an attempt to curtail and prevent any perceptions of 'acceptability' - unless, of course, we wish to follow some of our European partners in accepting evasion as a moral duty!

Stability

We mentioned earlier, that one of the functions of tax and tax systems is a contribution to the management of the economy. To economists and others, the use of the tax system in managing the economy ought to promote 'stability'. The Meade Report emphasised the need 'for a certain stability in taxation in order that persons may be in a position to make reasonably far-sighted plans. Fundamental uncertainty breeds lack of confidence and is a serious impediment to production and prosperity.'[15]

In promoting stability in the economy, taxation is a useful part of any government's armoury - yet, at an apparently contradictory level, taxation must allow flexibility and change. The flexibility and change is required in order to respond to different political views and changes and different trends and thinking in economic policy. The tax system must be able to respond and adjust to monetary policy or fiscal policy while providing and supporting economic stability.   Economic stability and stabilisation demands recognition of the relative merits of the various taxes; the size of the tax base; the speed of adjustment and influence of tax changes (the 'implementation' and 'response lag'); and the development of built-in flexibility methods, such as progressive tax rates.   Within these considerations it is clear that a good tax system must permit a change of emphasis in economic policy in order to reflect changes in government and thinking but appreciate that 'Such changes of emphasis will show themselves in the trade-off which is preferred among the various objectives of a good tax system.'[16]

Tax Reform

Tax reform requires a 'tax system which looks like someone designed it on purpose.' (W. E. Simon, former Secretary to US Treasury). Such a system would, presumably, address the principles and functions of taxation and demonstrate and achieve appropriate distributions and contributions. In the

[15]   Supra n8.
[16]   Supra n8.

United Kingdom we have, at times, seen aspects of reform and consolidation, but little in terms of a coordinated review and reform of our overall tax system and burdens[17], perhaps because the process of review and reform contains a number of fundamental difficulties. An interesting, unofficial review of the UK tax system was conducted by the Meade Committee, on behalf of the Institute of Fiscal Studies.[18] Although both the Committee and its Report have been subject to much criticism and comment, the Report is useful in identifying anomalies and areas of concern in the UK tax system, and in providing a comparison with an expenditure tax system. It is also believed that the Report will influence and make a contribution to future tax reform.

An Expenditure Tax

The Meade Committee was set up in mid-1975 and reported in 1978. Its brief was to 'take a fundamental look at the UK tax structure'. It must be noted that to make its task 'manageable' the Committee quickly decided to exclude consideration of some taxes, in particular excise taxes, local rates, stamp duties, petroleum revenue taxes and aspects of value added tax. In reaching its conclusions, the Meade Committee considered that the present anomalies in the UK system ought not to remain and that it would be necessary to move to a pure income tax or to a pure expenditure tax.[19] The Committee, for reasons that we shall explore, preferred the option of an expenditure tax. An expenditure tax involves a calculation of an individual's consumption expenditure not an individual's expenditure *per se*. For example, one might start by calculating an individual's income for any period and add to that income any capital receipts and borrowing. This would enable us to calculate an individual's 'spending power'. Sensible and desirable spending in the form of savings and investment would then be deducted from that 'spending power'. The remaining balance would represent the individual's consumption expenditure and it is that 'expenditure' (consumption) which would be subject to tax - progressive or otherwise.[20]

The concept of an expenditure tax is not new. It can be traced back to the writings of Thomas Hobbes and of John Stuart Mill. Nor is the concept of an expenditure tax confined to this country. In 1977 the US Treasury produced a 'Blueprint for Basic Tax Reforms' based on expenditure tax principles; similarly in 1978 the Swedish Royal Commission on Taxation proposed reforms along the lines of an expenditure tax. Despite these

---

[17]   We have experienced periods of consolidation, and periods of occasional and limited reforms, such as the reform of the unit of assessment to permit independent taxation of husband and wife (introduced on 6 April 1990).

[18]   Supra n8.

[19]   The anomalies and concessions that concerned the Committee included, (i) the distortions in the capital markets through preferential treatment of some investments (eg Pensions), (ii) the disincentive of progressive rate tax and the use of wasteful fringe benefits, (iii) the tax capitalisation problems of some concessions, such as mortgage interest relief. Others have suggested that the UK tax system ought to be considered for reform because (i) the costs of administration are comparatively high, (ii) the system is not internationally compatible; and (iii) historically, the PAYE system is out-of-date and unnecessary.

[20]   An 'expenditure tax' ought to be regarded as (or even called) a 'cash-flow income tax'. See Kay, *Fiscal Studies*, Vol 7, No 4, page 9.

proposals the only known experience of expenditure tax systems were in India and Ceylon in the 1950s.   In both instances, the systems were impractical and were abandoned - an event that was not considered by the Meade Committee.

The perceived advantages of an expenditure tax are: that it increases incentives to save and invest; it avoids the need to distinguish capital from income (although one would have to distinguish 'saving' from 'expenditure or consumption'); it provides a base to tax an individual on what he takes out of (or 'consumes') rather than on what he puts into the economy (although some economists believe 'consumption' is economically beneficial).

Even if one accepts the basis and principles of an expenditure tax, one wonders whether it is practically possible to consider its total introduction into the United Kingdom.   For example, some tax concessions have been capitalised into assets.   A sweeping removal of those concessions would remove the value of those assets and penalise those who had purchased or invested on the basis of existing concessions.   Similarly, those individual enjoying retirement might constantly be 'taking out' of the economy monies to support their day-to-day activities.   Those monies might derive from lifelong capital investments and pensions.   To penalise such 'consumption' might be perceived as inequitable.   When he was Chancellor of the Exchequer, Mr N. Lawson was caused to remark that a system of expenditure tax was 'quite impracticable, even if it was desirable' (1984 Budget Speech).

Credit must be given to the Meade Committee in recognising possible transitional problems and responding by suggesting two alternative approaches to the introduction of an expenditure tax.   The first approach involved the introduction of a universal expenditure tax based on the consumption principle and applicable to all taxpayers.   The second approach involved the introduction of a two-tier expenditure tax.   The lower tier would consist of a single rate of tax levied on expenditure or consumption through a form of value added tax (VAT or ITVAT as the Committee calls it).   The upper tier would be a 'universal expenditure tax' but limited in its 'universal' application to higher rate taxpayers with higher levels of expenditure - a sort of surtax on the higher level consumers.   It would be intended that over time the threshold for the application of the universal tax to those in the upper tier would eventually be lowered to a degree where the universal tax would be truly universal in its coverage and then the special VAT would be removed - proposal one, the favoured proposal, would then have been achieved.

As mentioned earlier, the Meade Committee and its Report were subject to criticism and comment.[21] Some critics referred to the unofficial nature and actual composition of the Committee; many critics commentated on the practical problems of the introduction of an expenditure tax - particularly transitional problems and the ultimately heavy reliance on a process of self-assessment; and some critics were concerned over the suggested benefits of an expenditure tax. Some economists perceive that consumption is economically beneficial and ought not to be discouraged or penalised.

Similarly, some particular (alleged) benefits of an expenditure-based tax have come under scrutiny. For example, it has been suggested that although an expenditure tax might increase the return to saving there was little evidence to suggest that it would substantially increase the level of saving. There is also some belief that expenditure tax would result in higher tax rates (needed to offset the loss of capital tax receipts) which in turn might present a disincentive to work, especially in instances of immediate consumption. Nor is it firmly believed that an expenditure tax would necessarily promote equity; a person's wealth might indicate a person's ability to pay but careful placing of that wealth (through exempt savings and investments) removes the obligation and liability to pay.

It is interesting to note that one of the driving forces behind the Meade Committee's appointment and proposals, the need to consider the removal of anomalies and concessions and the development of a coordinated and principled tax system, might itself be in danger should the Committee's proposals ever be formally adopted. It is clear that in any process of tax reform special interest groups are capable of obtaining *ad hoc* concessions and contribute to the development of anomalies through the process of 'pressurising'. There is little to suggest that such interest group concessions and anomalies would not be present in the process of change to an expenditure tax.

Finally, although there has not been a wholesale introduction of expenditure tax into the United Kingdom it is beginning to appear in the form of influencing recent tax developments. For example, the introduction of Personal Equity Plans (PEPs) in the 1986 Budget stirred the reaction that this represented

> ... the transfer of quoted shares from the category of 'no fiscal privilege' to that of 'Expenditure Tax' or better ... the principle that

---

[21]   See Prest 1978 BTR 176.
[22]   J. A. Kay, *Fiscal Studies*, 1986 Vol 7, No 2, at page 35.

direct personal investment in equities is intended to be a privileged form of saving has now been clearly established ....'[22]

A Comprehensive Income Tax

The Meade Committee reported that the UK tax system fell somewhere between a pure (or comprehensive) income tax system and an expenditure tax system. Its principal reason for dismissing reform in favour of the former was that

> ... it would be extremely difficult, if not impossible, to introduce all the features of a comprehensive tax. In particular, we think that many of the measures which would theoretically be necessary to index the system for proper capital income adjustments against inflation would not be practicable.[23]

Despite any apparent practical difficulties, the development of a comprehensive income tax has been the subject of serious consideration, particularly in Canada.[24] In essence a comprehensive income tax, often referred to as a tax on the 'accretion of economic power', requires that tax is imposed on actual or imputed increases in wealth or economic power. The increase in wealth would include consideration of 'wealth' at the beginning and at the end of the tax period together with a consideration of consumption during that period.

In 1966, the Carter Report[25] was presented to the Federal Government of Canada with the recommendation that a comprehensive income tax be introduced. The Report attracted the accolade that 'it must rank as the most comprehensive and detailed blueprint for tax reform ever created.'[26]

The recommendations of the Carter Commission included the introduction of a new comprehensive base for income tax. This new base would enable tax to be imposed on all gains in purchasing power. Such gains, whether they occurred from actual or deemed capital disposals, would be classed as taxable 'income'. At the same time, the Commission proposed a general reduction of the tax rate, a reduction that could be achieved through the

---

[23]   Supra n8 at p500.
[24]   It must be recognised that the debate and discussions of the Carter Commission will influence the reform debate in other countries. This was apparent in the tax base rate reforms in the United States in 1986.
[25]   The Report of the Royal Commission on Taxation, Canada, 1966. Chaired by Kenneth Le M Carter.
[26]   Sandford, [1987] BTR 148.

widening of the tax base.

Other recommendations of the Carter Commission included the integration of personal and corporate income tax and the removal of capital investment and allowance incentives. The latter were perceived as important in removing major sources of tax avoidance.

It is interesting to note that the Carter Commission considered the functions and principles of tax and was concerned at the need to reconcile any conflicts in terms of economic growth, stability, individual freedoms and Government policy. The Commission's overriding objective in supporting the introduction of a comprehensive income tax was the promotion of 'horizontal equity'. It was the Commission's view that the development of 'fair taxes should override all other objectives'; the comprehensive income tax was perceived as providing a good indicator and measure of the ability to pay.

Although the Carter Commission's Report was initially welcomed, it appears that little of it has been implemented or enacted.[27] Much of that 'failure' must be accounted for by the particular political changes in Canada. However, it is probable that the Carter proposals, like the Meade Committee proposals, would face common problems and barriers in the process of tax reform. These include the following.

Pressures from Special Interest Groups

We mentioned in relation to expenditure tax that anomalies and concessions could develop as a consequence of special interest groups. Examples of the 'pressurising' that might be experienced are found in some of the responses to the Carter proposals. It is reported that the 'business lobby' and the 'farm lobby' made strong representation in respect of the proposed treatment of death and gift taxes.

Social and Economic Views

It has been suggested that one of the reasons why the Carter proposals may have failed to have been implemented is that the economic arguments and base of the proposals are no longer 'vogue'. Social attitudes change in terms of priorities and 'horizontal equity' might not now be appropriate. Regional policies selective investment policies and redistribution might now

---

[27]   See Sandford, ibid.

be priorities. An extreme example of difference in social attitudes can be found in some jurisdictions where tax evasion is socially acceptable and often encouraged. By contrast, in the United Kingdom, tax evasion and avoidance is believed to attract social stigma.

Short-term Political Goods

It is clear that if any sweeping tax reforms are to succeed, they must enjoy political support. This need raises two problems. First, the proposals themselves ought to be as a consequence of political initiative and emanate from an official committee. The Meade Committee Report, initiated and appointed by the Institute of Fiscal Studies, failed to enjoy the necessary 'official' status. Second, both the expenditure tax system and the comprehensive income tax system require a long-term commitment and ability to withstand public criticisms and concerns. Despite the long-term benefits of enjoying a tax system based on a coherent set of principles, it is highly probable that those who suffer during the transition would vehemently pursue their own short-term goals of defeating the changes and restoring their benefits. That 'short termism' might also apply to the politicians. Apart from the amount of Parliamentary time that sweeping changes would absorb, it is unlikely that the Parliamentary term of a government would be sufficient to facilitate long-term changes and withstand short-term unpopularity. Any attempt at introducing wholesale changes might realistically be viewed as political suicide.

British politicians used to be told that if they changed the tax system the gainers would not thank them and the losers would not forgive them. If a Chancellor really wanted to make a reputation as tax reformer, he was advised to lie down until the feeling had passed.[28]

Role of Inland Revenue

It has been suggested that tax reform in Britain will never substantially take place unless we reform the Inland Revenue first.[29] Criticism is placed at the dominant policymaking role performed by the Inland Revenue. Not only is this comparatively unique, but also inappropriate. The Inland Revenue does not possess the necessary awareness or expertise to contribute to and consider the socio-economic and political realities of reform, it is merely equipped to consider administrative criteria and perform administrative functions. It has been suggested that the Inland Revenue's role should be

---

[28] J. A. Kay, *Fiscal Studies*, 1990, Vol 7, No 4, at p1.
[29] Ibid at p3.

confined to the latter and that tax policy and reform should clearly be placed in the hands of the Treasury, perhaps assisted by a body of advisors. Recent developments, Mr Lamont's body of 'wise men', might constitute a tangible response to this area of criticisms and concerns. This body of independent tax advisors (the wise men) has been continued by Mr Lamont's successors.

Finally, despite these procedural and process difficulties it is widely accepted that the 'British tax system is complex, inefficient and unfair' and that reform is necessary.[30] The manner and method of reform is subject to opinion and debate but it is agreed that it must be coherent and caused on principle, and probably incremental in approach and implementation.

The Plain Language and Structure of Tax Legislation

One of the criticisms and perceived barriers to the reform of tax law is directed at the language and mass of detail of tax legislation: in fact it was reported that in November 1995 there were nearly 6,000 pages of Inland Revenue primary legislation, representing an increase of over 50 per cent since 1988.

A number of initiatives have been taken to address concerns over language, structure and volume. The Institute of Fiscal Studies set up a Committee back in 1994 to examine these concerns. It subsequently recommended that a pilot project be adopted to see if an expensive rewrite could be justified: it estimated that a rewrite would take about five years and involve a team of up to 40 people. The Institute's Final Report on Tax Legislation was published in June 1996. In the meantime the Inland Revenue delivered to Parliament its Report, 'The Path to Tax Simplification', in December 1995. Subsequently the Inland Revenue has published another consultative document, August 1996, setting out proposals for carrying out the review and rewrite recommended in the Institute of Fiscal Studies Final Report on Tax Legislation. The Revenue aims to make the rewritten laws as easy as possible to understand, through logical ordering of the provisions, directness of expression and clear and simple layout. Difficult decisions exist in terms of layout: should it take an activity-based approach or one that reflects type of taxpayer, or type of tax or subject-base ? Should it rewrite all the legislation at the same time and go for a 'big-bang' introduction, or

---

[30] For a useful discussion on reform and principle see M. Wilson, *Taxation*, Chapter 12.

should it seek to reap the benefits of incremental reform through a staged introduction ? Who should comprise the reform/rewrite team: public/private sector experts or a combination ?

Whatever the answer to these and the many other questions raised by the Reports, it is interesting to note the recognition of the problems and of the time-scale to achieve a revision of the problems of language, detail and volume. Perhaps the system and experiences of 'self-assessment' might increase public awareness and experiences of the problem. One suspects that until public opinion is strong enough that successive governments will avoid the costs and disruption of a sweeping rewrite of tax legislation whatever the perceived long-term benefits, albeit that the 'Tax Law Rewrite' project has commenced.

Commentators on the early experiences of the rewrite suggest that it is likely to be an extremely long document in that it is an attempt to rewrite the law and practice of income tax, not just current legislation. The essence is an attempt to change the wording of laws without trying to change the meaning.   It should embrace extra-statutory concessions and rules for practice in addition to principles from case law and legislation. It is indeed a big challenge although the Government has confirmed that it is 'committed to proceeding with the rewrite project on the basis of full consultation in that the aim is to prepare a series of rewrite Bills, the first Bill likely to be ready for exactment is the capital allowances rewrite Bill.'[31] The following main Acts are to result, but from a steady progressive introduction rather than any 'big bang' event.

Income Tax (either tax-based or individual-based).

Corporation Tax (either tax-based or company-based).

Capital Allowances.

Capital Gains (computational provisions).

Stamp Duties.

Inheritance Tax; and Management.

EU and International Influence

The operation of our tax system and its development and reform must

---

[31]   See http://www.inland revenue.gov.uk/

consider EU and international influences. International influences have always been present. For example, there is a need to consider comparative treatment of the taxation of individuals and corporations. High tax rates might result in emigration of individuals and corporations. Similarly, the tax treatment of capital will influence investment decisions and locations. It is clear that the tax-induced mobility of these factors of production will have a distorting effect on the locality and transfer of these factors; the tax system is not neutral but is influential in determining the allocation and location of scarce resources. One need only refer to the intentions of the Government in the Republic of Ireland, when it set a corporation tax of 10 per cent in the hope of attracting manufacturing industry and corporations, to illustrate the distorting effect of taxation.

Other international effects of taxation include concerns over jurisdiction and enforcement. These involve the difficulty of negotiating double tax treaties and international cooperation. The fiscal and economic needs of some countries present difficult, and at times insurmountable, hurdles to cooperation on jurisdiction and enforcement matters. The OECD has a model code and agreement but this model is not binding and is often viewed as biased in favour of the economies of Western Europe. Other models have been suggested and developed, but they also suffer from perceived prejudice and favour.

Through its membership of the European Union, the United Kingdom has participated in the debate on aspects of tax reform in areas where barriers and distortions are apparent. It is important to appreciate that tax reform is necessary if the Union aims to facilitate the free movement of goods, services, people and capital and the freedom of establishment is to be fulfilled. This demands that the European Union considers and embarks on an ambitious harmonisation programme of both direct and indirect taxes. Thus far it has been progressing reform and harmonisation in areas of corporation tax and indirect tax in the form of VAT reforms. Its progress in the area of corporation tax reform will be considered at a later stage in the chapter on Corporation Tax - suffice to say at the moment that the Commission's progress has been slow and somewhat disappointing. The issue of indirect tax reforms has also been slow but is beginning to come to fruition. The operation and rates of VAT have had a distorting effect on the transfer of goods and services.[32] In a series of Directives the European Union has accepted a framework for a common system of VAT and the Union countries are working toward the ultimate aim of a harmonised system of rate bands, although political difficulties remain. As part of the

---

[32]   Since 1967, the Community has been working on the approximation of VAT and to this effect it adopted a long line of directives. For example, see the First and Second Directives (67/227/EEC and 67/228/EEC) which required member states to adopt a system of VAT. The comprehensive rules on VAT are to be found in the Sixth Directive (77/388/EEC) entitled 'harmonisation of the laws of the Member States relating to turnover taxes - common system ofvalue added tax and uniform basis of assessment'. Numerous directives and decisions have been adopted to limit or amend Directive 77/388 (see Directive 83/181).

push for the creation of the 'internal market', transitional measures came into force on 1 January 1993 and remained in force until 31 December 1996. These transitional measures involved a limited harmonisation and a response to the abolition of fiscal frontiers. The 'measures' were included in the Finance Bill 1992[33] and involve (broadly) amendments whereby exports from a member state to other member states will no longer be subject to VAT, while imports from other member states would be (an 'acquisitions' principle). Tax charged in one member state will be deductible in another member state ('reverse charge' principle); whereas imports from non-EU countries will still be subject to taxation. The precise details of the operation of VAT are outside the scope of this work, but it is important for the reader to appreciate that VAT is one of those areas of taxation where we are beginning to experience EU-driven reforms.

Increasingly there has been a call for European tax powers giving to Europe its own 'tax sovereignty'. Thus far this has been resisted, although some countries, including Belgium, believe that some formula must be found for a Europe-wide tax to replace contributions to the EU budget. The latest Budget Committee Report (March 1999) suggests that the EU should gain direct responsibility both for raising and spending revenue with the conclusion that EU taxes would have to come 'sooner or later'.

---

[33]   The transitional system is an amendment of Directive 77/388 (Directive 91/680/EEC).

chapter two
The Territorial Scope

Introduction

United Kingdom taxation is subject to a territorial limit, the cardinal principle being that the tax legislation does not extend beyond the jurisdiction. As far as income tax is concerned, this territorial aspect of income tax can be formalised into two propositions, which were clearly expressed by Lord Wrenbury in *Whitney v IRC*[1].

The policy of the Income Tax Act is to tax the person resident in the United Kingdom upon all his income whencesoever derived, and to tax the person not resident in the United Kingdom upon all income derived from property in the United Kingdom. The former is taxed because (whether he be a British subject or not) he enjoys the benefit of our laws for the protection of his person and his property. The latter is taxed because, in respect of his property in the United Kingdom, he enjoys the benefit of our laws for the protection of that property. The rules applicable in respect of other taxes are roughly similar, although they may differ in important respects.

This territorial limit to income tax was approved as still being a correct statement of the law by Lord Hailsham LC in *National Bank of Greece SA v Westminster Bank Executor and Trustee Co (Channel Islands) Ltd*.[2]

More recently, in *Clark v Oceanic Contractors Inc*[3], a case in which the principle of territoriality was applied to UK legislation generally, Lord Wilberforce said that, as a statement in respect of liability to pay income tax, it is 'still broadly correct'. This territorial principle, as far as it applies to UK legislation generally, is a principle of construction only, and can give way to express words or necessary implication. As far as it relates to income tax, it is to be found in the income tax Acts themselves.[4] There are a number of possible explanations for the existence of this territorial limit in the tax statutes. First, it may be, as Lord Scarman said in *Clark v Oceanic Contractors Inc* that Parliament is simply recognising the 'almost universally accepted principle that fiscal legislation is not

1   (1925) 10 TC 88 at 112; see also Lord Herschell in *Colquhoun v Brooks* (1889) 14 App. Cas. 493 at 504; also, the Royal Commission on the Taxation of Profits and Income, First Report, Cmnd 8761 para. 8 (1953).
2   [1971]1 All ER 233 at 236.
3   [1983] 1 All ER 133 at 143-4.
4   See Lord Scarman in *Clark v Oceanic Contractors Inc*, [1983] 1 All ER at page 139.

enforceable outside the limits of the territorial sovereignty of the kingdom', and that fiscal legislation is therefore drafted in the knowledge that 'it is the practice of nations not to enforce the fiscal legislation of other nations'[5].

On the other hand, it may be a case of Parliament not wanting to'go beyond its rights with regard to the comity of nations'.[6] It may also be a question of practicality. It is unlikely that the UK tax gatherer will be able to collect any tax charged on a person who is not present in the UK, and who has no UK income or property.[7]

The Connecting Factors

The main factors which connect a person to the UK's territorial limits for tax purposes are residence, ordinary residence, nationality (citizenship), and domicile. Of these, residence is by far the most important, while nationality is, by itself, not of great significance. Practicality, as referred to above, and yield may be the most important reasons why residence, as opposed to nationality, is preferred by the tax system as the main connector. Using nationality as the connector would result in substantial loss of tax because foreign citizens working in the UK would escape tax, while it might be impossible to collect tax from UK citizens who live and work abroad. This result may of course be commended by the fact that it would attract foreigners to the UK and thereby generate more revenue to circulate within the economy generally. But the loss of tax revenue to the exchequer may not be recouped by the spending power of the foreigners, and there may be reasons why the UK might not want to encourage such an influx of fiscal refugees. The residence connector avoids the problems inherent in the nationality connector, but both might, for different reasons, lead to adverse results for the exchequer in cases of increased emigration and/or birth rate.[8]

As connecting factors, the terms 'residence' and 'ordinarily resident' are normally used in United Kingdom tax legislation to describe a situation arising in a year of assessment, and not in relation to some longer or shorter period. The question that has to be decided is generally whether or not a person is resident or ordinarily resident in the United Kingdom in the year of assessment.[9]

This is generally the same question that has to be decided in respect of the domicile of a person. The 'United Kingdom' in this context refers to England,

5   Ibid.
6   See Lord Esher MR in *Colquhoun (Surveyor of Taxes) v Heddon*, (1890) 2 TC 621, at 625; compare Fry LJ at 630.
7   See generally E.. C. D. Norfolk (1980) BTR 70.
8   For a discussion about the emigration of persons and capital see A. Park (1976) BTR 20.
9   See Inland Revenue Statement of Practice, IR 20, para. 7.

Scotland, Wales and Northern Ireland and does not include the Isle of Man and the Channel Islands.[10]

There are a number of general points to note with respect to the territorial scope of United Kingdom tax. Generally, a United Kingdom resident is taxable in respect of all income and capital gains wherever arising. Such a person will also be liable to inheritance tax, unless he is not domiciled in the United Kingdom and he has no United Kingdom property. A non-resident will be taxable on income arising from sources within the United Kingdom, and will be liable to capital gains tax, if he is ordinarily resident, or if he is trading through a branch or agency in the United Kingdom and he disposes of assets used for the purposes of that branch or agency. There may be liability to inheritance tax unless the non-resident is also not domiciled here, and has no property here.

Residence[11]

While residence is the most important of the territorial connectors for liability to United Kingdom tax, the term is not defined by statute. This lack of a definition serves to ensure that the application of legislation in which the term is used 'is haphazard and beyond all forecast.'[12] This led Viscount Sumner to voice a powerful criticism of the situation that then was, and, regrettably, still is.

T]he subject ought to be told, in statutory and plain terms, when he is chargeable and when he is not. The words 'resident in the United Kingdom', 'ordinarily' or otherwise, and the words 'leaving the United Kingdom for the purpose only of occasional residence abroad', simple as they look, guide the subject remarkably little as to the limits within which he must pay and beyond which he is free. This is the more likely to be a subject of grievance and to provoke a sense of injustice when, as is now the case, the facility of communications, the fluid and restless character of social habits, and the pressure of taxation have made these intricate and doubtful questions of residence important and urgent in a manner undreamt of by [the introducers of income tax]. The Legislature has, however, left the language of the Acts substantially as it was in their days, nor can I confidently say that the decided cases have always illuminated

10   Inland Revenue Statement of Practice, IR 20, page 3.
11   For a general discussion see A. Sumption (1973) BTR 155.
12   Viscount Sumner in *Levene v IRC* (1928) 13 TC 486 at 502.

matters. In substance persons are chargeable or exempt, as the case may be, according as they are deemed by this body of Commissioners or that to be resident or the reverse, whatever resident may mean in the particular circumstances of each case. The tribunal thus provided is neither bound by the findings of other similar tribunals in other cases nor is it open to review, so long as it commits no palpable error of law, and the Legislature practically transfers to it the function of imposing taxes on individuals, since it empowers them in terms so general that no one can be certainly advised in advance whether he must pay or can escape payment. The way of taxpayers is hard and the Legislature does not go out of its way to make it any easier.

In spite of the criticisms, Viscount Sumner was of the view that the statutory provisions in which the terms referred to are employed are 'plain'[13].

Thus for example, Lord Warrington of Clyffe said in the same case that the term 'has no special or technical meaning' for tax purposes[14], and it is often said that, since 'residence' has no special meaning for tax purposes, it has to be given its plain and ordinary meaning. This view found its earliest expression in *Re Young*[15] where the Lord President said that the court must deal entirely with the statute in reference to the 'natural and proper meaning' of the words. In *Lysaght v IRC*[16] Viscount Sumner said that the meaning of the word is its meaning in the speech of plain men, and that the question to be asked is whether plain men would find that the result of the facts found is 'residence' in its plain sense. The best known formulation is however found in the words of Viscount Cave LC in *Levene v IRC*[17].

The word 'reside' is a familiar English word and is defined in the Oxford English Dictionary as meaning 'to dwell permanently or for a considerable time, to have ones settled or usual abode, to live in a particular place'. No doubt this definition must for present purposes be taken, subject to any modification which may result from the terms of the Income Tax Act and schedules, but, subject to that observation, it may be accepted as an accurate indication of the meaning of the word 'reside'.

The concept of residence being related to a person's 'home' is evident from this definition, for it refers to the place where a person has his or her usual

[13]   Ibid.
[14]   (1928)13 TC 486 at 509.
[15]   (1875) 1 TC 57 at page 59.
[16]   (1928) 13 TC 511 at 529.
[17]   (1928)13 TC at page 505.

place of abode, or where he or she lives. This concept also appears frequently in judicial *dicta*. For example, the Lord President in *Lloyd v Sulley*[18] referred to the place where a person's 'ordinary place of abode'and 'home' is situated. Similarly in *Levene v IRC* Viscount Sumner said[19] that the taxpayer 'continued to go to and fro during the years in question, leaving at the beginning of winter and coming back in summer. His home thus remained as before. He changed his sky but not his home'. On this basis, the taxpayer was resident in the UK even during long trips abroad. While this concept of where the taxpayer's home is located is seen in many cases[20], as we shall see, the dictionary definition of residence, and the view that the word must be given its ordinary meaning, are both often honoured as much in the breach as in the observance. There have been cases in which individuals have been held to be resident in the United Kingdom who could neither be regarded as dwelling here 'permanently or for a considerable time', nor as having their 'settled or usual abode', or their 'home' here, nor indeed, as 'living' here. This situation is of course largely due to the factors pointed out by Viscount Sumner in his powerful criticism of the lack of statutory definitions in *Levene v IRC* (above). Be that as it may, it does sometime contradict the assertion that the plain and ordinary meaning of the term is to be used.

The principal question with regard to residence is whether a person is resident in the United Kingdom or not, and not whether a person is resident in this country or in another country. That is to say, the question is: 'is X resident in the United Kingdom?' and not for example: 'is X resident in France or in the United Kingdom?', for X may well be resident in the United Kingdom for United Kingdom tax purposes while at the same time resident in France under French law, and in Germany under German law. The Revenue and the courts in this country are not generally concerned with the last two situations, except perhaps in the context of double taxation agreements. As the Lord President said in *Cooper v Cadwalader*[21], it is not necessary in order for a person to be chargeable that he shall have his sole residence in the United Kingdom, and it has been recognised as far back as the 19th century that 'a man cannot have two domiciles at the same time, but he certainly can have two residences.'[22]

This principle has been incorporated into the Inland Revenue's code which states thus:

It is possible to be resident (or ordinarily resident) in both the UK and

---

[18]   (1884) 2 TC 37 at 42.
[19]   (1928) 13 TC at page 501.
[20]   See for example, Viscount Cave LC (dissenting) in *Lysaght v IRC*, 13 TC 511 at page 532.
[21]   (1904) 5 TC 101 at 106-107.
[22]   Per the Lord President in *Lloyd v Sulley* (1884) 2 TC 37 at 41. For an even earlier expression of the principle, see *AG v Coote* (1817) 2 TC 385 at 386 (Wood B).

some other country (or countries) at the same time. If you are resident (or ordinarily resident) in another country, this does not mean that you cannot also be resident (or ordinarily resident) in the UK[23].

While it is clear that a person may be resident in more than one place, it may be that a person cannot be resident nowhere. According to the Lord President in *Rogers v IRC*[24], 'a man must have a residence somewhere.' Why this is so is not clear, but as early as 1875 it was stated that this proposition does not require the aid of decisions or authority[25]. Thus a sailor who spends most of his time at sea nevertheless must have a residence on land, because a residence is a dwelling place on land[26], and the court cannot recognise 'that he lives so entirely on the sea as to have no residence on the land[27].'

Since both *Rogers v IRC* and *Re Young* involved sailors, it may be that this principle applies to sailors only, although it is difficult to see why that should be so.

Grammatically, the word 'resident' indicates a quality of the person to be charged to tax - it is not descriptive of his property, real or personal[28]. The relation between a person and a place which is predicated by saying that a person 'resides' there includes, *inter alia*, the element of time, duration, or permanence. However, that element, essential and importance as it is, is not the sole criterion, and thus whether a person is resident in the United Kingdom or not is essentially a question of fact and degree. The determination of whether or not the degree extends so far as to make a person resident or ordinarily resident here is for the Commissioners and it is not for the courts to say whether they would have reached the same conclusion[30].

---

[23]   IR 20, para. 1.4. Note that the situations in which a person may be resident in the United Kingdom and in another country in the same year are normally covered by double taxation agreements.
[24]   (1879) 1 TC 225 at 227.
[25]   See Lord Deas in *Re Young* (1875) 1 TC 57 at 61-62.
[26]   Per the Lord President in *Re Young*, 1 TC 57 at 59.
[27]   Per Lord Ardmillan in *Re Young*, 1 TC 57 at 63.
[28]   Per Viscount Sumner in *Lysaght v IRC* 13 TC at 528.
[29]   Lord President Clyde in *Reid v IRC* (1926) 10 TC 673 at 678.
[30]   Per Lord Buckmaster in *Lysaght v IRC* 13 TC at 534.

The Residence of Individuals

The determination of an individual's residence must be made for each relevant year of assessment (Viscount Cave in *Levene v IRC*). However, the taxpayer's conduct in years previous and subsequent to the relevant year of assessment is often relevant in determining whether the taxpayer was resident in that year. The Revenue have produced a fairly detailed Statement of Practice on the residence and ordinary residence of individuals (IR 20), which contains a code of principles that seems to be based largely on decisions in their favour. We shall refer to this code at various stages of our discussion.

The Revenue position is that, strictly speaking, each tax year must be looked at as a whole, that a person is to be treated as either resident or not resident for the whole year, and that he cannot be regarded as resident for part of the year and not resident for the remainder[31].

The Revenue will however split the year, by concession[32], if the person is a new permanent resident; or if the person comes to the United Kingdom for at least two years (provided that he has not been ordinarily resident in the United Kingdom); or if the person has left the United Kingdom for permanent residence abroad (provided that in so doing he ceases to be ordinarily resident in the United Kingdom); or, subject to certain conditions.

The conditions are that the absence from the United Kingdom and the employment itself both extend beyond a complete tax year, and any interim visits to the United Kingdom during the period do not amount to 183 days or more in any tax year, or an average of 91 days or more in a tax year. In this respect, the average will be taken over the period of absence up to a maximum of four years if the person goes abroad under a contract of employment. In the first two cases the person is treated as resident only from the date of arrival in the United Kingdom, and in the last two, he is treated as not resident from the date of departure.

There are a number of factors (derived both from case law and the Inland Revenue code IR 20) which are applied in the determination of the residence status of an individual. Some of them are of conclusive effect in themselves while some others, while not necessarily conclusive may, in combination with others, suffice to make an individual resident in the United Kingdom in a relevant year of assessment. Furthermore, some of the factors apply only to certain classes of individual while others apply generally. The discussion that follows examines these factors.

[31]   1IR 20, para. 1.5.
[32]   See ESC A11, 7th Feb. 1996.

Period of Physical Presence in the United Kingdom

Section 336(1) of the ICTA 1988 provides that an individual who is in the United Kingdom for some temporary purpose only, and not with a view to establishing his residence there, will not be charged to income tax as a person resident in the United Kingdom in any year of assessment, if he has not 'actually' resided in the United Kingdom for a period equal in the whole to six months in that year. Section 9(3) of the Taxation of Chargeable Gains Act 1992 has a similar provision in respect of Capital Gains Tax.

The corollary to this is that if an individual has actually resided in the United Kingdom for a period amounting to six months in any tax year, he will be taxed as a resident (s.336(1)(b)).

This provision relates only to the taxation, under Schedule D, of profits or gains received in respect of foreign possessions or securities. However section 336(2) extends the rule to tax charged under Cases I, II and III of Schedule E (income from offices, employments, etc), and the Revenue code IR 20 applies the rule generally.

The rule as stated could be seen as an exempting clause. In this context, its import was succinctly expressed by the Lord President in *Lloyd v Sulley*[33].

> The meaning of it is this: if a foreigner comes here for merely temporary purposes connected with business or pleasure, or something else, and does not remain for a period altogether within the year of six months, he shall not be liable for a certain portion of taxation imposed by Schedule D. He would have been liable but for this exemption; he would have been a person de facto residing in Great Britain. But it is thought that it would be rather hard to charge him when it is merely a visit here for a temporary purpose, and therefore this exemption is introduced. But that so far from derogating from the force of the words by which the tax is laid on in Schedule D, only confirms the view which I have taken of the true force of these words, because it shows that residence for a temporary purpose would have subjected to the tax if it had not been for this clause of exemption.

On the other hand, it could also be seen as a charging clause. Consider these words of Lord Shand in *Lloyd v Sulley*[34].

> It rather occurs to me that although the provision in section [336(1)] is

---

[33]   (1884) 2 TC 37 at 42.

in the language of exemption, as I have indicated in the course of the argument, it rather appears to me to be a section which is intended to impose liability, or to show that liability will be imposed upon persons who come to this country, but who are the subjects of other realms.

Lord Shand's is a lone voice, since most of the authorities assume that the rule is an exempting clause. However, the provisions of section 336(1)(b) that an individual who has actually resided in the UK for six months will be chargeable as a person residing here can be seen (because of the form of words employed) as one which does impose a charge. In any event, it seems not to make a lot of difference which way it is regarded.

What Constitutes Six Months?

The period of six months referred to in section 336 is calculated in terms of calendar months, rather than lunar months. In *Wilkie v IRC*[35] the Revenue argued for the use of lunar months (ie 28-day months), whereby six months would be equal to 168 days. Donovan J rejected this, saying:

> I see no rational purpose behind a provision that the months shall be lunar months. When one is determining how long a foreigner or a Briton from abroad should be allowed to stay in the United Kingdom before contributing, through income tax, to the expenses of the State, there is something at least intelligible, if arbitrary, about selecting one-half of the fiscal year. But to tax him because he has been here for 168 days out of 365 is unintelligible and merely whimsical[36]'

In *Wilkie* the taxpayer was of Scottish origin and was domiciled in Scotland, but lived in India. He arrived in the United Kingdom for temporary purposes at about 2pm on June 2 1947. He left the the United Kingdom at about 10am December 2 1947, his departure having been delayed for about two days as a result of a compulsory cancellation by the airline of his earlier departure reservation. The question was whether he had 'actually' resided in the UK for six months in that tax year. Donovan J[37] said that it was right to add up the number of days in which an individual had been actually resident in order to see whether those days, continuous or discontinuous, equaled the number of days in six calendar months. There was however the problem of what to do about fractions of a day, since an individual's stay will almost

---

[34]   2 TC 37 at 44.
[35]   [1952] 1 All ER 92
[36]   At 94.
[37]   Ibid.

always begin and end with a fraction of a day. The Revenue had argued for treating fractions of a day as a whole day, with the effect, as they argued, that both the days of arrival and departure were whole days within which the taxpayer was actually resident in the UK. By this interpretation, the taxpayer would have been resident in the UK for 184 days in the year 1947-48 and so would have been here for more than six months. This of course leads to difficulties. There is no reason why a taxpayer could not also also claim under that principle to have been actually resident outside the UK on the days of arrival and departure, since he was actually outside the UK for fractions of those days. The problem was thus presented by Donovan J[38].

> By applying the rule about fractions of a day one gets the absurdity that the taxpayer is actually resident outside the UK for more than six months and actually resident inside the UK for more than six months. In other words, he is both exempt and chargeable under the rule.

Unsurprisingly, Donovan J rejected the rule about fractions in favour of a rule taking account of a lower unit of time than a complete day 'to arrive at the truth and avoid a fiction'[39].

This required an examination of the actual number of hours spent here, which in this case was some four hours below the limit. Arguments by the Revenue as to the administrative inconvenience that such a rule would cause were rejected on the basis that the burden of proving the facts justifying exemption under the six month rule lay on the taxpayer who has to establish his case for exemption[40].

No doubt in consequence of this decision, the Revenue practice now is to consider only whole days, but leaving the days of arrival and departure out of the calculation, thus avoiding the type of problems encountered in *Wilkie*. Under the IR 20, six months is equated with 183 days, whether or not the year is a leap year, ignoring the days of arrival and departure, and a person is who in the United Kingdom for this 183 day period in one year of assessment will, without exception, be treated as resident[41].

The Exemption

It is noteworthy that the six-month period specified in the rule relates to the time spent in the UK in each year of assessment - so it is possible in theory for a visitor to actually spend more than six months in the United Kingdom

---

[38]   At 96
[39]   Ibid.
[40]   At 97.
[41]   IR 20, para. 1.2.

without being resident, if the period is spread over two years of assessment (for example, from February to August). This point should be taken with care, because if the visits become regular, even though each one is for a duration which is less than six months in each tax year, it is still possible, taking into account other factors, for an individual to be resident. It is also quite easy to fall foul of the terms of the exemption itself. According to Lord McLaren in *Cooper v Cadwalader*[42]:

> this six month exemption is 'one that walks upon two legs'. It requires, first, that the party is here for a temporary purpose only, and secondly, that he is here not with a view or intent of establishing a residence. If the argument is lame on one of the legs, then the party does not get the benefit of the exemption, because he must be able to affirm both members of the double proposition.

The interpretation of the first part of the exemption, the meaning of 'temporary purpose', is pertinent to the issue of visits being spread over two years of assessment. In this respect Lord McLaren said[43].

> Temporary purposes mean casual purposes as distinguished from the case of a person who is here in the pursuance of his regular habits of life. Temporary purpose means the opposite of continuous and permanent residence. Nobody ever supposed that you must reside twelve months in the year in order to be liable for Income Tax, and therefore 'temporary' does not mean the negation of perpetuity, but means that it is casual or transitory residence, as distinguished from a residence, of which there may be more than one, but which may be habitual or permanent.

The vital words here are 'regular habits', 'casual' and 'transitory'. An individual who spends eight months in the United Kingdom spread over two years of assessment may well be stretching those words to their limits, since it is not entirely clear when the visit may be considered to have ceased to be casual or transitory. That the courts sometimes take a strict view of the matter is evident from *AG v Coote*[44].

In that case the taxpayer was domiciled in Ireland, and lived there for most of the year. He bought and furnished a house in London, where he stayed for a few weeks from time to time. The question was whether he was taxable

---

[42]   (1904) 5 TC 101 at 108-109.
[43]   At 109.
[44]   (1817) 2 TC 385.

as a UK resident in respect of his profits received here from his possessions in Ireland. The Barons of the Court of Exchequer held that he was. Graham B said[45] that it was 'quite impossible to say that the residence of the defendant in England was occasional, or for a temporary purpose' since at any period of the year he might have come to London, where he would have found his house ready for him. Wood B said that if the taxpayer had come to reside in London for a temporary purpose, he might have qualified for exemption, but said that 'it is clear that his residence here, while it continued, was for all manner of purposes.[46]'

With regard to the taxpayer's house, he said[47] that 'if this were a temporary residence, he would probably change it sometimes, but in fact it is his own house.' But for recent legislation (see the discussions below on the 'place of abode rule'), this type of statement would have raised serious issues as to whether any foreigner who owns a house in this country would ever be able to qualify for this exemption. However, more pertinent to this present discussion is the Wood B's statement that the taxpayer was here for 'all manner of purposes.' Presumably then, 'temporary purposes' is not the same thing as 'all manner of purposes', or to put it differently, 'all manner of purposes' extends beyond 'temporary purposes', and is therefore not permissible. Temporary purposes may therefore signify some sort of cohesiveness or singularity of purposes, all of which are 'temporary'.

With respect to the words 'view or intent of establishing his residence' in the second part of the exemption, the situation is just as interesting. In *AG v Coote*[48],

Richards CB said:

> The fact of the defendant's domicile has nothing to do with the question, nor has the time of his residence any effect on the construction of the words of the Act; for if the defendant came here for the purpose of establishing a residence, it were enough, although he should reside here only two weeks. The sole question is, whether he came here to reside with such a view as exempts him.

In the same case Graham B asked rhetorically, 'if a man dies two days after forming his establishment, is he not within the Act?'[49]

The answer presumably was 'yes, he is within the Act'. Thus in this context Lord McLaren said in *Cooper v Cadwalader* that there seemed to be a recognition of what may be called 'a constructive residence as distinguished

---

[45]   At 385.
[46]   Ibid.
[47]   At 386.
[48]   2 TC 385.
[49]   Ibid.

from actual residence'. According to him[50]

> It is not that you take a house or country place with a view or an intention of establishing a residence, although you may not have had time to become a resident. Still, if you are looking forward to it, apparently that makes you liable to taxation, because in order to get the benefit of the exemption you must say that you have no view and no intention of acquiring a residence there.

What Lord McLaren is saying is that this part of the exemption contains a very subjective element: did the taxpayer in fact have the view or intention of establishing his residence here? If subjectively this is found to be so, then he cannot claim the benefit of section 336(1). It therefore seems that the exemption thus granted to people who visit the United Kingdom is fairly limited in scope. Those who visit the United Kingdom for temporary purposes will be well advised to actively seek not to 'look forward to' establishing a residence here, and to avoid actively all activities which may be so construed.

Absence for a Whole Tax Year

It is possible for an individual to be resident in the UK even when he or she has not been physically present in the UK at any time during that year[51]. However, if an individual is absent from the United Kingdom for the whole of a year of assessment, it is more difficult for the Revenue to assert that he is resident in the UK in that tax year. This point is illustrated by *Turnbull v Foster*[52].

The taxpayer carried on business for about 40 years as a merchant in Madras where he had his residence. His children lived in the family home in the United Kingdom and he had over the years visited them for short periods nearly every year. The taxpayer and his wife were not in the United Kingdom at any time during the year in which the Revenue sought to assess him as a person residing in the United Kingdom. Not surprisingly, the Revenue's attempt failed. The fact that he was never in the country during the year was vital. The Lord Justice Clerk said that to hold the taxpayer resident in those circumstances 'would require a pretty strong case indeed'[53].

It is important to note however that the taxpayer in *Turnbull v Foster* had not

---

[50]   5 TC at 109.
[51]   See Nicholls J in *Reed v Clark* (1985) 58 TC 528 at 547.
[52]   (1904) 6 TC 206.
[53]   At 209.

previously been ordinarily resident in the United Kingdom, a fact noted by the court. For example, the Lord Justice Clerk said[54]: 'This gentleman has a usual residence in Madras - a usual residence - and he was in that usual residence for the whole of the year of assessment.' Lord Trayner also referred to the taxpayer's 'usual residence' being in Madras, and equated his usual residence with ordinary residence[55].

In the case of an individual who has previously been ordinarily resident, other factors may apply to make him resident, even though absent from the United Kingdom throughout the tax year. One of these is the 'place of abode' rule (below), and another is the principle that an individual must have a residence somewhere. So for example, in *Rogers v IRC* (above), a master mariner whose wife and family lived in the United Kingdom throughout the year in which he was abroad was taxed as a resident notwithstanding his absence for the whole year. According to the Lord President[56]:

> The circumstance that Captain Rogers has been absent from the country during the whole year to which the assessment applies does not seem to me to be a speciality of the least consequence. That is a mere accident. He is not a bit the less a resident in Great Britain because the exigencies of his business have happened to carry him away for a somewhat longer time than usual during this particular voyage.

Ordinary Residence in Previous Years

An individual's ordinary residence in the United Kingdom in years prior to a year of assessment in which his residence status is at issue is statutorily relevant only in respect of Commonwealth citizens or citizens of the Republic of Ireland. The relevant rule is in section 334, which provides that, if a Commonwealth citizen or a citizen of the Republic of Ireland who has been ordinarily resident in the United Kingdom leaves the United Kingdom for the purpose only of occasional residence abroad, he shall be assessed and charged to income tax as a person residing in the United Kingdom, notwithstanding such absence.

Compare paragraph 2.1 of IR 20 which simply states: 'You are resident and ordinarily resident in the UK if you usually live in this country and only go abroad for short periods only - for example, on holiday or on business trips.' This paragraph says nothing about the person being a Commonwealth

---

[54]   At 210.
[55]   Ibid.
[56]   1 TC 225 at 227.

citizen or a citizen of the Irish Republic. If it is intended to apply to individuals who are not Irish or Commonwealth citizens, its legality is doubtful.

This rule is, in spite of its wording (starting as it does with a reference to assessments, thereby appearing to be of a procedural nature), a substantive charging provision[57].

The rationale therefore has been thus expressed:

> Now that is a very important provision as extending the meaning of the words in the taxing clause, 'residing in the United Kingdom.' It extends it to a person who is not for a time actually residing in the United Kingdom, but who has constructively his residence there because his ordinary place of abode and his home is there, although he is absent for a time from it, however long continued that absence may be[58].

With respect to the terms used in this rule, the individuals who have the status of 'Commonwealth citizen' are described in section 37 of the British Nationality Act 1981. We shall discuss the meaning of 'ordinary residence' later in this chapter, and we shall consider now the meaning of 'occasional residence' abroad.

Occasional Residence Abroad

Section 334 applies to Commonwealth or Irish citizens who have left the UK for the 'purposes of occasional residence' abroad. What does this phrase mean in this context? The term been considered in a number of cases. It seems that the words 'purpose', 'residence', and 'occasional' are each vital here. Combined, they seem to refer to what the individual was seeking to achieve by going abroad. In ascertaining this, it is valid to examine the taxpayer's conduct in the relevant year of assessment as well as in other years of assessment, as this may throw light on the purpose with which the first departure from the UK took place. Such examination may go to show 'method and system' and so remove doubt which might be entertained if the years were examined in isolation one from the other[59].

It has been held that all the reasons underlying a person's being in a particular place are relevant[60]. So for example, a master mariner who has a

---

57   Per Nicholls J in *Reed v Clark*, 58 TC 528 at 552.

58   Per the Lord President in *Lloyd v Sulley* (1884) 2 TC 37 at 42.

59   See Viscount Sumner in *Levene v IRC* 13 TC 486 at 501.

60   Per Nicholls J in *Reed v Clark*, 58 TC 528 at 556.

home in this country, but spends considerable amounts of time abroad with his ship, cannot be considered to have gone abroad for the purposes of occasional residence. According to Lord Deas in *Re Young*[61]:

> He does not go into foreign parts beyond the seas for the purpose of occasional residence. He must live at the port he trades to for a considerable time. He may live on shore or on board the ship according to his mind, but he goes there, not for occasional residence, not for residence at all, but for the purposes of his trade.

By this token, it would seem that a business person who is merely going abroad on a business trip, no matter for how long, is only going abroad for his or her trade, and not for the purpose of residence - 'occasional' or not. Lord Deas seems to require that, in order for that phrase to be satisfied, there must at least be a purpose to reside abroad. This is the same thing as saying that the individual must be purposing or intending to live abroad, or to make his home abroad. So, a trading purpose is not necessarily a residence purpose, since trading abroad does not necessarily imply living abroad or making one's home abroad. It seems clear also that a prolonged stay abroad due only to enforced circumstances does not equate to a residence purpose[62]. In this respect, Nicholls J said in Reed v Clark[63]:

> There is nothing in the language or in my view the context of [s 334] to show that regardless of the circumstances a person can never be said to have left for the purpose only of occasional residence abroad if his residence abroad extends throughout an entire tax year. A man ordinarily resident here may go to live abroad in March intending to return some months later but through serious illness of himself or others or other unforeseen change of circumstances not return until the end of the following March. I can see no reason why, depending upon all the facts, such a man may not fall within [s 334]. If that is right, it would be absurd that such a man should fall outside [s 334] if the emergency which kept him abroad should chance to last for a week or two longer and not permit his return until after 5 April.

But if an individual is actually purposing to reside or live abroad, can this correctly be considered to be a purpose of occasional residence only? Since residence refers to a person's 'home', would an individual who purposes to live or make her home in France for a defined period - say, six months - be

[61]   1 TC 57 at 62.
[62]   See Hanna J in *Iveagh v Revenue Commissioners* [1930] IR 386 at 422.
[63]   58 TC at 553.

living in France for occasional residence only, or would the intention to make a home abroad necessarily connote something else? What then is a purpose of occasional residence? Let us examine some interesting cases. In *Levene v IRC*[64] a retired businessman who had previously been both resident and ordinarily resident in the United Kingdom went (in December 1919) to 'live abroad'. From the date of departure until some time more than five years later, he maintained no fixed place of abode anywhere, but stayed in various hotels, both in this country and abroad. In 1925, he finally was able to secure a flat in Monte Carlo for himself and his wife. During the years that he spent abroad, he spent an average of 20 weeks each year in the United Kingdom, his purpose being to obtain medical advice, to visit relatives, to take part in certain Jewish religious observances, and to deal with his income tax affairs. It was held by the House of Lords that the taxpayer originally left the United Kingdom and went to live abroad for occasional residence only, and so was resident in the United Kingdom in the years in question. According to Viscount Sumner[65]:

> The evidence as a whole disclosed that Mr. Levene continued to go to and fro during the years in question, leaving at the beginning of winter and coming back in summer, his home thus remaining as before. He changed his sky but not his home. On this I see no error in law in saying of each year that his purpose in leaving the United Kingdom was occasional residence only. The occasion was the approach of an English winter and when with the promise of summer here that occasion passed away back came Mr. Levene to attend calls of interest, of friendship and of piety.

In this case, the court thought that it could identify an 'occasion' which led to the occasional residence abroad - the English winter. In another case, no such occasion was identifiable, and thus the decision went the other way. In *IRC v Combe*[66] the taxpayer, who had been both resident and ordinarily resident in the United Kingdom left for the purpose of a three-year apprenticeship under a New York employer. The object of his apprenticeship was to qualify him as European Representative of the New York firm, and his employment accordingly made it necessary for him to visit Europe, and especially the United Kingdom from time to time on his employer's business (at times spending almost six months). On these visits he lived in hotels and throughout the three years he had no house and no fixed place of abode in this country. Instead, his business and residential headquarters were

[64]   (1928) 13 TC 486.
[65]   At 501.
[66]   (1932) 17 TC 405.

permanently in New York throughout the three years. It was held that the taxpayer's departure was not a departure for the purpose of occasional residence abroad and he was not resident in the United Kingdom in the years in question. Lord President Clyde said[67] that 'occasional residence' is residence taken up or happening as passing opportunity requires in one case, or admits, in another, and contrasts with the residence, or ordinary residence, of a person who is 'resident' or 'ordinarily resident' in some place or country. Lord Sands, concurring, noted that there was a 'distinct break'in the nature of the taxpayer's residence when he departed for America[68].

This concept of distinct (or definite) break was applied by Nicholls J in *Reed v Clark*[69]. The taxpayer left the United Kingdom for the USA with the firm intention of living in Los Angeles throughout the relevant year of assessment but to return to the United Kingdom shortly after the end of that year. He was away for a 13-month period which spanned the whole of the tax year, living for the most part in a house rented for him by a company under his control. Nicholls J held that, considering all the circumstances underlying the taxpayer's departure, including the fact that there was a definite break in the pattern of his life, his departure for the USA was not for occasional residence only. He ceased living in London, and for the whole tax year, he lived in or near Los Angeles, mostly in one fixed place of abode. He worked from there and for that year Los Angeles was his headquarters. The inescapable conclusion from the primary facts was that for the whole of the relevant year his home and place of business were in Los Angeles. He was thus not resident in the United Kingdom in the year in question. Nicholls J said that the meaning to be given to 'occasional residence' in the context of the relevant section was a question of law[70] and that occasional residence was the converse of ordinary or usual residence[71].

According to Nicholls J[72] a British resident's departure abroad for a period of a few weeks or months with the firm intention of returning to live here as before at the end of that period would most likely be always a departure for the purpose only of occasional residence. However, a firm intention to return to live as before is not necessarily indicative of occasional residence[73].

The difference is a question of degree, and 'there is an area where different minds may reach different conclusions.[74]'

So, a period of one year is 'long enough for a person's purpose of living where he does to be capable of having a sufficient degree of continuity to be properly described as settled'. Nicholls J thus concluded that the foreign country could be the place where, for that period, the individual was

---

i
67   At 410.
68   At 411.
69   58 TC 528; [1985] 3 WLR 142.
70   58 TC at 554.
71   Ibid.
72   At 555.
73   Ibid.
74   Ibid.

ordinarily and not just occasionally resident The Commissioners had found that the taxpayer's journey to America was not made as a matter of 'passing opportunity'. His business activities had previously taken him, and still took him to America, every year and on that particular trip he had established himself in a way which would make him both resident and ordinarily resident there under the United Kingdom rules. Summing up the matter Nicholls J said[75]:

> In this case there was a distinct break in the pattern of Mr. Clark's life which lasted (as from the outset he intended) for just over a year. He ceased living in London and for that year he lived in or near Los Angeles, mostly in one fixed place of abode, and he worked from there. For that year Los Angeles was his headquarters. He did not visit this country at all. On the whole I do not think that he can be said to have left the United Kingdom for the purpose only of occasional residence abroad. In my judgment the conclusion of the Commissioners on this was correct.

Thus perhaps it is easiest to look at 'occasional residence' first from the point of view of what it is not. It seems that a purpose to establish a settled residence (or to settle) abroad is not a purpose of occasional residence. Neither, it seems, is a purpose to establish a planned residence, not as passing opportunity requires or admits, but as part of a defined plan for a new lifestyle, either forever or for a specific limited period. A purpose of occasional residence on the other hand seems to be a purpose to reside abroad, but not for settled purposes - or perhaps a purpose to live, but not to settle abroad. The duration of the actual residence abroad does not seem to be the crucial factor[76], since for example prolonged residence abroad due to ill health does not necessarily impact on the original purpose for leaving this country. However, the duration of the proposed residence abroad may be important, as this may be indicative of whether there was a plan to settle (for a defined or indefinite term). Furthermore, the fact that the plan to reside abroad is motivated by fiscal reasons is not material. As Nicholls J said in *Reed v Clark*[77]:

> The presence of a tax avoidance intention may help to show, for instance, why a person went abroad at all, or at the particular time he did, how long he intended to remain away, or where his home in fact was in the year of assessment. But residence abroad for a carefully

---

[75]   AT 556.
[76]   *See Iveagh v Revenue Commissioners*, above.
[77]   58 TC at 556.

chosen limited period of work there (if that is what the facts establish) is no less residence abroad for that period because the major reason for it was the avoidance of tax. Likewise with ordinary residence.

The concept of a plan or purpose to live abroad seems clear enough. But the case of *Levene v IRC* appears to muddy the waters. Mr Levene and his wife had formed an 'intention to live abroad'. Both he and his wife had indifferent health, and had been advised by their doctors to live in the South of France and to avoid the UK in winter. In pursuance of his intention to 'live abroad', he sold his furniture, surrendered the lease of his house, and eventually went abroad. While abroad, he endeavoured to find a suitable flat in Monaco, but failed to find one until several years later. Viscount Sumner referred[78] to the rule charging the taxpayer as a UK resident if he had left the UK for the purpose only of occasional residence abroad, and asked 'Was that the only purpose of his leaving so far as residence is concerned?' This presumably presupposes that, if Mr Levene had any residential purpose which was not 'occasional', then the rule would not apply. The Special Commissioners had answered Viscount Sumner's question in the affirmative, and he felt that there was evidence before them on which they could so decide. According to Viscount Sumner[79]:

> His only declaration was that he meant to live abroad, not saying whether it was to be an occasional or a constant, a part time or a whole time sojourn. He was advised by his doctor to seek a better climate, which is consistent with returning to England when English weather minds. He had gone out of business in England and had broken up his establishment, but he still had in England business interests connected with his Income Tax assessments, and ties of filial piety and religious observance, for his father was buried at Southampton and he was himself a member of the English community of Jews.

With all respect to Viscount Sumner, it is difficult to see why any of these factors should matter. It seems clear that the taxpayer had formed an intention to live abroad, and to stop living in England. The fact that he had closed his English establishment and was looking for suitable accommodation in Monaco would be indicative of that. This fact was pointed out by Lord Warrington of Clyffe who said[80] that 'Since he gave up his house in 1918 he has had no intention of again taking a house or flat in

78   13 TC 486 at 500.
79   Ibid.
80   At 509.

the United Kingdom.' It is clear that an individual may easily decide to settle in another country while maintaining ties with his country of origin. Most emigrants do just that, and it would be odd if they did not. It would be impossible for an emigrant to also transplant all his family and friends, even if they were agreeable to the idea. Many emigrants will (financial and political considerations permitting) continue to visit their countries of origin frequently and for any number of reasons. Expatriate academics often do this during the summer vacations. Neither the retained ties nor the visits necessarily have any bearing on their original intention or purpose to emigrate from their home country and settle in another country.

In Levene's case, the Commissioners were 'satisfied' that Mr Levene had formed the intention of living abroad for the greater part of the year, but of returning to the UK each year and remaining here 'for considerable periods' in the year. Therefore, taking into account his past and present habits of life, the regularity and length of his visits here, his ties with this country, and his 'freedom from attachments' abroad, they came to the conclusion that, until 1925 when he took a lease of a flat in Monte Carlo, he continued to be resident in the UK. It seems that it was generally agreed that he ceased to be resident in the UK from the time that he acquired the flat. Contrast Lord Warrington of Clyffe[81], who preferred to leave that particular question open. Viscount Cave LC made reference to this 1925 event[82].

> He then went abroad from time to time, but continued to live in hotels either here or in France and he did not actually find a home abroad until the month of January, 1925, when he took a lease of a flat at Monte Carlo. The result is that during the period from the end of 1919 until January, 1925, he went much abroad, partly for the sake of his own and his wife's health, partly no doubt to search for a house or flat, and partly (as may be inferred from the finding of the Commissioners) in the hope of escaping liability to the English Income Tax.

Viscount Cave then went on to say that none of these purposes of going abroad was 'more than a temporary purpose'. In so doing, he referred to the fact that Mr Levene 'regularly returned to England for the greater part of the summer months though for less than one half of each year'.

Again, with respect to Viscount Cave, the fact that Mr Levene did not succeed in finding 'a home abroad' (obviously not from want of trying) does not seem to be a valid criterion for deciding what his purpose was in going

[81] AT 510.
[82] At 506.

abroad. It is not entirely clear how Viscount Cave came to the conclusion that none of Mr Levene's purposes was more than a 'temporary purpose'. What was so obviously temporary about all of them? If it was accepted that his leasing of a flat in 1925 changed his purpose of going abroad from temporary residence to a settled residence, what actually precipitated that change? Suppose that Mr Levene had succeeded in finding a suitable flat in 1920 - would this have meant that he had not gone abroad for occasional residence only? That would seem to follow from the reasoning of the Commissioners and the courts. It is true that a temporary purpose can change to a settled one. This would be the case if for example an individual went abroad to learn a foreign language for, say, four months, and while there, fell in love, got married, and decided to settle in that country. However, a lot of this would be directly related to the individual's own intentions. Clearly, Mr Levene had 'formed an intention to live abroad'. He had sought for accommodation, but only succeeded in finding one after a few years. It would seem to be obvious that his lack of success had nothing to do with his intentions, which seemed clear enough. The inescapable conclusion is that his inability to secure adequate accommodation operated against him by being somehow linked by the courts to his intentions or purposes in going abroad. This does not seem to be a correct way to looking at the matter.

Perhaps *Levene v IRC* can be explained from the point of view that the question involved was a question of fact and the courts were not prepared to disturb the Commissioners findings of fact without compelling reasons - a factor of some prominence in the speeches in the House of Lords. However, in applying this principle, statements were made which raise as many questions as they answer.

Regularity of Visits to the United Kingdom

The case of *Levene v IRC* (above) shows that where an individual makes regular visits to the United Kingdom for periods which are less than six months in any year of assessment, such an individual can still be treated as resident even if he has no home, business, or residential establishment in the UK. The crucial question is whether the visits are sufficiently regular to be part of his normal life. This point is illustrated even more vividly in *Lysaght v IRC*[81].

The taxpayer, born in England of Irish parents, was a Managing Director of an English company. After retiring from this post, he was appointed an advisory director to the company. He thereupon sold his house in England and went to live in Ireland, maintaining no definite place of abode in this country. His new position as a consultant to the company brought him to England every month for directors' meetings, on which visits he stayed for about one week, in hotels. The Commissioners held that he was resident and ordinarily resident in the United Kingdom in the year in question and this was upheld by the House of Lords (Viscount Cave LC dissenting). Viscount Sumner noted[84] that it was the shortness of the aggregate time during which Mr Lysaght was in the United Kingdom that constituted the principal point in his favour, but also noted that the question of longer or shorter time, like other questions of degree, is one peculiarly for the Commissioners. He did not doubt that the Commissioners had understood the word 'resident' in its proper legal signification and so applied it. Therefore their decision could not be interfered with. It is interesting however that Viscount Cave LC (dissenting) thought that the Commissioners could not rightly have arrived at their decision. His argument was powerful[85]:

In the present case the Respondent, Mr. Lysaght, has a permanent home in Southern Ireland where he lives with his family; but he comes to England once a month for business purposes, stays at an hotel and, when his business (which usually occupies about a week) is concluded, he returns home. It is unnecessary for me to repeat the observations which I have made in the previous case [*Levene v IRC*] as to the meaning of the expressions 'reside' and 'ordinarily reside'; and it is enough to say that, on the view which in that case I have taken as to the meaning of those expressions, there appears to me to be no reason whatever for holding that the Respondent is resident or ordinarily resident in this country. It is true that he comes here at regular intervals and for recurrent business purposes; but these facts, while they explain the frequency of his visits, do not make them more than temporary visits or give them the character of residence in this country. That he has a small account at a bank in Bristol - doubtless for use during his visits to this country - and a club in London to which he hardly ever goes, appear to me to be trivial circumstances which cannot affect the decision. If the Respondent is held to reside here and to be taxable accordingly, there would appear to be no reason why those many foreigners who periodically visit this country for business purposes, and having concluded their business go away, should not be made subject to a like burden.

Viscount Cave was a lone voice however, although his position seems to accord better with common sense than the position of the majority. Thus Mr Lysaght found himself to be a resident of two countries for tax purposes. The result then is that an individual may be held resident even if he has no place of abode (or home) at all (*Levene v IRC*) or no place of abode (or home) in the United Kingdom (*Lysaght v IRC*) if he makes habitual and substantial visits to the United Kingdom. For these purposes, 'substantial' means (as per the Revenue code IR 20) that the average annual period(s) of the visits amounts to three months (91 days) or more per tax year

Days spent in the UK for exceptional purposes beyond the taxpayer's control will be discounted for these purposes (see IR 20, para. 3.3). An example given in IR 20 of this scenario relates to illness of the taxpayer or a member of his family. The question here is what happens if the whole purpose of the visit is for medical treatment (no doubt derived from Mr Lysaght's visits of one week every month amounting to twelve weeks in a year), and 'habitual' means that this pattern has been followed for four consecutive years. In such a case, the Revenue will treat the individual as being resident from the fifth year[86].

If it is clear that the individual intends to follow this pattern from the beginning, he may be treated as resident from the beginning[87]. Presumably, the decision of whether an individual 'intends' to follow the pattern from the beginning can take cognisance of subsequent events.

The Purpose of the Visits to the United Kingdom

Closely connected with the last point is the purpose of the taxpayer's visits to the United Kingdom. If the person is merely in the United Kingdom as a traveller, and not as part of his regular order of life, the visits *per se* will probably not be sufficient to make him resident. For example in *IRC v Zorab*[88] the taxpayer was a retired member of the Indian civil service, who in the course of his habitual travels in Europe spent about five months in England each year, the sole purpose being to visit friends. He was held not to be resident by the commissioners, and this was upheld by Rowlatt J. Rowlatt J said[89] that one had to consider not only the time that the taxpayer was here but also the nature of his visit and his connection with this country. According to Rowlatt J, in this case the gentleman seemed to be a mere

---

[86]   See IR 20, para. 3.3.
[87]   See IR 20, para. 3.3.
[88]   (1926) 11 TC 289.
[89]   At 291.

traveller. He was a native of India and had retired from his work there, after which be began to travel extensively in Europe. In these circumstances there was sufficient evidence for the commissioners to hold that he was not resident.

It should be noted that this test as to the purpose of the taxpayer's visit is not conclusive, since a person may still be resident in the United Kingdom even if he is here for reasons beyond his control. That this is so can be established from the cases. In *Lysaght v IRC* (above) for example, the taxpayer only came to the United Kingdom for the purpose of board meetings, and not for the purpose of living here. This fact seemed to influence the Court of Appeal, which decided (by a majority) in his favour. However, that decision was reversed by the House of Lords. The inconclusiveness of volition is further illustrated by *Inchiquin v IRC*[90].

The taxpayer was an Irish peer, who had succeeded to the ancestral titles and estates (including a castle in Ireland) on the death of his father, but who was living in England. On the outbreak of the Second World War in 1939 he was called up for military service and became an officer in the British Army. In 1940 during the course of the war his mother, who was living in the castle in Ireland, died. The prevailing circumstances made it desirable that he should return to Ireland to live in the castle and look after the estate, and in particular to avoid being called an absentee landlord. However his military duties occupied him and he was not relieved until 1942 upon which he took up permanent residence in the castle in Ireland. The commissioners held that he was resident in the years 1940-41 and 1941-42, in spite of the fact that he had always wanted to return to Ireland but was forced to stay here. This decision was upheld by the Court of Appeal. Tucker LJ said[91] that he derived most assistance from the speech of Lord Buckmaster in Lysaght's case in which Lord Buckmaster said:

> A man might well be compelled to reside here completely against his will; the exigencies of business often forbid the choice of residence and though a man may make his home elsewhere and stay in this country only because business compels him, yet ... if the periods for which and the conditions under which he stays are such that they may be regarded as constituting residence, it is open to the commissioners to find that in fact he does so reside.

In this case there was sufficient evidence for the Commissioners to decide

90   (1946-50) 31 TC 125.
91   At 133-134.

as they did.

Place of Abode in the United Kingdom

The availability of accommodation or a place of abode to an individual is a factor that often points strongly to residence, because it indicates some sort of mental connection with the place where the place of abode is located. It may be indicative of an intention to establish a residence in that place. However, as we have seen in the context of regular visitors to the UK (Levene and Lysaght above), it is possible for an individual to be resident in the United Kingdom even though he has no home or place of abode here. The Lord President (Lord Clyde) noted this point in *Reid v IRC*[92].

> Take the case of a homeless tramp, who shelters to-night under a bridge, to-morrow in the greenwood and as the unwelcome occupant of a farm outhouse the night after. He wanders in this way all over the United Kingdom. But will anyone say he does not live in the United Kingdom? - and will anyone regard it as a misuse of language to say he resides in the United Kingdom? In his case there may be no relations with family or friends, no business ties, and none of the ordinary circumstances which create a link between the life of a British subject and the United Kingdom; but, even so, I do not think it could be disputed that he resides in the United Kingdom.

The point was reiterated by Viscount Cave LC in *Levene v IRC*[93].

> Where the person sought to be charged has no home or establishment in any country but lives his life in hotels or at the houses of his friends, and if such a man spends the whole of the year in hotels in the United Kingdom, then he is held to reside in this country; for it is not necessary for that purpose that he should continue to live in one place in this country but only that he should reside in the United Kingdom.

So, the lack of living accommodation or of an 'establishment' does not necessarily operate in favour of a taxpayer as pointing to non-residence. However, availability thereof may operate against the taxpayer as pointing to residence. We have noted earlier in this chapter that the concept of where

---

[92]   (1926) 10 TC 673 at 679.
[93]   13 TC 486 at 505.

an individual's 'home' is located appears regularly in the cases. It may be very difficult for an individual who has a home or a residential establishment in a country to claim that he does not have a view or intention to establish his residence in that country. Why then would he have an establishment there? Furthermore, the lack of a residential establishment anywhere abroad might operate against an individual who has left the UK to live abroad to indicate that he is still resident in here[94].

But once such an establishment is acquired, the taxation situation may change miraculously[95]. Thus the presence of living accommodation may introduce a presumption as to the individual's intentions - but of course this presumption, if it exists at all, must be rebuttable. Is this really the case?

It is interesting to examine the Revenue's practice in this respect. The Revenue's position used to be that, if an individual has a permanent place of abode or accommodation available in the United Kingdom for his use, he is resident here for any tax year in which he visits the United Kingdom, however short the visit may be[96].

There may have been a number of explanations for this type of rule. The sailors' cases referred to earlier (*Rogers v IRC* and *Re Young*) both involved individuals who had residential establishments in the UK, and this fact played a role in the decisions to hold them resident even though they were out of the UK for long periods (indeed, in *Rogers*, the absence was for the whole tax year). It was of course material in these cases that the sailors had no home or establishment anywhere else on land. *AG v Coote* (above) was another case in which the existence of a residential establishment in the UK played a major role in the decision to hold the taxpayer resident, even though his visits to the UK were for relatively short periods. This time, the fact that the taxpayer possessed a house in London went to establish that he had not come to visit the UK for 'temporary purposes' only, and so could be held resident even though he was here for less than six months. A more celebrated case in point is *Cooper v Cadwalader*[97].

The taxpayer in this case was an American barrister who had his ordinary residence in New York and who rented a house in Scotland, with exclusive shooting and sporting rights over the grouse shootings of the property, and fishing rights in the rivers and streams within the bounds of its territory. The house was furnished and was kept up for the taxpayer and placed at his disposal to go to at any time of the year that he chose. He and his valet, whom he brought with him from America, normally resided at this property continuously for a period of about two months each year during the grouse

---

[94]   *Levene v IRC* (above).
[95]   Ibid.
[96]   See IR 20 paras. 3.3 and 4.1. This rule, as far as it relates to temporary visitors, has recently been changed - see ICTA 1988, s.336(3).
[97]   (1904) 5 TC 101.

shooting season. He had no place of business in the United Kingdom, and, during his stay here, maintained and kept open his residence in New York so he could return to it at any time. It was held that he was resident in the United Kingdom. According to the Lord President[98] the taxpayer had, in effect, a lease of heritage in Scotland, occupied personally the properties let to him for a considerable portion of each year, and when he was absent in America, these properties were kept in readiness for his return. It was clear that his occupation of the property was not of a casual or temporary character. Rather, it was substantial, and as regards some of its incidents, it was continuous.

The Lord President said[99] that if a person continues to have a residence in the United Kingdom, he is resident there in the sense of the Acts, and that a person may have more than one residence, if he maintains an establishment at each. This is may be regarded as strong support for the proposition that the existence of accommodation introduces a presumption as to intention to establish a residence. Although the context in which the statement was made does not suggest that any visit, no matter how brief, will be sufficient, it is arguable that cases like *AG v Coote* could be interpreted as pointing to such a result (at least, perhaps in respect of property owned by the taxpayer).

It also seems that *dicta* in *Thomson v Bensted*[100] provide support for the proposition. In that case the taxpayer had his home in Hawick, wherein lived his wife and family. He worked for a company which required him to live in Nigeria, where he spent eight months in the relevant year, the remaining four months being spent at his Hawick home in the UK. The question was whether he was resident in the UK during the relevant year. The taxpayer argued that he was not resident in this country inasmuch as he was required to reside in Southern Nigeria during the whole period of his employment by the company, and that his residence must therefore be deemed to be in that country. The Court of Session held that he was resident in the UK. Lord Dundas referred to his home in Hawick, and said: 'That is a place of residence, and if he occupies that place of residence for a portion of a year, he then is within the meaning of this clause, as I read it, residing there in the course of the year[101].

This was so far the most direct statement of the 'place of abode' rule, and it may have been the direct source of the Revenue's original position on the matter. The Court of Session in this case placed reliance on *Cooper v Cadwalader*. However, there is nothing in *Cooper v Cadwalader* that justifies

---

[98]   At 105.
[99]   At 106.
[100]   (1918) 7 TC 137.
[101]   7 TC at 146.

this statement by Lord Dundas. The statement seems to be an extension of *Cooper v Cadwalader*, and that in a way that was not necessary for the decision in *Thomson v Bensted* itself. That the statement is not supported by *Cooper v Cadwalader* itself is clear. For example, there was nothing in the statement of the Lord President in *Cooper v Cadwalader* to suggest that the six month rule in section 336(1) cannot apply in appropriate cases to negate the rule that he had stated. This would seem to indicate that any presumption that may exist as to intention to establish a residence is rebuttable. Indeed the possibility of the six month rule being applicable to negate the place of abode rule was explored, albeit unsuccessfully, by counsel in *Cooper v Cadwalader* itself. In response to the argument of counsel that Mr Cadwalader fell within the six month exemption, the Lord President said[102]:

> This provision appears to be directed to prevent temporary residents for less than six months in one year from being charged in respect of profits received from abroad, but it does not appear to me to apply to a case like the present. I do not think that the Appellant can reasonably maintain that he is in the United Kingdom 'for some temporary purpose only, and not with any view or intent of establishing his residence therein', in the sense of the section, as he took [the property in which he had shooting rights] with the view of establishing his residence there during a material part of each year and maintaining his connection with it as tenant during the rest of the years, and he has a residence always ready for him if he should choose to come to it.

What may be deduced from this answer is that if Mr Cadwalader's visit had been for some temporary purpose only, and if he had never had any intention of establishing his residence in the rented property, section 336(1) may have availed him, notwithstanding that he had an establishment or place of abode available for his use. This is very far from Lord Dundas' statement in *Thomas v Bensted* (and the Revenue's old stance) that any visit will automatically be sufficient to attract a resident status if an individual has a place of abode. Indeed, none of the early cases which may be regarded as favourable to the Revenue (eg *AG v Coote*, *Re Young*, *Rogers v IRC*) expressed any universal and immutable principle in this respect. While some of them did indicate that the existence of a residential establishment may be strongly indicative of the taxpayer's state of mind (or purpose) when coming

---

[102] Ibid.

to this country, it was never stated that any presumption in that respect could not be displaced by clear evidence.

The Revenue rule could clearly work hardship to foreign visitors who just happened to have some available accommodation in the UK, and it might even have eventually served as a strong disincentive to property deals in the UK. It is not surprising therefore that the rules governing the application of the place of abode were changed[103].

The change relates to those who are in the United Kingdom for temporary purposes only. In this respect, section 336(3) provides that the question whether an individual is in the United Kingdom for some temporary purpose only and not with the intention of establishing his residence there shall be decided without regard to any living accommodation available in the United Kingdom for his use[104].

Thus, an individual whose normal place of residence is outside the UK and who comes to visit the UK will not be resident here simply because he has accommodation available here for his use. However, other factors may still apply to make him resident. The only change in the rule is simply to remove, in respect of visitors to the UK, any presumptions that they are not here for temporary purposes only, and that they had an intention to establish a residence here, that seemed to arise out of the availability of accommodation - and the effect is simply that the availability of accommodation is in itself no longer a sufficient criterion to make a visitor resident. The situation is thus now much the same as that which was envisaged in *Cooper v Cadwalader:* the place of abode rule affects those who have some stronger connection with the United Kingdom than the mere availability of accommodation here. This stronger connection is most likely to be found in the lifestyles of the individuals concerned, vis-a-vis the UK (for example, that they come here every year, have business or family connections here, etc). The connection, if it exists, may then be fortified (but not established) by the availability of accommodation, which may operate in addition to the other factors to indicate a particular lifestyle (of residence here).

Compare the Revenue code IR 20 (paras. 3.7 and 3.11) which now applies the place of abode rule to 'longer term visitors' (ie those who visit for a purpose that will entail a stay of at least two years). In such cases the fact that accommodation is available will render the visitor resident from the date of arrival. For those who 'come to and remain' in the UK availability of accommodation is said to be relevant in determining their status (para. 4.6).

---

[103]   The changes took effect on 6th April 1993; see ICTA 1988, s.336(3).

[104]   Compare s 9(4) of the TCGA 1992 for similar provisions with respect to Capital Gains Tax.

The issue of the taxpayer's intentions in respect of the UK then becomes a distinct matter to be established by evidence, as does the issue of whether he is in the UK for some temporary purpose only.

This may have taken the real sting out of the place of abode rule, for its original sting (at least, as far as the Revenue's rule was concerned) was in relation to temporary visitors who happened to have accommodation available for their use. It is of course arguable that the sting never ought to have been there at all. The Revenue's old rule seems to bear no relationship to the *ratio* of the authority (*Cooper*) that it was supposed to have been based on, since it seems clear that *Cooper* never intended to apply any presumption to people who were clearly temporary visitors. In *Cooper* it was clear to the court that the taxpayer was not here for 'temporary purposes.' The evidence for this lay not in any presumption that the availability of the accommodation raised but, rather, in the lifestyle of Mr Cadwalader. That lifestyle may itself have been sufficient to make him resident, even if he had lived in hotels when he came here (*Lysaght v IRC*). That he also had a 'home' in the UK made his case even weaker. Viewed in this light, it is questionable whether the place of abode rule now serves any purpose in its own right. It is not really appropriate to people whose homes are in the UK, since the fact that this is where they 'live' means that they are resident here. It is not relevant to those who have no 'home' at all (eg wanderers and vagrants). It no longer raises any presumption in respect of those whose homes are outside the UK but who come to visit the UK temporarily. It appears that the availability of accommodation in the UK now merely serves as a corroborative factor, where other factors are present. The Revenue's new rule of treating it as establishing residence in certain situations seems suspect.

Question of Fact

Whether or not an individual has a place of abode available for his use is a question of fact, and as *Lowenstein v De Salis*[105] shows, an individual does not even have to own or rent the property if it is *de facto* available for his use. In that case a Belgian national, who had his residence in Brussels, visited the United Kingdom each year, and occupied for varying periods property in England, which comprised of a hunting box, together with the hunting stables, garage and gardens, and which belonged to a company of which he was a director and majority shareholder. It was admitted that the taxpayer could, when in the United Kingdom, use the said residence, stables and

[105]   (1926) 10 TC 424.

garage, without obtaining formal permission. In no year was he in this country for up to six months. The main factor that distinguished this from *Cooper v Cadwalader* was that in this case the taxpayer was neither the owner nor the lessee of the property. According to Rowlatt J, it really came to this: whether it is of the essence of the case that a man should be treated as coming here with a view to establishing his residence, and not for a temporary purpose only, that he should have at any rate a proprietary interest, such as a lease or something of that sort, in the house which he occupies when he is here. Rowlatt J held that it was not. He could not see what difference it made. The house was *de facto* available for the taxpayer's occupation whenever he came to this country and that was sufficient. Rowlatt J, concluding the matter, said[106]:

> When you are considering a question like residence, you are considering just a bundle of actual facts, and it seems to me that in a case like this you can quite well say that here this man had this house at his disposal, with everything in it or for his convenience, kept going all the year round, although he only wanted it for a short time. Luckily, he was in relation with a Company who were the owners of it, and he could do that without owning it. It is an accident. It might have been that he could do that with a relation, or a friend, or a philanthropist, or anybody; but in fact there was this house for him; and a lease would not put him in any better position so far as having the house and the availability of it, and the power of coming to it were concerned, so far as I understand the facts. Now I think that it is a case in which you do say you look at the substance of the matter. You do not look at the substance of the matter and say the man is the Company, - that is inaccurate, but you look at the substance of the matter and say: This is the house in which he could reside and did reside. It might have been held that he must not do it any longer, but up to the present time in history there has been no change for the last two or three years. There it is. He has got this house to come to when he likes; he does not own it; he has got no proprietary interest in it, but it is just as good as if he had for the purpose of having it for a residence, and there it is. I am bound to say that I do not think there can be any question upon the facts as clearly found in this case, giving the Appellant the benefit of anything that may be doubtful upon the case ... stated.

Not surprisingly, the fact that *de facto* availability is the crucial point is

---

[106]   At 437-438.

reiterated in the Revenue's code[107]. However, the Revenue have a lot more to say on the question whether accommodation is available for a person's use. According to the Revenue code, a house which a person owns, and which he lets out on a lease under the terms of which he has no right to stay in it, or which is left empty of furniture or which is undergoing extensive refurbishment, so that it is not in a state to be lived in, will not be treated as being available for his use[108].

Any accommodation rented for use during a temporary stay in the United Kingdom may be ignored if the period of renting is less than two years in the case of furnished accommodation, and one year in the case of unfurnished accommodation[109].

A house owned or rented by one spouse will usually be considered available for the use of the other, and accommodation provided by an employer may be regarded as available in certain circumstances[110].

Overseas Duties

Apart from section 336(3) ICTA 1988 (availability of a place of abode disregarded for certain purposes in respect of temporary visitors), there is another statutory qualification to the place of abode rule. Section 335(1) ICTA 1988 provides that, where a person works full-time in a trade, profession, vocation, office or employment, and no part of the person's duties are carried on in the United Kingdom, then the question of residency in the United Kingdom shall be determined without regard to any place of abode maintained in the United Kingdom for his or her use.

With respect to the question whether, for the purposes of this statutory qualification, any part of the duties of an office or employment was performed in the United Kingdom, an allowance is made for 'incidental' duties. Section 335(2) provides that where the duties of an office or employment fall substantially to be performed outside the United Kingdom in any year of assessment, duties performed within the United Kingdom which are merely incidental to the performance the duties performed abroad will be treated as if performed outside the United Kingdom[111].

The question when a duty performed in the United Kingdom can be taken to be 'merely incidental' to one which is performed abroad was confronted in *Robson v Dixon*[112]. The taxpayer was employed as a pilot by KLM Airlines, his base being at Schiphol Airport, Amsterdam. He and his wife had their family home in Hertfordshire, meaning that he had a place of abode in the

---

[107]   See IR 20, para. 4.3.
[108]   Para 4.4.
[109]   Ibid.
[110]   Para. 4.3.
[111]   See also IR 20, para. 4.5.
[112]   [1972] 3 ALL ER 671.

United Kingdom. His duties always commenced in Amsterdam but he would sometimes land at Heathrow en-route to Amsterdam. In the years in question the total number of take-offs and landings made by the taxpayer in all the countries that his flights took him to was 811. Of this number, only 38 took place in the United Kingdom and such stop-overs were normally for a duration of some 40 to 60 minutes. It was held that, while the duties performed by the taxpayer in the United Kingdom were small quantitatively in comparison with the duties performed by him outside the United Kingdom, they were qualitatively of a nature similar to those duties, and were not duties the performance of which was merely incidental to the performance of the duties performed abroad. According to Pennycuick VC[113]

> the expression 'merely incidental to' must be given effect according to the ordinary meaning of those words. The words are on their ordinary use apt to denote an activity (here the performance of duties) which does not serve any independent purpose but is carried out in order to further some other purpose. He concluded[114]:

> The duties performed by the taxpayer, apart from his duties at Schiphol, mainly consisted of taking a plane up at Schiphol, flying it to whatever its destination was and then bringing it down. In the case of the flights from Schiphol to some destination (normally in America) on which there was a stop at England, his duties consisted of taking the plane up at Schiphol, flying it to England, bringing it down at Heathrow or elsewhere, and then taking it up again and flying it again to the next destination, in America. With the best will in the world, I find it impossible to say that the activities carried on in or over England are merely incidental to the performance of the comparable activities carried on in or over Holland or in or over the ultimate destination in America. The activities are precisely co-ordinate, and I cannot see how it can properly be said that the activities in England are in some way incidental to the other activities.

It was said however[115] that a single landing might be disregarded under the *de minimis* rule. Furthermore, landings due to an emergency, such as weather conditions or mechanical trouble, or due to a diversion, might be regarded as incidental to the performance of the duties performed abroad. A situation that presents borderline questions would be one in which 'a

---

[111]   At 677.
[112]   Ibid.
[115]   At 677.

pilot's normal route did not touch on the United Kingdom but on one or two occasions he landed in the United Kingdom while acting as substitute for some other pilot who was ill'[116].

There exists an argument that this provision in section 335(1) speaks only in respect of a place of abode which is maintained in the United Kingdom (as opposed to one which is actually used), such that if the place of abode is not used at all, then the provision may assist the taxpayer, but that if a person visits that place of abode then the provision will not help him. This type of issue was not raised in *Robson v Dixon* and, considering that, if correct, it would by itself alone have been fatal to the taxpayer's case, it seems that the argument is of doubtful force.

Partnerships

Section 111(2) of the ICTA 1988 provides that, where a trade or profession is carried on by persons in partnership, and any of those persons is chargeable to income tax, the profits, gains, or losses arising from the trade or profession will be computed for income tax purposes as if the partnership were an individual who is resident in the United Kingdom. If any of the partners is not resident in the United Kingdom, then s.111 would apply in respect of that person as if the partnership were an individual who is not resident in the United Kingdom[117].

Corporations

According to Lord Loreburn LC in *De Beers Consolidated Gold Mines v Howe*[118] it is easy to ascertain where an individual resides, but when the inquiry relates to a company, which, 'in a natural sense, does not reside anywhere, some artificial test must be applied.'

J. Prebble in 'Should Tax Legislation be written from a Principles and Purpose Point of View or a Precise and Detailed Point of View?'[119]talks about the 'unreality' of the process of ascribing a notional residence to companies. The author states that it 'becomes even more divorced from facts and fictions that exist in the world or in the legal system when one bears in mind that companies are themselves already artificial, fictitious, creations'.

In applying such an artificial test, one may adopt a number of approaches. First, one may take a company to be resident where it was incorporated. Such an approach would have the 'merits of simplicity and certitude[120]'.

[116]   Pennycuick V-C at 677.
[117]   S.112(1). The section also deals generally with partnerships which are controlled abroad.
[118]   (1906) 5 TC 198 at 212.
[119]   (1988) BTR 112 at 116)
[120]   Per Lord Loreburn LC, ibid.

It would however open up tremendous planning opportunities. For as long as UK taxes remain residence-based, a company would be able to avoid UK (and other) taxes by the simple expedient of being incorporated in a tax haven. Secondly, one may take a company to be resident where its directors (or the majority of them) are resident. This might raise a number of problems, and would also have planning implications. Thirdly, a company might be taken to be resident wherever its centre of operations is. This would accord with the reality of the company's situation.

The UK, pragmatic as always, adopts a mixture of the first and third approaches. The third approach was given voice by Lord Loreburn LC in the De Beers case, when he said[121]:

> In applying the conception of residence to a Company, we ought, I think, to proceed as nearly as we can upon the analogy of an individual. A company cannot eat or sleep, but it can keep house and do business. We ought, therefore, to see whether it really keeps house and does business. An individual may be of foreign nationality, and yet reside in the United Kingdom. So may a Company. Otherwise, it might have its chief seat of management and its centre of trading in England, under the protection of English law, and yet escape the appropriate taxation by the simple expenditure of being registered abroad and distributing its dividends abroad ... [A] Company resides, for purposes of Income Tax, where its real business is carried on ... and the real business is carried on where the central management and control actually abides.

This is acknowledged to be the basic common law test for the residence of corporations. What the test means, is, according to Madden J in *John Hood & Co Ltd* v *W E Magee*[122], that the residence of a company is to be determined, 'not by the place of abode for the time being of its managing director, but by the place where the company permanently keeps house, where it can make and re-make its officers, including its managing director, prescribe their duties, including the place of their residence, and call them to account.'

The first approach referred to earlier in this discussion was adopted by the UK as a further test for the residence of corporations by section 66(1) of the FA 1988[123]. By this provision, any company which is incorporated in the United Kingdom is resident here with effect from 15 March 1988 and the

---

[121]   5 TC at 212-213.
[122]   (1918) 7 TC 327 at 355.
[123]   See generally, D. Sheridan (1990) BTR 78.

place of central management and control will no longer be taken into account. Transitional provisions existed in Schedule 7 of the FA 1988, for example, providing a five year period of grace for existing companies. There is however no corollary to this statutory test for residence. The De Beers test has been described as still being 'alive and well[124]'.

Thus it would seem that companies which were incorporated outside the United Kingdom would still be subject to the common law rule of control and management. The Exchequer can 'have it both ways' in that those companies which were incorporated here are resident here automatically, and those which were not incorporated here are still resident here if their central management and control is exercised here.

Ordinary Residence

Ordinary residence is of far less importance for the purposes of United Kingdom tax than residence. It is however important in several respects. First, as we have seen above, section 334 ICTA 1988 applies to treat Commonwealth citizens and citizens of the Republic of Ireland, who are ordinarily resident in the United Kingdom, and who go abroad for the purposes of occasional residence, as being resident in the United Kingdom during their absence. Secondly, section 65(4) and section 65(5) ICTA 1988 provide that a Commonwealth citizen or a citizen of the Republic of Ireland who satisfies the Board that he is not ordinarily resident in the United Kingdom is to be taxed on foreign income under Cases IV and V of Schedule D only on income which is remitted here (and not on all income arising). Thirdly there is a general anti-avoidance provision in section 739(1) of the ICTA 1988 which deals with the transfer of assets by a person who is ordinarily resident to a person who is not resident or not domiciled in the United Kingdom. And fourthly, the persons chargeable to United Kingdom capital gains tax are defined by section 2(1) of the Taxation of Chargeable Gains Act 1992 as persons who are resident or ordinarily resident in the United Kingdom.

In spite of its importance in the contexts mentioned above, the term 'ordinary residence' is neither defined in statute, nor given a special technical meaning for tax purposes[125]. The words must bear their natural and ordinary meaning as words of common usage in the English language[126].

It is clear from the discussions above that ordinary residence is not synonymous with residence, that the word 'ordinary' qualifies the word

[124] See J. D. B Oliver, (1996) BTR 505; compare D. Sheridan (1990) BTR 78.
[125] See Lord Warrington of Clyffe in *Levene v IRC* 13 TC at 509.
[126] See Lord Scarman in *R v Barnett LBC*, ex parte Shah [1983] 2 AC 309 at 341.

'residence'[127], and that there is thus a need to examine the judicial definitions. The early cases equated ordinary residence with an individual's 'usual' residence[128].

In *Levene v IRC*, Viscount Cave said that ordinary residence 'connotes residence in a place with a degree of continuity and apart from accidental or temporary absences[129]'. Worryingly, he then added that, so understood, the expression 'differs little' from the meaning of the word 'residence' as used in the tax legislation, and that he found it difficult to imagine a case 'in which a man while not resident here is yet ordinarily resident here[130]'.

In the same case Lord Warrington of Clyffe[131] defined it as meaning residence 'according to the way in which a man's life is usually ordered'. In *Lysaght v IRC*[132] Viscount Sumner said that the converse of 'ordinarily' is 'extraordinarily', and that part of the regular order of a man's life, adopted voluntarily and for settled purposes, is not 'extraordinary'. In the non-tax case of *R v Barnet LBC ex parte Shah*[133] Lord Scarman, after a review of the case law (including *Lysaght* and *Levene*) said:

> Unless, therefore, it can be shown that the statutory framework or the legal context in which the words are used requires a different meaning ... 'ordinarily resident' refers to a man's abode in a particular place or country which he has adopted voluntarily and for settled purposes as part of the regular order of his life for the time being, whether of short or of long duration.

Lord Scarman added[134] that a settled purpose does not require an intention to stay indefinitely, but that the purpose, while settled, might be for a limited period only. All that is necessary is that the purpose of living where one does live has a sufficient degree of continuity to be properly described as 'settled'. In this context, a specific limited purpose, such as education, can be a settled purpose. However, in spite of the reference to a voluntary adoption of a way of life, volition is no more a necessary ingredient of ordinary residence than it is of residence. Thus, in *Re Mackenzie*[135] for example, a woman who was domiciled in Australia and who came to visit this country and who was detained as a person of unsound mind, was held to be ordinarily resident in the United Kingdom when she died here, still detained, some 50 years later. According to Norton J[136], 'If ... she was not ordinarily

[127]   Lord President Clyde in *Reid v IRC* (1926) 10 TC 673 at 678.
[128]   See for example *Turnbull v Foster* (6 TC 206) - the Lord Justice Clerk at 210; Lord Trayner, ibid.
[129]   13 TC at 507.
[130]   Ibid.
[131]   At 509.
[132]   13 TC at 528.
[133]   [1983] 2 AC 309 at 343. For comment, see J. L. Wosner (1983) BTR 347.
[134]   At 344.
[135]   [1941] Ch 69.
[136]   AT 77.
[137]   (1926) 10 TC 673.
[138]   See also Lord Warrington of Clyffe in *Levene v IRC* 13 TC at 509.

resident in England during the last 52 years of her life, she was not ordinarily resident anywhere else'.

This question, like that of residence, is a question of fact, and there are many examples in the cases. The taxpayers in *Levene* and *Lysaght* for example, were held to be ordinarily resident as well as resident. These cases have already been discussed earlier. We will examine two other cases. First, *Reid* v *IRC*[137].

The taxpayer, a British subject, was in the habit of travelling abroad on the continent of Europe for the greater part of the year, spending only the summer months in the United Kingdom. While abroad, she had no fixed place of abode in this country, staying in hotels both when she was here and when she was abroad. She however had family and business ties here, and her personal belongings, which were not required when she was travelling, were kept in store in London. It was held by the Commissioners that she was ordinarily resident in the United Kingdom and this decision was upheld by the Court of Session. The Lord President (Clyde) rejected the suggestion that the meaning of the word 'ordinarily' is governed wholly or mainly by the test of time or duration[138].

According to Lord Clyde[139], from the point of view of time, 'ordinary' would stand in contrast to 'casually'. In this case the taxpayer was not a 'casual' visitor to her home country. Lord Clyde said he would hesitate to give the word 'ordinary' any more precise interpretation than 'in the customary course of events[140]'.

In response to the argument of counsel that the taxpayer 'ordinarily resided' on the Continent rather than in this country because she spent nearly three times as much of her life abroad as here, Lord Clyde said that there was nothing impossible in a person ordinarily residing in two places. Lord Blackburn, concurring, said[141]: 'It is quite true a man may have more than one ordinary residence; he may have half-a-dozen; and each might be described quite fairly as an ordinary residence.' He also noted[142] that a person may be ordinarily resident in the United Kingdom without having any particular house or spot in the United Kingdom which could be described as his 'ordinary residence'. According to Lord Blackburn, such a person may stay in a different hotel every day of the 365 days in the year. Nobody could say in such situation that the person had an ordinary residence, but everyone would agree in saying that he had been 'ordinarily resident' for the whole of the year within the confines of the United Kingdom. That conclusion would be reached entirely from the fact that he had physically

[137]   (1926) 10 TC 673.
[138]   See also Lord Warrington of Clyffe in *Levene v IRC* 13 TC at 509.
[139]   At 680.
[140]   Ibid.
[141]   At 682.
[142]   At 681.
[143]   (1957) 37 TC, 493.

resided in the United Kingdom and no other fact, as far as Lord Blackburn could see, is material in construing the expression 'ordinarily resident'.

The second case that we shall examine is *Miesegaes v IRC*[143]. The taxpayer was a Dutch national. He and his father had originally come to this country as refugees at the beginning of the Second World War. When his father left this country for Switzerland at the end of the war, he remained at boarding school in England. He was at all material times domiciled outside the United Kingdom, and spent his school holidays with his father in Switzerland. It was held that he was ordinarily resident in the United Kingdom. Wynn Parry J at first instance said[144] that the correct test was whether the taxpayer had been here in the ordinary course of his life during his adolescence. The commissioners had applied the test correctly and he could see no justification for interfering with their decision. He was upheld by the Court of Appeal. Pearce LJ, referring to the statement of Lord Buckmaster in *Lysaght v IRC* that volition was immaterial, said[145]:

Lord Buckmaster's remarks as to the exigencies of business seem equally applicable to the exigencies of education. Education is a large, necessary and normal ingredient in the lives of adolescent members of the community, just as work or business is in the lives of its adult members. During the years of youth education plays a definite and dominating part in a boy's ordinary life. In this case the school terms at Harrow dictated the main residential pattern of the boy's life. Education is too extensive and universal a phase to justify such descriptions as 'unusual' or 'extraordinary'. It would be as erroneous to endow educational residence with some esoteric quality that must, as a matter of law, remove it from the category of residence, or ordinary residence, as it would be to do so in the case of business residence. The argument based on the institutional or compulsory nature of a boy's life at school is misleading. The compulsion is merely the will of his parents, who voluntarily send him to that school. It would be hazardous, and in my opinion relevant, to investigate whether adolescents are residing voluntarily where their lot is cast and how far they approve of their parents' choice of a home or school. The Appellant's argument might lead to the unreal conclusion that a boy whose parents were in the Far East and who was therefore boarded with a tutor, or at an educational establishment where boys remain all the year round, would not reside anywhere at all. The educational and institutional nature of the

---

[143]   (1957) 37 TC, 493.
[144]   At 499.
[145]   At 501.

residence are, of course, factors to be taken into account; but it would be wrong to hold that such residence cannot be ordinary residence.

The Revenue practice is to treat ordinary residence as being equal to habitual residence[146] (usually for three successive years). A person who is non-resident for a year because he is physically absent from this country for that whole year may still be treated by the Revenue as ordinarily resident, if he 'usually lives' here[147].

It may be that the only case in which an individual would be held to be resident but not ordinarily resident is when he comes from abroad to this country for some temporary purpose but remains for more than six months in the tax year[148]. With respect to students, a person who comes to the United Kingdom for a period of study or education which is expected to last for more than four years will be treated by the Revenue as resident and ordinarily resident from the date of his arrival[149]. If the period of study is not expected to exceed four years, the person may be treated as not ordinarily resident, but the result will depend on whether or not he has accommodation available here, whether he intends to remain here at the end of his period of education, or whether he proposes to visit the United Kingdom in future years for periods of three months or more per year of assessment[150]. And with respect to other long term visitors, a person who comes here (whether to work or not) will be treated as ordinarily resident from the date of his arrival if it is clear that he intends to remain here for three years or more[151].

Domicile

The domicile of a person is often of much less importance than his residence or ordinary residence. However, it is still important for certain purposes. First, section 65(4) and (5) of the ICTA 1988 charge the foreign income of a non-domiciled person on a remittance basis[152]. Secondly section 192(1) of the ICTA 1988 defines 'foreign emoluments' as the emoluments of a non-domiciled person from an office or employment with an employer who is non-resident (excluding employers in the Republic of Ireland), and thirdly, section 6(1) of the Inheritance Tax Act 1984 defines 'excluded property' as property situated outside the United Kingdom, of which the person

[146] IR 20, para. 1.3 ('year after year'); para. 2.1 ('if you usually live in this country'). See also paras. 3.4 to 3.13.
[147] Para. 1.3.
[148] Ibid.
[149] IR 20 para. 3.13.
[150] Ibid.
[151] IR 20, para. 3.8.
[152] Compare s 12(1) of the TCGA 1992.

beneficial entitled thereto is domiciled outside the United Kingdom.

Domicile bears its general Conflicts of Laws meaning. The common law of domicile in the UK has been described as being 'of a highly capricious nature[153]'. Detailed discussion is beyond the scope of this book and can be found in books on Private International Law[154]. Here, we will just identify a number of general features. Domicile generally refers to a person's permanent home. Every one must have a domicile and only one. A domicile of origin is acquired at birth and a domicile of choice can be acquired by adults, the requirements being a change of residence to another place and an intention to stay there permanently. The domicile of choice can be abandoned by acquiring another one or by revival of the domicile of origin.

Citizenship

Citizenship is largely relevant only in respect of Commonwealth citizens or citizens of the Republic of Ireland, and then only in certain clearly defined situations (see for example, s.65 and s.334 of the ICTA 1988, both discussed above). Citizenship is determined according to general law. Relevant provisions can be found in the British Nationality Act 1981.

---

[153]   S. Green (1991) BTR 21. See also D. Sheridan's analysis of the Joint Report of the Law Commission and the Scottish Law Commission of 31 July 1987 (1989) BTR 230.

[154]   See also IR 20, paras. 5.1 to 5.9, for the Revenue's summary of the position.

chapter three
Income Tax - the Concept

By comparison to other taxes, income tax is by far the largest source of revenue in the United Kingdom. For example, in 1989 income tax accounted for approximately 26per cent of the total tax revenue; corporation tax accounted for 11per cent; and the combined revenue of capital gains tax and inheritance tax accounted for two per cent of the total tax revenue.

It is in the first part of this book that we develop a consideration of the rules and principles that apply to income tax. The problem we initially face is that of seeking to ascertain and present a definition of income. It has often been stated that income tax is a tax on income; but an economist would reply and explain that the flow of revenue from capital is also income. Clearly income tax for our purposes (and for the purposes of the Inland Revenue) does not include income from capital. This calls for a consideration of the distinction between income and capital. Exhaustive and conclusive definitions of income and capital are not provided by the legislature. There exists a further need to consider the schedular system and the definitions within that and the roles that the various schedules perform.

Capital v Income: the Distinction and its Importance

The distinction between an income and a capital item of expenditure or receipt has assumed a lesser importance than it previously enjoyed. Its past importance reflected the absence of a capital gains tax (until its introduction in 1965) and the consequent ability, prior to 1965, to enjoy tax- free capital gains. It was eventually conceded that the absence of a capital gains tax presented not only an avenue for tax planning or avoidance, but also supported the possible 'injustice' of not taxing those with the ability to pay on the grounds that their income was of a particular type and derived from a particular source (a capital gain).

The introduction of a capital gains tax has not removed the need to recognise the distinction between income and capital: at the very least the distinction is of importance in recognising and advising upon the correct tax principles. The distinction may have practical importance in that the rates applicable to income gains and those applicable to capital gains have not always been the same.[1] For example, capital gains tax enjoyed a maximum rate of 30per cent for a number of years, whereas income tax rates reached 60per cent during the same period. Today's assimilation of the rates provides stronger recognition of the often indistinguishable distinction between income and capital and of the need to tax the latter.[2]

In doing so it raises the issue of whether the capital/income distinction matters. In response to this one must acknowledge that the assimilation of rates does not amount to as assimilation of taxes: the income and capital tax regimes remain distinct and separate. For example, differences remain in the following areas.

- The Bases of Computation
- The annual CGT exemption is higher than the income tax personal allowance
- The ability to use 'loses'
- The dates for payment
- Different reliefs

One of the major problems in determining the distinction between income and capital is the absence of precise definitions or determining theories. Judicial comments have confirmed that the question '... must depend in large measure upon the particular facts of the particular case'[3], and that 'in many cases it is almost true to say that a spin of a coin would decide the matter almost as satisfactorily as an attempt to find reasons.'[4]

Although the revenue law student should recognise the difficulties in this area, the good student must also possess an awareness of the application of the distinction in relevant case law. We will present a discussion of the more important cases when we consider income receipts and revenue

---

[1]   Today the rates are the same, except that any capital gain is always to be taxed as the top slice of one's income and thus at any marginal rate of income tax.

[2]   It is widely believed that the previous practice of taxing income and capital gains at different rates distorted investment decisions and contributed to the development of a tax avoidance industry.

[3]   Per Abbott J, in *Oxford Motors Ltd v Minister of National Revenue* (1959) 18 DLR 712.

[4]   Per Greene MR in *CIR v British Salmson Aero Engines Ltd.* [1938] 2 KB 482 at 498.

expenditure in Schedule D Cases I and II. For the moment, we will simply highlight the competing theories that have been presented as assisting or explaining the distinctions between capital and income.

Fixed and Circulating Capital

This theory has enjoyed a great deal of support and involves a recognition that fixed capital is 'capital' whereas circulating capital is merely 'income'. The fixed capital is the   structure (permanent or semi-permanent) that generates the income.   The income is often represented through the disposal of the circulating capital items. Those circulating capital items are the creation of the fixed capital.

For example, in *Golden Horse Shoe (New) Ltd v Thorgood*[5], the court was required to decide whether the sale of dumps generated at a Gold Mine was a sale of capital. Romer LJ summarised the issue by stating that, '... the question to be decided in this case is whether the dumps are to be regarded as fixed capital or circulating capital.'

In conclusion, the dumps were regarded as circulating capital : their existence and creation was caused by and was an aside to the fixed capital - the mines.

Fruit of the Tree

In a similar fashion to fixed and circulating capital theory, the 'fruit of the tree' theory suggests that the tree represents the capital and the fruit represents income items that are generated by and grow out of and from the capital.

Accretion to Economic Power

This theory involves a recognition that income is the gain generated out of the application of capital. It has been suggested that the accretion to economic power theory is perhaps a more accurate description of the distinction between income and capital, albeit that the other theories are more frequently cited by the judiciary.

Ultimately the issue is one of fact and, as we shall see in our later discussions, the suggestion that the matter could, as easily and as predictably, be determined by a 'spin of a coin' is very close to the truth! For the moment is useful to look at the following cases as an illustration of the

5   [1933] All ER 402.

difficulties in this area.

In *Gray (Inspector of Taxes) v Seymours Garden Centre*[6] , the taxpayers, who carried on the trade of nurserymen, erected a planteria to protect growing plants and to maintain the quality of the plants until they were sold. The planteria enjoyed an internal layout that permitted customers to view and select plants. The taxpayer sought to claim allowances on the cost of the construction of the planteria on the grounds that it constituted 'plant'.

The case ultimately revolved around the meaning of 'plant'. This is where we begin to see the limits of our capital allowance system. To enjoy the allowances, investments must be channelled in certain directions. Included in the permitted directions is 'plant'. Unfortunately no statutory definition of this term is provided: it is left to the judiciary to determine its meaning and scope and hence the scope of this element of our capital allowance system. As one might expect, the meaning of 'plant' has caused much debate and concern over the years. In the current case, Vinelott J was prepared to conclude that the planteria was not just plant and thus not deserving of allowance status: 'In my judgment on the evidence before the Commissioners a planteria falls well on the premises side of the line wherever it may be drawn.'[7]. The dividing line referred to was the consequence of the application of the business test and the premises test as explained and applied by Hoffman J in *Wimpey International Ltd v Warland*[8]. In fact Vinelott was at pains to point out that in *Gray* the Commissioners overlooked the crucial distinctions recently emphasised by Hoffman J. Those tests and the distinctions emanate from a long line of decisions, summarised and referred to by Hoffmann J, and evolve and emanate from the often-quoted dictum of Lindley LJ, that plant:

> ...in its ordinary sense, includes whatever apparatus is used by a businessman for carrying on his business, not his stock-in-trade which be buys or makes for sale; but all goods and chattels, fixed or moveable, live or dead, which he keeps for permanent employment in his business.[9].

Subsequent acceptance and application of this *dictum* evolved into a recognition of a number of tests and distinctions (and a lot of confusion and ambiguity). In the recent case of *Gray v Seymour* Vinelott J placed great emphasis on the Commissioners' failings in not accepting and applying the 'business test' and the 'premises test' advocated by Hoffman J in *Wimpey v*

---

6   [1993] 2 All ER 809.
7   *Gray v Seymours* (loc cit, 814).
8   [1988] STC 149 at 172.
9   *Yarmouth v France* (1887) 19 QBD 647 at 658.

Warland. These tests and their application invite a two-tier approach to the determination of the meaning of 'plant'. The first tier (the 'business test') demands that the item in question is used in the carrying on of the business. The second tier (the 'premises test') disallows items that are used in the business as premises or as the place upon which the business is conducted. This second tier could also be called the 'stock-in-trade test', for following the distinctions adopted by Lindley LJ, stock-in-trade would also be disallowed at tier two.

Vinelott J's overriding acceptance of the two-tier approach with the emphasis on the prevailing nature of the premises test, is disappointing: it creates the impression that premises can never constitute plant - untrue - and it ignores the value of the 'functional' approach. It has been through the proper use of the functional approach that 'premises' have in the past succeeded as being 'plant'. The case of *IRC v Barclay, Curle and Co.*[10] is a well-known example where the costs of excavating and constructing a dry dock were allowed as expenditure on 'plant'. The Revenue had argued, unsuccessfully, that the excavation and construction related to an industrial building and not plant.

The taxpayers were able to succeed with their claim in *IRC v Barclay, Curle and Co.* because the court properly considered the role of 'function'. Lord Reid carefully and correctly suggested that if a structure fulfilled the function of 'plant' then it should be presumed to be 'plant'[11]. The scope of the functional approach is enhanced if we recognise that the function can be performed passively and that the same item could constitute both 'plant'and 'premises'.

The difficulty raised by this decision is how to incorporate the 'functional'approach into the business premises dichotomy and approaches in *Wimpey* and *Gray*. Interestingly, in *Gray* Vinelott J was prepared to recognise that the property in question, a planteria, could constitute plant, but did not explain the relationship between this possibility and the business/premises dichotomy adopted in the case. One suspects that the possibility was based on 'function'. It is likely that the functional approach will operate as an exception to the prevailing nature of the tier-two premises test. As such it will provided proper recognition that premises can constitute and function as plant. In a sense it also completes the circle, in that the business/premises approach begins by considering whether the asset functions as part of the carrying on of the business (the business test), and then moves to consider (negatively) whether that contribution is as an

[10]   [1969] 1 All ER 732.
[11]   *loc cit*, p 740.

excluded item, such as stock-in-trade or premises. The functional approach completes the circle and returns us to our functional beginnings (the business test) by allowing function to prevail in the determination of excluded assets: a *prima facie* excluded asset, premises, will not be excluded if it functions as part of the business (the 'business test' and performs the particular functions of 'plant' (the functional approach).

In *Lawson v Johnson Matthey plc*[12] the facts of the case involved a parent company's (Johnson Matthew plc) injection of monies (50 million) into one of its wholly-owned subsidiaries, Johnson Matthey Bankers Limited (JMB). The cash injection was part of a scheme to facilitate the disposal of JMB to the Bank of England. The background of the scheme revealed that JMB had fallen into difficulties on its commercial loan business; large advances had been made on what turned out to be inadequate security. The parent company, Johnson Matthey plc, discussed these difficulties at a board meeting on the night of September 30/October 1, 1984, and concluded that:

■ JMB was insolvent and could not open its doors for business later that day unless further financing, which Johnson Matthew plc could not afford to supply, was made available.

■ The cessation of business by JMB, and the resulting damage to confidence in Johnson Matthey plc, was likely to lead to demands by lending institutions for the repayment of metals and moneys owed to them by Johnson Matthew plc and that Johnson Matthey plc would be unable to meet its obligations as they fell due in the absence of further financial support, which did not seem to be available. Johnson Matthey plc would therefore have to cease trading.

■ There was no alternative to the winding up of JMB and that a liquidator should be appointed.

■ They should do everything in their power to protect the interests of Johnson Matthey plc's shareholders and employees and to facilitate the orderly disposal of Johnson Matthey's assets, in which unsecured creditors would be dealt with on an equitable basis, and that therefore they would ask for the appointment of a receiver for Johnson Matthey plc.

■ These decisions to ask for a liquidator for JMB and a receiver for Johnson Matthey plc should be implemented an hour later at 1.30am.

[12]   (1992) STC 466.

The Bank of England was immediately informed of this decision and, concerned at the possible effects on the stability of the United Kingdom banking sector, the Bank of England proposed a 'rescue package'. This consisted of two elements: the Bank would acquire the issued share capital of JMB for the sum of one pound and, prior to this sale, Johnson Matthew plc must inject 50 million into JMB.

Johnson Matthew plc responded to this scheme by noting that the only practical alternative to the Bank's proposals was to implement the previous decision to ask for the appointment of a receiver and that, in the circumstances, the injection of 50 million might appropriately be regarded as expenditure necessary to retain goodwill and confidence in all the remaining group companies and enable them to stay in business. Consequently, Johnson Matthey plc agreed to inject 50 million into its wholly-owned subsidiary and then transferred the whole of the issued share capital of that subsidiary, JMB, to the Bank of England for one pound. Johnson Matthey plc then sought to deduct the 50 million injection monies as a trading expense in its accounts for the year ending March 31, 1985. It was that deduction and the nature of the expenditure that formed the basis of this dispute. It is clear that in order to be deductible the expenditure must be of a revenue nature and that it must be 'wholly and exclusively' incurred for the purposes of the trade.

The General Commissioners took the view that the 50 million payment was of a revenue and not capital nature because its purpose was to preserve the trade of Johnson Matthey plc from collapse. On appeal, the High Court expressed disagreement with the General Commissioners, preferring to treat the expenditure as part of the disposal of a capital asset - the shares in JMB. The Court of Appeal followed the High Court's opinion in treating the expenditure as capital expenditure:

> ...(i) JMB was a capital asset to the taxpayer company; (ii) the taxpayer company disposed of JMB to the Bank; (iii) the only terms on which the Bank was willing to acquire JMB was on payment of the 50 million by the taxpayer company to JMB. . . the payment seems to me to be a payment by the taxpayer company to get rid of a capital asset. . . . In my view the common sense of the matter is that the 50 million was capital expenditure...

Leave to appeal was granted by the House of Lords.

The speeches in the House of Lords appear to present two very different approaches to the determination of the capital versus revenue expenditure issue - albeit both approaches, in this particular instance, admit of the same conclusion: the expenditure was of a revenue nature! The first approach we can attribute to Lord Templeman. Lord Templeman began by confirming that the purpose of the expenditure has a limited use in contributing to the requirement of 'wholly and exclusively', but that the finding that the purpose of the expenditure was to 'preserve the trade of Johnson Matthew plc did...not automatically enable the taxpayer company to deduct 50 million... the deduction can only be made if the 50 million was a revenue expenditure and not a capital expenditure.' Thus the nature of the expenditure is not determined, nor perhaps even influenced, by the purpose of the expenditure.   The nature of the expenditure was determined by Lord Templeman by consideration of and application of existing authorities despite an earlier acknowledgement and approval of Lord MacMillan's observation on the fallibility of the criteria adopted in those authorities. The first authority referred to by Lord Templeman was that of *British Insulated and Helsby Cables Ltd v Atherton* and the proposition of Viscount Cave LC that a 'once and for all payment bringing into existence an asset or advantage for the enduring benefit of the trade' was capital expenditure. On the basis of that proposition, Lord Templeman was able to conclude that the protection of the taxpayer company from insolvency was not expenditure on an 'advantage for the enduring benefit of the trade.' Many people might quite reasonably disagree with Lord Templeman's perception of the benefit received by the taxpayer company, unless Lord Templeman's emphasis on the need to directly relate the expenditure to the transfer of an existing identifiable and tangible asset is a narrowing of Viscount Cave's enduring test to include only the bringing, or the procurement, of an asset into existence - not the protection of an existing asset of the existence, the goodwill and the business of Johnson Matthey plc.

In a similar vein, Lord Templeman distinguished *Associated Portland Cement Manufacturers Ltd v IRC* in that the payment in that case was capital. The expenditure in that case was designed to improve the goodwill of the business and would thus follow earlier categories of capital expenditure being expenditure on the acquisition or the improvement of capital assets. In *Johnson Matthey* the expenditure was not to acquire or improve its goodwill, but to preserve it - a vital distinction according to Lord Templeman; although one might question the degree of difference between the preservation and the improvement of goodwill.

Finally, reference was made to Lord Wilberforce's *dicta* in *Tucker [Inspector of Taxes] v Granada Motorway Services Ltd* that, in determining the distinction between capital and revenue expenditure, the courts can do little better than form an opinion as to where the balance of indicators lie. In Johnson Matthey plc, Lord Templeman formed the opinion that the balance of indicators supported the conclusion that the 50 million was '...paid, and paid solely, to enable the taxpayer company to continue in business...' As such it was a revenue expense: not a capital expense attributable to the disposal of the worthless shares in JMB.

The other approach apparent in the House of Lords can be found in the speech of Lord Goff. Lord Goff acknowledged that the agreement between the taxpayer and the Bank of England was reduced to a written document that made no mention of the rescue plan but referred solely to the agreement for the sale and purchase of the shares of the wholly-owned subsidiary, JMB. If that agreement was the sole matter that the court elected to examine, then the logical conclusion would be to treat the expenditure as capital expenditure attached to the disposal of a capital asset. Lord Goff concluded that that type of analysis is '...too narrowly construed, and ignores the reality of the situation...' The reality and the true analysis according to Lord Goff was that the payment was a 'contribution to the rescue of JMB planned by the Bank, which was a prerequisite of the transfer of the shares in JMB to the Bank for a nominal consideration. As such it was a revenue payment.' The conclusion reached was the same as that of Lord Templeman but with a less mechanistic and perhaps more practical reality approach.The appeal was allowed.

Sources of Income and the Schedular System

Having ascertained that the funds received are of an income nature, the next stage in determining any tax liability is the need to ascertain whether that type of income is taxable. Some guidance is provided by the legislature through the declaration that certain types of income are non-taxable. These include an array of items representing political and policy considerations; for example among the items are : certain social security benefits; war widows pension; redundancy payments; education scholarship and foreign services allowances for civil servants.

Apart from the statutory declared non-taxable incomes, income will be taxable or non-taxable depending upon the application of the doctrine of source and recognition of the schedular system. The schedular system reflects an historical contribution to the UK tax system having been originally developed by Addington during the early 1800s. The schedular system remains today - subject to a number of refinements and the pending 'tax law rewrite' (which may threaten its future existence). The significance of this system is that income in any tax year will not be taxable unless it can be traced to a source identified in a schedule. Thus, for income to be taxable it must be caused, for example, by employment (Schedule E) or trade (Schedule D). Section 1, (TA 1988), supports this conclusion by declaring 'Income is taxable if it falls within one or other of the Schedules'.

Today's Schedules are as follows :

Schedule A

Income from rents and other receipts from land in the UK

Schedule D

Case I   Profits of a trade in UK

Case II   Profits of a profession or vocation in UK

Case III Interest, annuities and other annual payments

Case IV Securities out of the UK

Case V Profits from foreign possessions

Case VI Annual profits or gains not falling under Cases I-V and not charged by virtue of any other Schedule

Schedule E

Income from offices, employments

Cases I, II and pensions

and III

Schedule F Dividends and distributions by companies.

Exclusivity

Although Income tax is one tax its computation must reflect the individual contributions from the Schedules A-F, and the computations within those Schedules. This leads us onto the need to recognise the mutual exclusivity of the Schedules and the rules therein. For example, assessment of income under Schedule E will prevent the assessment of the same income under Schedule D (or vice versa). This was confirmed at an early stage by the House of Lords in *Fry v Salisbury House Estate Ltd.*[13] Here the taxpayer owned a building and let parts of it. The taxpayer was initially assessed under Schedule A on the basis of the building and services and then reassessed for the services under Schedule D. The House of Lords dismissed the reassessment on the grounds that having assessed the rental incomes under Schedule A, '... there is no possibility of subsequently dealing with them under Schedule D.'

As between the Cases within the Schedules, it appears that, subject to statutory direction to the contrary, the Inland Revenue may elect under which case to charge income. For example, in *Liverpool and London and Globe Insurance Co v Bennett*[14] a fire and life insurance company was entitled to 'invest money, not immediately required, in such manner as might from time to time be determined.'

Using this power the Company invested money in the USA and those investments subsequently yielded interest. The interest was received by the Company abroad but never remitted to the UK (although it did appear on the Company's balance sheet). The Company was assessed under Case 1 of Schedule D (ITA 1842) in respect of the 'interest received'. The assessment was upheld by the court. The Company had unsuccessfully argued that they ought to be assessed under Case IV only. The advantage of Case IV was that it would only attach to interest from securities abroad if that interest had been received in the UK in the current year. In hearing the case, Lord Shaw of Dunfermline stressed that :

> ... it is well settled that if a sufficient warrant be found in the statute for taxation under alternative heads the alternative lies with the taxing authority. They have selected Case 1. It appears to me that this selection is ... founded upon the soundest and most elementary principle of business ....[15]

Doctrine of Source

The schedular system led to the development of the doctrine of source. The

---

[13]   [1930] AC 432.

[14]   [1913] AC 610.

[15]   Ibid at 616.

doctrine of source demands that in the current tax year the source of the income must be an identifiable activity and that activity must be recognised as falling within one of the Schedules. This doctrine has proved problematic when income is identifiable but the source of that income (the activity) is no longer identifiable in the current tax year. For example, in *Bray v Best*[16], a payment in respect of employment that no longer was in existence, nor had it been in existence during the year of assessment, was not taxable. The payment referred to previous employment. Lord Oliver stressed that :

> For an emolument to be chargeable to income tax under Schedule E not only must it be an emolument FROM employment but it must be an emolument FOR the year of assessment in which the charge is sought to be raised.

(This particular payment is now dealt with by statute - but it is still a useful illustration of the requirements of the doctrine of source).

One of the logical developments from the doctrine of source requirements is the development of a residual schedule or case to catch and sweep-up all sources of income other than those specified in the other schedules or cases. The provision of a 'catch-all' or 'sweeping' case would prevent the possible non-taxable income or source (other than those to be declared as exempt by statute). On first impressions Schedule D, Case VI (see later discussion) might be regarded as that residual, catch-all case, but on closer examination its comprehensiveness appears to be incomplete and defective.

The Tax Unit

Before we examine some of the detailed rules and principles of the various Schedules, we must briefly consider the unit of assessment. In essence, the unit of assessment requires that we make a choice as to how we tax husbands and wives. We may, for example, wish to adopt separate taxation, whereby we treat husbands and wives as if they were single people. Under a system of separate taxation marriage would attract no fiscal incentives or disincentives, nor would there be any disincentives to a married woman seeking and obtaining employment.

An alternative to a system of separate taxation, might be a system of

---

[16]   [1989] 1 All ER 969.

splitting income. This would involve computing the total joint income and splitting (or dividing) that income by two. Tax liability would then be assessed on an individual basis with each partner's taxable income representing their share of the split income. For example, a disproportionate individual income of £20,000 for one partner (husband) and £15,000 for the other partner (wife) would be split to represent taxable income of £17,500 per partner (individual). Under a split system fiscal advantages are apparent where income is unequally earned or if one partner only is working.

Finally, a system of aggregation could apply to the income of husbands and wives. Under the principles of aggregation the income of the husband and wife are summed to represent joint income. Tax liability would then be assessed and determined according to the joint income. For instance, if we use the example above, the assessable income would not be £17,500 per individual but £35,000 per married couple.

Until 1990, the system of aggregation applied in the United Kingdom. Legislation declared that 'a woman's income chargeable to tax shall be deemed for income tax purposes to be his [the husband's] income and not to be her income.'[17]

The selection of the family unit as the tax unit was not all bad news : the husband became entitled to a married man's personal allowance to help him support his 'dependent' wife.

The system of aggregation was subject to much criticism and concern. In the Meade Report, reference was made to the perceptions of dependency as 'becoming less and less compatible with modern attitudes to the relationships between men and women.'[18]

The Government announced the possibility of change through its Green Paper in 1980[19], and changes were introduced in the treatment of husbands and wives in the reforms of 1990. These reforms abolished the system of aggregation, and husbands and wives are subject to individual assessment on their income (both earned and investment income). However, an element of discrimination does remain in that a 'married couple's allowance' is available to either the husband or the wife. In practice it is normally attributed to the husband and as such may represent an implicit acceptance of 'dependence'.

Critics of the 1990 reforms emphasise that the married couple's allowance does little to recognise or assist the needs of the family unit. It is suggested that if the married couple's allowance was abolished, then child benefit

[17]   TA 1988, s.279. Repealed by FA 1988, s.32 for the year 1990-91 and subsequent years of assessment.

[18]   'The Structure and Reform of Direct Taxation : Report of a Committee' chaired by Professor J. E. Meade. The Institute of Fiscal Studies (1978) p377.

[19]   'The Taxation of Husband and Wife', 1980 Cmnd 8093.

provision could be doubled. The belief is that a change in that direction would move adequately and effectively represent and assist the needs of the family unit.

Further criticisms of the 1990 reforms are directed at the treatment of investment income. It is now possible for the transfer between husband and wife of investment income profit to reduce tax liability. A higher rate tax partner might transfer his investment income to his wife in order that the income is subject to basic rate liability in her hands (assuming she is a basic rate taxpayer). Some critics believe that investment income ought still (on equitable grounds) remain subject to a system of aggregation.

In a budget declared to give to families support when they needed it, the Chancellor announced on 9 March 1999 that a child tax credit would replace the married couple's allowance from April 2001. The child tax credit would be worth £416 but would offer nothing where one earner received income of £38,000 or more per annum. Nothing is offered to assist childless married couples.

The System of Self-Assessment

In March 1993, the Chancellor of the Exchequer announced that the direct tax system would move to a system of self-assessment[20]. The intention was that the procedures for assessment and collection would be more 'straightforward and fairer.' It was also expected that the new system would free up time for the Revenue to investigate matters rather than be involved in detailed tax calculations. Self-assessment applies to tax returns for the 1996/97 tax year onwards.

In essence the system allows the taxpayer a choice as to whether they want the Inland Revenue to calculate their tax liability or whether they wish to calculate their own liability. Different deadlines exist for the completion of complex forms (or free of charge floppy disk) for Schedule E taxpayers with automatic penalties for late returns. The Inland Revenue will provide 'Help Sheets' providing guidance on particular topics.

An example of the timescale can be given for the tax year of 1996/97. If you want the Revenue to calculate your tax liability you will have to send in the return for the year ended 5 April 1997 by 30 September 1997 (or within two months after your receive the return if later). Otherwise you will have until 31 January 1998 to send in the return. There are automatic penalties for late

---

[20]   See Sanford (1994) BTR 674.

returns. Also you will be charged interest on any underpaid tax from 31 January following the tax year according to the amount of tax finally found to be due.

The Revenue have nine months from the date they receive your return to correct obvious errors, and you have a year from the filing date to make amendments yourself. If, however, the Revenue decide to make enquiries about your return, you cannot make amendments either to the return or to a claim until the enquiry is completed. The Revenue will normally have a year from the filing date for the return to notify you that they intend to enquire into it. It has recently been reported[21] that during the first year of operation the Revenue has flooded accountants with notices dated 29 January but arriving after the deadline of 31 January. As a result 'some accountants have questioned whether notices that arrived after January 31 are valid and have threatened to ignore the request.' Of course, the one-year period does not apply in instances of fraudulent or negligent conduct.

The timescale for the payment of any tax due provides that payments on account should be made on 31 January in the tax year and 31 July following, with the balance payable or repayable on the following 31 January. A *de minimis* exception applies in that payments on account are not required if the amount of tax you were due to pay direct to the Revenue was less than £500.

In February 1998 the Revenue issued an invitation (contained in a press release) for people to send in views and suggestions on the operation of the self-assessment scheme. Over 400 responses were received and a report was issued in December 1998.[22] It was concluded that there was a considerable degree of consensus on the main aspect in need of improvement which was summarised in a quote[23]:

The new system is an improvement on the old system. With a little more attention to the organisation with tax offices and a little more clarity of the notices which are issued to taxpayers, the new system could be a very considerable improvement on the old.

---

[21]   The *Times,* 22 February 1999.

[22]   'Assessing Self Assessment. Response to the Public Consultation on Self Assessment'.

[23]   At para 33.

chapter four
Schedule E - Employment Income

Schedule E[1] provides the basis for the taxation of emoluments [2] and income from [3] 'offices and employment'. Schedule E contains three cases of which Case I is discussed in this chapter. Case I states that 'it applies to any emoluments for any year of assessment in which the person holding the office or employment is resident and ordinarily resident in the United Kingdom.'

Case II and Case III involve the need to deal with employment and employment income from overseas.

Office or Employment?

One of the initial problems to be determined in discussion of the scope of Schedule E is the meaning of 'office' or 'employment'. In the absence of any statutory definition or guidelines, we need to turn to judicial comment and guidance. The accepted meaning, or perhaps the characteristics, of an office appear to be those enumerated by Rowlatt J in *Great Western Railway Co v Bates*[4] and repeated in *Davies v Braithwaite*[5]. Rowlatt J emphasised the non-personal nature of an office, stating that :

> ... it was something which had an existence independent of the person who filled it. It was something which was held by tenure and title rather than by contract and which continued to exist, though the holders of it might change and it was fulfilled by successive holders.[6]

These characteristics of an office were recently approved of in *Edwards v Clinch*[7] although the decision in *Edwards v Clinch* is not without difficulty. Mr Clinch had been appointed as inspector at a number of separate public local

[1] The TA 1988 s19(1) levies Income tax under Schedule E.
[2] TA s.131 - emoluments include 'all salaries, fees, wages, perquisites and profits whatsoever.'
[3] As we shall discuss later, not all income from employment is caught under Schedule E. Schedule E is concerned with the taxation of income caused by the employment : a distinction that is of vital importance.
[4] [1920] 3 KB 266.
[5] [1931] 2 KB 628.
[6] Ibid at 635.
[7] [1981] 3 All ER 543. Lord Salmon confirmed the meaning of the word 'office' is, 'a subsisting, permanent, substantive position which has an existence independent of the person who fills it.'

inquiries. The issue was one of whether Mr Clinch held an 'office' at each inquiry or was he merely exercising his profession. The court concluded that Mr Clinch's appointment at each inquiry was not the appointment to an 'office'. Having repeated the accepted characteristics of an office, Lord Salmon accepted the words of Ackner L J[8] that Mr Clinch's appointment was a 'temporary, *ad hoc*, appointment to a position that did not have an existence of its own, nor any quality of permanency'.

This strict adherence to the suggested characteristics of an 'office' might result in 'few' offices being accepted as such.[9] One wonders to what extent the decision in *Edwards v Clinch* gives effect to the suggestion that the deliberately vague term (office) should be applied according to the ordinary use of language and the dictates of common sense.[10]

It has been suggested that the inclusion of the term 'employment' was to extend the scope of Schedule E and might possibly be viewed as a residual category.[11] Today the issue and determination of employment focuses on the distinction between a contract of service and a contract for services. The former is equated with employment.[12] Previous analysis of employment centred on the suggestion that employment 'means something analogous' to an office.[13] It is now clear that a person employed by a company is an employee - except where the company and the individual might in fact be treated as the same. Employment lawyers will remind us that a difficulty exists when an employee is seconded to work for an other firm. This situation involves a determination of fact and a recognition of tax concessions.[14]

It has been recognised that the exercise of a profession or trade can co-exist with the exercise and engagement of employment. For example, *Mitchell and Eden v Ross*[15] raised the possibility that a consultant radiologist could be in private practice exercising his profession and, in the same year of assessment, receive income from employment with a Regional Hospital Board. The income attributed to the profession (the private practice) would be assessed under Schedule D Case II whereas the employment income would be assessed under Schedule E.

Although the distinction between 'office and employment' is assumed to be of little importance[16], the distinction between an office or employment and a

8   [1981] Ch 1 at 17-18.
9   Examples include, a director of a company, an executor and a company auditor.
10 Lord Wright in *McMillan v Guest* [1942] AC 561 at 566. Cited by Lord Salmon an 'office' and neither earnings from a profession or vocation.
12 *Andrews v King* [1991] STC 481.
13 Rowlatt J in *Davies v Braithwaite*, supra 5, at 635. Also, see Lord Wright in *McMillan v Guest* [1942] AC 561 at 566: The word employment has to be construed with and takes its colour from the word 'office'.
14 Extra-statutory concession A37 (1988) declares that fees paid to the individual but accounted for to his firm should not be treated as his taxable income and subject to PAYE.
15 [1961] 3 All ER 49.
16 This distinction has been described as being of importance. The example often given is that of the Taxes Act 1988, s.291(2) disqualifying an employee but not an officer from holding shares, under the BES scheme, in a connected company.

'profession' is often a source of concern and importance.[17]   In *Davies v Braithwaite*[18] the issue was whether an actress who performed in plays, films and radio productions was exercising a profession in doing so (Schedule D Case II) or merely engaging in contracts of employment (Schedule E).   In determining the matter, the court preferred to look at the context of the activities (rather than each isolation activity) and the general arrangements and activities of the taxpayer.   By taking such a wide perspective the court was able to conclude that :

> ... where one finds a method of earning a livelihood which does not consist of the obtaining of a post and staying in it, but consists of a series of engagements and moving from one to another - then each of those engagements cannot be considered an employment, but is a mere engagement in the course of exercising a profession ....[19]

In a more recent case, *Fall v Hitchen*[20], the courts were prepared to take a more restrictive approach in concluding that the engagement of a ballet dancer involved a contract of employment.   This decision is difficult to reconcile with that in *Davies v Braithwaite*.   In both instances one would suggest that the nature of the livelihood envisaged contemplated the entering into of a series of engagement and that each engagement ought not to be viewed in isolation from the nature of the livelihood and from the arrangements and activities of the taxpayer.   Perhaps any reconciliation or explanation lies in the apparent change of focus.   The focus today appears to involve the analysis of the isolated contract under dispute in an attempt to determine whether that contract - irrespective of other commitments or expectations - was one for services or of service[21].   The emphasis, therefore, appears to be one of determining whether that is a contract of employment rather than consider whether it is in one sense employment but in reality part of the arrangement and exercise of a profession.[22]

Further guidance on the relevance of this distinction can be seen in *Hall v Lorimer*[23] [1993] BTC 473 where Nolan J provided a list of indicators on the issue of employee versus self-employed. These included such matters as whether the person performing the services had set up a business-like

---

[17]   See later discussion.

[18]   Supra 5.

[19]   Per Rowlatt J, supra 5 at 635. Although Rowlatt J did, rather unhelpfully add, : '... every profession and every trade does involve the making of successive engagements and successive contracts and, in one sense of the work, employments ...'.

[20]   [1973] 1 All ER 368.

[21]   On the basis of such an analysis the conclusion of employment was unavoidable in *Fall v Hitchen*. The contractual details indicated that it was a full-time contract and prohibited the employee from taking on outside activities without the employer's consent.

[22]   A further element of explanation can be found in the judgement of Rowlatt J in Davies V Braithwaite, where emphasis is placed on the historical background to the introduction of the word 'employment' to Schedule E. Rowlatt J appears to suggest that 'employment' is a residual category. If the activity is neither an office nor the exercise of a trade or profession, then we must turn to 'employment' to plug the gap and catch the activity. If that suggestion is accepted, then Rowlatt J's analysis of the activities in Davies v Braithwaite would begin and end with 'trade or profession'.

[23]   [1993] BTC 473.

organisation of his own; the degree of continuity in the relationship between the person performing the services and the person for whom he performs them; how many engagements he performed and whether they were performed mainly for one person or for a number of different people. On the issue of compiling a list we are warned that:

> No exhaustive list has been compiled and perhaps no exhaustive list can be compiled of considerations which are relevant in determining that question [distinguishing between a contract of service and a contract for services], nor can strict rules be laid down as to the relative weight which the various considerations should carry in particular cases[24].

This appears to have been confirmed by the Court of Appeal in *Hall v Lorimer*[25] where the emphasis was placed on the overall effect and circumstances of the particular case rather than on any ·definitive checklist.

Emoluments

Tax under Schedule E is charged on emoluments from the office or employment.[26] Emoluments are defined as including 'all salaries, fees, wages, perquisites and profits whatsoever.'[27] Special rules exist to catch benefits in kind and related benefits - those rules are discussed later in this chapter. At this point, discussion will focus on the requirement that the emolument must, for the purposes of Schedule E[28], be from the office or employment. The insistence on 'from' or 'therefrom' (by reference to the office or employment) is acknowledged to represent a test of causation[29] and demands consideration of the question : when is a fee, salary, reward etc received in respect of the employment, or in respect of a personal characteristic or circumstance?

The importance of the test of causation is that is correctly places the focus on the cause and reason for the receipt rather than on the timing or status of the giver. Thus, receipts from non-employers and/or receipts received before or after employment are capable of being treated as caused by the employment and therefore 'emoluments' taxable under Schedule E[30].

[24]   Per Cooke, J in *Market Investigations Ltd* v *Minister of Social Security* [1969] 2QB 173.
[25]   [1994] STC 23.
[26]   TA 1988, s.19.
[27]   TA 1988, s.131.
[28]   In accordance with the Schedules system, emoluments not caused by and, therefore, not caught under Schedule E might be assessed to tax elsewhere. It has even been suggested that they might be regarded as capital as opposed to income, and conceivably taxable as capital. See Jarrold v Boustead [1964] 3 All ER 76.
[29]   [1959] Ch 22 at 33.
[30]   See more recently in *Mairs v Haughey* [1993] BTC 339, where it was decided that a payment made to employees to relinquish their contingent rights under a non-statutory redundancy scheme was not taxable because the character of the payment took that of the payment it replaced, namely a redundancy payment. Such a payment was caused through being unemployed rather than being employed!

The often quoted words of Upjohn J in *Hochstrasser v Mayes* confirm this :

> ... the payment must be made in reference to the services the employee renders by virtue of his office and it must be something in the nature of a reward for services past, present or future.'[32]

Although it should be noted that the causation has not enjoyed overwhelming support. Lord Simon criticised the test as 'outmoded and ambiguous' and subsequently suggested a 'far less begging test' by asking whether it was paid to taxpayer as an employee.[33] Lord Simon's criticisms were not followed in the subsequent case of *Tyrer v Smart*[34] nor in *Mairs v Haughey*[35] where the House of Lords relied on Lord Radcliffe's speech in *Hochstrasser* where he considered the test was whether the payment had been made for acting as or being an employee - 'from' the employment or caused by the employment?

The facts of *Hochstrasser v Mayes* provide a useful illustration of the causation requirement. Here the employer, ICI Ltd, operated a relocation scheme for its employees whereby ICI Ltd would reimburse any loss suffered on the selling price of the employees house. An employee, Mayes, was required to relocate by ICI Ltd He did so and sold his house for £350 less than the purchasing price of three years earlier. The Inland Revenue sought to assess the £350 receipt as an emolument under Schedule E - an assessment that failed.

The House of Lords emphasised that the sum of £350 was paid to the taxpayer in respect of his personal situation as a house-owner and not because of or caused by any services given by him. Emphasis was also placed on the 'favourable' salary of the employee (the £350 was not a disguised salary payment) and on the fact that the onus is on the Revenue to establish that the reward was for the employees' services[36].

The fine dividing line between a payment being caused by your employment and a payment being caused by some other reason is illustrated in *Hamblett v Godfrey*[37]. Employees at GCHQ who wished to continue in employment following the removal of their rights to belong to a trade union were given

---

[31] Practical problems can result from a future sum being received following the termination of employment, or vice versa. The Finance Act 1989 provides some relief by adopting a receipts basis and charging tax by reference to the year of receipt irrespective of the fact that that receipt might not have any source in that year, ie the taxpayer is not an employee in that year of receipt and assessment. Objections to the absence of source can be answered by understanding that the tax liability will be by reference to the relevant year of employment: '

[32] [1959] Ch 22 at 33.

[33] See *Brumby v Milner* [1976] 2 All ER 636.

[34] [1979] STC 34.

[35] [1993] STC 569.

[36] Concern has been expressed at the anomaly consequent on this decision. Depending on the nature and manner of provision, housing benefit or contribution may be taxable. For example, the provision of rent free (full or partial) would attract a tax assessment. Similarly mortgage contributions and concessions will attract the attention of an assessment - but contributions in the form of a guarantee against loss or relocation will not (according to the decision in Hochstrasser v Mayes)!

[37] [1987] 1 All ER 916. See also *Bird v Maitland* [1982] STC 603 where a compensatory sum paid to employees following the withdrawal of a hire care provision was an emolument.

£1,000 each in recognition of the withdrawal of those rights. The Court of Appeal agreed with the Revenue that the sum of £1,000 was an emolument caused by their employment and thus assessable to tax under Schedule E. Purchas LJ explained that the approach that the court should adopt is one of considering the 'status of the payment and the context' in which it was made. The status of the payment was one of compensation for loss or rights as an employee.   The context was one of employment.   Purchas LJ emphasised that : '... if the employment did not exist, there would be no need for the rights in the particular contract in which the taxpayer found herself.'[38]

One might respond that the context of the payment in *Hochstrasser v Mayes* was also one of employment. If Mayes had not been in employment with ICI Ltd he would not have been in the situation of the need to relocate albeit on favourable terms. Perhaps the solution, or at least reconciliation, lies in the emphasis and degree placed on the dominant cause of the payment.[39]

In *Hamblett v Godfrey* the rights subject to compensation were stated as being 'directly connected with the fact of the taxpayer's employment'. That 'direct connection' places emphasis on and indicates the dominant cause of the payment - the employment situation and the employee status.   In contrast, the emphasis in *Hochstrasser v Mayes* was placed on the status of house-owner as the dominant reason and cause for the receipt. This type of analysis indicates the fine line and distinctions that are necessary and not all too obvious in this area of law.

The categories of cases selected below are used as a matter of convenience to place and introduce some decisions that illustrate the fine distinctions and degree(s) of emphasis adopted by the courts. The cases also illustrate the breadth of coverage of s.19, including payments from non-employees and payments by reference to past, present and future services.[40] It must be appreciated that the distinctions are issues of fact and, in determining fact, the courts will look to the reality of the situation in true Ramsay fashion. Thus in *O'Leary v McKinlay*[41] the court looked beyond a trust to the reality of the provision of funds to an employee.

Similarly, in *Shilton v Wilmhurst*[42] Southampton paid a £325,000 transfer fee to Nottingham Forest in order to secure the services of Peter Shilton, a well-known professional footballer. Southampton also paid an £80,000 signing-on fee to Shilton. In addition, Nottingham Forest paid £75,000 to Shilton in

---

[38]   Ibid.
[39]   'Apportionment' suggests itself as an equitable, if not practically onerous, solution.
[39]   'Apportionment' suggests itself as an equitable, if not practically onerous, solution.
[40]   It is possible that the scope for the inclusion of payments for past services as emoluments has been limited. Lord Templeman in *Shilton v Wilmshurst* ([1991] STC 88, at 91) indicated that section 19 includes (*et al*) as emoluments sums paid 'as a reward for past services and as an inducement to continue to perform services'. Although Lord Templeman stated that the 'authorities are consistent' with his analysis, it is not entirely settled that payments for past services must also be an inducement as to future services in order to be treated as an emolument under section 19.
[41]   [1991] STC 42.
[42]   [1991] STC 88.
[43]   Noted by R. Kerridge, 1991 BTR at 311.

order to secure the transfer to Southampton. The reality of the situation was that Nottingham Forest was to receive a net sum of £250,000 (£405,000 - £80,000 - £75,000) and Shilton was to receive £155,000 (75,000 + £80,000). The final outcome of a series of appeals gave effect to this arithmetic reality - albeit the reasoning did cause some difficulty.[43]

Examples

Inducement payments/signing-on fees - The courts have been required to determine the status of inducement payments paid in return for persuading one to adopt employment or leave employment. In most cases, the payments are made by the new employer. Although the inducement payments appear to have made in return for an agreement to enter into employment, it has been possible for the courts to conclude that such payments, albeit 'flowing' from employment, were not caused by the employment[44] - as different cause might be identifiable, such as the foregoing of some personal advantage or right such as amateur status and rights appertaining to such status.

In Jarrold v Boustead[45] the taxpayer received a signing-on fee from Hull Rugby League Club of £3,000. In determining the status of this signing-on fee the Court of Appeal was prepared to look outside the terms of the agreement under which it was paid[46] to conclude that the signing-on fee was not an emolument but an award of compensation to Mr Boustead for relinquishing forever his amateur status and the advantages that flowed from that status.[47] By contrast, in *Riley v Coglan*[48] a sum of £500 paid as a signing-on fee by York Rugby League Club was treated as an emolument from and caused by the employment. The distinction appears to be that in *Riley* the sum was clearly related to the services to be performed : it was repayable if the player failed to serve for the stipulated period (proportionate repayment) and was classified as 'a running payment for making himself available to serve the club when required to do so'.[49]

In *Pritchard v Arundale*[50], a senior chartered accountant (Mr Arundale) surrendered his accountant and senior partner status, and took up an appointment as a joint managing director of a company. In return Mr Arundale received a full salary and a stake in the business consisting of 4,000 shares. On the issue of whether the transfer of the shares amounted

---

[44]   A distinction drawn by Megarry J.

[45]   [1964] 3 All ER 76.

[46]   At first instance Pennycuick J held that it was not permissible to look outside the terms of the agreement under which the £3,000 was paid. It is submitted that the Court of Appeal's approach was correct in ignoring expressions of consideration and agreement but focusing on the reality of the payment

[47]   By relinquishing his amateur status, Mr Boustead, was barred from playing for or visiting and using the facilities of a rugby union club.Byelaw 24 of the Rugby League provides : 'A player who relinquishes his amateur status is permitted to receive a signing-on fee from the club with which he first registers as a professional player. No club shall pay, or offer to pay a signing-on fee to a player who has previously been registered as a professional player with the League.'

[48]   [1968] 1 All ER 314.

[49]   Ibid, per Ungoed-Thomas J.

[50]   [1972] Ch 229, [1971] 3 All ER 1011.

to an 'emolument from employment' the court concluded that it did not. Factors influencing this conclusion included (1) the shares were transferred not by Mr Arundale's new employer but by a third party[51]; (2) under the agreement Mr Arundale was entitled to the transfer of shares 'forthwith' (a full six months in advance of entering into employment as a joint managing director)[52]; and (3) Mr Arundale was to receive a full salary at a commercial rate as an employee.

This analysis was confirmed and followed in *Glantre Engineering v Goodhand*[53] where a £10,000 sum paid to Mr Wells in return for his agreeing to leave a firm of accountants and join another company was held to be an emolument from employment. In this case, Mr Wells received the payment direct from his new employers and it was not regarded as severable from the other benefits to which Mr Wells became entitled under the employment agreement - it was an emolument from that employment agreement and that employment situation. Following an analysis of the arguments that the sum of £10,000 was to compensate Mr Wells for the surrendering of his chartered accountant status (a *Jarrold v Boustead* attempted analogy), the court remained unconvinced : the loss of status was 'a less important factor than the loss of security that Mr Wells would suffer as a result of leaving the employment of the firm of accountants.'[54]

The more recent decision in *Shilton v Wilmhurst*[55] must be added to this discussion. As indicated above, the case involved the transfer of Peter Shilton from Nottingham Forest to Southampton Football Club. Under the transfer arrangement, Southampton were to pay a transfer fee of £325,000 to Nottingham Forest, and a signing-on fee of £80,000 to Peter Shilton. Peter Shilton also demanded and received a fee of £75,000 from Nottingham Forest. The courts were required to determine the status of the £75,000 fee and concluded that it was a fee paid for 'being or becoming an employee' and therefore an emolument from employment and taxable irrespective of the fact that it came from Nottingham Forest rather than from Southampton. The decision clearly permits a signing-on fee as taxable even if paid by your ex-employer (cf *Pritchard v Arundale*, above). The difficulty is in determining when a payment made as a signing-on fee will not be classed as an emolument from employment. The distinctions adopted in *Pritchard v Arundale* and in *Jarrold v Boustead* remain valid and are a guide in this area. The decision in the Shilton case appears to be chipping away at those distinctions (without removing them) and widening the scope of the

---

[51] The third party consisted of the major shareholder of the company. One might suggest that the major shareholder was for all intents and purposes the Company - although the decision in *Salomon v Salomon & Co Ltd* [1897] AC 22, illustrates the difficulty in supporting that suggestion.

[52] It was suggested that the distinction was apparent in that the taxpayer might have died between receiving the shares and entering into the contract of employment. The suggestion was that the shares would still be part of the deceased's estate.

[53] [1983] 1 All ER 542.

[54] See Warner J, ibid.

[55] Supra, n42.

[56] See earlier discussion.

'emolument' to include payments and signing-on (or leaving) fees paid by ex-employers. The decision in the Shilton case made fiscal sense when one views the financial and arithmetic reality of the situation.[56] It also makes sense by closing the door on an area of potential in tax planning and evasion - but, what the decision fails to do is provide sufficient guidance on its own limitations; in particular, when we can apply a *Pritchard v Arundale* or *Jarrold v Boustead* analysis in the determination of whether a payment, from a third party in particular, is made in return for one 'being or agreeing to become an employee'.

If we search the judicial reasoning in *Shilton v Wilmshurst* we begin to find some, albeit inconclusive, guidance. The Court of Appeal expressed agreement with Morritt J that the emolument from a third party (here an ex-employer) would only be an emolument 'from the employment' if that third party could be shown to have an 'interest' in the performance of the employment contract.[57] The problem with that analysis was that it gave the wrong result. Nottingham Forest had no interest in the performance of the contract : Nottingham Forest's interest was in the formation of the contract only.   Adopting the requirement of 'interest' and the distinction between 'interest in performance' and 'interest in formation' led the Court of Appeal to the conclusion that the payment of £75,000 was not an 'emolument from employment' (arithmetically incorrect!).   The House of Lords rejected the Court of Appeal analysis and held the £75,000 to be taxable as an 'emolument from employment' (arithmetically correct!).[58] Lord Templeman in rejecting the 'interest' requirement, emphasised that it should not and did not matter whether the payment be received from Southampton or from Nottingham Forest; the crucial analysis was whether it was paid for 'acting, being or becoming an employee'. In determining this we are to include '... emoluments which are paid as inducements to enter into contracts of employment and to perform services in the future.'[59]

Rewards and Gifts[60] - It is possible that rewards and gifts received by employees might be treated as caused other than from the office or employment and therefore they would not be taxable under section 19. Such 'gifts', rewards and other payments have been found to have been caused by the desire to recognise and acknowledge achievements[61] or to

---

[57]   [1990] STC 55 at 62.

[56]   Supra n40.

[59]   Ibid.The use of the word 'and' is significant. It, perhaps, sets the boundaries and acts as guidance for later courts.(It might also raise doubts as to the correctness of the Shilton case). One might suggest that the requirement of having to show that payment was not only a signing-on fee (or leaving-fee) but also paid on the basis of the 'performance of services in the future' (albeit thoseservices might be performed for a new employer) is analogous to the need to establish an 'interest' in the employment contract, the interest being one of the 'performance of services'. If that is so, then we have not, in substance, removed the Court of Appeal's requirement of the need to establish an 'interest of performance'.

[60]   Although some members of the judiciary and commentators have referred to the testimonial principle, it has been emphasised that the 'testimonial principle and the personal gift principle' are not categories to be defined or explained, but merely examples of transactions that do not fall within the taxable category of remuneration for services (per Megarry J in Pritchard v Arundale (1972) 47 TC 680 at 686). Megarry J clearly and correctly emphasised that there does not exist a range of categories.

[61]   See discussion on Moore v Griffiths [1972] 3 All ER 399 and Seymour v Reed [1927] AC 554, above.

indicate ones appreciation or goodwill at times of celebration or occasion:

> ... the question is not one of which of two [or more] straitjackets the transaction best fits, but whether it comes within the statutory language, or else, failing to do so, falls into the undefined residuary class of cases not caught by the Statute ....

We would do well to remember this advice? Note also the non-taxable award to a bank employee in recognition of his achievements in his professional examination in *Ball v Johnson*[62] The issue is one of fact and degree and is illustrated by the following decisions.

In *Moore v Griffiths*[63], Bobby Moore captained the England football team which was the World Cup in 1966. He then received a bonus of £1,000 from the Football Association. The court decided that this bonus was not taxable as a reward for services; it was of the nature of a testimonial. Brightman J identified six factors that contributed to this conclusion: (1) the payment had no foreseeable element of recurrence; (2) there was no expectation of the award which came as a surprise to Mr Moore and was not a contractual right or expectation; (3) the payment was not made or announced until after the World Cup had been won and the Association had dispensed with the services of the players; (4) a gift was consistent with the Association's nature and functions of promoting the sport and recognising appropriate achievements; (5) the intention of the giver (the Association) was clearly one of benevolence and not one of employer; (6) all players, irrespective of the service rendered, received the same award of £1,000 - it was not proportionate to services rendered.

By contrast, a proportionate 'gift' in *Laidler v Perry*[64] was held to be an emolument from employment. Here an employing company gave each of its 2,300 employees a Christmas 'gift' of a £10 voucher. Any employee who had not been with the company for one full year would not receive the full £10 but a proportionately reduced amount. The court concluded that, despite the expression of 'gift' and the time of year of its presentation, Christmas, the voucher was an emolument[65]. It did not distinguish between the personal achievements and contributions of the employees (upon

---

[62]   1971 47 TC 155.In Calvert v Wainwright [1947] 1 All ER 282, a tip to a taxi driver was held to be taxable. Atkinson J stated that it was a tip "... given in the ordinary way as remuneration for services ...". Atkinson J, further stated that : "... supposing at Christmas, or, when the man is going for a holiday, the hirer says : "You have been very attentive to me, here is a £10 note", he would be making a present, and I should say it would not be assessable because it has been given to the man because of his qualities, his faithfulness, and the way he has stuck to the passenger ..."It is that distinction that is of importance!

[63]   Supra n610.

[64]   [1965] 2 All ER 121.

[65]   In *Seymour v Reed* a professional cricketer with Kent County Cricket Club was, under the club regulations, granted a benefit match. The grant of the benefit match was not of right but discretionary. It was the Committee of the County Cricket Club that exercised the discretion in favour of the taxpayer. Following the benefit match, the taxpayer received the gate monies and subscriptions. The Revenue claimed the money was taxable as an emolument from the taxpayer's employment. The Court disagreed. The benefit match and monies collected were an appreciation and acknowledgement of the cricketer's contributions and personal qualities. The income was more in the nature of a testimonial to mark appreciation at the end of a professional cricketer's career.

qualifying, they would all received a flat rate of £10) but did relate the payment to length of employment.

In Moorhouse v Dooland[66]the Revenue successfully persuaded the court that monies and gifts received by a professional cricketer employed by Lancashire Cricket Club were taxable as emoluments from employment. The monies and gifts here consisted of a contractual entitlement to receive one guinea for every 50 runs scored or six wickets taken, and a right to 'collections' for meritorious performance.[67] In concluding that these sums were emoluments from employment, Jenkins LJ identified four issues for consideration: (1) the perceptions of the receiver: did he believe it to be a gift or testimonial, or did he believe it be derived from or caused by his employment?; (2) was the income part of a contractual entitlement and expectation or was it a purely voluntary payment?; (3) was the payment of a recurring nature?; (4) did the circumstances indicate a gift, a payment according to personal needs or qualities?[68]

Payments for Entering into Restrictive Covenants - Under ICTA 1988, s.313, a payment made in respect of an undertaking given by the employee to restrict his activities is deemed to be an emolument. The restriction(s) must be caused by the undertaking as opposed to interest or professional restrictions on the employee or their position.[69] Payments made after 8 June 1988 will be subject to income tax at the appropriate base or higher rate, and the sum paid will be a deductible income expense of the employer. Payments made prior to 8 June 1988 did offer some tax advantages in allowing the employee to enjoy a 'grossed up' amount equivalent to basic rate liability : only those employees with higher rate liability would be taxed on the payment received at the appropriate higher rate - lower paid employees (basic rate) would in effect receive a tax-free sum!

Payments Made in Respect of the Variation and/or Termination of Employment - It is necessary to have an awareness of the general principles and of the statutory rules. The general principles attempt to give effect to the issue of causation. They respect the need to consider, as a matter of reality and fact, whether the payment was an emolument caused by the employment in accordance with the requirements of TA 1988, s.19. Thus we find that on the matter of payments in respect of the variation and removal of contractual rights we need to carefully consider the 'right' and its context.[70] For example, a payment made in respect of the removal of pension rights was not a payment caused by employment, as required by

---

[66]   [1955] 1 All ER 93, 36 TC 12.

[67]   The latter was a right found in the League rules rather than expressly in the contract with Lancashire Council Cricket Club.

[68]   These issues can be contrasted with the six factors identified by Brightman J in *Moore v Griffiths* (see discussion, above).

[69]   In *Vaughan-Neil v IRC* [1979] 3 All ER 481, a payment made to a barrister for his agreeing not to practice escaped tax. The payment was made upon the barrister taking-up an appointment with a building contractor - inherent in taking-up such employment was a prohibition on a barrister practising at the bar (professional restriction and prohibition).

[70]   See earlier discussion.

s.19.[71] Strictly speaking the pension is not paid in return for services rendered - albeit it tends to be viewed today as part of the remuneration package!

The need to focus on the exact variation and the focus of the payment or compensation received is illustrated in *Holland v Geoghegan*.[72] In that case the 'totting' rights (rights to sell salvaged property) of refuse collectors were terminated. The refuse collectors went on strike and subsequently received a lump sum in respect of terminated rights. The court, however, viewed the lump sum payment as a inducement to return to work and not, primarily, as a payment of compensation. On that basis the lump sum paid was taxable as an emolument from employment.

In *Hunter v Dewhurst*[73] a taxpayer waived his retirement rights under the contract and thereby continued in his office as director. In return he received £10,000 and agreed to renounce all rights of compensation. The House of Lords held that this sum was not an emolument caused by the office or employment. The House of Lords treated this sum as a payment of compensation for the surrender of retirement rights.

When payments are received in respect of the termination of employment, *Dale v De Soissons*[74] indicates the danger of including termination rights and payments in the initial contractual terms. The contractual terms stipulated that the company would have the right to terminate the contract after only one year. The contract also stated that if the company did exercise it's right to terminate after only one year's service, the company would pay a sum in respect of the services and a further sum on the termination. In *Dale v De Soissons*, the company exercised this contractual right and terminated the employment after only one year. The company also paid a sum of £10,000 to the employee, at termination, caused by the employment (albeit paid at termination) because is was part of the employee's rights under the terms and contract of employment.

Finally, as part of the general principles, we must mention the decision in *Shilton v Wilmshurst*.[75] The decision of the House of Lords seems to suggest that a payment made (by your employer) at the termination of your employment will be an emolument if paid by reference to the beginning of your employment with another employer (Southampton Football Club).

The relevant statutory principles are to be found in TA 1988, section 148 (note a redrafting of section 148 took place in the FA 1998). Section 148 is an important residual section in that it applies to payments that are not

---

[71] See *Tilley v Wales* [1943] 1 All ER 280. [1972] 3 All ER 333.
[73] (1932) 16 TC 605. There is some concern over the status of the decision in *Hunter v Dewhurst*. In the case, four judges found for the taxpayer (three being in the House of Lords) and five found for the Revenue. In later cases, it has been suggested that *Hunter v Dewhurst* be confined to its special facts. This illustrates the difficulties and uncertainties faced in this area.
[74] [1950] 2 All ER 460. See also EMI Group Electronics Ltd v Coldicott [1997] STC 1372.
[75] Supra n42.
[76] TA 1988, s188(4); FA 1988, s74(1). Hence in *Shilton v Wilmshurst*, the debate took place in recognition that if the sum paid by Nottingham Forest was not an emolument under the general principles, then it would be caught by section 148 subject to the £30,000 exemption provided by section 188.

taxable as emoluments under the general principles (experience as 'not otherwise chargeable to tax'). It applies to payments made and other benefits not otherwise chargeable to tax which are received in connection with the termination of a person's employment, or any change in the duties of or emoluments from a person's employment, which are chargeable to tax under this section if and to the extent that their amount exceeds £30,000 (s. 148 (i)).

Benefits are defined as items which would have been emoluments 'had the employment continued' (s.148(2)). Also any part of the payment not covered by the exemption is treated as received in the tax year 'when the payment or benefit is actually received' (s.148(3) - note previously it was when the termination, etc, occurred)[76]. A number of types of payment are excluded from s.148 including any payment that is 'otherwise chargeable to tax.'

Fringe Benefits ('Benefits in Kind')

In addition to salaries, fees and wages, the term 'emoluments' includes benefits in kind[77] (perquisites and profits). The rationale for attempting to include the value of benefits in kind in calculating tax liability was expressed by the Royal Commission on the Taxation of Profits and Income as necessary in order to promote equality and equity between taxpayers.

> If advantage can be taken of any weakness in the tax treatment of such benefits, there is an obvious temptation to resort to them as a means of part remuneration. And the harm that results is not merely the absolute loss of revenue : it is unfairness in the distribution of tax as between one taxpayer and another.[78]

The above quote also indicates the importance of not leaving any 'gaps' in the taxation of benefits. One assumes that any 'gaps' will promote tax planning and tax advantages to the detriment of the equality and equity among taxpayers. Whether the rules on the taxation of fringe benefits achieves or substantially contributes to any desired equal treatment of taxpayers is debatable.[79] Economists point out that an income tax system which exempts or fails to catch income in kind will encourage individuals toward self-sufficiency and trade by barter and influence the allocation of resources. An often-given example of that influence on the allocation of

---

[77]   An appropriate definition of a benefit in kind can be found in the Final Report of The Royal Commission on the Taxation of Profits and Income, Cmnd 9474 (1055) at para 208 : '... the law includes in its conception of income a benefit having money's worth even though it is only received in kind.'

[78]   Ibid.

[79]   See The Royal Commission's Report, ibid at para 211: '... all benefits in kind received in the course of employment and attributable to it are a form of remuneration and should rank as taxable income, since otherwise one taxpayer's income is not equitably balanced against another's.'

[80]   [1892] AC 150.

resources is of a man painting his own house rather than employing someone else to paint his home. The latter transaction would attract tax. The result is an incentive towards do-it-yourself work where it may be more efficient for individuals to specialise in the occupations at which they have a comparative advantage. The complexity of the rules and principles applying to the taxation of fringe benefits illustrates, or perhaps contributes to, the difficulties in this area. The principles demand that we ask two questions: (1) is the benefit taxable in the hands of that particular taxpayer? (a 'status' and 'benefit' issue); (2) if the benefit is taxable, what is the appropriate value of the benefit? In answering these questions we must consider both common law and statutory rules. Our starting point is consideration of the principle of convertibility.

Convertibility

This principle was established by the House of Lords in *Tennant v Smith*.[80] At its purest level, this principle states that a benefit is taxable only if the taxpayer is able to convert the benefit into money. Thus in *Tennant v Smith* the provision of free accommodation (valued at £50) to a bank employee was not taxable because it was non-convertible. The bank employee was to act as custodian of the premises and conduct special bank business after bank hours. He was not allowed to sublet the premises nor to use them for any purpose other than the bank's business. It was confirmed that the benefit 'is not income unless it can be turned to money'.[81]

The principle of convertibility has subsequently developed to include the convertible value of benefits that could not be assigned or sold but could be converted into monetary value. For example, in *Heaton v Bell* the taxpayer partook of his employer's car loan scheme. In return for the use of a car, the taxpayer received an amended lower wage (a deduction of just over £2 per week). It is important to appreciate that the employer would enjoy the use of the car but it was an unassignable (to a third party) right. The House of Lords held that the benefit was convertible. It could, at any time, be converted into money by the employee giving notice to his employers that he wished to relinquish his right to use the car and his employers would then be obliged to increase his wages by an amount equal to the amount by which his wages had been reduced by the car loan scheme (£2 per week).[82]

Similarly, in *Abbott v Philbin*[83] a non-assignable share option was convertible in that it could be used to raise monies. Alternatively, the right to exercise

---

[81] Lord Halsbury, ibid at 156.
[82] n Lord Upjohn dissented explaining that the benefit (the use of the car) could not be turned into money: 'In my opinion, this personal unassignable right for use of the car was not equivalent to money while it continued and that, surely must be the test ...'.
[83] [1961] AC 352.

the option enabled the taxpayer to obtain shares from the company. Those shares would be property rights of value and freely convertible into money.

It is interesting that in both *Abbott v Philbin* and in *Heaton v Bell*, the benefit was expressed to, or appeared to be, unassignable (directly) to a third party. It is perhaps asking too much of one to accept that both decisions are authorities for allowing the Revenue to ignore expressed or actual restrictions on assignment. In *Tennant v Smith* the court did not appear to look beyond the expressed non-assignability of the benefit as found in the terms of employment and occupation. In *Abbott v Philbin* Lord Radcliffe criticised the 'not very precise language' used in *Tennant v Smith*, and suggested that there exist many uncertainties that have yet to be cleared up, including the following:

> must the inconvertibility arise from the nature of the thing itself, or can it be imposed merely by contractual stipulation? Does it matter that the circumstances are such that conversion into money is a practical, though not a theoretical, impossibility; or, on the other hand, that conversion, though forbidden, is the most probable assumption.[84]

The test of convertibility not only determines the taxability or otherwise of the benefit, but it also provides the answer to the question of the 'value' of the benefit provided. The value of the benefit provided equals the convertible value at the date of provision. Thus in *Wilkins v Rogerson*[85] an employee who was provided with a suit was assessed on the second hand value of the suit at the date of provision (the convertible value). The second hand value was lower than the cost to the employer of providing the benefit but it reflected the value that the employee would expect if he elected to convert the benefit into money.[86]

In *Heaton v Bell* the converted value was of £2 per week - the amount by which the taxpayer's wages would increase if he had elected to withdraw from the car loan scheme and the amended lower wage benefit.

Statutory Rules - Despite judicial efforts, the convertibility rule remains limited in its scope and, particularly in times of high tax rates, ineffective in controlling and dealing with the growth in fringe benefits.[87] The legislature has responded to this situation by declaring that certain types of benefit and benefits provided to certain types of employee, will be taxable irrespective

---

[84]   Ibid, at 378-9.
[85]   [1961] 1 All ER 358.
[86]   The suit cost the employer £14 15s to provide, but the taxpayer was attributed as receiving a benefit to the value of £5 only (the second hand value of the suit).
[87]   It has been reported that the use of recognised fringe benefits is far higher in the UK than in any other European country.
      The limitations of the principle in Tennant v Smith may not have been of concern in 1892 when the standard rate of income tax was only 2.5% : the incentive to substitute income with a fringe benefit was clearly not prominent or strong.

of the fact that those benefits would not be convertible under the principle established in *Tennant v Smith*.

Living Accommodation[88]

Where living accommodation is provided for a person (or to his family) by reason of his employment, its value to him, less anything he pays himself, is taxed under Schedule E.[89] The charge only applies to the provision of living accommodation, not to ancillary services such as heating, lighting and furniture (although the provision of such services to 'higher paid employees' may be assessable under other statutory provisions). It is also important to establish that the accommodation was provided by reason of the employment.[90]

The assessment is based on the value to the employee of the accommodation provided. The TA 1988, section 837 explains that the value to the employer is the annual value, and that the annual value is the rateable value of the property or the rent paid by the employer to provide the accommodation (if the latter presents a higher figure).[91]

An additional charge is imposed an employees who are provided with living accommodation that costs more than £75,000 to provide.[92] The additional charge involves the application of a formula taking into account the actual cost of provision and any rent paid by the employee.[93]

The statutory rules do permit some relief to those who occupy living accommodation provided by their employer in 'non-beneficial circumstances'. The following classes of non-beneficial occupation and provision will not be chargeable :

(a) where the accommodation is deemed necessary for the proper performance of the employee's duties;

(b) where the employment is one where it is customary to provide living accommodation and the accommodation is provided for the better performance of the employment duties;

(c) where the occupation of the premises is part of special security arrangements.

[88] TA 1988, ss145, 146.
[89] Note that this rule does not apply if the accommodation is made subject to a charge to him as income tax elsewhere. For example, if the accommodation is convertible then it will be taxed in accordance with the *Tennant v Smith* principles and not by an application of these statutory rules and valuations.
[90] In practice, if the accommodation is provided by your employer it is deemed to have been provided by reason of your employment.
[91] Section 837 initially provides that the annual value is a 'fictitious rent' equating to that 'which might reasonably be expected to be obtained on a yearly letting if the tenant undertook to pay rates and taxes and the landlord undertook to pay for repairs and insurance.' In practice, it is the rateable value rather than the value of the 'fictitious rent' that is used for assessment purposes.
[92] TA 1988, s146. (Introduced by FA 1983, s21).
[93] The formula provides : [(cost of providing accommodation) minus £75,000 x official rate of interest] minus any excess rent paid by the employee.
[94] See Vertigan v Brady [1988] STC 91.
[95] [1988] STC 91.

The nature of your employment and your contractual responsibilities will help determine whether you are able to enjoy the 'non-beneficial' occupation exceptions. For example, it is probable that hotel staff will enjoy exception (a). Similarly, in *Tennant v Smith* the obligation to occupy the premises was related to the performance of contractual duties. The requirements in situation (b) of 'customary' and 'better performance' might present an additional burden. 'Customary' will demand an examination of 'industry wide' practices and an examination of the history and length of those practices.[94] This burden can be balanced against the requirement in exception (a) to show that the occupation was 'necessary' for 'proper performance' rather than merely promoting 'better performance'.

In *Vertigen v Brady*[95], Mr Vertigen was a very experienced nurseryman and a 'key worker.' His employer bought him a bungalow in which Mr Vertigen lived rent free. Mr Vertigen could not afford to buy his own bungalow. Mr Vertigen was assessed under s.145, TA and appealed on the grounds that the provision was either: necessary for the proper performance of his duties, or for the better performance of duties of his employment and was the kind of employment in which it was customary to make such provision.

Mr Vertigen's arguments were rejected. Knox J explained that the 'necessity' required for ground (a) was a necessity based on the relationship between proper performance and the dwelling house, not a 'necessity based on the personal exigencies of the taxpayer in the shape of his inability to finance the acquisition of suitable accommodation.'

The claim on the second ground also failed. It was accepted that the provision of the bungalow was for the better performance of Mr Vertigen's duties but that the prudent practice had not become customary! According to Knox J the issue of 'custom' demanded consideration of three factors:

■ Statistical Evidence - How common is the practice statistically?

■ Longevity: how long has the practice gone on? A custom can hardly come into existence overnight.

■ Trade acceptance: has it achieved acceptance generally by the relevant employees?

Vouchers and Credit Tokens

If an employee receives a voucher or credit token that can be exchanged for goods and/or services, he will be taxed on the cost of provision, ie the

---

[96]   TA 1988, s.141, 142 and 144. Note, TA 1988 ss.143, 144 - If a voucher is exchangeable for cash, the exchange value of the voucher is chargeable under the PAYE Scheme. A cash voucher is one which can be exchanged for a sum of money.

[97]   The 'convertibility' principle did develop to recognise an element of the cost of provision or, more accurately, the debts incurred by the employer in providing the benefit. For example, in *Nicholl v Austin* (1935) 19 TC 531 a company paid an employee's debts and the court held that the benefits provided were convertible into a sum equating with the costs to the employer of providing those benefits (the cost of settling those debts).

amount that it cost the employer to provide the voucher or token (except in the case of a cash voucher where the exchange value will apply).[96] Prior to the introduction of legislation covering this area, the convertibility principle would have caught many vouchers and, possibly, credit tokens.[97] Problems did occur with the growing use of non-convertible credit tokens, such as credit cards and non-transferable season tickets. Here the voucher or token remained in the physical possession of the employee and, although it may have been used to acquire goods or services, it remained non-converted. Under today's legislation, convertibility is irrelevant and the credit token or voucher will be taxable on the value of 'the cost of provision.'

Special Statutory Provisions Applying only to Directors and 'higher paid employees'

In 1948 special rules were introduced to tax certain benefits provided to directors and higher paid employees that were not 'otherwise chargeable to tax.' In other words, these benefits will be taxable even though they are not convertible within the principle of *Tennant v Smith*. The relevant rules can now be found in the TA 1988, Part V, Chapter II and Schedules 6 and 7. The statutory rules began life in 1948 as an attempt to control the tax avoidance benefits provided through the use of expense account provisions. Today the rules apply to a wider range of benefits and attempt to provide some recognition of the practice of providing remuneration and benefit packages. The main specific benefits which are chargeable to income tax by the TA 1988, Part V, Chapter II are : (a) expense allowances; (b) benefits in general; (c) beneficial loan arrangements; (d) expenses connected with living accommodation; (e) cars and petro; and (f) scholarships.

It is important to appreciate that this legislation only applies to (a) directors and employees with emoluments of £8,500 or more, per annum[98] and (b) directors with emoluments of less than £8,500, except where those directors work full-time in the company and control less than five percent of the company.[99] In computing the employees emoluments for the purposes of the £8,500 threshold level, it is assumed that the rules in TA 1988, ss153 and 154 are applicable and sums computed on the basis of ss153 and 154 are included within the initial computation of the employees' emolument level. Such sums will later be ignored if the initial emolument level does not reach the £8,500 threshold level.

---

[98]   The FA 1989, s53, explains that employees earning over £8,500 are no longer to be described as higher paid. We shall continue to use the term as one of convenience.

[99]   'Directors' need not be formally appointed as 'directors' in order to be caught by the legislation (TA 1988, s168).The 5% requirement relates to 5% of ordinary share capital or distribution rights and satisfies the statutory requirement of 'material interest' (TA 1988, s167).

[100]   TA 1988, s.153.

[101]   To be deductible, expenses must satisfy the tests laid down in TA 1988 ss198, 201 and 203.

[102]   TA 1988, s.154.

Payments for Expenses and Expense Allowances[100]- Any sum paid to an employee, by reason of his employment, in respect of expenses is treated as income of that employee or director. This includes expense allowances and the reimbursement of expenses. The expenses are caught under this provision unless 'otherwise chargeable to tax'. Furthermore genuine expenses[101] are deductible and are not treated as emoluments.

Benefits in General[102]-This requires that certain benefits provided to directors or higher paid employees are to be treated as emoluments from their office or employment. The benefits caught by section 154 include sums spent on or in connection with the provision of (a) accommodation, other than living accommodation; (b) entertainment; (c) domestic or other services; and (d) other benefit 1988, section 154 requires that certain benefits provided to directors or higher paid employees are to be treated as emoluments from their office or employment.

Rendell v Went[103] illustrates that the charge on the benefit provided is upon the 'cost of the benefit'. The cost of the benefit demands that we recognise the expenses 'incurred by the employer in or in connection with' securing the provision of the benefits. Thus in *Rendell v Went*[102] the cost of the benefit provided was the full cost to the employer of £641.

Assessing the cost of the provision of an in-house service, such as reduced rate or free travel to airline employees, has proved difficult and might possibly lead to absurd results[104]. The obvious (and perhaps logical) solution would be to follow the approach of most other OECD countries and insert market value as the cost of provision. Another sensible choice would be to use the 'marginal cost' of the provision as the relevant employer's cost. Unfortunately, the legislation appears to indicate that the appropriate cost is the 'actual cost' of provision[105].

Thus in *Pepper v Hart*[106]employees of Malvern College had taken the benefit of a scheme whereby their sons were educated at the school at one-fifth of the fees normally charged. The employees submitted that the cost of the benefit should be the marginal cost, and that in this instance the marginal cost of the boys' education represented some additional expenditure on items such as food, laundry and stationery. It was clear that the presence of the boys did not increase the other expenses of running the school : staff

---

[103] [1964] 2 ALL ER 464.

[104] Provision for an employee or for members of his family or household, by his employer, are deemed to be made by reason of the employment.

[105] TA 1988, s.155 contains many exemptions from the s154 charge. These include : the provision of accommodation and supplies used at the employee's place of work and used solely for work purposes, canteen meals provided for the staff generally, expenses incurred in the provision of any pension, annuity or other like benefit for the director or employees and their families upon the employee's death or retirement, medical insurance and treatment for foreign visits. [1964] 2 All ER 464. The actual cost must include 'a proper proportion of any expenses relating partly to the benefit and partly to other matters.'

salaries, insurance, heating and maintenance of buildings, maintenance of grounds, remuneration of administrative and other staff, and so on. Nor would the absence of the boys have reduced these 'other expenses'. Unanimously the Court of Appeal rejected the submissions of the taxpayers. Nicholls LJ explained[107] that the 'statutory formula is concerned with one specific calculation : the amount of the expense incurred by the employer in providing the benefit.'

Applying that calculation it was clear that each place in the school cost the school as much as every other place. Thus the expense incurred by the school in providing the benefits to the assistant school masters and bursar must include a proper portion of the general running expenses of the school; that portion represents the statutory requirement of including 'a proper proportion of any expenses relating partly to the benefit and partly to other matters.'

The taxpayers were properly assessed on the full cost rather than the marginal cost of the benefit; Nicholls LJ admitted[108] that the necessary rateable apportionment of the relevant expenses would produce a figure close to the amount of the ordinary school fees - thus removing the benefit!

Initial academic and press response suggest that this decision may have adverse and absurd effects on existing fringe-benefit concessions.[109] The suggestion is that employees may be assessed on a cost basis that may exceed the cost of the benefit to non-employees. For example, airline staff occupying otherwise empty seats on an aircraft amounts to very little in marginal costs but amounts to an excessive amount if the cost is to include an apportionment of full costs.[110]

An appeal by the taxpayers to the House of Lords was successful. The taxpayers were charged on the marginal cost of provision. The House of Lord's decision is important in a wider context in the pronouncements made on the issue of statutory interpretation and the use of supplementary material, including the use of Hansard. On the less important issue of the value to be attributed to the benefit provided there appear to be two approaches. In the minority, Lord Mackay LC insisted that once the benefit to be taxed has been identified, one must then consider whether that benefit was received as of right or as result of the exercise of the provider's discretion[111]. If it was as a result of the exercise of discretion, then the surplus (marginal) costs of exercising that discretion and providing, in this case the surplus school places, must be the cost of provision.

---

[106] [1990] STC 786.
[107] Ibid at 791.
[108] Ibid at 788.
[109] For an initial response see J. Dyson, [1990] BTR 122 and D. Wright, the Sunday Times, 18 November 1990, at 11.
[110] [1992] STC 898.
[111] [1992] STC 898 at 901.

Lord Browne-Wilkinson (representing the majority) expressed disagreement with the approach of Lord Mackay on the ground that the distinction proposed was 'not reflected in the parliamentary proceedings'. Lord Browne-Wilkinson preferred the approach of accepting that the relevant statutory provisions were ambiguous and thus he referred to the debate in Hansard and in particular to the responses given by the, then, Financial Secretary to the Treasury, which made it clear that the absurd consequence of apportioning total costs to those enjoying an in-house provision or benefit was never intended. Nor was it intended that market price should apply (an original provision that was withdrawn during debate). Lord Browne-Wilkinson concluded that Parliamentary debate reveals that the value of the benefit provided (in house) was intended to be and should represent and reflect the marginal costs of provision. Commenting on the difficulties that a reference to Hansard and Parliamentary debate might cause, Lord Brown-Wilkinson suggested that he did not believe that the practical difficulties arising from this approach to statutory interpretation were '... sufficient to outweigh the basic need for the courts to give effect to the words enacted by Parliament in the sense that they were intended by Parliament to hear...'[112].

The Legislature has been able to predict and make provision in other potentially difficult areas. For example, where the provided (the benefit) remains the property of the employer, the employee is taxed on the 'annual value' of the asset, plus any other expenses of provision excluding acquisition and production costs.[113] The 'annual value' for the provision of land is its rateable value. For other assets, the annual value is 20 percent of their market value at the time that they are first provided by the employer.[114]If the ownership of the asset is subsequently transferred to the employee the employee may be charged on the value of the item when he first received it less any annual value charges that may have been applied.[115] This is an anti-avoidance provision preventing the abuse of the normal rule[116] of market value at the date of transfer in circumstances of depreciating assets.

If the expense incurred by the employer is partly to provide a benefit to the employee and partly for some other identifiable purpose, section 156 allows 'apportionment' to take place. The employee is only taxed on the proper proportion of the expense and the benefit. For example, in *Westcott v Bryan*[117] a managing director was required by his employers to live in a large house, close to the Potteries in Staffordshire. The Managing Director would have preferred to have lived in London and would have preferred a much

---

112   [1992] STC 898 at 921.
113   TA 1988, s.156(4).
114   TA 1988, s.156(5).
115   TA 1988, s.156(4).
116   TA 1988, s.156(3).
117   [1969] 3 All ER 564.
118   It is significant that in *Rendell v Went* [1964] 2 All ER 464, apportionment of the legal fees was not allowed on the grounds that 'no part of the money was spent on something that did not benefit the taxpayer'. The taxpayer enjoyed all the money in that it was all spent to cover his legal fees.
119   TA 1988, s.163.

smaller property. His employers were concerned over the need to entertain clients and the convenience of the location. The employers paid most of the running costs of the house. The court held that the taxpayer was to be assessed on only a proportion of the running costs provided by his employers. The money spent by his employers was partly for the taxpayer's benefit and partly for the benefit of others.[118]

Living Accommodation (ancillary services)[119]- The general rules in TA 1988 section 145 covering the provision of living accommodation are supplemented in the case of directors and higher paid employees to facilitate the taxation of services provided with the accommodation (such as furniture, heating, telephone, etc). The 'general benefits' provisions in section 154 will normally attach to the provision of 'ancillary services'. However, where those ancillary services are provided in relation to non-beneficial occupation some relief is provided in section 163. Section 163 provides that in instances of non-beneficial occupation the provision of sums in respect of heating, lighting, cleaning, repairs, furniture etc, must not exceed 10 per cent of the emoluments of the employment - a maximum charge for the provision of those services and benefits.

Low Interest or Beneficial Loans[120] If the employer provides the

employee with a low-interest or interest-free loan, the employee is taxed on the cash equivalent of that loan. The cash equivalent represents a computation of the benefit received by calculating the difference between the amount of interest that would have been paid at an official rate and any interest actually paid.

Some relief is provided in that a *de minimis* exception applies[121] and loans for 'qualifying purposes' are excluded. A 'qualifying purpose' is one that is generally recognised as deductible from total income. For example, loans to purchase one's main residence are eligible for interest relief under the general law (although a £30,000 limit applies).

Should the employer release or write off (whole or in part) the amount due, a charge will be imposed on the amount so released or written off (the benefit provided). This will also apply to the release or writing off of loans made for a qualifying purpose.[122]

---

[120]   TA 1988, s.160 and Sched. 7.
[121]   TA 1988, s.161. The de minimis limit means that the employee is not treated as receiving an emolument where the aggregate amount of all beneficial loans outstanding in a tax year does not exceed £5000.
[122]   A benefit has been provided in that the outstanding amount of the loan (and interest) are no longer repayable.

Cars and Fuel[123]

If an employee is provided with the use of a car, that benefit may be taxable, except where that car is a 'pool car'. A 'pool car' is a car that is genuinely available to more than one employee; is not regularly garaged at an employee's house; and any provided use is purely incidental to its business use.[124]In all other cases, the provision of the car will be a taxable benefit. The value of the benefit provided is represented by a cash equivalent fixed by statute. Some concerns have developed as to whether the statutory regime adequately taxes the private value of the 'company car' and some changes have been introduced to try to reflect concerns. Provided below is an outline of both the 'old' regime and the 'new' rules. These provide a useful comparison in the often debated area of the benefit of a 'company car', one of the more visible 'fringe benefits'.

'Old' Rules - Under the 'old' regime a declared cash equivalent is reduced by 50 per cent if the car is used preponderantly for business travel (at least 18,000 miles *per annum*). Conversely, if business travel is below 2,500 miles *per annum* the cash equivalent is increased by 50percent - the personal benefits exceed the car's business utility.[125]

If the employer also provides the employee with free petrol for private motoring, a statutory scale of charges similarly applies. The scale and charge is reduced by 50 per cent if business mileage exceeds 18,000, BUT, the charge is not increased if business mileage is less than 2,500 miles *per annum*.

'New' Rules -   The 'old' rules were changed with effect from 6 April 1994. The new rules will tax cars on a cash equivalent of 35 per cent of the list price of the car based on the   full cost (ie car price including VAT and cost of any accessories and delivery) subject to a list price ceiling of £80,000 with a third reduction for 2,500 plus business miles and a reduction of two-thirds for over 18,000 business miles *per annum*. A further reduction of one third may be made if the car is four years old or more at the end of the year (section 157, schedule 6).

Relief still remains for pool cars. Similarly the car 'related benefit' of fuel for private use still raises a tax charge (section 158), on the basis of a scale charge.   The 1998/99 scales are as follows: Petrol Engine Size (Cash Equivalent) Up to 1400cc (1010)1400cc 2000cc(1280) Over 2000cc(1890). Diesel Engine Size (Cash Equivalent) 2000 or less(1280) Over 2000(1890).

---

[123]   TA 1988, ss.157 and 158. On 30 July 1992, the Inland Revenue issued a Consultative Document, 'Company Cars - Reform of Income Tax Treatment'.The document contains the broad aims of (i) ensuring that the tax charged is a fair reflection of the benefit received; (ii) avoiding distortions in the car market; (iii) minimising incentives to drive less fuel efficient cars; (iv) keeping administrative costs to a minimum. The central proposal is that the car cash equivalents should be based on a percentage of the price of the car supplied. No charges are proposed to the apportionment rules or to the 'business deductions' rules. Although the general aim of 'neutrality' is accepted, some critics have suggested that the proposals fall short of satisfying the declared aims, and that the proposals fail to recognise that the majority of company cars are work cars - figures reveal that less than eight percent of 'company cars' travel less than 2,500 business rules per annum whereas over 26 per cent travel 18,000 plus, business rules *per annum* (see K.Paterson [1992] BTR 368).

[124]   TA 1988, S.159.

[125]   TA 1988, s.168(5); TA 1988, s.157 and Sched. 6.

In March 1999 the Chancellor announced further reform of the company car tax regime seeking to move toward a system of company car taxation based on carbon dioxide emissions rather than mileage from April 2002. The Government wants companies and staff to choose more fuel-efficient cars. At the same time the Government has announced reductions in the business mileage and age-related discounts from April 1999. Essentially these are:

- If you drive between 2,500 and 18,000 miles the tax charge will be 25 per cent of the car price instead of 22 per cent

- If you drive more than 18,000 miles the tax charge is 15 per cent instead of 11.66 per cent

- If your car is four or more years old, you will knock off just 25 per cent of the resultant tax figure rather than one third

- The tax paid on free fuel for private use has been increased by 20 per cent

Scholarships[126]

If a member of a director's or higher-paid employee's family receives a scholarship (directly or indirectly) from the employer, the director or higher-paid employee will be taxed on the value of the scholarship. Some relief is available in that the charge can be avoided if it is shown that the scholarship was from a trust or similar scheme and that such payments do not represent more than 25 per cent of payments made from that fund in that year.

Mobile Phones[127]

Although aspects of the provision of a mobile phone might be caught under section 156, the Finance Act 1991 introduced a scale charge of £200 whenever a mobile phone is provided and is available for private use. The rules are contained in section 159A TA. In March 1999 the Chancellor announced that the tax charge for workers who use mobile phones provided by their employers would be scrapped from April 1999, perhaps encouraging greater use of the dreaded mobile phone!

Employee Shareholdings

Section 162 TA introduced controls to recognise the growing use of

---

[126] TA 1988, s.165.
[127] TA 1988, S.159A added by FA 1991, s.30(2).

employee share schemes. This 'use' often reflected elements of the following: the use of partly-paid shares or shares acquired at less than market value; and the   use of 'stop loss' arrangements consisting of arrangements to protect against a fall in the value of the shares after the employee acquired them (for example, through an option for the company to buy back the shares at the employee's acquisition cost).

Section 162 imposes a charge on the benefits connected with employee shareholdings where 'an employee (or a person about to be employed) acquires shares at an undervalue in a company (whether from the employer or not) in pursuance of a 'right or opportunity available by reason of the employee's employment'.

The charge applies by deeming there to be a 'notional loan' to which the 'beneficial loan' provision (s.160) apply. The amount of the notional loan is the amount of the undervalue represented by the difference between the market value of fully paid shares at the date of acquisition less any payment made for those shares. The notional loan continues until the amount outstanding is made good or the shares are disposed of.

Deductible Expenses

The rules and principles in the deductibility of expenses have been described as 'notoriously narrow in their application' and 'notoriously rigid, narrow and restricted in their operation'.[128] Certainly when one compares the deductibility rules in Schedule E with the Schedule D taxpayer, the Schedule E employee does appear to be at a disadvantage. The Schedule D taxpayer enjoys a deductibility test of wider application.

It is normal to draw a distinction between (a) expenses connected with travelling, and (b) other expenses. The TA 1988, 198(1) as amended by the FA 1988 explains that if the holder of an office or employment is obliged to incur and defray out of the enrolments of the office or employment - qualifying travelling expenses, or any amount (other than qualifying travelling expenses) expended wholly, exclusively and necessarily in the performance of the duties of the office or employment, there may be deducted for the emoluments to be assessed the amount so incurred and defrayed. 'Qualifying travelling expenses' means amounts necessarily expended on

---

[128]   See the Final Report of the Royal Commission on Taxation of Profits and Income. Cmnd 9474 (1955).The Report also reveals the opinion that the 'existing rule drew the line as fairly as could be expected of any general rule and that no other form of wording would be an improvement upon it'.

[129]   See Ricketts v Colquhoun [1926] AC 1, '... the expense had to be one which each and every occupant of the particular office was necessarily obliged to incur'.

travelling in the performance of the duties of the office or employment, or other expenses of travelling which are attributable to the necessary attendance at any place of the holder of the office or employment in the performance of the duties of the office or employment, and are not expenses of ordinary commuting or private travel.

Thus it appears from these provisions that travelling expenses need only be incurred 'necessarily' or be expenses which are not expenses of 'ordinary commuting' but which are 'attributable' to the necessary attendance at a place of work. This is different to the 'wholly, exclusively and necessarily' incurred requirement for the deduction of other expenses.

the application of section 198 involves the application of two tests :

- Was the taxpayer necessarily obliged to incur those expenses?
- Were the expenses necessarily incurred in the performance of the taxpayer's duties?

The test of 'necessary' travel expenses appears to be an objective test demanding consideration of whether the class of employee (or potential employee) would necessarily incur those travel expenses as part of their duties[129]. In some instances, the class of employee might be so small as to demand an assessment of whether it was necessary for an individual to incur those expenses as part of his or her duties. In *Ricketts v Colquhoun*[130] the class of employee (or potential employee) was wide and could have included those who lived in the Portsmouth area where the work was to be undertaken rather than in London. The taxpayer's decision to reside in London was a personal decision and his travel expenses from London to Portsmouth were not necessarily incurred as a consequence of his employment or office in Portsmouth. By contrast in *Taylor v Provan*[131] the class of potential employee was very narrow; it consisted of the need to acquire the services of one particular individual. The question of whether he would necessarily have to incur travel expenses from Canada to London in the performance of his duties became a personal question and was answered in the affirmative : the employers could only employ him and must accept his decision on residence.

The second part of the section 198 test demands consideration of whether the travel expenses were incurred in the performance of the duties of employment. It seems that the application of this part of the test invites the

[130] Ibid.
[131] [1974] 1 All ER 1201.

following general rules.

1. The costs of travelling to work from home are not deductible on the grounds that the travel does not involve the 'performance of your duties': your duties commence when you arrive at work, not on your way to work.

2. The costs of travelling from one place of employment to a place of different employment are not deductible. Once again you are not travelling in the course of your employment: you are travelling from one employment to another employment.

3. In contrast to (2) above, if you are travelling from one place of employment to another place of the same employment, it is likely that you are travelling in the performance of your duties. In such a case, it is likely that any expenses incurred will be deductible as necessarily incurred in the performance of your duties (provided, of course, that the employee is obliged to travel within the same employment).

4. It is possible that the employee's 'home' can be classed as a point where work commences (a place of work) and travel between that point to another point of the same work will be deductible, as a continuation of those duties.

The following decisions indicate the complexity of the above rules and of the distinctions adopted.

The case of *Ricketts v Colquhoun*[132] involved a barrister who resided in London. His earnings from the bar were assessable under Schedule D, Case II. The barrister also took up an appointment as Recorder of Portsmouth (Schedule E appointment). The barrister sought to deduct the costs of travelling from his home in London to Portsmouth. His claim failed. The costs of travel were not necessarily incurred. As explained above, he could have elected to have lived in Portsmouth. Nor were the costs incurred in the performance of his duties : his duties as Recorder did not commence until he reached the office in Portsmouth - when travelling to that office he was travelling to his employment, and not in the course of that employment.

In *Owen v Pook*[133] the taxpayer, a medical practitioner, worked as a general practitioner at his home in Fishguard. The taxpayer also held a part-time appointment as an obstetrician and anaesthetist at Haverfordwest, 15 miles

---

[132]   Supra 129.
[133]   [1969] 2 All ER 1.

from Fishguard. The part-time appointments included 'stand-by' duties. These duties required the taxpayer to be accessible by telephone: he often gave advice by phone. The costs of travelling between the taxpayer's home in Fishguard and the hospital in Haverfordwest were deductible. Lord Guest explained that the taxpayer had, in contrast to *Ricketts v Colquhoun,* two places where the duties were performed. Dr Owen's duties commenced at the moment he was first contacted by the hospital authorities. He took responsibility for a patient as soon as he received a telephone call. He often advised treatment by telephone :

> ...there were thus two places where his duty is performed, the hospital and his telephone in his consulting room. If he was performing his duties at both places, then it is difficult to see why, on the journey between the two places, he was not equally performing his duties...

In *Taylor v Provan*[134] the taxpayer was appointed as a director of an English Brewery Company. The taxpayer was resident in Canada but was appointed by the English Company because of his very special knowledge and skills on matters of amalgamation and merger within the brewing industry. The taxpayer completed most of his work in Canada but frequently made visits to England. He did not receive any remuneration for the work completed, but he did receive income to cover the travel expenses to England. The House of Lords held by a majority of 3:2 that the expenses were an allowable deduction. The reasoning of the majority is not altogether settled and certain. Lord Morris and Lord Salmon appear to accept that the taxpayer was travelling between two places of the same employment and was thus travelling in the course of, and in the performance of, his duties of employment. More controversially, Lord Reid in his search for the *ratio* of *Owen v Pook* appeared to accept that the expenses were deductible on the grounds of 'necessity'.[135] If the latter is the sole reasoning of Lord Reid and of *Owen v Pook*, then it fails to recognise the dual requirements of 'necessity' and 'performance' of section 198 - unless the latter requirement was implicitly accepted as present on the facts presented in both cases.

One of the more interesting concerns expressed by Lord Reid was the danger of adopting a test on the ground of one's home being regarded as a place of work. Lord Reid expressed concern that the majority in *Owen v Pook* did not intend to

[134] Supra 131.
[135] [1974] 1 All ER 1201, at 1207.

decide that in all cases where the employee's contract requires him to work at home he is entitled to deduct travelling expenses between his home and his other place of work. Plainly that would open the door widely for evasion of the rule. There must be something more.[136]

It has been suggested that the emphasis should not be upon where the work started (is your home a place of work?) but on when the work started[137] If the emphasis is then placed on the issue of when duties will be deemed to have commenced any necessary travelling will be in the performance of those duties.

Finally, it is generally accepted that if travel expenses are allowable then any incidental expenses of the travel will also be allowed. A provision was introduced through section 198 (1A)(b) TA (FA 1997) to recognise 'triangular travel'. It enables those employees who do not have a normal place of work but who perform their duties at a number of different sites to get relief for their travelling expenses. The detail covers travelling expenditure which does not comprise 'ordinary commuting' or 'private travel' but which is attributable to the necessary attendance by the employee at 'any place' where his or her attendance at that place is in performance of the duties of the office or employment.[138]

Other Expenses

Expenses, other than travel expenses, are deductible if they are 'wholly, exclusively and necessarily incurred in the performance of duties'.[139] As a matter of convenience this test can be broken down into three parts.

Performance of Duties - As with travel expenses, other expenses are only deductible if those expenses are incurred in the performance of duties. This requirement excludes expenses incurred in enabling an employee to acquire qualifications or training to facilitate later performance or performance at a different level of employment - preparation costs. For example, in *Lupton v Potts*[140] a solicitor's clerk was not allowed to deduct the expenses of Law Society Examination fees, partly on the ground that the fees and the examinations were not part of the performance of his duties - they were part of preparation costs for new duties. Similarly, a schoolteacher in *Humbles v Brooks*[141] was not allowed to deduct the costs of a weekend course in history on the grounds that he was not performing his duties by attending the course merely getting background information.

---

[136]   Ibid.
[137]   BUKTG, p209.
[138]   The normal example is the allowance for airline pilots and staff. See *Nolder v Walters* (1930), 15STC 380.
[139]   TA 1988, s.198(1).
[140]   [1969] 3 All ER 1083.
[141]   (1962) 40 TC 500.

A recent decision of the House of Lords confirms that the expenses must be incurred in the performance of duties not in preparing to perform duties. The decision involved the consolidated appeals of *Fitzpatrick v IRC* and *Smith v Abbott*[142]. These were conflicting English and Scottish decisions at a lower level. Each case involved journalists who bought newspapers each day which they read before they went to work. The purpose of the reading was to give them some ideas for stories, etc and to ensure that they did not repeat news which had been reported by competitors. In the Fitzpatrick case in Scotland, it was held that the expenses were not necessarily incurred, in the Abbott case in England it was held that they were.

The House of Lords held that the question of whether an expense was necessarily incurred was a mixed question of fact and law. Lord Templeman said that the two decisions could not stand together. He reviewed the cases and decided in law that the expenses were not necessary: like the schoolmaster in *Humbles v Brooks* the journalists read the papers to enable them to perform their duties, not in performance of their duties!

Necessarily Incurred- As explained above, the test of whether an expense is necessarily incurred is an objective test based upon the question of 'whether the duties could be performed without incurring that expense'.[143]Thus, we ignore the personal attributes of the individual employee, and look to the attributes a reasonable class of employees and the requirements of the employment. For example, one employee with defective eyesight could not recover the costs of glasses on the ground that the expense would not necessarily have been incurred by the employment : the objective test would raise the issue of the reasonable class of employee, including many good sighted persons.[144] Similarly in *Lupton v Potts*, above, Plowman J explained that the duties of the taxpayer under the contract of employment were perfectly capable of being performed without incurring the expense of Law Society Examination fees. In *Humbles v Brooks*, the course fee was not deductible; the court explained that he was not 'necessarily obliged' to attend the weekend course. Finally, in *Brown v Bullock*[145] a bank manager was not allowed to deduct the costs of a club membership as membership of that club was not necessary for the performance of his duties; although it was admitted that membership might assist the manager in developing 'local contacts'.

Wholly and Exclusively- The test of 'wholly and exclusively' is not totally objective. We need to consider whether the individual derives any personal, private, benefit or advantage from the expenditure. Thus, for example, in

---

[142]   [1994] 1 All ER 673
[143]   *Brown v Bullock* (1961) 40 TC 1, per Donovan LJ, 'The test is not whether the employer imposes the expense but whether the duties do, in the sense that, irrespective of what the employer may prescribe, the duties cannot be performed without incurring the particular outlay.'
[144]   *Roskams v Bennett* (1950) 32 TC 129.
[145]   Supra, 140.

Brown v Bullock the bank manager would obtain the private benefits of 'club membership'. The test of wholly and exclusively does, however, permit some private benefit provided that the sole object of the expenditure was incurred in performance of the employee's duties and that any private benefit was an unintended but inescapable incidental result or effect of that expenditure :a test that is very difficult to satisfy. For example, in *Ward v Dunn*[146] a taxpayer claimed an allowance in respect of clothing worn for work purposes. The claim failed. Walton J explained that the expenditure on the clothing was not wholly for the purposes of his employment.

> ... when Mr Dunn purchases a suit he purchases it, maybe partly with a view to going round the sites [his employment] but, at any rate, partly with a view to wearing it in the ordinary course as one wears clothing for comfort and for covering one's nakedness [intended private benefit] ...'[147]

The requirement of 'wholly and exclusively' is not without relief in that apportionment appears to be available in appropriate instances. For example, where a telephone is used partly for business calls the taxpayer can deduct the expenses of those business calls as they are 'wholly and exclusively' intended for business purposes : costs of private calls are obviously not deductible. Any telephone rental charges are not deductible because the intention of the rental agreement and expenses is a dual intention of business and private use.[148]

Entertainment Expenses

Legislation has been introduced to supplement the section 198 requirements in relation to entertainment expenses. The Taxes Act, 1988, section 577 prohibits the deduction of entertainment expenses subject to a number of exceptions including a *de minimis* exception. However, should an employee receive an entertainment allowance s.577 allows the employee to escape liability on that part of the expenditure that satisfies the requirements of section 198 that the expenditure was wholly, exclusively and necessarily incurred in the performance of duties.

---

[146]   [1979] STC 178.
[147]   Walton J did appear to suggest that 'the matter would be very different if the clothes that Mr Dunn wore were special clothing worn only at, and for, places of work rather than clothing that could be used for ordinary wear'.
[148]   *Lucas v Cattell* (1972) 48 TC 353.

Concessions

A number of extra-statutory concessions exist to assist the employee. This includes allowances for the cost of upkeep of tools or special clothing (ESC A1); travel by directors and other 'higher paid' employees between two or more group companies (ESC A4); and the cost of meals purchased away from home by lorry drivers (SP 16/80).

chapter five
Schedule D Cases I and II - Income from Trades, Professions and Vocations

The income tax charge on the profits of trades, professions and vocations is to be found in section 18 of the Taxes Act. By s.18(3), tax is charged under Case I of Schedule D on the 'annual profits or gains' of a trade carried on in the United Kingdom or elsewhere[1], and tax is charged under Case II on the annual profits or gains of a proffesion or vocation[2] not contained in any other schedule. Taxpayers who are resident in the UK are charged in respect of annual profits or gains arising or accruing:

(i) from any property whatever, whether situate in the UK or elsewhere, and

(ii) from any trade, profession or vocation whether carried on in the UK or elsewhere.[3]

Non-residents are charged on profits from any property whatever in the UK, or from any trade, profession or vocation exercised within the UK.[4] Generally, the tax is chargeable on and paid by the persons entitled to or receiving the relevant income.[5]

Scope of the Charge

As we have just seen, the charge under Schedule D Cases I and II is limited to persons carrying on or exercising either a 'trade', or a 'profession', or a 'vocation'. What do these words mean, and what guidance do we get from

[1]   S.18 TA 1988. The term 'elsewhere' is redundant in that the House of Lords have declared that Sch. Case I does not apply to a trade carried on wholly outside the United Kingdom (See *Colquhoun v Brooks*, (1889) 2 TC 490).
[2]   Note that although s.18 refers to 'profits or gains', 'gains' do not include capital gains. The charges raised under Schedule D apply only to income gains not contained in any other Schedule.
[3]   ICTA 1988, s.18(1).
[4]   Ibid.
[5]   S. 59 (1)

the legislation on the issue? With regard to the terms 'profession' and 'vocation', we get no guidance from the statute. Thus we must again look to case law for definitions.

Profession

The word 'profession' is not a term of art, and does not appear to have any special or technical meaning for income tax purposes. It used to be confined to the three 'learned' professions - the church, medicine, and law. However, it now has a much wider meaning[6] and can include all sorts of occupations. Judges quite rightly are wary of attempting to produce a comprehensive definition.[7] The rationale for such wariness, according to Scrutton LJ in *Currie v IRC*[8], is that

> it is impossible to lay down any strict legal definition of what is a profession, because people carry on such infinite varieties of trades and businesses that it is a question of degree in nearly every case whether the form of business that particular man carries on is, or is not, a profession.

While the vastness of the range of activities in which humans may engage would preclude an all-embracing definition, general principles are ascertainable. Some of these emerge from this statement of Scrutton LJ in *IRC v Maxse*[9]

> A 'profession' in the present use of language involves the idea of an occupation requiring either purely intellectual skill, or of any manual skill, as in painting and sculpture, or surgery, skill controlled by the intellectual skill of the operator, as distinguished from an occupation which is substantially the production, or sale, or arrangements for the production or sale of commodities. The line of demarcation may vary from time to time.

A journalist is exercising a profession.[10] So is an author[11], a 'man of letters', [12] an actress,[13] an editor,[14] a painter, sculptor, and, of course, anyone in the

---

6   See Scrutton LJ in *IRC v Maxse* (1919) 12 TC 41 at 61.
7   See Scrutton LJ in *IRC v Maxse*, Supra
8   (1921) 12 TC 245 at 264.
9   12 TC at 61.
10   IRC v Maxse, supra.
11   Swinfen Eady MR in *IRC v Maxse* 12 TC at 58.
12   Swinfen Eady MR in *IRC v Maxse* 12 TC at 58.
13   *Davies v Braithwaite* [1931] 2 KB 628; 18 TC 198.
14   Scrutton LJ in *IRC v Maxse*, 12 TC at 61.

three 'learned professions'.[15] An accountant may or may not be exercising a profession - no hard and fast rule can be laid down about it.[16]

On the other hand, a proprietor of a periodical or newspaper who is not responsible for the selection of the artistic or literary contents is not exercising a profession.[17] A company cannot carry on a profession even if its members are professionals.[18] According to Rowlatt J in *William Esplen v IRC* (at 734), it is of the essence of a profession that the profits should be dependent mainly upon the personal qualifications of the person by whom it is carried on, and that can only be an individual. There can be no professional qualifications except in an individual.

Although it appears that it is a question of fact whether or not an individual is carrying on a profession, the issue is not so straightforward, as was thus explained by Lord Sterndale MR in *Currie v IRC*[19].

> Is the question whether a man is carrying on a profession or not, a matter of law or a matter of fact? I do not know that it is possible to give a positive answer to that question, because it must depend upon the circumstances with which the Court is dealing. There may be circumstances in which nobody could arrive at any other finding than that what the man was doing was carrying on a profession; and therefore, taking it from the point of view of a judge directing a Jury, or any other tribunal which has to find the facts, the judge would be bound to direct them that on the facts they could only find that he was carrying on a profession. That reduces it to a question of law. On the other hand, there might be facts on which the direction would have to be given the other way. But between those two extremes there is a very large tract of country in which the matter becomes a question of degree; and where it becomes a question of degree, it is then undoubtedly, in my opinion, a question of fact; and if the Commissioners come to a conclusion of fact without having applied any wrong principle, then their decision is final upon the matter.

In the same case Scrutton LJ said[20] that the question 'in the last resort' is a question of fact. So it seems that the correct answer is that 'it is prima facie

---

[15]   Scrutton LJ in *IRC v Maxse*.
[16]   *Currie v IRC* 12 TC 245. See especially Scrutton LJ at 264. In *Currie v IRC*, the Commissioners found that an accountant who was practising as a tax consultant was not carrying on a profession. Rowlatt J held that the issue was one of law, and that the Commissioners were wrong. On appeal, both Lord Sterndale MR and Scrutton LJ had 'great difficulties' with the Commissioners' finding that a man who was a member of an organised profession with recognised standard of ability was himself not exercising a profession, but still upheld the findings on the ground that it was a question of fact. With respect, this is a questionable outcome.
[17]   Scrutton LJ in *IRC v Maxse*, 12 TC at 62; compare Warrington LJ at 60.
[18]   See *William Esplen v IRC* [1919] 2 KB 731
[19]   (1921) 12 TC 245 at 259.
[20]   12 TC at 263.

and in the last resort a question of fact - but it depends on the circumstances.' It is clear from *Currie v IRC* (*supra*) that a finding of the Commissioners on the question will not be overturned unless there is either no evidence to support their finding, or they have misdirected themselves in law.

Vocation

Again, the word 'vocation' does not appear to be a term of art. For income tax purposes, it is normally given its plain and ordinary meaning 'according to common sense and according to the ordinary use of language'.[21]

In *Partridge v Mallandaine*[22] Hawkins J said that 'vocation' and 'calling' are synonymous terms. Denman J said in the same case[23] that 'vocation' is a strong word, that it is analogous to the word 'calling', which is 'a very large word indeed', and that 'it means the way in which a person passes his life'. In this case, the taxpayers attended races, and systematically and annually carried on the business of bookmakers. It was held that they were carrying on a vocation. According to Hawkins J,[24] 'if anybody were asked what was the calling or vocation of these gentlemen, the answer would be 'professional bookmakers.' Everybody knows what professional bookmakers are'.[25]A jockey is carrying on a vocation.[26] But a film producer is not carrying on a vocation[27] neither is a man who is 'continually betting with great shrewdness and good results, from his house or from any place where he could get access to the telegraph office'.[28]

According to Rowlatt J in *Graham v Green*[29] to say that such a person was carrying on a vocation would produce very startling results

> because a loss in a vocation or a trade or an adventure can be set off against other profits and we are face to face with this result, that a gentleman earning a profit in some recognised form of industry but having the bad habit of frequently, persistently, continuously and systematically betting with bookmakers, might set off the losses by which he squandered the fruits of his industry, for Income Tax purposes, against his profits - a very remarkable result indeed.[30]

---

[21]   Denman J in *Partridge v Mallandaine* (1886) 2 TC 179 at 181.
[22]   2 TC 179 at 181.
[23]   2 TC at 180.
[24]   2 TC at 181.
[25]   Compare *Graham v Arnott* (1941) 24 TC 157.
[26]   *Wing v O'Connell* [1927] IR 84.
[27]   *Asher v London Film Productions Ltd.* [1944] KB 133.
[28]   *Graham v Green* (1915) 9 TC 309.
[29]   9 TC at 312 - 313.
[30]   Contrast the American case of *CIR v Groetzinger*,(94L.ed.2d. 25) where the US Supreme Court held that a full time gambler was engaged in a 'trade' or 'business'.

Trade

The Taxes Act attempts to define 'trade'. Section 832(1) provides that trade 'includes every trade, manufacture, adventure or concern in the nature of 'trade'. From this definition[31] we can extract a number of principles. First, trade includes every trade. This is of course circular and rather helpful.[32]

It still leaves us with the question 'what then is a trade?'. However, the expression 'trade includes every trade' may be deemed to refer to those activities which have specifically been declared to be trades by the statute, in addition to those which may be construed to be trades in particular instances by the courts. There are several such statutory trades, examples of which are: all farming and market gardening in the UK[33]; the occupation of land for any purpose other than farming or market gardening, if the land is managed on a commercial basis with a view to the realization of profits[34];mines, quarries, railways, and other specified concerns (eg fishings, railways and other ways, ironworks, gasworks, alum mines, canals, etc).[35]

So we learn that, first of all, for the purposes of the charge to tax under Schedule D Cases I and II, 'trade' includes all those statutory trades referred to above. The second thing that we learn from the statutory definition is that trade includes every 'manufacture',[36]thereby bringing a whole range of manufacturing industries within the charge under Schedule D Case I.

According to Lord Donovan in *Ingram v Callaghan*, the definition shows that manufacture is to be regarded as more than a means to an end. Thirdly, we learn that trade includes every 'adventure' in the nature of trade, and fourthly, we learn that it includes every 'concern' in the nature of trade. The last two points are not easily assimilated because of the appearance of the word 'trade' therein. This presupposes that we already know what a trade is, before we can begin to consider whether a particular 'adventure' or 'concern' has the nature of a trade. For these purposes, it may be that the words 'adventure' and 'concern' relate to different things.

The Concise Oxford Dictionary[37] defines concern as 'a business' or 'a firm', and defines adventure as 'a daring enterprise', 'a hazardous activity', and 'a commercial speculation'. Thus, an 'adventure' seems refer to an isolated activity, whereas a 'concern' may relate to an on-going or continuous activity. This means that any single speculative activity or continuous activity which has the nature of a trade is caught within the Schedule D Case I

---

[31]   In *Van Den Berghs Ltd. v Clark,*((1935) 19 TC 390 at 428) Lord Macmillan said that this definition involves 'a fine disregard of logic'.

[32]   Note however the statement of Scott LJ in *Smith Barry v Cordy* ((1946) 28TC 250 at 257) that, since the definition includes the very word 'trade' without qualificiation, that word must be used in its ordinary dictionary sense, and the oter words must necessarily be intended to enlarge the statutory scope to be given to the word 'trade' in Schedule D.

[33]   s.53(1), ICTA 1988.

[34]   s.53(3).

[35]   s.55.

[36]   In *Ingram v Callaghan*, Lord Donovan said (45 TC at 166) that this definition is not worth very much, unless it is to be implied that the definition assumes in this respect that the goods manufactured will be sold.

[37]   9th edn, 1995

charge. This is a major factor distinguishing trades from professions and vocations, since the last two presuppose continuity. Thus, there is no such thing as an adventure in the nature of profession, or an adventure in the nature of vocation.

After analysing the statutory definition of trade, one seems still to be left with the task of ascertaining what constitutes a trade.[38] The authorities indicate that there is no single, infallible test for determining this question. A few examples will suffice. Lord Denning in a much-quoted passage said in *Griffith v JP Harrison* (Watford) Ltd[39]

> Try as you will, the word 'trade' is one of those common English words which do not lend themselves readily to definition, but which all of us think we can understand well enough. We can recognize a 'trade' when we see it, and also an 'adventure in the nature of a trade.' But we are hard pressed to define it ... short of a definition, the only thing to do is to look at the usual characteristics of a 'trade' and see how this transaction measures up to them.

Similarly, Lord Wilberforce said in *Ransom v Higgs*[40]: 'Trade cannot be precisely defined, but certain characteristics can be identified which trade normally has. Equally some *indicia* can be found which prevent a profit from being regarded as a profit of a trade'.

While the courts have often stated that a precise definition of trade is not possible, they have not shied away from venturing opinions on the characteristics of a trading activity. This is not surprising seeing that Lord Denning suggested in *Griffith v JP Harrison* (Watford) Ltd.[41] that we should try to identify the characteristics of trade and measure any transaction against those characteristics. With respect to what those characteristics are, Lord Wilberforce said in *Ransom v Higgs*[42]

> Trade involves normally, the exchange of goods, or of services, for reward, not of all services, since some qualify as a profession, or employment, or vocation, but there must be something which the trade offers to provide by way of business. Trade moreover presupposes a customer.[43]

Lord Reid said in the same case that trade is 'commonly used to denote

---

[38]   See generally D de M Carey (1972) BTR 6.

[39]   [1963] AC 11 at 20.

[40]   [1974] 1 WLR 1594 at 1610.

[41]   [1963] AC at 20.

[42]   [1974] 1 WLR 1594 at 1611.

[43]   Compare Palles CB in *Dublin Corporation v M'Adam* (2 TC 387 at 397) 'No man, in my opinion, can trade with himself; he cannot, in my opinion, make, in what is its true sense or meaning, taxable profit by dealing with himself...'

operations of a commercial character by which the trader provides to customers for reward some kind of goods or services'.[44]

From these *dicta* we observe that one who is involved in a trade has 'something' (goods or services) to trade in, and that a trader must have 'someone' (a customer, or, exceptionally, himself or herself)[45] to trade with. While these points are helpful, they do not tell the whole story. The question whether a person is trading or not is a question of fact and each case depends on its own circumstances. In analysing such circumstances, there are several factors which may legitimately be taken into account. These factors are the so-called 'badges of trade'. The Royal Commission on the Taxation of Profits and Income (the Radcliffe Commission) identified six such badges[46] which we will use as the basis of the discussion that follows. The Commission, after an analysis of competing principles and methods of ascertaining which profits to charge to income tax, concluded that there should be no single fixed rule. It pointed out that the general line of enquiry that has been favoured by Commissioners and encouraged by the courts is to see whether a transaction bears any of the badges of trade. According to the Commission, this is the right line, which has the advantage 'that it bases itself on objective test of what is a trading adventure instead of concentrating itself directly with the unravelling of motive'. The Commission therefore set out to produce a summary of what it regarded as 'the major relevant considerations that bear upon the identification' of the badges of trade. The avowed intention of the Commission was to address the issue of 'lack of uniformity in the treatment of different cases according to the tribunals before which they have been brought'[47]. It is important to note that these badges of trade harbour no magic. None of the badges is conclusive in itself[48], and some of them are of negligible value. The question which the Commissioners and the courts must answer in every case is whether, on a true analysis of the activities and circumstances of the taxpayer, the taxpayer is trading. This seemingly simple question may rightly lead to different results on apparently similar facts. It may even rightly lead to results which may be considered by others to be suspect. According to Browne-Wilkinson VC in *Marson v Morton*[49] the most that is detectable from the reading of the authorities is that there are certain features or badges which may point to one conclusion rather than another. The discussion that follows needs to be viewed in this context.

---

[44]   [1974] 1 WLR at 1600.
[45]   See *Sharkey v Wernher* [1955] 3 All ER 493.
[46]   Cmnd 9474, para 116.
[47]   The Commission suggested that, in future, all tax appeals that raise this issue should go before the Special Commissioners, instead of various bodies of General Commissioners (see para. 117).
[48]   See Browne-Wilkinson VC in *Marson v Morton*, (1986) 59 TC 381 at 392.
[49]   (1986) 59 TC 381 at 391.

The Badges of Trade

The Subject Matter of the Realisation

This particular badge addresses itself to the situations where the 'thing' which the taxpayer is alleged to have traded in consists of goods (as opposed to services). The badge normally comes into play when a person has disposed of goods at a profit, without having been running an established business of dealing in those goods. In such cases, the transaction is either a trading transaction or a capital transaction.[50]

The latter would not be subject to income tax, but may (given the right factors) be subject to capital gains tax. It is not difficult to see the position which the Revenue would take in such matters. If the transaction results in a profit, the Revenue would almost certainly claim that it is a trading transaction. On the other hand, if it results in a loss, the Revenue would almost certainly claim that it is a capital transaction not eligible for loss relief. For a taxpayer who has made a profit, the resolution of the question would no longer in most cases result in a significant difference in tax liability. Before the introduction of capital gains tax in 1965, a decision against the Revenue would have resulted in the taxpayer completely escaping tax on the transaction. This result would only follow today if the capital transaction also somehow manages to escape capital gains tax. However, even if capital gains tax is chargeable, there may still be a benefit to the taxpayer in having the transaction classified as a capital transaction - the taxpayer might be able to benefit from the capital gains tax 'annual exemption'. Thus, the question is not entirely moot.

The badge of trade under discussion involves an examination of the nature of the goods in which the taxpayer is alleged to have traded. The purpose is to ascertain whether there could be any valid reason other than commercial speculation ('adventure') explaining the taxpayer's initial acquisition of the goods. The application of this badge is based on certain premises. First, that certain types of property are more likely to be acquired as investments than with the view to trading in them. This is typically true of income-yielding assets. Some other types of goods, while yielding no income, might provide aesthetic enjoyment and pride of possession for the owner. With these types of goods, the inference of trading is difficult to draw from an isolated transaction of selling them at a profit. On the other hand, there are commodities which give no pride of possession, deliver no aesthetic enjoyment, and which are unsuitable for long-term investment. When such

---

[50]   See generally Rowlatt J in *Ryall v Hoare* (1923) 8 TC 521 at 525; Lord Keith in *IRC v Reinhold*, (1953) 34 TC 389 at 396.

goods are bought and sold (especially if bought in large quantities exceeding the taxpayer's personal requirements), the inference of trading is easier to draw. The nature and/or quantity of the goods may be such that they could only have been acquired as the subject of a 'deal' (ie a commercial speculation).

The explanation of this badge by the Radcliffe Commission is thus[51].

> While almost any form of property can be acquired to be dealt in, those forms of property, such as commodities or manufactured articles, which are normally the subject of trading are only very exceptionally the subject of investment. Again, property which does not yield to its owner an income or personal enjoyment merely by virtue of its ownership is more likely to have been acquired with the object of a deal than property that does.

While the Commission's explanation does not deal with the issue of quantity, as we shall see, the quantity of the items purchased can be a decisive factor against the taxpayer.

The case law relevant to this badge is both interesting and sometimes conflicting. Some cases are perhaps quite clear. The first two involve the purchase and sale of goods of such quantity that they could never have been intended for personal consumption. In *Martin v Lowry*[52] the taxpayer was a wholesale agricultural machinery merchant who had never had any connection with the linen trade. He purchased from the Government some 44 million yards of its surplus stock of aeroplane linen, 'with the sole intention of selling it again at a profit'. He proceeded to sell the linen piecemeal by an extensive series of transactions spread over a period of seven months, using an organisation set up for that purpose. The Revenue argued that the profits derived from the sale were profits from a trade. The taxpayer on the other hand argued that he did not carry on a trade or business, but only engaged in a single adventure not involving trading operations. The Commissioners held that he did carry on a trade. Upholding this finding, Viscount Cave LC said[53] that, having regard to the methods adopted for the resale of the linen, to the number of operations into which the taxpayer entered, and to the time occupied by the resale, the Commissioners could not possibly have come to any other conclusion.

Rutledge v IRC[54] was similar. The taxpayer was a money lender and cinema proprietor. On a business trip to Berlin, he made a deal with a bankrupt firm

51   1955, Cmnd 9474 para 116.
52   (1927) 11 TC 297 (HL).
53   11 TC at 320.
54   (1929) 14 TC 490.

of paper manufacturers to purchase one million rolls of toilet paper for £1,000. Within a short time after his return to the United Kingdom, he sold the whole consignment to one person at a substantial profit. The Court of Session held that he had been involved in an adventure in the nature of trade. The Lord President (Clyde) said[55] that the taxpayer had certainly been in an adventure - for he had made himself liable for the purchase of this vast quantity of toilet paper obviously for no other conceivable purpose than that of reselling it at a profit. Thus, the element of adventure entered into the purchase from the first. On the question whether this adventure was 'in the nature of trade', Lord Clyde said[56] that the question was not whether the taxpayer's isolated speculation in toilet paper was a trade, but whether it was an 'adventure ... in the nature of trade'. He said that the question whether a particular adventure is 'in the nature of trade' or not must depend on its character and circumstances. However, if, as in this case, the purchase is made for no purpose except that of resale at a profit, there was little difficulty in arriving at the conclusion that the deal was in the nature of trade, even though it may be wholly insufficient to constitute by itself a trade.[57] In the circumstances, it was:

> quite plain (1) that the [taxpayer], in buying the large stock of toilet paper, entered upon a commercial adventure or speculation; (2) that this adventure or speculation was carried through in exactly the same way as any regular trader or dealer would carry through any of the adventures or speculations in which it is his regular business to engage; and therefore (3) that the purchase and re-sale of the toilet paper was an 'adventure ... in the nature of trade' within the meaning of the Income Tax Act ...

Whilst expounding on the issue of adventures and their nature, Lord Clyde did not say much about the subject matter. Lord Sands dealt with that point. He said[58] that the nature and quantity of the subject dealt with exclude the suggestion that it could have been disposed of otherwise than as a trade transaction. According to him, 'neither the purchaser nor any purchaser from him was likely to require such a quantity for his private use', thus it was quite a reasonable view for the Commissioners to have taken that the transaction was in the nature of trade.

The third case on this point is *IRC v Fraser*.[59] The taxpayer, a woodcutter, bought three lots of whisky, which he sold at a profit. He had no special knowledge of the whisky trade, did not take delivery of the whisky, nor did

[55] At 496.
[56] At 496-497.
[57] At 497.
[58] 14 TC at 497.
[59] (1924) 24 TC 498.
[60] At 502-503.

he have it blended or advertised. The purchases and sales were operated through an agent, and this type of purchase was a common type of transaction in the neighbourhood. This was an isolated transaction on the taxpayer's part, but it was still held to be an adventure in the nature of trade. The Lord President (Normand) in a most enlightening passage said[6]:

> But what is a good deal more important is the nature of the transaction with reference to the commodity dealt in. The individual who enters into a purchase of an article or commodity may have in view the resale of it at a profit, and yet it may be that that is not the only purpose for which he purchased the article or the commodity, nor the only purpose to which he might turn it if favourable opportunity of sale does not occur. In some of the cases the purchase of a picture has been given as an illustration. An amateur may purchase a picture with a view to its resale at a profit, and yet he may recognise at the time or afterwards that the possession of the picture will give him aesthetic enjoyment if he is unable ultimately, or at his chosen time, to realise it at a profit. A man may purchase stocks and shares with a view to selling them at an early date at a profit, but, if he does so, he is purchasing something which is itself an investment, a potential source of revenue to him while he holds it. A man may purchase land with a view to realising it at a profit, but it also may yield him an income while he continues to hold it. If he continues to hold it, there may be also a certain pride of possession. But the purchaser of a large quantity of a commodity like whisky, greatly in excess of what could be used by himself, his family and friends, a commodity which yields no pride of possession, which cannot be turned to account except by a process of realisation, I can scarcely consider to be other than an adventurer in a transaction in the nature of a trade ... In my opinion the fact that the transaction was not in the way of the business (whatever it was) of the Respondent in no way alters the character which almost necessarily belongs to a transaction like this. Most important of all, the actual dealings of the Respondent with the whisky were exactly of the kind that take place in ordinary trade.

These three cases are more or less straightforward cases. Regardless of the intentions of the taxpayers at the time of purchase, the nature of the items was that they could not be held as investments, and they yielded no aesthetic enjoyment or pride of possession. Furthermore, the sheer quantity of the items purchased was a giveaway. These two factors could not have led to any conclusion other than that the taxpayers had been engaged in commercial speculations. What is not so straightforward however is the case of land. Lord Normand in the passage just referred to indicated that land by its nature is capable of yielding income and pride of possession. But it is also something of which no more is being created and therefore tends to appreciate in value - thus, it is often a sound investment. Does this then mean that sales and purchases of land inevitably will be capital and not trading transactions? Such a proposition cannot possibly be right - and again, here, the result depends on the circumstances. Cases dealing with land can often produce conflicting outcomes. We will examine a few of them.

In *IRC v Reinhold*[61]the taxpayer, a company director, bought four houses in 1945 and sold them almost three years later at a profit. He admitted that he had bought the property with the view to resale and that he had instructed his agents to sell whenever a suitable opportunity arose. The Revenue assessed him to tax on the profits on the basis that that they were profits from an adventure in the nature of trade. The General Commissioners, being equally divided on the issue, allowed his appeal. The Revenue's appeal against this decision failed. The Revenue had contended that, if a person buys anything with a view to sale that is a transaction in the nature of trade. They argued that the purpose of the acquisition in the mind of the purchaser is all-important and conclusive, and that the nature of the thing purchased and the other surrounding circumstances do not and cannot operate so as to render the transaction other than an adventure in the nature of trade. This argument was rejected.

According to Lord Russell[62], the argument, as formulated, was 'too absolute'. Lord Russell said that it took no account of a variety of circumstances which are or may be relevant to the determination of such a question.[63]Such factors included whether the article purchased, in kind and in quantity, is capable only of commercial disposal and not of retention as an investment or of use by the purchaser personally, and whether the transaction is in the line of business or trade carried on by the purchaser. These factors were not present in the case, and the mere fact of the intention to resell was not conclusive. The transaction was prima facie an investment capable of yielding an income[64] , and the Revenue had not discharged the burden of showing that it was an adventure in the nature of trade. Lord Keith

[61]   (1953) 34 TC 389.
[62]   At 394-395.
[63]   At 395.
[64]   At 395-396.

agreed that it was not enough for the Revenue to show that the subjects were purchased with the intention of realising them some day at a profit.[65]He said that this is the expectation of most, if not all, people who make investments. According to him, 'heritable property is a not uncommon subject of investment and generally has the feature, expected of investments, of yielding an income while it is being highway.'[66]

In the present case the property yielded an income from rents, and so was clearly capable of being held as an investment. Lord Carmont dealt in greater depth with the question of the subject matter of the transaction. Referring to property which can be held as an 'investment', he said[67] that this referred to the purchase of 'something normally used to produce an annual return such as lands, houses, or stocks and shares.' He said that the term would cover the purchase of houses as in the present case, but would not cover 'a situation in which a purchaser bought a commodity which from its nature can give no annual return.' According to him, this is just another way of saying that certain transactions show inherently that they are not investments but incursions into the realm of trade or adventures of that nature, and that it is because of the character of such transactions that it can be said with additional definiteness that certain profits are income from trade and not capital accretion of an investment.[68]The conclusion therefore was that

> although in certain cases it is important to know whether a venture is isolated or not, that information is really superfluous in many cases where the commodity itself stamps the transaction as a trading venture, and the profits and gains are plainly income liable to tax.

A similar case is *Marson v Morton*.[69]A potato merchant bought land with the benefit of planning permission in July 1977 and sold it in September 1977 at a profit. The General Commissioners, relying on *IRC v Reinhold*, held that the transaction was not an adventure in the nature of trade, because it was in the same category as normal investments in stocks and shares, and it was far removed from the taxpayer's normal trading activities. Browne-Wilkinson VC upheld their decision. He said that the case fell in the 'no-man's-land', where different minds might reach different conclusions on the facts found.[70]

The subject matter - land with planning permission - is an item of property which is 'neutral' (in the sense that it could have been bought for investment purposes). Although it is a commodity which is dealt with by way of property

[65]   Ibid.
[66]   At 392.
[67]   Ibid. Lord Carmont gave as an example the purchase and sale of whisky in *IRC v Fraser, supra*.
[68]   (1986) 59 TC 381.
[69]   At 392.
[70]   At 393.

deals, it is not the same as whisky or toilet paper, which is incapable of realisation or in relation to which profit is incapable of being realised other than by a quick sale.[71]

With respect to the Revenue's argument that the land did not yield any income, Browne-Wilkinson VC said[72] that 'in 1986 it is not any longer self-evident that unless land is producing income it cannot be an investment', and added that the mere fact that land is not income-producing should not be decisive or even virtually decisive on the question whether it was bought as an investment.

Cooke v Haddock[73] is also relevant. The taxpayer, a solicitor, purchased 72 acres of farm and land. He obtained planning permission in respect of the property. The rental value of the property was £167 *per annum*, while the interest charged on the mortgage secured to purchase it was £320 *per annum*. He did not take any steps to advertise the property. He later sold the property at a profit. The taxpayer claimed that the property had been bought as a long-term investment. The Special Commissioners held that the transaction was an adventure in the nature of trade. They held that it must have been obvious to the taxpayer at the time of the purchase that he must either himself develop the land or sell it in whole or in part to developers, because the transaction would otherwise have been quite uneconomic due to high level of the interest payment compared to the rental value. This decision was upheld by Pennycuick J.

These cases can be contrasted with *Page v Pogson*.[74] The taxpayer, who was at the time an unemployed former clerk of works and local authority building inspector, bought some land and built a house on it for himself and his wife. After completing it, he lived in it with his wife, and then sold it six months later. He then bought another piece of land and built another house on it. He and his wife lived in this house until he was able to secure employment in another part of the country, upon which he sold the house in order to take up residence where his new job was located. The Commissioners held that he had not built his first house with the idea of resale or of carrying on the business of a builder, but that the success of the first transaction encouraged the him to build the second house as a business venture and that the profits on the second house were taxable. Upjohn J felt himself unable to reverse the Commissioners' decision with respect to the second house, although he felt that the taxpayer showed a number of 'cogent reasons' why the Commissioners were wrong, although doubting whether he himself would have reached that decision.

[71]   Ibid.
[73]   (1960) 39 TC 64.
[74]   (1954) 35 TC 545.

It is not clear what lessons can be learnt from *Page v Pogson*. It is probably best consigned to the realm of decisions on their own facts, since one cannot help feeling that the right result might not have been reached in the case. Perhaps this case just goes to illustrate further the principle that this issue is essentially a question of fact.

The sum of the preceding discussion is that when property is dealt in, in an isolated transaction, much depends on the nature of that property in the determination of the question whether the transaction is an adventure in the nature of trade. Where the nature and/or quantity of the property is such that it is only capable of commercial realisation, this might be decisive of the question - the adventure or speculation in respect of that property would be in the nature of trade. With respect to other types of property, one would have to examine the whole range of circumstances. In this respect, Browne-Wilkinson VC suggested in *Marson v Morton* that, 'in some cases perhaps more homely language might be appropriate by asking the question, was the taxpayer investing the money or was he doing a deal?'[75]

Length of the Period of Ownership

The Radcliffe Commission said in respect of this badge that 'generally speaking, property meant to be dealt in is realised within a short time after acquisition. But there are many exceptions from this as a universal rule.'[76]

Normally, investment items presuppose an intention to hold onto an item for a long period. On the contrary, if property is resold 'very swiftly after the purchase', this would, in the ordinary case point to an intention to trade rather than invest.[77]

However, the last statement in the explanation by the Radcliffe Commission (above) is pertinent. This badge is not of very much value because of the 'many exceptions'. For example, a long period between acquisition and sale will only negative a finding of trading where other factors do not lead to an opposite conclusion - and the fact of a quick resale is of itself inconclusive. The best that can be said is that a quick resale attracts attention. Cross J presented a good assessment of this badge in *Turner v Last*[78].

> The fact that [the taxpayer] did resell [the property] very soon is obviously not conclusive. A man may buy something, whether it be land or a chattel, for his own use and enjoyment with no idea of a quick resale, and then, quite unexpectedly, he may receive an offer to buy which is too tempting to

---

[75]   (1986) 59 TC 381 at 392.
[76]   1955, Cmnd 9474 para 116.
[77]   See Browne-Wilkinson VC in *Marson v Morton*, 59 TC at 393.
[78]   (1946) 42 TC 517 at 522-523.

refuse. That is a perfectly possible state of facts: but the fact that there was a quick resale naturally leads one to scrutinise the evidence that it was not envisaged from the first very carefully.

The Frequency or Number of Similar Transactions by the Same Person

According to the Radcliffe Commission[79] if realisations of the same sort of property occur in succession over a period of years or there are several such realisations at about the same date a presumption arises that there has been dealing in respect of each.

This badge deals with a question which is different from that which was raised in the 'adventure in the nature of trade' discussions. A person who has been held to be chargeable to income tax in respect of an isolated speculative activity does not thereby become a trader in the subject matter of the transaction. He or she would have been on an adventure and no more. Income tax is chargeable in those cases simply because Parliament has decreed that it be so if the adventure had the nature of trade. As we have seen earlier, not all speculative adventures have the nature or character of trade. In fact, many may not even properly fit the description of an 'adventure', but would fall better within the description of an 'investment'. What the present badge deals with is those situations where a single transaction in a thing is not an adventure in the nature of trade, but then the transaction is repeated. This repetition takes us from the realm of adventure into the realm of pattern. Traders trade according to patterns, and the existence of a pattern of profitable deals, speculations, or 'investments' may mean that the person engaged therein has now become a trader in the subject matter. This principle can be seen in the judgment of the Lord President (Clyde) in *IRC v Livingston*[80]

> I think the profits of an isolated venture ... may be taxable under Schedule D provided the venture is 'in the nature of trade.' ... If the venture was one consisting simply in an isolated purchase of some article against an expected rise in price and a subsequent sale it might be impossible to say that the venture was 'in the nature of trade'; because the only trade in the nature of which it could participate would be the trade of a dealer in such articles, and a single transaction falls as far short of constituting a dealer's trade, as the appearance of a single swallow does of making a summer. The trade

[79]   1955, Cmnd 9474 para 116.
[80]   (1926) 11 TC 538 at 542.

of a dealer necessarily consists of a course of dealing, either actually engaged in or at any rate contemplated and intended to continue.

Thus the presence of a pattern of dealing is strongly indicative of trading. The courts may even categorise retrospectively an activity as trading by examining subsequent, similar, acts. Consider the following words of Rowlatt J in *Pickford v Quirke*.[81]

> Now, of course, it is very well known that one transaction of buying and selling a thing does not make a man a trader, but if it is repeated and becomes systematic, then he becomes a trader and the profits of the transaction, not taxable as long as they remain isolated, become taxable as items in a trade as a whole, setting losses against profits, of course, and combining them all into one trade.

In *Pickford v Quirke*, the taxpayer had, during a boom in the Lancashire cotton spinning industry, engaged in transactions which were known in the area as 'turning over a mill'. The transactions usually involved the purchase by a syndicate of the shares of an existing mill, liquidation of the company, and formation of a new company to purchase the old company's assets at a profit to the syndicate. The taxpayer engaged in this on four different occasions. In each of the transactions he formed a syndicate with different people for the purpose of the transactions, making a profit in each one. The Commissioners found that the four transactions, considered separately, were capital transactions, and the first transaction, considered by itself, would not have constituted a trade. However, since there was more than one transaction, they asked the question whether, when all the four transactions were regarded together, the taxpayer could be said to have entered 'habitually' into profitable contracts in such a sense as to constitute the four transactions into a trade, ie 'did he make a business of turning mills over?'. This question they answered in the affirmative, meaning that the profits were taxable. They were upheld by Rowlatt J and the Court of Appeal. Lord Hanworth MR said that the Commissioners had addressed their minds to the right questions, and the point could not be taken that they were adverting their minds to facts known to them beforehand in previous related cases involving the taxpayer.[82]

According to him[83]:

---

[81]   (1927) 13 TC 251 at 263.
[82]   13 TC at 269-270.
[83]   At 269; compare Sargant LJ at 275.

You may have an isolated transaction so independent and separate that it does not give you any indication of carrying on a trade ... When, however, you come to look at four successive transactions you may hold that what was, considered separately and apart, a transaction to which the words 'trade or concern in the nature of trade' could not be applied, yet when you have that transaction repeated, not once nor twice but three times, at least, you may draw a completely different inference from those incidents taken together.

A similar approach was taken in *Leach v Pogson.*[84] The taxpayer established a driving school, and sold it to a company at a profit, in return for cash and shares. This type of transaction was repeated 29 more times. The Special Commissioners found that he carried on one trade of running motoring schools, by way of selling driving lessons and selling schools. Thus the receipts from the sale of the driving schools were taxable as receipts from a trade. On appeal to the High Court, the taxpayer admitted that the Commissioners' decision was correct in respect of all the transactions except the first, but argued that the first was of a different character. Ungoed-Thomas J held that the Commissioners were entitled to take into consideration the subsequent 29 transactions to throw light upon the nature of the original transaction, and to come to the conclusion that, at the time the of the first transaction, the taxpayer had intended to embark, and was in fact embarking, upon a course of trade consisting of selling driving schools of motoring.

Finally, in *Smith Barry v Cordy*[85] a man spent a substantial part of his fortune in purchasing about 63 endowment policies taken out on the lives of other people. The purpose of the purchases was to enable him to derive an annual income sufficient for him to live on. Consequent upon war injuries he was advised to seek warmer climes, upon which he decided to settle in India. He thereupon sold most of the policies which had not matured. He was assessed to income tax on the profits of 'dealing in insurance policies'. On appeal to the Special Commissioners, the Commissioners held that he had been engaged in a 'concern in the nature of trade', and was therefore taxable on the profits. The Court of Appeal held that the Commissioners' finding was conclusive unless there was no evidence to support it. According to Scott LJ[86]:

There appears to us to be abundant evidence to support this finding. The Case is conclusive that he made up his mind to utilise the

84   (1962) 40 TC 585.
85   (1946) 28 TC 250; 2 ALL ER 396.
86   At 260.

commercial market in endowment life policies for the express purpose of getting a means of livelihood at the average rate of £7,000 a year over a long period of years. He showed great mathematical skill - an element in the business of an average adjuster, an underwriter, a banker or a financier. He continued to make his purchases in the commercial market over a period of eighteen months, i.e., until he had planted enough trees to yield him the fruit he wanted over the series of seasons for which he was making his purchases.

All these decisions clearly establish that repetition points strongly to trading. It may even be stronger than that - repetition may be determinative in some cases. The difficult question here concerns how many times a transaction in a thing has to be repeated before the repetition leads to a finding that the taxpayer is 'dealing in' that thing. *Page v Pogson* (*supra*) may indicate that one instance of repetition may be sufficient. This raises questions about those activities which people may not consider to be dealing in a thing such as the pensioner who makes home-made tarts and who occasionally sells some of them to her friends, or a man who regularly sells things at car boot sales. Such individuals may well find themselves being regarded by the Revenue as traders.

Supplementary Work on or in Connection with the Property Realised

This badge often comes into play in connection with isolated activities (that is, adventures or speculations). As with the 'subject matter' badge, the question when applying this badge is often whether the relevant adventure or speculative activity has the nature of trade. The essence of the badge was thus explained by the Radcliffe Commission.

If the property is worked up in any way during the ownership so as to bring it into a more marketable condition; or if any special exertions are made to find or attract purchasers, such as the opening of an office or large-scale advertising, there is some evidence of dealing. For when there is an organised effort to obtain profit there is a source of taxable income. But if nothing at all is done, the suggestion tends the other way.[87]

---

[87]   1955, Cmnd 9474 para 116.

The implication of this statement is that supplementary work on an item of sale may convert what would have been a capital transaction into one having the nature of a trade. This is not self-evident, and it is clearly not a conclusive factor. However, there is ample authority for its applicability. One aspect of this badge - special exertions to find or attract purchasers - is exemplified by *Martin v Lowry* (supra), which involved the purchase of 44 million yards of aircraft linen. In order to facilitate the disposal of the linen the taxpayer created a business structure, including the appointment of sales staff and the rental of premises. This, in addition to the nature and quantity of the materials dealt in, provided a strong indication of trading.

The other aspect of the badge - property is worked up in any way during the ownership so as to bring it into a more marketable condition - is illustrated by several cases. In *Cape Brandy Syndicate v IRC*[88] the taxpayers, a group of wine merchants, formed a syndicate to buy what amounted in total to 3,100 casks of brandy from the Cape Government. They then proceeded to blend the brandy with French brandy and recask it, before resale in lots over a period of some 18 months. None of the taxpayers had previously or since been engaged in a similar transaction, and they contended that they carried out an isolated transaction of a speculative nature, which was not a trade or business. The Special Commissioners held that they were trading and were upheld by Rowlatt J and the Court of Appeal. According to Rowlatt J[89], the case presented some curious features.

> It is quite clear that these gentlemen did far more than simply buy an article which they thought was going cheap, and re-sell it. They bought it with a view to transport it, with a view to modify its character by skilful manipulation, by blending, with a view to alter, not only the amounts by which it could be sold as a man might split up an estate, but by altering the character in the way it was done up so that it could be sold in smaller quantities. They employed experts - and were experts themselves - to dispose of it over a long period of time. When I say over a long period of time I mean by sales which began at once but which extended over some period of time. They did not buy it and put it away, they never intended to buy it and put it away and keep it. They bought it to turn over at once obviously and to turn over advantageously by means of the operations which I have indicated.

IRC v Livingston[90] provides another illustration of the principle. In this case, three individuals purchased as a joint venture a cargo vessel, with a view to

---

[88]   [1921] 2 KB 403; 12 TC 358.95
[89]   TC 358 at 364.
[90]   (1926) 11 TC 538.

converting it into a steamer-drifter before resale. They completed the conversion after extensive repairs and alterations, and sold it at a profit. It was held that this was an adventure in the nature of trade. The Lord President (Clyde)[91] compared the case with *Martin v Lowry (supra)*. According to him, the disposal of the aircraft linen in that case involved the organisation of a number of selling agencies similar to those required for the purpose of marketing a large stock in the course of any ordinary trade, and lasted seven months. Similarly, in the present case, the conversion of the cargo vessel into a steam-drifter required a more or less extensive reconstruction and alteration of the vessel similar to what is required in order to market second-hand vessels in the ship-building and ship-repairing trades, and the operation of the venture lasted for nearly four months. Lord Clyde said[91] that the test which must be used to determine whether a venture such as was undertaken in the case was in the nature of trade is 'whether the operations involved in it are of the same kind, and carried on in the same way, as those which are characteristic of ordinary trading in the line of business in which the venture was made'. In this case, the activities of the taxpayers fell within the test, and they were trading.[92]

However, as indicated earlier, it not necessarily the case that that supplementary work will always convert an isolated transaction from a mere capital speculation into an adventure in the nature of trade. There is nothing magical about supplementary work in itself, if it does not show a pattern of operation that is consistent with ordinary trading in the line of business wherein the property is dealt. Even if the supplementary work is consistent with the activities of those who ordinarily trade in that property, that still is not conclusive.[93]

For example, a man who wishes to sell the family car, and who proceeds to get it serviced, cleaned, repainted, and fitted with new tyres, does not thereby engage in an adventure in the nature of trade, even if he takes steps to advertise the car for sale. However, these are the normal steps that any sensible dealer in used cars might take before selling a car. So what would be the decisive factor? The answer would lie in the whole set of circumstances surrounding the transactions. So, for example, if the same man who had taken the above steps in respect of the family car had instead taken the same steps in respect of a used car recently purchased by him, that might very well constitute an adventure in the nature of trade. The distinction between the two scenarios is simply that the circumstances are quite different. On the one hand (the case of the purchase and sale of a used

---

[91]   At 542.
[91]   Ibid.
[92]   See also *Iswera v CTC*, [1965] 1 WLR 663.
[93]   See for example Wynn-Parry J in *West v Phillips* (1958) 38 TC 203 at 213- 214.
[94]   (1961) 39 TC 636.

car), the whole transaction from the beginning (purchase) to the end (sale) is no different from what a used car dealer would do. On the other hand (the sale of the family car), only the end (sale) showed any resemblance with the normal activities of a used car dealer. The beginning (purchase) was of a totally different character.

This means that the circumstances of the purchase of an asset may negative any inference of trading that may be drawn from supplementary work done on it before sale. This is illustrated by *Jenkinson v Freedland*.[94]The taxpayer bought two metal stills which were covered with a thick coating of sticky, tenacious, and highly inflammable resinous substance. He removed the resinous substance by a process of his own invention, and restored them to good working order. He thereafter sold them to companies under his control. The Commissioners held that this was not trading, and they were upheld by the Court of Appeal. With regard to the question whether the adventure was an adventure in the nature of trade, Harman LJ said that the first question which arose was, 'whose trade?'.[95]

He said that it must be profits of the taxpayer's trade which are to be taxed. So far as the evidence went, the taxpayer never engaged in the trade of buying or selling equipment for the chemical trade except in connection with the two companies to which he sold the stills. According to Harman LJ, further inferences that could be drawn from the facts were that the taxpayer would never have embarked on the deal except with a view to the advantage of the companies, that he never intended to market the stills in the ordinary course of trade but rather to supply them as equipment for the companies (which although an advantage to him having regard to his interest in the companies, was not a trading advantage to himself), and that the so-called profit on the sale was the result of fiscal and not trading considerations (*viz* that the high price would allow the companies to claim greater tax allowances).

A stronger case is *Taylor v Good*[96]. The taxpayer and his wife carried on two retail businesses, one as a grocer, and the other as a newsagent and post office. He bought a house at an auction for possible residence with his wife. On inspection, the condition of the house was such that it was not practicable for them to live in it. He subsequently obtained planning permission and sold it at a profit. The Special Commissioners held that the transaction was an adventure in the nature of trade. On appeal, the Revenue conceded that the circumstances of the purchase could not be regarded as having been part of an adventure in the nature of trade. However, they

[95]   At 646.
[96]   (1974) 49 TC 277.

argued that the subsequent activities of the taxpayer pointed to such an adventure. The Court of Appeal rejected the Revenue's claim. Russell LJ, after reviewing some of the relevant cases said[97]:

> All these cases, it seems to me, point strongly against the theory of law that a man who owns or buys without present intention to sell land is engaged in trade if he subsequently, not being himself a developer, merely takes steps to enhance the value of the property in the eyes of a developer who might wish to buy for development.

He therefore concluded[98]that there was no ground at all for holding that activities such as those in the present case, designed only to enhance the value of the land in the market, are to be taken as pointing to, still less as establishing, an adventure in the nature of trade.

In short, merely taking steps to enhance the value of something that one has decided to sell does not point to (much less establish) an adventure in the nature of trade. According to Wynn-Parry J in *West v Phillips*,[99] such steps are by themselves 'colourless'.

The Circumstances that Were Responsible for the Realisation

The Radcliffe Commission said in respect of this badge[100]: 'There may be some explanation, such as a sudden emergency or opportunity calling for ready money, that negatives the idea that any plan of dealing prompted the original purchase.'

This badge is essentially a negative badge. The circumstances for realisation might point to reasons of disposal other than for trading profit or gain. In *West v Phillips*[101] the taxpayer, a builder, built a large number of houses to hold as an investment (the 'A' houses). He also built others for sale (the 'B' houses). When faced with rent controls, high taxation, and high cost of repairs which meant that the houses built for investment were no longer a profitable investment, he changed his mind and sold them. Wynn-Parry J, reversing the Special Commissioners, held that the profits on the houses originally built for investment were not taxable as income of a trade. He said that the circumstances of the sales precluded any finding that the investment houses had been incorporated into trading stock with the 'B' houses. According to him[102]:

97   At 296.
98   At 297.
99   38 TC 203 at 214.
100   1955, Cmnd 9474 para 116.
101   38 TC 203.
102   At 212-213.

Mr. West changed his intention in regard to class 'A' houses and decided to sell such of them as became vacant or whenever a sitting tenant made a suitable offer. There was a number of reasons for this change of policy. The combination of a rise in the cost of repairs and of higher taxation with the existence of rent control during and after the war made the class 'A' houses no longer a profitable investment. Furthermore, all hope of paying off his mortgages to building societies out of the net yield from rents had ... entirely disappeared ... It is those reasons which in my view must be borne in mind all through the consideration of this case. It comes to this. The house property had become more of a liability than a profit; he had to find moneys to clear his liabilities to his bankers, to the building societies, and in respect of arrears of taxation ...

This principle can also work against the taxpayer, as is illustrated by *Stott v Hoddinott*.[103] The taxpayer, an architect, surveyor and engineer, was contractually obliged to take up shares in milling companies granting him contracts. The shares were subsequently sold at a loss. The sales were necessary to finance the purchase of shares from other companies under similar contracts. The General Commissioners held that the taxpayer was not a dealer in shares, that it was not a part of his business to deal in shares, and that the losses on sales by him of shares so taken up by him were a loss on capital and could not be allowed to he set against or deducted from the profits or gains of his business as an architect, surveyor and engineer. Their decision was upheld by Atkin J.

Like other badges, the fact that there exists an explanation for the sale does not necessarily always lead to a conclusion that the taxpayer was not trading. We saw this earlier in *Page v Pogson (supra)*, where a decision of the Commissioners that the taxpayer was trading when he sold a house occupied by him and his wife was upheld by the court even though he clearly had a good and reasonable explanation - the fact that he had secured a job in another part of the country - for selling his house.[104]

Motive

The final badge of trade referred to by the Radcliffe Commission is motive.[105] This is a difficult item of consideration and the authorities are not always consistent. The Radcliffe Commission's own explanation of the

---

[103]   (1916) 7 TC 85.
[104]   See also *Mitchell Bros v Tomlinson* (1957) 37 TC 224; *Wisdom v Chamberlain* (1968) 45 TC 92..
[105]   See generally, J. F Avery-Jones (1983) BTR 9; I. Saunders (1990) BTR 168.

badge is not very helpful either. According to the Commission[106]

> There are cases in which the purpose of the transaction of purchase and sale is clearly discernible. Motive is never irrelevant in any of these cases. What is desirable is that it should be realised clearly that it [i.e., motive] can be inferred from surrounding circumstances in the absence of direct evidence of the seller's intentions and even, if necessary, in the face of his own evidence.

In this statement, the Commission claimed that motive is never irrelevant - but it is not clear whether they were stating that as an absolute rule, or whether that statement only relates to those cases 'in which the purpose of the transaction and sale is clearly discernible.' If it was intended as an absolute statement, then it is clearly incorrect, at least today - for the courts have consistently maintained that motive itself is not relevant. If the statement refers only to cases in which the purpose of the transaction is clear, then it is still difficult to see how motive can be relevant in cases of such clarity. Whatever the statement means, it does not tell us very much, because it says nothing about the weight to be accorded to motive even if it is relevant in every case. As we have seen earlier in this discussion, the Radcliffe Commission took the view that objective tests of what is a trading adventure are preferable to a test that concerns itself directly with 'the unravelling of motive'.[107]

This is an eminently sensible approach, which is undermined subsequently by the Commission's own explanation (above) of this badge of trade. The task of inferring motive in the 'absence of direct evidence of the seller's own intentions' is not an enviable one. The task of inferring it 'in the face of' the seller's own evidence is even more unsavoury. Regardless of any denials, such a task must involve an assumption that the seller is being untruthful. It may perhaps have been better for the courts to steer away completely from issues of motive and to disclaim any relevance thereof.

In the event, the case law is often confusing and the state of the authorities leaves much to be desired. On one hand, we can see from the cases an attempt to apply an objective standard which represents that the presence or absence of a profit motive is inconclusive. So we see in *IRC v Reinhold* (*supra*) a taxpayer who purchased four houses and sold them three years later at a profit, who also admitted that he had purchased the houses with a view to making a profit on them and that he had instructed his agents to sell

---

[106]   1955, Cmnd 9474 para 116.
[107]   1955, Cmnd 9474, para. 116.
[108]   34 TC at 397.

as soon as a suitable opportunity arose. In spite of this admission as to his intentions, it was held that he was not trading. The Revenue had argued that the intention of a buyer at the time of purchase stamps the venture as in the nature of trade if his intention is to sell. This argument was rejected outright. We have already referred to the statement of Lord Keith in that case that it is not enough for the Revenue to show that the objects were purchased with the intention of realising them some day at a profit, and that this is the expectation of most, if not all, people who make investments.[108]

We have also already referred to the statement of Lord Normand in *IRC v Fraser* that an individual who enters into a purchase of an article or commodity may have in view the resale of it at a profit, and yet it may be that that is not the only purpose for which he purchased the article or the commodity, nor the only purpose to which he might turn it if favourable opportunity of sale does not occur.[109]

Thus, we have a clear indication from these cases of the inconclusiveness of the profit motive. In *IRC v Reinhold*, Lord Keith said[110] that the facts were, at the worst for the taxpayer, 'equivocal'. This meant that the Revenue had to tilt the scales in their favour by showing other factors (apart from the intention to make a profit) that pointed to trading.

On the other hand, one case has accorded great weight to the presence of profit motive. In *Wisdom v Chamberlain*[111] the actor Norman Wisdom had a substantial amount of savings. With this he bought a quantity of silver bullion, as a 'hedge' against the devaluation of sterling that seemed imminent. In the event, the expected devaluation did not materialise, but other events led to a marked appreciation in the value of the silver bullion. He subsequently sold the bullion at a profit. The taxpayer had contended that silver was not a commodity which he would have bought if he had intended to make a quick profit, and that the object of the transactions was to minimise possible loss through devaluation. However, the Commissioners held that the profit was taxable as the profit of an adventure in the nature of trade. Goff J reversed them on the grounds that the silver was purchased as a hedge against devaluation, but the Court of Appeal restored the Commissioners' decision. Harman LJ said[112]

> It seems to me that, supposing it was a hedge against devaluation, it was nevertheless a transaction entered into on a short-term basis for the purpose of making a profit out of the purchase and sale of a commodity, and if that is not an adventure in the nature of trade I do

---

[108] 24 TC a 502.
[110] 34 TC at 397.
[111] (1968) 45 TC 92.
[112] At 106.

not really know what is. The whole object of the transaction was to make a profit. It was expected that there would be devaluation, and the reason for wanting to make a profit was that there would be a loss on devaluation; but that does not make any difference, it seems to me, to the fact that the motive and object of the whole transaction was to buy on a short-term basis a commodity with a view to its resale at a profit. That, as it seems to me, is an adventure in the nature of trade.

It is difficult to know what to make of this statement, for it seems unduly wide and sweeping. Two things emerge therefrom. First, although the taxpayer disclaimed any profit motive, Harman LJ ascribed such a motive to him. This supports the Radcliffe Commission's statement that a particular motive may be attributed to the seller in the face of the seller's own evidence. Secondly, Harman LJ appeared to be suggesting that the presence of a profit motive in the taxpayer is decisive - a statement that cannot possibly be correct, especially when viewed in the light of *IRC v Reinhold*. If this be the case and Harman LJ was not really suggesting that the presence of a profit motive is decisive, the question arises of what he was actually trying to do. Was he trying to apply some kind of objective standard (involving a constructive profit motive)? And how does the absence (or alleged absence) of a profit motive fit into an objective standard?

It seems clear from the authorities that the absence of a profit motive does not necessarily exculpate the taxpayer. The principle can be seen from the following passage in the judgment of Lord Coleridge CJ in *IRC v Incorporated Council of Law Reporting*[113].

> It is not essential to the carrying on of a trade that the persons engaged in it should make, or desire to make, a profit by it. Though it may be true that in the great majority of cases, the carrying on of a trade does in fact, include the idea of profit, yet the definition of the word 'trade' does not necessarily mean something by which a profit is made.[114]

The principle so expressed is established by a long line of cases. In *Mersey Docks and Harbour Board v Lucas*[115] the board had to use its profits for certain statutory purposes. It was still held that its profits were taxable. In *Grove v YMCA*[116] it was said that the YMCA was a society established for the

---

[113]   (1888) 22 QBD 279 at 293.
[114]   Contrast Lord Wilberforce in *Fletcher v Income Tax Commissioner* [1971] 3 All ER 1185 at 1189 - 'one of the criteria of a trade is the intention to make profits.'
[115]   (1883) 2 TC 25 (HL).
[116]   (1903) 4 TC 613.

improvement of the spiritual, mental, social and physical condition of young men. It established a restaurant, operated on the usual commercial principles, which was open to the public. It was held that the restaurant was a trade even though it was clear that it would still have been kept running if it did not make a profit. In *Iswera v CTC*[117] the taxpayer wished to be near her daughters' school. She negotiated to buy a plot on a building site close to the school, but the owner would only sell the whole site. She accordingly bought the whole site, and sold off nine of the other ten lots to sub-purchasers. She retained two lots, while the remaining one was reconveyed to the vendor. The sale of the lots yielded a profit. The Ceylon Board of Review held that the dominant motivation of the transaction which she ultimately undertook appeared to be: a blocking-up of the premises; the selling of these blocks so as to make a profit on the transaction, and; obtaining a block for herself below the market value. Therefore, it was an adventure in the nature of trade. This decision was upheld by the Supreme Court of Ceylon, and by the Privy Council. Lord Reid in a famous statement said[118]

> Before their Lordships, counsel for the appellant came near to submitting that, if it is a purpose of the taxpayer to acquire something for his own use and enjoyment, that is sufficient to show that the steps which he takes in order to acquire it cannot be an adventure in the nature of trade. In their Lordships' judgment that is going much too far. If, in order to get what he wants, the taxpayer has to embark on an adventure which has all the characteristics of trading, his purpose or object alone cannot prevail over what he in fact does. But if his acts are equivocal his purpose or object may be a very material factor when weighing the total effect of all the circumstances. In the present case not only has it been held that the appellant's dominant motive was to make a profit, but her actions are suggestive of trading as regards the greater part of the site which she bought. She had to and did make arrangements for its subdivision and immediate sale to the nine sub-purchasers before she could carry out her contract with the vendor of the site.

In this case, as in *Wisdom v Chamberlain*, we see that the taxpayer was attributed a profit motive, in the face of her own evidence as to her purposes. It is clear that she only bought any land in the area because of a desire to live near the school attended by her daughters. It is also clear that,

[117]   [1965] 1 WLR 663 (PC).
[118]   At 668.

had she had the option, she would only have bought one or two plots, and that she only bought the whole site because that was what the vendor demanded. Her actions subsequent to the agreement to purchase the land might have been anything, but certainly it seems harsh to attach a profit motive to the purchase itself. An alternative interpretation of the facts is that, having been forced to purchase a quantity of land which she neither wanted nor needed, she only took what amounts to sensible steps to obtain the best price for the 'excess baggage' that was forced upon her. On that analysis, it is difficult to see how a profit motive could have been attributed to her. On the other hand, and be that as it may, Lord Reid also pointed out that the taxpayer's purpose or object alone could not prevail over what she had in fact done, and that her actions were suggestive of trading. (In this case, the relevant actions bear very much on the 'supplementary work' badge of trade). Thus, it may be said that, independently of her motives, her activities, viewed objectively, pointed to trading.

Complications arise from the indifferent usage of terminology. Lord Reid said that the taxpayer's 'purpose or object' alone could not prevail over what she had in fact done. Her purpose or object was to be near her daughters' school. However, she also had a profit motive. This presupposes that a person's motive is a different thing from his or her purpose or object. The question is what is the difference, and, if there is indeed a real difference, which, in cases of conflicting motives and purposes, prevails for tax purposes.

The authorities do suggest that there is indeed a difference. In *Ensign Tankers (Leasing) Ltd v Stokes*[119] Millet J said[120] that, in order to constitute a transaction in the nature of trade, the transaction in question must possess not only the outward badges of trade but also a genuine commercial purpose. This point had already been made by Browne-Wilkinson VC in *Overseas Containers (Finance) Ltd v Stoker*,[121] where he also said that the commercial character of a transaction is normally determined objectively by the nature of the transaction itself (ie, whether it is a transaction of a similar kind to transactions of the same nature in the commercial world, and whether it is carried on in the same way).

Millet J then went on to say in *Ensign* that the purpose or object of a transaction must not be confused with the motive of the taxpayer in entering into it.[122] According to him, the question is not why the taxpayer was trading, but whether he was trading.

Thus, if the sole purpose of a transaction is to obtain a fiscal advantage, it

---

119   [1989] BTC 410; 1 WLR 1222 (reversed on other grounds [1991] BTC 74).
120   [1989] BTC at page 469. For a critical view of Millet J's approach, see V. Shrubsall (1990) BTR 52, especially at 58-59, where the author describes Millet J's distinction as 'artificial'.
121   [1989] BTC 153 at 159.
122   [1989] BTC at page 469.
123   At 469-470.
124   At 469.

is logically impossible to postulate the existence of any commercial purpose. However, it is possible to 'predicate a situation in which a taxpayer whose sole motive is the desire to obtain a fiscal advantage invests or becomes a sleeping partner with others in an ordinary trading activity carried on by them for a commercial purpose and with a view of profit'.[123] Millet J also said that where both commercial and fiscal purposes are present the question is not which purpose was predominant, but whether the transaction can fairly be described as being in the nature of trade.[124]

Therefore, motive is clearly different from purpose - but as we shall see, this statement in itself might be misleading if both terms are applied in relation to the taxpayer as opposed to some other thing.

Millet J's view in *Ensign* that the taxpayer's motive is not relevant to the issue was disapproved by the Court of Appeal, which held that motive is relevant in certain circumstances.[125]Browne-Wilkinson VC confirmed that 'a transaction which has all the features of trade must also have a commercial purpose'.[126] He also confirmed Millet J's view that motive, as such, is irrelevant. According to him, the only relevant question is 'what was the purpose or object of the transaction'? He said that it does not follow however that, in deciding the purpose of the transaction, the motives or intentions of the parties are immaterial.

Browne-Wilkinson VC said that where the acts of the taxpayer are equivocal, and the purpose may or may not have been commercial, the Commissioners are entitled to look at evidence of the subjective intention or motives of the relevant party. This is not because the legally relevant question is 'with what motive did the parties enter into the transaction?', but because such motive is evidence, sometimes compelling, on which to decide the legally relevant question: was the purpose of the transaction a trading purpose?[127]

We have already raised the question that, if there are mixed motives, or if there is a conflict between purpose and motive, which is to prevail for tax purposes? Browne-Wilkinson VC attempted a resolution of such questions in *Ensign*, saying:[128]

> If the Commissioners find as a fact that the sole object of the transaction was fiscal advantage, that finding can in law only lead to one conclusion, viz. that it was not a trading transaction. Since a fiscal advantage was the sole purpose there is no place for there being any commercial purpose; but ... if the Commissioners find as a fact only that the paramount intention was fiscal advantage, as a

[125]   [1991] BTC 74 (reversed on other grounds by the House of Lords, [1992] BTC 110).
[126]   [1991] BTC at 83.
[127]   At 84.
[128]   At 85; compare Browne-Wilkinson VC in *Overseas Containers (Finance) Ltd. v Stoker*, [1989] BTC, at 160.

matter of law that is not decisive since it postulates the existence of some other purpose (albeit not paramount) which may be commercial. In such a case, the Commissioners have to weigh the paramount fiscal intention against the non-fiscal elements and decide as a question of fact whether in essence the transaction constitutes trading for commercial purposes.

In other words, the question cannot be answered definitively by any statement of principle - rather, the Commissioners still have to weigh all the factors. This statement was rejected by Lord Templeman in the House of Lords. Lord Templeman did not consider that the Commissioners or the courts were competent or obliged to decide whether there was a sole object or paramount intention, or to weigh fiscal intentions against non-fiscal intentions.[129] Rather, 'the task of the commissioners is to find the facts and apply the law'.

In the present case, he felt that the facts were undisputed and the law was clear. With respect, this does not advance the situation at all. The facts are quite often undisputed. This is often why the Revenue would argue that the absence of an intention to make a profit does not prevent a finding of trading. Lord Templeman's response does not answer the question of the correct approach in cases of conflicting motives and purposes - something that is now left 'hanging in the air'. It may be that the Commissioners ought not to be facing the task of unravelling a person's paramount intention but it may be better still to relieve them of the burden of looking into the matter of intention at all, therefore rendering redundant the question which motive is to prevail.

Furthermore, contrary to Lord Templeman's claim, the law is, with respect, far from clear - particularly with regard to the question of the relevance of, and the weight to be accorded to, a seller's motives. The proof of this can be seen in the apparent inability of Lord Templeman to provide a clearer and more logical solution to the question than the solution of Browne-Wilkinson VC which he was rejecting. This fact that the law is not not so clear is especially evident when one considers the confusion engendered by the loose usage of terminology in the courts. To further compound the situation, Lord Reid in *Iswera v CTC* used the words 'purpose or object' to refer to the same things that Browne-Wilkinson describes as motive or subjective intention, saying that, if the taxpayer's acts clearly point to trading, the purpose or object alone cannot prevail over what he in fact does, but if the

---

acts are equivocal, the purpose or object may be a very material factor when weighing the total effect of all the circumstances.[130]

But as we have seen above, motive is a different thing from purpose. The issue has then variously been described as involving: the motive of the taxpayer; the object of the taxpayer; the intention of the taxpayer; the purpose of the taxpayer; the object of the transaction and; the purpose of the transaction. No water could be more muddied than this. When we are not even clear as to the terminology which we are employing in asking the question, how can we present a clear answer?

None of the above statements gives any indication as to what precisely is meant by the purpose of the transaction. However, one may deduce from them that the motive of the taxpayer and the subjective intention of the taxpayer both refer to the same thing - possibly the taxpayer's state of mind. Thus, the issue of a person's motive would logically seem to be an entirely subjective matter. If this be so, then it is difficult to see how any Board of Commissioners or court could sensibly attribute any motive to a person 'in the face of' that person's own evidence.

So what is the end of all this? Perhaps the answer to this apparent confusion over the terminology employed in asking the question lies not in an analysis of the differences (if any) between motive, purpose, and object, but in an analysis of what these terms are attached to. Thus, the motive of the taxpayer may be interpreted as referring to the same things as the purpose of the taxpayer, the object of the taxpayer, and the intentions of the taxpayer in entering into the relevant transaction. All of these may then be contrasted with the purpose of the transaction or the object of the transaction itself. The former concepts are clearly subjective - but the latter ones are primarily objective[131], only involving subjective factors if the transactions themselves are equivocal, and their purpose or object cannot be ascertained definitively from the facts alone. While this analysis advances the situation somewhat, it is not entirely convincing to pretend that one can ascertain the purpose or object of the transaction just by examining a state of facts, and without reference to the purpose, object, intention, or motive of the taxpayer, for one necessarily colours the other.

Leaving this particular problem behind, it seems clear in any event that the taxpayer's motive, subjective intention, object or purpose may, in some cases, be decisive as to the purpose of the transaction which he has entered into. This principle was applied to questionable effect in *Religious Tract and Book Society of Scotland v Forbes*[132]- a case which also illustrates the other

---

[131] See Browne-Wilkinson VC in *Ensign,* at 87.
[132] (1896) 3 TC 415.

aspect of the principle - that when a transaction has all the hallmarks of trade, the motive of the taxpayer is not relevant. In this case the object of the society was 'by the circulation of religious tracts and books, to diffuse a pure and religious literature among all classes of the community'. This object was to be carried out 'by the establishment of central and branch depositories and of auxiliary societies and by means of colportage and other agencies.' These 'depositories' were basically bookshops, which were found to be run according to commercial principles. On the other hand, the society's colporteurs were to a certain extent cottage missionaries, who were often found reading the scriptures, praying with the sick and others, or conversing with them on spiritual matters, and the directors attached importance to that aspect of their work. Instructions to colporteurs were to the effect that 'as the Society exists to spread the knowledge of the Gospel and promote the Kingdom of Christ by means of the press, and to circulate pure and healthy general literature, a colporteur's chief duty is to sell Bibles and the books and periodicals which are supplied to him.' The bookshops or 'depositories' were operated at a profit, but the colportage resulted in losses, and the question was whether these were trading losses that could be set against the profits from the bookshops. It was held that the colportage was not a trade, but that the bookshops were. The Lord President pointed out[133] that the object of the Society was not that of making profit, but the diffusion of religious literature. However, 'the business of bookselling cannot be taxable or not taxable according to the motive of the bookseller'. As far as the colportage was concerned, he said that the issue must depend entirely on whether it, as well as the shops, is a business, trade, or adventure, carried on for commercial purposes and on commercial principles. The facts negatived that view. The methods of the colportage were not commercial methods - 'that is to say, that the business carried on is not purely float of pushing the sale of their goods, but that on the contrary the duty of the salesman is to dwell over the purchase and make it the occasion of administering religious advice and counsel.' Lord Adam concurred, saying[134]

> I think the true question is whether this colportage system to which the profits of the shops are applied is or is not part of the trade of bookselling carried on by the Society. Now, we are told in this case that this colportage system is not a commercial system at all. It is not carried on for the purpose of making profit. It is not carried on as a trade speculation, because we are told in this case that it could not be carried on at a profit. It appears to me to be a very remarkable

[133]   At 418.
[134]   At 419.

trade as to which those who carry it on admit that they could not possibly make any profit out of it. It shows clearly that it is not carried on as part of the business of bookselling, but they carry on the business of bookselling for the purpose of making profit, and having made profit, they expend it on the charitable purpose for which this Society exists, namely, the sale of books by colporteurs.

It is not clear whether the *ratio* of this decision is that evangelism is not a trade, or whether it is that the colportage was not operated along commercial lines. Browne-Wilkinson VC thus explained the decision in *Ensign Tankers (Leasing) Ltd v Stokes*: 'A seller of religious tracts who travels from door to door selling his wares, appears to be conducting an ordinary business of sale and purchase. Yet if his object is to engage the customer in religious discussion so as to spread the gospel that intention is decisive and the selling of the tracts does not constitute trading.'[135]

Lord Templeman in the same case explained the case as deciding that a colporteur 'was a missionary and not a trader'.[136] If this be the true *ratio*, it does not follow that a missionary or evangelist cannot be a trader. If the *ratio* on the other hand is that the colportage was not operated on commercial lines, that is not very convincing either. It begs the question what 'commercial lines' means in this context. It also raises questions as to the basis of application of that definition to the action of selling books from door to door, as opposed to selling books from a fixed location.

Whatever the *ratio* of *Forbes*, it seems a questionable decision. If a taxpayer's subjective intention is only relevant where the facts are equivocal, then it is not clear how that subjective intention could have been relevant in this case. Viewed objectively, the activity of going from door to door selling anything seems to be very clearly an ordinary trading activity. Many businesses are run today on those lines, including milk delivery, pizza delivery, newspaper delivery, etc. If a person ran a pizza selling and delivery operation with the main or sole aim of engaging customers in religious discussion, and the operation was run at a profit, it is difficult to see how such an operation would not amount to trading. Similarly, if an individual operated a taxi with the same objective, and this was operated at a profit, it is difficult to see why it would not be a trade. There is nothing equivocal about these activities in themselves. It is only when viewed in the light of the seller's motives that questions can arise - but then that motive is only relevant where the activity itself is equivocal. It seems that a major factor in

---

[135]   [1991] BTC at 83.
[136]   [1992] BTC at 125.
[137]   Contrast *Grove v YMCA, supra*.

Forbes was that the colportage was operated at a loss. If it had operated at a profit, it is not certain that the decision would not have been that it was a trade.[137]

The real difficulty lies in the point which has been made earlier, that it may not be possible (especially where an operation is carried on at a loss) to determine what the purpose of the transaction is, or whether the taxpayer's activities are equivocal (for the purpose of admitting his or her motives) without prior reference to those motives. This can become quite circular. This then raises the question of when a transaction is equivocal. The issue was addressed in *Kirkham v Williams*.[138]

The taxpayer in this case was a general dealer and demolition contractor. His storage of some demolition equipment at his mother's house led to some problems with the local planning authorities. Subsequently, he contracted to purchase some land, 'principally to provide office and storage space' for his demolition and plant hire business. He used the site for the storage of materials for use in his business, and used part of a mill situated on it as his office. He grew a few crops on the land and bought a few calves for fattening up for resale. The level of the taxpayer's farming activities in this regard were very limited, to the extent that they were never recorded in his account books. After obtaining planning permission for the erection of an industrial/agricultural dwelling house, he built over a period of nine months a substantial four-bedroomed house on the site, although he never actually intended to live in it, and only occupied it temporarily. The taxpayer sold this property at a profit and soon completed the purchase of another piece of property from where he continued his business. The Revenue contended that the profit on the sale was derived from a trading activity. The Commissioners found that the site was acquired principally to provide office and storage facilities for the taxpayer's business but nevertheless decided that the sale was a trading venture and was thus assessable under Schedule D Case I. No reason was given for this conclusion. The Court of Appeal reversed the decision and held that the taxpayer was not trading. The issue of the taxpayer's intentions or purposes was crucial. Nourse LJ said[139] that the Commissioners' most significant finding was that the site was acquired principally to provide office and storage space for the taxpayer's business. But, according to him, the finding of a principal purpose also presupposes the co-existence with it of some subsidiary purpose, which the Commissioners had failed to specify. Possible subsidiary purposes were agricultural use of the whole or some part of the land available for such use,

---

[138]   [1991] BTC 196; 64 TC 253.
[139]   [1991] BTC 196 at 200.

development and sale of some part or parts of the site, and, development and sale of the whole site. Nourse LJ said that it was open to the Commissioners to infer from their findings of primary fact that the taxpayer's subsidiary purpose in acquiring the site was the development and sale of part or the whole of the property. This however did not answer the question and an analysis of the primary facts was essential. The facts showed clearly that the taxpayer had contracted to purchase the site before making any application for planning permission. It was not possible for him to develop the site without planning permission, and at the date of the contract, he was not certain as to whether or not he would be able to obtain such permission. Furthermore, if the principal purpose of the acquisition was the provision of office and storage space for his business, he must have intended to retain the site for the immediate future, perhaps for longer, and certainly not to dispose of it unless and until he had made alternative provision. Thus, if one were to look at the primary facts found by the Commissioners, and 'the inferences that could be properly drawn from them in the light that is least favourable to the taxpayer',[140]the position was thus: the taxpayer acquired the site in order to provide the office and storage space which he needed for his business as a result of the difficulties which he had experienced with the local authority over storage at his mother's address. He could also have intended to develop and sell the site as a whole if he could obtain planning permission to do so and if and when he had been able to provide himself with suitable office and storage space elsewhere. This was an event which could not occur in the immediate future, and might not occur for some time. Was this state of affairs a sufficient basis in law for the conclusion that the site was acquired as trading stock and not as a capital asset of the taxpayer's business? Nourse LJ said that the authorities were to the effect that the first question to be asked was whether a transaction was equivocal or unequivocal. If it is unequivocal, that is, if it has all the characteristics of trading, then the taxpayer's 'purpose or object alone cannot prevail over what he in fact does.'[141]

If an equivocal transaction is entered into for two different purposes, both must be taken into account when weighing the total effects of all the circumstances in order to decide as a question of fact whether the transaction constitutes trading for commercial purposes. With regard to a trading or profit making intention, the material intention was that which the taxpayer had at the time when he acquired the property.

According to Nourse LJ, the taxpayer's acquisition of the site was an

140   Nourse LJ at 201.
141   At 203.
142   Ibid.

equivocal transaction. This was because:

> If viewed on its own, it does not tell you whether the property was acquired as trading stock or as a capital asset of the taxpayer's business. It might have been either. So account must be taken of the two purposes which the commissioners had attributed to the taxpayer, in the one case by express finding and in the other by presumed inference.[142]

Here, any 'subsidiary purpose' which the taxpayer may have had of developing and selling the site could not have been implemented concurrently with his 'principal purpose' of providing office and storage space for his business.[143]First, there was no certainty that he would succeed in obtaining planning permission and, even if he did, he would not have been able to sell the site unless and until he had been able to provide himself with suitable office and storage space elsewhere. This was an event which might not have occurred for some time. This meant that the taxpayer's 'object' or 'purpose' or 'intention' with respect to the development and sale was severely circumscribed, and its implementation indefinite in point of time. It was therefore not capable of amounting in law to an intention sufficient to give the property the character of trading stock. Nourse LJ was of the view that it was not open to the Commissioners, having made a finding which was apt to characterise the transaction as an acquisition of a capital asset, to deny it that character by reason of an intention thus circumscribed and indefinite.

Lloyd LJ concurred with the outcome, but on a different analysis of the facts. On the issue of a subsidiary purpose, he said that the most conspicuous feature of the case was the absence of any finding as to the subsidiary purpose.[144]He felt that if the Commissioners had intended to find that the subsidiary purpose was a trading purpose they would have made an express finding to that effect, bearing in mind their express findings as to the principal purpose, and their conclusion. Thus, it was not open to anyone to draw an inference that the Commissioners had found that the subsidiary purpose was a trading purpose. He was convinced that the only subsidiary purpose which the Commissioners could have had in mind was the farming purpose. Although they had found that the level of farming was very limited, this limited nature of the purpose was irrelevant. A principal purpose implies a subsidiary purpose, but does not exclude a very subsidiary purpose.

[143]   At 204.
[144]   At 203.

On a fair reading of the case, Lloyd LJ was of the view that the case was not a dual-purpose case at all, since neither of the two purposes found or implied by the Commissioners was a trading purpose. The Commissioners must have held that the taxpayer was assessable because of a subsequent change of intention, but there was no evidence to support such a finding and it was not part of the Revenue's case.

So, in this case, the transactions were equivocal, and the taxpayer's intentions or purposes became relevant. Why were they equivocal? Because it was not clear whether the taxpayer had acquired the site as stock-in-trade, or as a fixed capital asset. Why was this not clear? Because it was not clear whether he had embarked on an adventure which had all the characteristics of trading. Why was this not clear? Because his activities, viewed on their own, could have been interpreted in many ways. Thus, it seems that a transaction is only unequivocal if, viewed by itself and without reference to any other factor, it clearly points in one direction.

To sum up the discussion on motive, it seems that the relevance of this as a badge is predicated upon a finding that the taxpayer's transactions are equivocal. Where the transactions bear all the hallmarks of trade, then an objective standard is applied - the taxpayer is trading, regardless of his motive (or, the court may ascribe a profit motive to him by some objective criteria). If the transactions do not bear all the hallmarks of trade, or, if it is not clear from the facts whether they do, then the courts have to decide whether the transactions have a commercial purpose. In deciding whether or not the purpose of a transaction is commercial, evidence of the taxpayer's own purpose, motives, or subjective intentions are relevant. This evidence may then tilt the scale in favour of trading or non-trading. Although this analysis (as we have seen earlier) is not without difficulty, it would seem to reflect the position that the courts currently take.

Mutual Trading

We have noted the suggestion that trade is bilateral or reciprocal, in the sense that the trader must trade with someone. The principle that (subject to specific exceptions) no-one can trade with himself or herself has led to the recognition of tax free surpluses of mutual associations.[145]

The question in cases of alleged 'mutuality' is, according to Lord Wilberforce

---

[145]   This has naturally attracted increasing attention from the Revenue - see D. Harris (1998) BTR 24. One effect of this attention can be seen in s.21C(3) TA 1988, in respect of 'mutual businesses' under Schedule A.
[146]   [1971] 3 All ER 1185 at 1189.
[147]   See generally R. Burgess (1976) BTR 361.
[148]   (1932) 16 TC 430 at 448.

in *Fletcher v Income Tax Commissioner,*[146]'is the activity, on the one hand, a trade, or an adventure in the nature of trade, producing a profit, or is it, on the other, a mutual arrangement which, at most, gives rise to a surplus?'.

The mutuality principle applies where a number of people contribute to a common fund for their mutual benefit, and there is any refund of the surplus contributions.[147]According to Lord MacMillan in *Municipal Mutual Insurance Ltd v Hills,*[148]since the common fund is composed of sums provided by the contributors out of their own moneys, any surplus arising after satisfying claims obviously remains their own money, and 'such a surplus resulting merely from mis-calculation or unexpected immunity cannot in any sense be regarded as taxable profit.' Thus, for example, if ten tenants contribute regularly to a fund for the maintenance and improvement of the facilities of their block of flats, and at the end of a certain period, they discover that the expenses of such maintenance were lower than their contributions to date, if they then distribute the surplus between themselves, the Revenue cannot be heard to say that the sums so distributed are the profits of a trade. This principle is illustrated by *New York Life Insurance Co v Styles.*[149]In this case, the only members of the taxpayer life insurance company were the holders of participating policies, who also owned all the assets of the company. Every year, surpluses of the premiums over the expenditure referable to the policies were returned to the policy holders as bonuses. The House of Lords held that these were not taxable as profits arising from a trade. Lord Watson said[150]:

> When a number of individuals agree to contribute funds for a common purpose, such as the payment of annuities, or of capital sums, to some or all of them, on the occurrence of events certain or uncertain, and stipulate that their contributions, so far as not required for that purpose, shall be repaid to them, I cannot conceive why they should be regarded as traders, or why contributions returned to them should be regarded as profits.

In order to obtain recognition as a mutual association, or to obtain recognition of mutual trading, the situation must be such that an identifiable class of persons (members) contribute to funds and enjoy and participate in the surplus, and there must be complete identity between the contributors and participators. Lord Macmillan said in *Municipal Mutual Insurance Ltd. v Hills*[151] that the cardinal requirement is that all the contributors to the common fund must be entitled to participate in the surplus and that all the

[149]   (1889) 2 TC 460.
[150]   At 471.
[151]   16 TC at 448.
[152]   See Lord Watson in *New York Life Insurance Co. v Styles*, 2 TC at 471.
[153]   See Lord Wilberforce in *Fletcher v Income Tax Commissioner*, [1971] 3 All ER at 1190.

participators in the surplus must be contributors to the common fund; in other words, there must be complete identity between the contributors and the participators. If this requirement is satisfied, the particular form which the association takes is immaterial. Thus, such an identity, if it exists, is not destroyed or even impaired by the fact that the members form themselves into a corporation,[152] or by the fact that the contributions of members are not equal.[153]

Two points must be noted in relation to mutual trading. First, if a mutual association trades with outsiders (non-contributors) then any surplus from those dealings will be trading profits and thus taxable. For example in *Carlisle and Silloth Golf Club v Smith*[154] although the annual subscriptions received from members were not taxable because those members were also participators, the green fees from non-members were taxable as trading income. As the non-members were not entitled to participate in profits or surpluses, there was no mutuality. Secondly, it has been suggested that the mutuality, and, in particular, the participation, must be genuine. For example, in *Fletcher v Income Tax Commissioner*,[155] hotel owners paid subscription fees to a members' club as part of an arrangement to allow the hotel guest access to some private bathing areas. The Privy Council declared that no mutuality was present. Lord Wilberforce said[156] that it is not an essential condition of mutuality that contribution to the funds and rights in it should be equal. However, 'if mutuality is to have any meaning there must be a reasonable relationship, contemplated or in result, between what a member contributes and what ... he may expect or be entitled to draw from the fund: between his liabilities and his rights'.[157]

In the present case it was clear that such a relationship was not reasonable. The hotel owners were required to contribute much more and were entitled to much less than the other members in the club. The disparity, as regards surpluses, between their interest and that of ordinary members was of a substantial scale, and the result was a distortion of the mutuality principle.

Illegal Trading

The issue of whether the profits of illegal or criminal activities are taxable has long been debated.[158] It is now clearly established that the taxpayer cannot raise the illegality of his or her activities as a defence to an assessment to income tax. In effect, trade, profession, or vocation does not necessarily presuppose legality. This principle was recognised even in the 19th century.

---

[142]   (1889) 2 TC 460.
[143]   At 471.
[154]   [1913] 3 KB 75; 6 TC 198.
[155]   [1971] 3 All ER 1185.
[156]   At 1191.
[157]   Ibid.
[158]   See generally, G. Graham (1966) BTR 309; K. Day (1971) BTR 104; M. Mulholland and R. Cockfield (1995) BTR 572.
[159]   (1886) 2 TC 179 at 181.

It was Denman J who said in *Partridge v Mallandaine*[159]:

> But I go the whole length of saying that, in my opinion, if a man were to make a systematic business of receiving stolen goods, and to do nothing else, and he thereby systematically carried on a business and made a profit of £2,000 a year, the Income Tax Commissioners would be quite right in assessing him if it were in fact his vocation. There is no limit as to its being a lawful vocation, nor do I think that the fact that it is unlawful can be set up in favour of these persons as against the rights of the revenue to have payment in respect of the profits that are made. I think this does come within the definition of the word 'vocation' according to common sense and according to the ordinary use of language.

In this case, a bookmaker's profits were taxable as the profits of a vocation, even though wagering contracts were unlawful. In *Minister of Finance v Smith*[160] the profits of illegal brewing were held to be taxable, and in *Mann v Nash*[161] the profits of automatic 'fruit' and 'diddler' machines used for illegal gambling activities were held to be taxable. It is interesting to note that the court does not necessarily view the taxing of proceeds of illegal activities as the State participating in unlawful gains. Rowlatt J explained that the State would merely be taxing a man in respect of his resources.[162] More recently, in *IRC v Aken*[163] the profits of prostitution were held to be taxable.[164]

It is well enough to state that the profits of illegal activities are taxable in principle. This however raises serious questions. How, for example, would one ascertain those profits? The Taxes Act does not levy tax on proceeds, but on profits. Profits presuppose expenses. The question is, what expenses of illegal activities (if any) are deductible? For example, if a man rents some premises and buys personal computers and peripherals for the purpose of making illegal copies of software, which illegal copies he then sells systematically at a huge profit, can he claim any deductible expenses? Presumably the expenses of the premises would be deductible - and presumably, he would be able to claim capital allowances in respect of the plant and machinery used for the copying. If not, why not? Presumably also, he will be able to deduct any costs incurred in avoiding detection by the police - and if not, why not? And what happens if there is a police raid, all his equipment and 'trading stock' are all confiscated, and he is forced to pay substantial damages to those whose copyright he is breaching by his illegal copying? Would any of these be deductible? If the principle of taxing illegal

---

[160]   [1927] AC 193.
[161]   (1923) 16 TC 523.
[162]   *Mann v Nash* (1923) 16 TC 523 at 530-531.
[163]   [1990] BTC 352; STC 497.
[164]   Note that Parker LJ said ([1990] BTC at 359) that, in England, prostitution is not illegal - the deal between a prostitute and her client is immoral and unenforceable, but it is not illegal.

trades is to be carried to its logical conclusion, there is no reason why such expenses cannot be deducted. But if they are deductible, that raises all sorts of other questions, both moral and legal.

Furthermore, supposing that, in the example given by Denman J in *Partridge v Mallandaine* above, some of the stolen goods are later recovered by the police or by their rightful owners before the 'trader' can sell them, can the 'trader' then deduct the cost of having knowingly bought these stolen goods? There would appear to be no reason in principle why this should not be the case. However, Parliament has stepped in to determine that, in certain situations, expenses will not be deductible. Section 577A(1) of the Taxes Act provides that no deduction shall be made for any expenditure incurred in making a payment, the making of which constitutes the commission of a criminal offence. Section 577A(2) provides that payments induced by demands constituting the offences of blackmail and extortion cannot be deducted. Section 577 A (1) would cover a situation such as a person paying for knowingly receiving stolen goods, but it would not cover the case of the dealer in illegal copies of computer software referred to above, since there is nothing criminal in paying for computer software or hardware. This means that lacunae still exist.

It would seem that this whole question of illegal activities needs to be investigated properly and resolved (by Parliament) once and for all. Perhaps the statement (which raises as many questions as it answers) of Lord Denning in *J P Harrison (Watford) Ltd v Griffiths* is a good starting point. Lord Denning said[165]

> [T]ake a gang of burglars. Are they engaged in trade or an adventure in the nature of trade? They have an organisation. They spend money on equipment. They acquire goods by their efforts. They sell the goods. They make a profit. What detail is lacking in their adventure? You may say it lacks legality, but it has been held that legality is not an essential characteristic of a trade. You cannot point to any detail that it lacks. But still it is not a trade, nor an adventure in the nature of trade. And how does it help to ask the question: If it is not a trade, what is it? It is burglary, and that is all there is to say about it.

While this arguably goes against the trend of the authorities, it seems to be a perfectly sensible approach to the question. But if it indeed be true that burglary is not a trade, why does the same principle not apply to receiving

---

[165]   (1962) 40 TC 281 at 299.

stolen property or supplying illegal gambling machines? And, if receiving stolen property can amount to a trade, why not burglary? It should be interesting to see how (if ever) Parliament resolves this question.

The Basis of Assessment

The basis of assessment under Schedule D Cases I and II used to be known as the 'preceding year' basis. In practice, application of the preceding year basis of assessment means that the owner of a business will be assessed for every year of assessment ending April 5 on the profits of his or her accounting year ending in the previous year of assessment. For example, if a trader makes up his or her accounts to December 31 in each year, he or she would be assessed for the year 1999-2000 (ie, the year ending April 5 2000) on the profits of the account ending December 31 1998. The rationale for this type of assessment was simple: the profits of a year which has already ended are easily ascertainable since the trading activities of that year are concluded and set in stone. This basis of assessment also gives businesses some 'breathing space' in which to finalise their accounts. However, the preceding year basis of assessment can lead to anomalies and difficulties. Some of the anomalies were addressed by differential rules for opening and closing years of trading. One major problem however was the propensity of the preceding year basis to engender cash flow problems for the trader in years of falling profits or high investment costs. Another problem was the delay in recovering tax revenues in years of increasing profits. While this particular problem might have been seen as problematic for the Revenue, traders could benefit immensely by paying tax on the profits of a year of low profits, in a year of high profits.

The choice and application of basis of assessment has been a source of debate and concern. Prior to the introduction of the preceding year basis, a rather complicated system of assessing the average profits of the three accounts years preceding the year of assessment existed. The preceding year basis was introduced in 1927-28 (by the Finance Act 1926) following the recommendations of the Royal Commission on Income Tax, 1920. One alternative to the preceding year basis is the 'current year' basis - one which charges tax in each year of assessment on the profits of the trader's accounting period ending in that year. Theoretically, this would avoid the anomalies and difficulties inherent in the preceding year basis. However, it would also lose one of the benefits of the preceding year basis - the

---

[166]   Cmnd 9474, (1955).
[167]   Cmnd 8189 (1951).

'breathing space' would be gone, and businesses would have to rush to finalise their accounts. Some may find it difficult to meet the deadlines for submission of returns. Also, in this type of rush, mistakes may be made. The Revenue can then capitalise on either of these scenarios and impose penalties. It is interesting in this respect to note that both the Radcliffe Committee[166] and the Committee on the Taxation of Trading Profits[167]concluded that a true current year basis of assessment of profits under Schedule D could not be achieved.

To add to the debate on the issue, in the 1991 Budget speech, a consultative document on the basis of assessment, was proposed. The document, 'A simpler system for taxing the self-employed: Proposals for the reform of the administrative arrangements for taxing the self-employed and the basis of assessment', was published on 14 August 1991. As the title of the document suggests, the broad aim was to make the system of assessment 'easier and cheaper to administer and to reduce dealings between the Inland Revenue and the taxpayer'. Two options for changing the basis of assessment were proposed: current year basis, and accounting period basis. The proposals relating to the current year basis still took the preceding year into account. The proposal was for interim payments to be made on 1 January and on 1 July (before actual profits are known) with an adjustment following the computation of actual profits, on 1 January of the following year. The profits and performance of the preceding year were to be the basis for the calculations needed to ascertain these 'interim payments'. On the other hand, the proposals relating to the accounting period basis were an attempt to follow the corporation tax rules of demanding a return of income in respect of a stated accounting period. However, unlike corporation tax, payments would be made either by two instalments, 9 and 15 months after the start of the accounting periods, each equal to 50 per cent of the final liability for the last period; or one payment, 12 months after the start of the accounting period. This attempt to bring the basis of assessment in line with that operated in relation to companies contributed to the declared aim of 'neutrality'. The proposals represented an attempt to bring the basis of assessment for all businesses 'into line', so that 'the form of business vehicle chosen would be irrelevant from a tax perspective'. Initial response to these proposals suggested that the detail would not achieve the stated aims, and that further consultation and clarifications was needed.[168]

In the March 1993 Budget, the Chancellor announced further developments, including the introduction of a self-assessment system. The Chancellor also

---

[168]   See A. J. Shipwright (1992) BTR 12.

explained that the preceding year basis of taxation was 'one of the least attractive features of our present tax system', and declared that he proposed a 'major simplification' through the introduction of a current year basis of assessment and taxation of the self-employed. These two proposals are now in effect. The Finance Act 1994 (s.200) introduced a new Section.60 into the Taxes Act 1988. This took effect in the 1994-95 year of assessment, with respect to trades, professions and vocations commenced on or after 6 April 1994. With respect to other trades, professions and vocations, it took effect in the 1996-97 year of assessment.

There are some transitional provisions in Schedule 20, para. 3, FA 1994. Section 60(1) of the ICTA 1988 provides that income 'tax shall be charged under Cases I and II of Schedule D on the full amounts of the profits of the year of assessment.' Thus, the normal basis of assessment is now the current year basis.

Special rules still exist for the opening and closing years of trading. In respect of the first year of trading (referred to in the statute as 'the commencement year'), the computation of the profits chargeable to income tax is made on 'the profits arising in that year'.[169] In respect of the second year of trading (described as 'the year next following the commencement year'), tax is charged generally on the profits of the first 12 months of trading.[170] In situations of cessation of trading (where a trade, profession or vocation is 'permanently discontinued'), tax is charged on the profits of the period from end of the basis period for the preceding year of assessment to the date of cessation[171] except where the cessation takes place in the second year of trading, in which case tax is charged on the profits of the period starting immediately after the end of the commencement year to the date of cessation.[172]

Application of Opening and Closing Year Rules

We have seen that, in spite of the change of the basis of assessment from the preceding to the current year basis, special rules still apply to the opening and closing years of the business. This means that the question whether and when a trade, profession or vocation was actually commenced or discontinued is pertinent. The commencement of a business is usually easy to ascertain. One of the major problems about commencement dates

[169]   S.61(1) TA 1988.
[170]   S.61(2) TA 1988.
[171]   S.63(b) TA 1988.
[172]   S.63(a) TA 1988.

(eligibility for deductible expenses) has been rendered moot by Section 401(1) of the Taxes Act. This subsection allows a trader to deduct expenditure incurred in the seven years before commencement of the trade by treating the expenditure has having been incurred on the date of commencement. However, the date of commencement is still important in respect of the application of the opening year rules.

Discontinuance

The question whether there has been a discontinuance of the business is more involved. It has been said that there is a discontinuance where a trader ceases to carry on the trade and where the trader ceases to trade in the way that he or she had previously traded.[173]

The first point is trite but the second raises questions. Obviously, not every change in trading practices will amount to a discontinuance, so the question necessarily arises as to how to determine whether a change has led to a discontinuance. The question whether a trade has been permanently discontinued within the meaning of the statute may, on one view of the matter, be a question of law. In *Kirk and Randall v Dunn*[174]Rowlatt J asserted that the question was one of law: 'the finding is that upon the construction of the Rule this case is not within it'. However, the question whether a change of activities results in a trade being permanently discontinued or whether it was merely suspended for a time, is a question of fact[175] and degree.[176]

This seems a different question from that posed by Rowlatt J in *Kirk and Randall v Dunn* and, to that extent, that statement is perhaps of doubtful authority.[177]The better view seems that the whole issue is one of fact and degree.

Some principles are discernible from the cases. First, the expression 'permanently discontinued' does not connote a discontinuance which is everlasting[178] even though a trade which is discontinued indefinitely would come within that expression.

Secondly, it seems that a trade is not discontinued if it is merely in abeyance, or if it lapses into a period of quiescence (ie, if there has been a temporary

---

[173]   Tiley and Collison's UK Tax Guide, (1997-98) para. 7:56.

[174]   (1924) 8 TC 663 at 670.

[175]   See The Lord President (Clyde) in *Gordon and Blair Ltd v IRC,* (1962) 40 TC 358 at 362; compare Lord Donovan in *Ingram v Callaghan* (1968) 45 TC 151 at 165.

[176]   Lord Guthrie in *Gordon and Blair Ltd v IRC,* 40 TC at 364; compare Lord Carmont (at 363). Note that 'a question of degree is typically a question of fact, and a decision on it is not in effect open to review'- per the Lord President (Normand) in *IRC v Fraser,* 24 TC at 502.

[177]   Contrast Rowlatt J in *Seldon v Croom-Johnson* (16 TC 740 at 746), where he said that the question whether a barrister who had been appointed as King's Counsel was carrying on a new and different profession was ' to a certain extent' a question of fact.

[178]   See Lord Donovan, in *Ingram v Callaghan* (1968) 45 TC 151 at 165.

cessation in activities). In *Kirk and Randall Ltd v Dunn*[179] the taxpayer company was the new owner of the business of a firm of contractors. It was engaged in the completion of the old contracts of the business but was unable to obtain new contracts. From December 1914 until February 1920, it had neither works nor plant, but during that period persistent but unsuccessful efforts were made by its directors to obtain contracts. The company at all times retained a registered office and held its statutory meetings yearly. The secretary's salary and directors' fees were paid, and substantial payments made for expenses, including those incurred by the directors in connection with their abortive efforts to obtain contracts. In 1920, with the introduction of fresh capital into the company, and the adoption of a different business policy, a number of profitable contracts were obtained, and fresh plant was acquired.

The special commissioners held that the trade ceased between 1914 and 1920, and that a new trade was commenced in 1920. This decision was reversed by Rowlatt J. He said[180] that the question here was: 'Is what this Company is doing carrying on a trade or business, or nothing at all?', because there is 'no question about it being anything else but a trade or business if it is carrying on anything'.

He noted that the company had 'persisted in seeking for business - business which, if they got, they would have had to finance somehow and to carry out; they would have had to acquire plant and workmen whether the business was in this country or elsewhere.' He also noted that, at all times, they still had directors and a secretary who drew fees, typing, legal, and travelling expenses. Rowlatt J said that the contention was unarguable that they only began their business in 1920 because for the first time somebody yielded to their solicitations for a contract - just as it would be unarguable to say that a person who in the middle of a great career failed for some time to obtain business despite all efforts had therefore ceased to be in business.[181]He thus concluded:

> As far as I understand it it is not a question that the field of business was not precisely the same. The Company solicited precisely the same class of business they did in the old days. They solicited just the same sort of business, and they got some. That is all there is.[182]

This case can be contrasted with *Ingram v Callaghan*.[183] The taxpayer company manufactured surgical and pharmaceutical rubber goods. It

[179]   (1924) 8 TC 663.
[180]   At 669.
[181]   at 669-670.
[182]   at 670.
[183]   (1968) 45 TC 151.

incurred losses due to competition from the plastics industry. In 1960 it was acquired by another company (R Ltd) which later decided to switch the company's business to plastics. In 1961 it ceased to produce rubber goods, sold off its stock and dismissed most of its staff. For a time, it sold plastic components manufactured by another company in the group (M Ltd), for products which were indistinguishable from those the company had previously been marketing. They were sold under the same brand name and the company's profits during this period were profits on goods invoiced to it by M Ltd. In 1962, the company was sold to another company (P Ltd), after which its trade was exactly the same as it was originally, except that the components which it manufactured (in factory space rented from P Ltd) were plastic instead of rubber. It claimed that it was carrying on the same trade as before and was entitled to carry forward losses incurred before 1961. The Special Commissioners held that, in 1961, the company had permanently discontinued the trade of manufacturing and selling rubber goods, that the trade of selling goods made by another company was a different trade, and yet a new trade was commenced in 1962. The company argued that the original trade had merely been in abeyance. Goff J accepted the company's argument and reversed the Commissioners. The Court of Appeal upheld the Commissioners' decision. Harman LJ said[184]

> [T]he learned Judge [held] that the conclusion reached by the Commissioners was an 'impossible' one, and that what had happened was in truth that there had been a mere suspension of the Company's business between 1961 and 1962 and no 'permanent discontinuance', so that the new business could be regarded as the same as the old one. I am unable to take this view of the facts. I cannot see any evidence that, when the Company's factory was closed and its machinery disposed of and its staff dismissed in 1961, there was any intention of merely keeping it in abeyance to resume at a favourable opportunity. I think that at that time anyone would have said that the business was at an end. If the receipt by the Company from [M Ltd.] during the next year of some part of the proceeds of [M Ltd.'s] activities is to be regarded as a trading activity, I think it was a different and new trade, and the manufacturing business started up in the [P Ltd.] factory in 1962 seems to me to have been a fresh venture. Even if this be to go too far and supposing it to be wrong, I cannot see how there was no basis for such a conclusion so that it was one at which the Commissioners were not entitled to arrive. It was, in my

[184]   At 747.

judgment, a justifiable conclusion.

Gordon and Blair Ltd v IRC[185] was another case involving a change from one type of activity to another. The taxpayer company carried on business as brewers. It also sold beer on the open market. In October 1953, after making losses, it ceased to brew its own beer. At this time, some of its staff became redundant and were dismissed. The company continued to bottle and sell beer, but this was in respect of beer supplied to its specification by another brewery company. The company claimed that it carried on the same trade before and after October 1953, so that losses sustained prior to that date could be set against subsequent profits under Section 342(1) ICTA 1952. The Special Commissioners held that, as from 1953, the company ceased trading as brewers, and commenced a fresh trade of selling beer. The Court of Session held that the Commissioners were entitled to decide as they did. The Lord President (Clyde) said[186] that the question was primarily, if not wholly, a question of fact, depending on the circumstances of each case.

The last two cases show the types of problems that can arise in respect of new activities taken on by trader. In the context of a change in the nature of the taxpayer's activities, as seen in the cases just examined, the real question is whether the taxpayer is thereby discontinuing one trade and commencing a new one, or whether the original one is in abeyance, waiting to be revived at some future date.

There are situations however wherein the taxpayer does not stop any particular activity, but still takes on a new role. In such cases, is the taxpayer merely extending his or her business or commencing a new one? This issue came up for decision in *Seldon v Croom - Johnson*.[187]The taxpayer was a barrister and he was appointed as a King's Counsel during the year of assessment. Before his appointment as King's Counsel, the taxpayer carried on his practice partly in Bristol and partly in London. Before making his application to be appointed as King's Counsel, he was given to understand that his application would not be considered unless he was prepared, in case he should be appointed, to have professional chambers and a professional address in London only. Immediately upon his appointment, he accordingly gave up the occupation of his chambers at Bristol and commenced to practice from London only. By the practice of the Bar, a King's Counsel was not allowed to draw pleadings, to settle interrogatories or a notice of appeal, to advise on evidence, or to appear before any court without junior counsel, except in cases in which he may have already been

[185]   (1962) 40 TC 358.
[186]   40 TC 358 at 362.
[187]   [1932] 1 KB 759; 16 TC 740.

engaged before his appointment. From the date of his appointment as King's Counsel, the taxpayer began to appear in a class of cases in which he had not appeared for some years before his appointment and to be instructed by clients, many of whom were different from those by whom he had been previously instructed. He was also engaged in few, if any, of the class of cases in which he had normally been engaged as a junior counsel in the years immediately preceding his appointment. His earnings in the relevant year were lower than those of the preceding year and he contended that the profession he carried on as a King's Counsel was different from the one that he carried on as barrister-at-law.

The General Commissioners held that the taxpayer had permanently discontinued his profession as barriser-in-law and had commenced a new profession as King's Counsel. Their decision was reversed by Rowlatt J. He said[188] that a change of residence or a change of chambers from one town to another did not throw any light on the question of identity of profession. He further said[189] that the position involved in becoming a King's Counsel in all ordinary cases of practising barristers is quite simple - they always fall under the same rule. They carry on the same profession, 'only they occupy a higher rank or degree within it and therefore are in fact more selective in the business which they do. That is all it comes to.' Thus, there was no evidence upon which the Commissioners could properly come to the conclusion to which they did.

These cases all go to illustrate that, in the final analysis, the question must depend on the available evidence (and perhaps also on what the judges know, since Rowlatt J's knowledge of the barristers' profession may be seen as having had a significant effect on the decision in *Seldon v Croom-Johnson*. Therefore decisions will normally be taken on a case by case basis, and decided cases will be useful mainly as illustrations.[190]

Succession and Changes in Ownership

A change in the ownership of a business results, for income tax purposes, in the business being permanently discontinued, and a new business being commenced on date of the change. This principle is mainly relevant to cases where the business is being carried on in partnership, but it is also relevant in cases of succession (ie, where a business carried on by one person is transferred as a going concern to another).[191]The relevant provision is

---

[188]   16 TC 740 at 746.
[189]   At 747
[190]   See Lord President Clyde in *Gordon and Blair Ltd. v IRC*, 40 TC 358 at 362.
[191]   See *Watson Bros v Lothian* (1902) 4 TC 441.

Section 113(1) of the Taxes Act which provides:

> Where there is a change in the persons engaged in carrying on any trade, profession or vocation chargeable under Case I or Case II of Sch. D ... the amount of the profits of the trade, profession or vocation on which income tax is chargeable for any year of assessment and the persons on whom it is chargeable, shall be determined as if the trade, profession or vocation had been permanently discontinued, and a new one set up and commenced, at the date of the change.

However, where there is a continuing partner after the change, the trade, profession or vocation is not treated as discontinued.[192]

Partnerships

Before we go further, it is useful at this stage to note some general issues in respect of the income tax treatment of partnerships. Unless the contrary intention appears, a partnership is not treated as an entity separate and distinct from the partners.[193] If any of the partners is liable to income tax, then the profits of the partnership's business will be computed for income tax purposes as if the partnership were an individual who is resident in the UK[194]Each partner's share in the profits and losses of the business will be determined according to his or her interest in the partnership.[195] Where a partnership includes a company, the profits of the partnership's trade are computed, for Corporation Tax purposes, as if the partnership were a company[196] The share of the profits attributable to the member company will be subjected to Corporation tax[197], and income tax will be charged on the profits of the partners who are not companies.[198] As already seen above, a change in the partners leads to a discontinuance of the existing trade, and a commencement of a new trade by different people, except where there is continuing partner. However, by virtue of Section 114(1)(c), where a company joins a partnership which did not originally include a company, there is a discontinuance, even if there are continuing partners.

Ascertainment of Profits

As indicated earlier in this discussion, income tax is charged under Cases I and II of Schedule D on the 'annual profits or gains arising or accruing' from the trade, profession or vocation.[199] The measure of the income that is

[192]   s.113(2) TA 1988.
[193]   TA 1988, s.111(1).
[194]   s.111(2).
[195]   s.111(3).
[196]   s.114(1).
[197]   s.114(2).
[198]   s.114(3).
[199]   S.18(1) TA 1988.

charged is described as 'the full amount of the profits of the year of assessment.'[200] Typically, the statute does not define 'annual profits or gains'. It is established however that, in this context, the word 'annual' means 'in any year,' and the words 'annual profits or gains' mean 'profits or gains' in 'any year as the succession of the years comes round.'[201] This definition was approved by the House of Lords in *Martin v Lowry*[202] in which case Viscount Cave LC also made the point that 'annual' does not denote any need for recurrence.[203]

For the purposes of the Schedule D charge, the words 'profits' and 'gains' bear the same meaning,[204] ie, the net increase (if any) enjoyed by the business in the relevant period. The word 'profits' is to be understood in its natural and proper sense - in a sense which no commercial man would misunderstand.[205]

Judicial comment explains that it is the 'difference between the price received on a sale and the cost of what is sold.'[206] According to Fletcher-Moulton LJ in *Re Spanish Prospecting Co Ltd*[207]

> Profits implies a comparison between the state of a business at two specific dates usually separated by an interval of a year. The fundamental meaning is the amount of gain made by a business during the year. This can only be ascertained by a comparison of the assets of the business at the two dates ... if the total of the assets of the business at the two dates are compared, the increase which they show at the later date as compared with the earlier date (due allowance of course being made for any capital introduced or taken out of the business in the meanwhile) represents in strictness, the profits of the business during the period in question.

The issue of the amount of the profits or gains made by a business is basically a question of fact. Profits and gains must be ascertained on ordinary principles of commercial trading.[208] This was confirmed by the Committee on the Taxation of Trading Profits when it reported the need to compute a balance of a profit and loss account[209]. The Committee also reported that it was settled that profits should be computed in accordance with established commercial accountancy principles[210].

[200]   S.60(1) TA 1988.

[201]   Rowlatt J in *Ryall v Hoare* (1923) 8 TC 521 at 526.

[202]   (1927) 11 TC 297. See Viscount Cave LC at 320; Viscount Sumner at 321.

[203]   At 320-321.

[204]   See Lord Selborne LC in *Mersey Docks and Harbour Board v Lucas* (1883) 2 TC 25 at 29; compare Lord Halsbury LC in *Gresham Life Assurance Society v Styles*, (1892) 3 TC 185 at 188 and 189.

[205]   Lord Halsbury LC in *Gresham Life Assurance Society v Styles* (1892) 3 TC 185 at 188.

[206]   Sir George Jessel MR in *Erichsen v Last* (1881) 8 QBD 414.

[207]   [1911] 1 Ch 92 at 98-99.

[208]   Lord Halsbury LC in *Gresham Life Assurance Society v Styles* 3 TC at 189; see also J Freedman (1995) BTR 434; G MacDonald (1995) BTR 484.

[209]   Cmd 8189 (1951).

[210]   Ibid. According to the Committee, this was settled following the House of Lords' decision in *Usher's Wiltshire Brewery Ltd v Bruce* [1915] AC 433.

As such, there is a clear principle that business accounts should be made up in accordance with ordinary accountancy practice, unless these contravene some legal rule.[211] Viscount Haldane explained this principle in *Sun Insurance Office Ltd. v Clark*[212]

> It is plain that the question of what is or is not profit or gain must primarily be one of fact to be ascertained by the tests applied in ordinary business. Questions of law can only arise when ... some express statutory direction applies and excludes ordinary commercial practice, or where, by reason of its being impracticable to ascertain the facts sufficiently, some presumption has to be invoked to fill the gap.[213]

Cash or Earnings Basis?

Ordinary principles of commercial trading pointed to two methods of ascertaining the profits of a business. First, the cash basis (or the conventional basis). This requires profits to be ascertained by simply deducting all sums actually expended from the sums actually received during the relevant period.[214] This was the normal method of computing the profits of authors and barristers[215]- the latter because of an archaic principle that they cannot sue for their fees, and the former because they are remunerated by royalties which cannot be computed accurately in advance. The cash basis, being a simple arithmetical calculation of incoming and outgoing sums has simplicity as its main virtue. However, it runs into problems in cases where the taxpayer both gives and receives credit, or carries trading stock at the beginning and the end of the relevant period. The earnings basis is more appropriate for these types of situations. This basis requires the business to bring into account its debts, credits, and trading stock, at the beginning and at the end of the relevant period. The resulting figure represents a more accurate profit figure. Originally the idea was that neither of these bases is necessarily more correct than the other, although the Revenue seemed to prefer the earnings basis. However, the principle was established that, an assessment on a particular basis for any year

---

[211]   For a general discussion see J Freedman (1994) BTR 468; R Burgess (1972) BTR 308.
[212]   [1912] AC 443 at 455.
[213]   See also *Odeon Associated Theatres v Jones* [1972] 2 WLR 331.
[214]   See generally, Lord Denning MR in *Mason v Innes* (1967) 44 TC 326 at 339.
[215]   See the Revenue Statements of Practice A3 (barristers), and A27 (others).
[216]   (1952) 32 TC 520 at 531.

necessarily precludes the application of the other. In *Rankine v IRC*[216]. Lord Keith thus explained this point:

> [A]nd if the taxpayer and the revenue agree, in circumstances of full disclosure, to the computation of the profits and gains upon a certain basis it is not, I think, open to the revenue to seek to reopen an assessment made on this agreed basis merely because the revenue finds that it would have been more profitable to the tax gatherer to have made the assessment on another basis.

The Labour Government announced in December 1997 that it was going to withdraw the cash basis. The promised reforms were implemented in the Finance Act 1998, the effect of which seems to be the imposition of the earnings basis in virtually all cases. Section42(1) FA 1998 provides that, for the purposes of Case I or II of Schedule D, the profits of a trade, profession or vocation must be computed on an accounting basis which gives a 'true and fair view'. Exemption from this rule is given for barristers and advocates who are in the first seven years of practice.[217]

The Revenue in a March 1998 Budget press release[218] explained the significance of the 'true and fair view' by saying that the approach's only concern is the computation of taxable profits and losses. In other words, it does not require accounts to be drawn up in any particular way - as long as the tax computations are made according to the true and fair view. Thus, a trader can still make up his trading accounts on a cash basis if he so chooses - but when the tax calculations start, he will then have to 'convert the profit to an earnings basis profit in the tax computations'. The release went on to state that the true and fair view does not require a true and fair view balance sheet to be prepared.

The question of course is why a trader would want to keep accounts on the cash basis knowing fully well that, for tax purposes, he or she would have to do the calculations on the earnings basis. More recently, the Revenue, in a joint statement with the Tax Faculty of the Institute of Chartered Accountants[219], claimed that this true and fair view imposed by the FA 1998 is nothing new at all, but is rather a mere adoption by Parliament of an approach which has been adopted by the courts over several years[220] They pointed out that the concept is one which is well known to accountants, and that the Accounting Standards published by the professional bodies have

---

[217] S.43 FA 1998.
[218] IR 29, para. 26.
[219] IR Tax Bulletin, December 1998, 606 et seq.
[220] The statement refers for example to the Court of Appeal's decision in *Gallagher v Jones* (1993), 66 TC 77, and the decision of Knox J in *Johnston v Britannia Airways Ltd* (1994) 67 TC 99.

recognised that certain accounts should be prepared in this way. In terms of practicality, the tax requirement for 'documents to show a true and fair view requires them to comply only with those parts of Accounting Standards that are germane to the calculation of profits.'[221]

It is not clear whether 'the true and fair view' necessarily equates to 'the earnings basis', as the Revenue and the ICA seem to think. It is arguable that if this is what Parliament intended; they could have said so in so many words. Is it the case that the cash basis can never present the true and fair view, or that the earnings basis always will? What for example would represent a true and fair view in respect of an author who is only paid by yearly royalties, but who regularly incurs business expenses on credit? Presumably such royalties are normally known to the author only when they are paid/received. Therefore it is sensible to bring them into account upon receipt (cash basis), as opposed to when they are arguably 'earned' (when the books are being sold in the bookshops). On the other hand, would such an author be able to brings his or her debts into account at the time when they are incurred (and not wait until he has paid the debts)? This might have to be so in order to present a true and fair view. But here we might have an application of a mixture of the cash basis and the earnings basis in the same trade - an idea which sounds absurd - and this in order to present a true and fair view! Perhaps a better approach is to say that Section 42(1) FA 1998 is just advocating a common sense approach wherein Accounting Standards are influential.

To conclude this part of the discussion, trading profits are, broadly speaking, equal to trading receipts minus trading expenditure. In *Mersey Docks and Harbour Board v Lucas*[222], Lord Selborne LC said that the word 'profits' as used in the statute means the incomings of the concern, after deducting the expenses of earning and obtaining them. As Lord Herschell put it in *Gresham Life Assurance Society v Styles*, 'whether there be such a thing as profit or gain can only be ascertained by setting against the receipts the expenditure or obligations to which they have given rise.'[223]This seemingly simple arithmetical formula for ascertaining the profits of a trade, profession or vocation actually involves a number of detailed legal principles for, once a person has been found to be trading, it is not the law that everything which he or she receives or earns is a trading receipt, or that everything that he or she spends or owes is a trading expense.

---

221   Ibid, para. 11.
222   2 TC 25 at 28.
223   TC at 194.

There is a glut of case law relating to these points just mentioned - whether something received or earned is a trading receipt, and whether something spent or owed is a trading expense. The next two chapters will address these questions.

chapter six
Schedule D Cases I and II -
Trading Receipts

Introduction

Trading receipts represent the consideration for the goods and services provided by a person carrying on a trade, profession or vocation. While the discussions in this chapter will focus almost entirely on the nature of sums of money received by a trader, payments in money's worth (to be brought into account at market value) also fall within the income tax charge. So, for example, payments in shares[1] or 'rent charge'[2] may well fall within a trader's trading receipts. The phrase 'trading receipts' is not defined in statute. It implies that 'there is a trader carrying on a trade or profession or and that the payment is received in the course of his trade or profession.'[3]

However, it is not the rule that every sum of money received by a trader is to be brought into account as a receipt of the trade. This is one area where the distinction between capital and income comes into play, for the principle is that only receipts of an income or revenue nature fall to be taken into account as trading receipts. When a trader receives a sum of money, there are two main questions - whether the money was income or capital in nature, and whether it was a receipt of the trader's business. Sums which represent capital in the hands of the taxpayer necessarily escape a tax which is only charged on income. Consider the famous words of Lord MacNaghten in *A G v London County Council*[4]: 'income tax, if I may be pardoned for saying so, is a tax on income. It is not meant to be a tax on anything else.'[5]

This is not to say that capital receipts will always escape the tax gatherer. There was a time when capital receipts escaped tax altogether but, today, capital receipts may well fall within the charge to capital gains tax. In spite of the fact that capital gains tax may be chargeable today, the distinction

---

[1]   *Gold Coast Selection Trust Ltd v Humphrey* [1948] 2 ALL ER 379; AC 459.
[2]   *Emery & Sons v IRC* [1937] AC 91.2
[3]   Per Lord Cameron in *IRC v Falkirk Ice Rink Ltd* (1975) 51 TC 42 at 51.
[4]   (1901) 4 TC 265 at 293.
[5]   Compare Sir Wilfred Greene MR in *IRC v British Salmson Aero Engines Ltd* (1938) 22 TC 29 at 42.

between capital and income is still important - and this despite the harmonisation of tax rates. For example, the differential rules for allowances and deductions for income tax and capital gains tax may be significant.

As indicated earlier, two questions arise when a trader receives a sum of money - was the sum income or capital, and, was it 'a receipt of the recipient's business'?[6] And there are two approaches to these two questions. First, it may be that the question whether a sum received by a trader is income or capital in nature comes first - the idea being that if it is capital in nature, then the question whether it is a receipt of the taxpayer's trade or business does not arise. This is the approach that has been taken in many leading cases[7], and, more recently, by Lord Hoffmann in *Deeny v Gooda Walker Ltd*.[8]

However, doubt was cast on this manner of ordering the questions by the other Law Lords in the case. Lord Browne-Wilkinson seemed to reverse the order, putting the question whether the sum is a receipt of the business first, and the question whether it is income or capital, second.[9]It is not clear whether he was thereby seeking to particularise this as the correct order, or whether he was simply listing the questions as it suited him. However, Lord Mustill was quite direct in preferring the second approach to the questions. He said that the question whether a particular receipt was a receipt of the taxpayer's trade 'must always come first.' He admitted that, in practice, the question will often be so closely linked to the question whether, if it is a receipt of the trade, it is in the nature of income or capital, that an affirmative answer to one will demand an affirmative answer to the other. He said however that this need not always be so.

Is there actually any significant difference between these two approaches, and, if so, which is to be preferred? It may be that much depends on what is meant by the phrase 'a receipt of the taxpayer's business'. On one view of the matter, it might seem odd (except perhaps in respect of cases which clearly have no connection at all with the taxpayer's trade) that the question whether a sum is a receipt of the trade can come before the question whether it is capital or income - because it is arguable that, by definition, a capital sum cannot ever be a receipt of the trade (or 'business') for income tax purposes. On this basis, it might be that Lord Hoffmann's approach, which seeks first to determine whether the sum is income or capital, is to be preferred. In this case, it is only after this hurdle has been crossed that the question whether it is a receipt of the trade will arise. However, as already indicated, it depends on what their Lordships meant by 'receipt of the

---

[6]   See Lord Browne-Wilkinson in *Deeny v Gooda Walker Ltd* [1996] BTC 144 at 146.
[7]   See, for example, *Glenboig Union Fireclay Co Ltd v IRC* (1922) 12 TC 427; *Van Den Berghs v Clark* (1935) 19 TC 390.
[8]   [1996] BTC 144, at 152-153.
[9]   At 146.

business'. If the term was employed loosely (to refer to anything that arises out of or is connected with the taxpayer's trading activities), then perhaps Lord Mustill's ordering is to be preferred. If the term was employed technically (referring to what amounts in law to a trading receipt chargeable to income tax) then Lord Hoffmann's approach may be preferable. However, perhaps an even better approach to the issue is to treat both questions as part and parcel of a single question (whether the sum is taxable as a trading receipt), in which case the question which of them 'comes first' must depend on the circumstances of each case. Thus, if a trader wins the National Lottery, the question whether the prize money is a receipt of his business would come first, in the sense of whether it actually has any relationship with his business. The situation might be the same if a trader receives an unsolicited gift from a former customer (see below), or if he sells an item of machinery used in his trade. However, all these situations might also arguably raise the question whether the sums are income or capital. Indeed, one might rightly say that if a sum is not a receipt of the trade, then it is capital[10] (or 'a windfall'[11]); and that if it is capital, then it is not a receipt of the trade - a point that hardly needs authority. In short, it does not seem to be an edifying task to take this issue too far. Thus, perhaps the courts should just take first the question that seems most appropriate to be so taken and not bother too much about the 'right' order (if such a thing exists). As Lord Mustill said, for practical purposes, in most cases, the answer to both questions is likely to be the same.

Income or Capital?

We have already identified and discussed at an earlier stage various theories relating to the proper distinction between income and capital. This distinction has been described as 'artificial'[12], and, according to Kay,[13] neither legislation nor case law has succeeded in creating an economically defensible justification for the distinction. Nevertheless, it is still necessary to ascertain whether a sum of money is income or capital. The word 'income' is not defined anywhere in the statute. Lord Wrenbury said in *Whitney v IRC*[14] that the word 'income' means 'such income as is within the Act taxable under the Act'. This statement however does not really advance the situation, and so we must seek assistance elsewhere. While theories such as the 'tree' and the 'fruit', and fixed and circulating capital and other formulations may be helpful in specific cases to resolve the matter, there are

---

[10]   See for example Lord Blackburn in *Burmah Steamship Company Ltd v IRC*, 16 TC at 75.
[11]   Per Lord Sands, ibid.
[12]   See Lord Sands in *Burmah Steamship Company Ltd v IRC* (1931) 16 TC 67 at 73; contrast Lord Macmillan in *Van Den Berghs Ltd v Clark*, (1935) 19 TC 390 at 428 -'in general the distinction is well recognised and easily applied'.
[13]   J. A. Kay, 'The Economics of Taxation' (1979) BTR 354 at 357.
[14]   (1925) 10 TC 88 at 113.

many transactions which do not fit readily into these categories, and care must be taken not to accord undue weight to these tests. Lord Radcliffe's warning in this respect is poignant[15].

> These phrases are, of course, used with intended reference to earlier judicial decisions that distinguish between capital and income for the purpose of assessing profit. Since a question of capital or income is always capable of giving rise to a question of law, such a form of argument is unavoidable in any legal system that governs itself by appeal to precedent. Nevertheless, it has to be remembered that all these phrases ... are essentially descriptive rather than definitive, and, as each new case arises for adjudication and it is sought to reason by analogy from its facts to those of one previously decided, a court's primary duty is to inquire how far a description that was both relevant and significant in one set of circumstances is either significant or relevant in those which are presently before it.

There are many cases wherein the distinction has been at issue. Here again, the authorities are not always consistent. Lord Sands said in *Burmah Steamship Company Ltd v IRC*[16] that 'some of the decisions may appear to be arbitrary', and, as Sir Wilfred Greene MR said in *IRC v British Salmson Aero Engines Ltd,*[17] there have been many cases which fall on the borderline, and 'in many cases it is almost true to say that the spin of a coin would decide the matter almost as satisfactorily as an attempt to find reasons.' Judges are not in the habit of spinning coins to decide matters such as these, and so attempts have been made to rationalise the case law under a number of categories of consideration. The discussion that follows employs some of these categories as a foundation for its analysis.

Payments in Lieu of Trading Receipts

Where a trader receives compensation payments in lieu of what would have fallen to be classified as receipts of his or her trade, the authorities have consistently held such payments to be of the same nature as the payments that they are replacing - in other words, income or revenue receipts, which will also be classified as trading receipts. The relevant principle was explained by Diplock LJ in *London and Thames Haven Oil Wharves Ltd v Attwooll*[18]

> Where, pursuant to a legal right, a trader receives from another

---

[15]   *Commrs. of Taxes v Nchanga Consolidated Copper Mines* [1964] AC 948 at 959.
[16]   16 TC at 73.
[17]   (1938) 22 TC 29 at 43.
[18]   [1966] BTC 144 at 153.

person compensation for the trader's failure to receive a sum of money which, if it had been received, would have been credited to the amount of profits (if any) arising in any year from the trade carried on by him at the time when the compensation is so received, the compensation is to be treated for income tax purposes in the same way as that sum of money would have been treated if it had been received instead of the compensation.

The principle of this statement was approved and applied by Lord Hoffmann in its entirety in *Deeny v Gooda Walker Ltd*.[19] It was also approved by Lord Browne-Wilkinson (the rest of their Lordships other than Lord Hoffmann concurring) in respect of the question 'whether such compensation falls to be treated as income or capital of the taxpayer's trade'.[20]

However, Lord Browne-Wilkinson had some reservations about the applicability of the statement to the question whether the compensation was a receipt of the taxpayer's business.[21]

According to Lord Browne-Wilkinson, in the ordinary run of cases the receipt of a sum by a trader as compensation for the failure to receive what would have been a receipt of his trade will normally demonstrate that the compensation is itself a receipt of that business. However he felt that 'there may be unusual cases where the test propounded by Diplock LJ might not be appropriate to the correct determination of the question whether the compensation is a receipt of the taxpayer's business.'[22] Thus, the principle, as explained by Diplock LJ, will cover most cases - but it admits of exceptions, perhaps in relation to the question whether the compensation is a receipt of the business. The principle applies, not only in respect of compensation for failure to receive a sum of money, but also to compensation for liability to pay a revenue expense.[23] It can be seen in a long line of cases. For example, in *Gray v Lord Penrhyn*[24], two employees of the taxpayer trader had misappropriated money by falsifying the wages accounts over a number of years. The taxpayer's auditors admitted negligence on their part in not making certain inquiries and paid compensation of a sum equal to the misappropriated amounts to the taxpayer. Finlay J held that the compensation payment had to be treated as simply a business payment and a business receipt. In *London and Thames Haven Oil Wharves Ltd v Attwooll* itself, the taxpayer owned jetties for discharging oil from tankers. One of its jetties was damaged by the negligent handling of a tanker and was out of service for over one year. The tanker

---

[19]   [1996] BTC 144 at 153.

[20]   See Lord Browne-Wilkinson at 146.

[21]   Ibid.

[22]   Ibid; compare Lord Mustill, ibid.

[23]   See *Donald Fisher (Ealing) Ltd v Spencer* (1989) 63 TC 168; BTC 112 (CA); *Deeny v Gooda Walker Ltd* [1996] BTC 144.

[24]   (1937) 21 TC 252.

owners admitted liability and the taxpayer recovered from the owners and its insurers the cost of repairing jetty and compensation for the loss of use of the jetty during its repair. The combined compensation received exceeded the cost of repairing the jetty by some £21,000, which the Revenue sought to tax as a trading receipt. The compensation for the loss of profit was held to be taxable as a trading receipt. Willmer LJ said[25] that if there had been no collision, the profits which the taxpayer would have earned by the use of the jetty would plainly have been taxable as a trading receipt. He then wondered why the same should not apply to 'the sum of money recovered from the wrongdoer in partial replacement of those profits'. If the taxpayer could escape tax in this type of case, Willmer LJ said that there would be something very much wrong with the law, for the consequence would be that a jetty-owner, such as the taxpayer company, would be better off by being subjected to a casualty of this sort (that is, by losing the use of his jetty and recovering damages therefor) than he would be if he were able to use it continuously for the purpose of making profits.

According to him, that would be 'a very strange result indeed.'

These cases both involved payments agreed between the parties (no doubt to avoid costly litigation). However, the way in which the payment came to be made is not material. The principle can apply in respect of payments made after litigation, compromised or otherwise[26].

It also applies to statutory payments. This can be seen in a number of cases. First, *IRC v Newcastle Breweries Ltd.*[27] Here, the government requisitioned one-third of the total stock of raw rum belonging to the taxpayers who were wine and spirit merchants. Compensation was paid for the rum. The taxpayers argued that the compensation was not a profit from their business at all, but was a sum payable by way of compensation for the compulsory taking by the Crown of a part of the their capital. The House of Lords disagreed and held that this must be treated as a sale of the rum and the fact that it was compulsory made no difference. Viscount Cave LC said[28]:

> It is true that the rum taken by the Crown had not been refined or blended and was not, therefore, in the state in which rum was usually sold by the Appellants; but it was rum which they had bought for the purposes of their business, and the cost of the rum was no doubt treated as an outgoing of the business. If the raw rum had been voluntarily sold to other traders, the price must clearly have come into the computation of the Appellants' profits, and the circumstance that

---

[25]   43 TC at 507.

[26]   See for example, *Roberts v WS Electronics Ltd* (1967) 44 TC 525; *Donald Fisher (Ealing) Ltd v Spencer* (1989) 63 TC 168;

[27]   (1927) 12 TC 927.

[28]   At 953.

the sale was compulsory and was to the Crown makes no difference in principle ... The transaction was a sale in the business, and although no doubt it affected the circulating capital of the Appellants it was none the less proper to be brought into their profit and loss account.

Similarly, in *Sutherland v IRC*[29] a steam-drifter used for herring fishing by the taxpayer was requisitioned by the Admiralty for hire. The taxpayer argued that his fishing industry was brought to an end by the intervention of the Admiralty and that the hiring by the Admiralty subsequently must be viewed as compensation to him for the stoppage of his business. The compensation (hire) payments were held to be trading receipts. The Lord President (Strathclyde) said[30]:

The Appellant acquired this ship, he acquired her as an instrument, or as ... a commercial asset, susceptible of being put to a variety of different uses in which gain might be acquired, and whichever of these uses it was put to by the Appellant and profits earned, he was carrying on the same business, even although alterations were necessary on the vessel for the changed purpose, provided that each of these uses was one for which she as a ship was adapted. It is true in a sense that fishing is a different industry from mine sweeping, or trading or patrolling, or watching a gap in a boom, or the like, but viewed form the standpoint of the ship-owner, they are the same business because in each his vessel, if she earns profits, is employed for gain. It is the same piece of machinery, or implement, or commercial asset which is used to acquire profit. In short the business is that of the employment of a ship for gain in ordinary ship owning business.

Finally, in *Lang v Rice*[31] the taxpayer ran cabaret clubs in Belfast which were completely destroyed by bombs. The Northern Ireland Office paid compensation for, *inter alia*, 'consequential loss'. This part of the compensation was 'confined to loss of net profit' in respect of a period of about 18 months. The Court of Appeal in Northern Ireland held that this was revenue payment because it was made in lieu of trading profits.

In fact, the principle that a payment in lieu of trading profits is income and taxable as a trading receipt is applicable regardless of the source of the legal

[29]   [1918] 12 TC 63.
[30]   At 69-70.
[31]   [1984] STC 172; 57 TC 80.

right of the trader to recover the compensation. This was clearly stated by Diplock LJ in *London and Thames Haven Oil Wharves Ltd v Attwooll*.

> It may arise from a primary obligation under a contract, such as a contract of insurance, from a secondary obligation arising out of non-performance of a contract, such as a right to damages, either liquidated, as under the demurrage clause in a charter-party, or unliquidated, from an obligation to pay damages for tort, as in the present case, from a statutory obligation, or in any other way in which legal obligations arise.[33]

In order to apply this principle to a particular case, it is necessary first to identify what the compensation was paid for.[34] The answer to this question also provides the answer to the question whether the compensation arose out of the trade.[35] If the compensation was paid for the failure of the trader to receive a sum of money, then the question has to be asked whether, if that sum of money had been received by the trader, it would have been credited to the amount of profits (if any) arising in any year from the trade carried on by him at the date of receipt.[36] For these purposes, the method by which the compensation has been assessed in the particular case does not identify what it was paid for; it is no more than a factor which may assist in the solution of the problem of identification.[37]

Lord Hoffmann put it slightly differently in *Deeny v Gooda Walker Ltd*.[38]

> The fact that damages are computed by reference to income which could have been earned does not mean that they are compensation for the loss of that income. The income which might have been expected to be received may be merely an element in the valuation of a different asset or interest.[39]

Compensation for the Sterilisation of Assets

Where a trader receives compensation for the sterilisation of business assets, the courts have normally held the compensation to be capital in nature. In *Glenboig Union Fireclay Co Ltd v IRC*[40] the taxpayer manufactured

---

[32] 43 TC at 515.
[33] Note however that payments under an insurance contract may sometimes be treated a capital receipts - see for example *Crabb v Blue Star Line Ltd* [1961] 2 ALL ER 424; 39 TC 482.
[34] Diplock LJ in *London & Thames Haven Oil Wharves Ltd v Attwooll* (ibid); compare Kerr LJ in *Donald Fisher (Ealing) Ltd v Spencer*, 63 TC at 186.
[35] Lord Hoffman in *Deeny v Gooda Walker Ltd* [1996] BTC at 153.
[36] Diplock LJ in *London & Thames Haven Oil Wharves Ltd v Attwooll*, ibid.
[37] Ibid.
[38] [1996] BTC at 153.
[39] Lord Hoffman referred to *British Transport Commission v Gourley* ([1956] AC 185) and *Lewis v Daily Telegraph* ([1964] AC 234) as examples of the proof of this proposition. For a general discussion of the Gourley principle see G. Dworkin (1967) BTR 315 and G. Dworkin (1967) BTR 373.
[40] (1922) 12 TC 427.

fireclay goods and sold raw fireclay. They were lessees of some fireclay fields in the neighbourhood of the Caledonian Railway, some of which ran under the lines of the Railway. The Caledonian Railway, after some litigation, in exercise of a statutory power, and upon payment of compensation, required the taxpayer to leave part of the fireclay unworked. The compensation payment was calculated on the basis of projected lost profits. In this case, it was the taxpayer (rather than the Revenue) that was claiming that the compensation was a trading receipt. The House of Lords held that the compensation was not a profit earned in the course of the taxpayer's trade, but was a capital receipt, being a payment made for the sterilisation of a capital asset. The taxpayer had referred to the fact that the compensation was in fact assessed by considering that the fireclay to which it related could only be worked for some two and a half years before it would be exhausted, and had argued that the compensation therefore represented nothing more than the actual profit for two and a half years received in one lump sum. Lord Buckmaster[41] rejected that argument as fallacious. He said that the compensation was a sum paid to prevent the taxpayer from obtaining the full benefit of the capital value of that part of the mines which it was prevented from working by the railway company. He said that it made no difference whether it is regarded as a sale of the asset out and out, or whether it is treated merely as a means of preventing the acquisition of profit that would otherwise be gained - because in either case, the capital asset of the taxpayer has, to that extent, been sterilised and destroyed, and it was in respect of that action that the compensation was paid. Lord Buckmaster concluded:[42]

> It is unsound to consider the fact that the measure, adopted for the purpose of seeing what the total amount should be, was based on considering what are the profits that would have been earned. That, no doubt, is a perfectly exact and accurate way of determining the compensation, for it is now well settled that the compensation payable in such circumstances is the full value of the minerals that are to be left unworked, less the cost of working, and that is, of course, the profit that would be obtained were they in fact worked. But there is no relation between the measure that is used for the purpose of calculating a particular result and the quality of the figure that is arrived at by means of the application of that test. I am unable to regard this sum of money as anything but capital money.

[41]   At 463.
[42]   At 463-464.
[43]   At 465-466.

Lord Wrenbury, concurring, said[43] that the answer to the question 'was that compensation profit?' may be supplied by the answer to the question 'Is a sum profit which is paid to an owner of property on the terms that he shall not use his property so as to make a profit?' He said that the answer must be in the negative. According to him, the whole point is that such an owner is not to make a profit and is paid for abstaining from seeking to make a profit. Lord Wrenbury presented two ways of looking at the question, each of which pointed to a capital payment[44].

> The matter may be regarded from another point of view : the right to work the area in which the working was to be abandoned was part of the capital asset consisting of the right to work the whole area demised. Had the abandonment extended to the whole area all subsequent profit by working would, of course, have been impossible, but it would be impossible to contend that the compensation would be other than capital. It was the price paid for sterilising the asset from which otherwise profit might have been obtained. What is true of the whole must be equally true of part. Again, a further point of view is this: had the working not been interfered with, the profit by the working would have extended over, say, three years; it would have been an annual sum. The payment may be regarded as a redemption of that annuity. Is the redemption of an annuity itself an annuity? If the currency of the annuity had been, say, ten years, and the beneficiaries were A for three years and B for seven years, could A have claimed all the compensation money on the ground that it was income of the first year? Clearly not.

This case can be contrasted with *Burmah Steamship Company Ltd v IRC*.[45] The taxpayers bought a second-hand ship which they committed to repairers for overhaul. The repairers exceeded the contractual time for completion of the overhaul and the taxpayers recovered damages (calculated on the basis of estimated loss of profits) for the late delivery of the ship. Here, it was the taxpayers that were claiming that the compensation was not a receipt of their trade, because it did not arise out of any actual trading with the vessel. They claimed that, on the contrary, it arose out of the breach of a contract, the object of which was not trading, but rather the acquisition of a capital instrument of trade. The Court of Session held that the compensation was a trading receipt. The Lord President (Clyde) gave[46] the example of someone who chartered one of the

---

[44]   Ibid.
[45]   (1931) 16 TC 67.
[46]   At 71.

taxpayers' vessels then breaching the charter, thereby exposing himself to a claim of damages. He said that, in such a situation, there would be no doubt that the damages recovered would be regarded as a trading receipt, the reason being that the breach of the charter was an injury inflicted on the taxpayers' trading, making a 'hole' in the profit. Thus the damages recovered could not therefore be reasonably or appropriately put by the taxpayer to any other purpose than to fill that 'hole'. He said that, if, on the other hand, one of the taxpayers' vessels was negligently run down and sunk by a vessel belonging to some other shipowner, and the taxpayers recovered as damages the value of the sunken vessel, there would be no doubt that the damages so recovered could not be regarded as a trading receipt, the reason being that the destruction of the vessel would be an injury inflicted, not on the taxpayers' trading, but on the capital assets of their trade, making a hole in those capital assets. The damages could therefore only be used to fill that hole.[47]

What then was the position in this case? Lord Clyde said[48]:

> Now in the present case, the injury inflicted on the Appellant by the repairers failure to make timeous delivery of the vessel is obviously not an injury to the Appellant's capital assets. Time sounds in money no doubt but the loss to the Appellant by the late delivery was in the form of loss of trading opportunities, not in the form of the loss of fixed capital ... it is very relevant to enquire whether the thing in respect of which the taxpayer has recovered damages or compensation is deprivation of one of the capital assets of his trading enterprise, or - short of that - a mere restriction of his trading opportunities.

It is important to note that what was stressed in both cases was that the measure by which the compensation is calculated is not the deciding factor - rather the crucial factor relates to the subject matter of the 'injury' or damage. If the injury or damage occurs in respect of a capital asset so as to make a 'hole' in that asset, compensation will be capital, since it will only go to fill the 'hole' in the capital asset (ie, to restore the capital asset, or to provide funds to replace it). If the injury or damage occurs in respect of trading opportunities, then compensation will be a receipt of the trade, filling, as it were, the hole in the trading opportunities. This all sounds straightforward enough. However, it would be a mistake to assume that the issue is so clear-cut that it can be expressed so definitively. It is not at all

---

[47]   At 71-72.
[48]   At 72.

self-evident that a hole in a capital asset cannot by the same token constitute a hole in trading opportunities. In the final analysis, each case has to be decided on its own facts.

Compensation for Cancellation of Business Contracts

Where compensation is received in return for the premature termination of a business contract one might reasonably assume that the receipt is of an income nature - after all, businesses sell their goods and services by entering into contracts. However the matter is not as simple as that. It is possible for a contract to be so important to a business that it might be regarded as a capital asset of the business - in which case compensation for the termination of such a contract might well be of a capital nature. For a contract to be so regarded, it appears that it must be more than just a profit-earning contract. The contract must constitute, or contribute substantially to, the provision of the profit earning apparatus of the trade.

The leading case is *Van Den Berghs Ltd v Clark*.[49] In this case, the taxpayers entered into agreements with a Dutch company to regulate competition between them. The agreements detailed prices and areas of supply of margarine. They also provided for a sharing of profits, and for a management arrangement. A dispute arose and the agreements were eventually terminated on the understanding that the Dutch company would pay compensation of £450,000 to the taxpayers for the termination. The House of Lords held that the deal between the two companies was a capital asset, and the payment for its cancellation was capital. Lord Macmillan[50] noted that the taxpayers were giving up 'their whole rights under the agreements for thirteen years ahead', and that the agreements which the taxpayers consented to cancel were not ordinary commercial contracts made in the course of carrying on their trade. Neither were they contracts for the disposal of their products, for the engagement of agents or other employees necessary for the conduct of their business, nor were they merely agreements as to how their trading profits when earned should be distributed as between the parties. Rather, the cancelled agreements related to the whole structure of the taxpayers' profit-making apparatus, regulated their activities, defined what they might and what they might not do, and affected the whole conduct of their business. Lord Macmillan thus concluded[51]:

The agreements formed the fixed framework within which their

---

[49]   (1935) 19 TC 390.
[50]   At 431.
[51]   At 432.

circulating capital operated; they were not incidental to the working of their profit-making machine but were essential parts of the mechanism itself. They provided the means of making profits, but they themselves did not yield profits. The profits of the Appellants arose from manufacturing and dealing in margarine.

A similar result was reached in *Barr Crombie and Co Ltd v IRC*.[52] The taxpayer company managed ships under certain agreements with a particular shipping company. About 98 per cent of its business came from a 15 year agreement with this company. The shipping company went into liquidation about seven years into the agreement, and the taxpayer company was paid compensation in respect of the eight years still to run before the expiry of the agreement. It was held that the compensation payment was capital and was not a trading receipt of the taxpayer company. The Lord President (Normand) noted[53] that virtually the whole assets of the taxpayer company consisted in the cancelled agreement, and that, when the agreement was surrendered or abandoned, practically nothing remained of the taxpayer company's business. Thus this fell within the principle of *Van Den Berghs v Clark*.

As indicated earlier, this principle relates strictly to contracts affecting the whole structure of the taxpayer's trade. If a contract is an ordinary trading contract, payments for cancellation will be income, and will form part of the trading receipts. This principle can be seen in *Kelsall Parsons and Co v IRC*.[54] The taxpayers were manufacturers' agents who held a number of contracts for several manufacturers. They would arrange, under these contracts, to sell the manufacturers' products in return for a commission. One of the agency contracts, a three-year agreement, was terminated at the end of the second year, and the taxpayers received compensation amounting to £1,500 for the termination. The Court of Session held that the compensation was an income receipt from trading. The loss of one agency contract did not affect the profit-making apparatus of the business. Such contracts were not part of the 'fixed framework' of the taxpayers' business. Rather, it was a contract which was incidental to the normal course of their business - a business which was to obtain as many contracts of this kind as they could. Also important was the fact that the cancelled contract had only one year left to run.[55]

Compensation for Restriction of Activities

A sum of money might be received in return for forgoing or giving up business and trade opportunity or activity. If the restriction is substantial or

---

[52]   (1945) 26 TC 406.
[53]   At 411.
[54]   (1938) 21 TC 608; see also *Rolfe v Nagel* (1981) 55 TC 585 (CA).
[55]   See generally, the Lord President (Normand) at 621; Lord Fleming at 622.
[56]   [1952] 1 Ch 311; 33 TC 136. Note that this case has been described as one which 'depended on its own particular facts' (per Lord Cameron in *IRC v Biggar* (1982) 56 TC 254 at 274. Some doubt has also been cast on it ('the Court of Appeal held, rightly or wrongly') by Lord Browne-Wilkinson in *Deeny v Gooda Walker Ltd* [1996] BTC 144 at 146.

results in removal of the profit-making apparatus (the 'tree') then sums received in return will be capital. In *Higgs v Olivier*[56] , Sir Laurence Olivier starred in the film *Henry V* and received a sum of £15,000 in return for agreeing that he would not, for a period of 18 months, appear as an actor in or act as producer or director of any film to be made anywhere by any other company. The Court of Appeal held that the sum of £15,000 was a capital receipt for a substantial restriction on the professional activities of the taxpayer. Sir Raymond Evershed MR said[57] that there is a true analogy between such an arrangement, or between a sale of one of a trader's capital assets and a restrictive covenant of a substantial character entered into by a trader relating to trading. This was to be contrasted with a restriction of 'a very limited or partial character'. In this case, even though the taxpayer was still free to act upon the stage and to take broadcasting work, the restriction on him still took a 'substantial piece' out of the ordinary scope of the professional activities which otherwise were open to him.[58]

Since the agreement was 'a restriction extending to a substantial portion of the professional activities which were open to' the taxpayer, the sum that he received for it could not properly be regarded as money which came to him from the ordinary course of the exercise of his profession. Singleton LJ said[59] that the money was not a profit or gain from the vocation of the taxpayer, but rather it was a payment for abstaining from his vocation.[60]

The crucial point in respect of this line of authority lies in the concept of 'substantial restriction'. Where an agreement is more regulatory than restrictive (for example, where it only determines the way in which a trader conducts his activities especially in a form in which it could be interpreted as an ordinary trading agreement), payments for the agreement may be income. For example, in *White v G and M Davies*[61] a farmer received an EEC subsidy for agreeing not to sell milk products and to restrict his dairy farming activities. Browne-Wilkinson J held that the subsidy represented trading income. It was a sum received for agreeing to work (trade) in a particular way. The facts also indicated that there was no substantial restriction on the farmer's activities. He could still farm the land, albeit not wholly for dairy farming purposes. Similarly, in *IRC v Biggar*[62] a farmer was paid some money under the EEC Dairy Herd Conversion Scheme for agreeing to switch from dairy farming to raising cattle for beef. The Court of Session, approving the decision of Browne-Wilkinson J in *White v G and M Davies*, held that the sum was a trading receipt. The Lord President (Emslie)[63] distinguished the case from *Higgs v Olivier*. He said that in *Higgs v Olivier*, Sir Laurence Olivier

[57]   33 TC at 146.
[58]   Sir Raymond Evershed MR at 147.
[59]   At 149.
[60]   See also *Murray v ICI* [1967] 2 All ER 980 (CA) - payments in return for 'keep out' agreements (agreements not to trade in specific countries) were capital.
[61]   [1979] STC 415; 52 TC 597
[62]   (1982) 56 TC 254.
[63]   At 264.

would, but for the restrictive covenant, have carried on acting in and producing and directing films as well as carrying on his vocation on the legitimate stage on radio and elsewhere. Thus the restriction which he accepted severely limited his ability to exploit his art and exposed him to inevitable loss. However, in the present case there was no question of there being a restriction of this kind which is capable of being equiparated with sterilisation of part of a taxpayer's capital assets. According to Lord Emslie[64];

> The Scheme was a conversion scheme in terms of which on the one hand the taxpayers agreed to stop producing milk and milk products and, on the other hand, to begin producing meat instead. They agreed, in short, to continue to farm to their full capacity. Only the product changed. There was no question, but for their entry into the Scheme, of the taxpayers producing both milk and meat and in any event there was no question of their being able to farm to better advantage. The Scheme itself recognised that those who entered it should not suffer, as a result of changing their product, any appreciable reduction in their income, and so far as the Case discloses, the taxpayers' entry to the Scheme exposed them to no loss of any kind. Their capital assets were not, in any sense, sterilised. They sold one herd (at a profit) and replaced it with another.

Finally, in *Thompson v Magnesium Elektron Ltd*[65] the taxpayers used chlorine in the production of magnesium. They were also able to produce caustic soda, a by-product of the use of chlorine. ICI then agreed to supply chlorine to the taxpayer at below market price in return for the taxpayer agreeing not to produce its own chlorine and caustic soda. ICI also paid a sum to the taxpayer to reflect the loss of caustic soda sales that the taxpayer was likely to suffer. ICI wished to protect its own market position in the production and sales of caustic soda. The Court of Appeal held that the payment was trading income representing the loss of trading profit on the sale of caustic soda. The agreement with ICI was simply a trading arrangement for the supply of chlorine.[66]

Sale of Information or Know-How

Statute has been introduced to deal with this type of receipt. Previously case law had suggested that if a trader disposed of a patent or know-how the sum received would be trade income unless the disposal was part of the

---

[64]   At 264-265.
[65]   (1944)1 All ER 126; 26 TC 1.
[66]   See Lord Greene MR, 26 TC at 11.
[67]   See *Evans Medical Supplies Ltd v Moriarty* [1957] 3 All ER 718.

disposal of a business interest and assets in a distinct area, normally a foreign country. The latter disposal would be one of capital (in part).[67] TA 1988 Sections 530-531 now provide that the receipts from the sale of know-how will be treated as trading income (S.531(1)) unless the sale is consequent on the sale of the business entity, in which case it will then be treated as a capital receipt (S.531(2))- although even here the taxpayer can elect to treat the sum received as an income receipt.(S.531(3))

Other Factors Affecting Trading Receipts

We have so far been concerned primarily with the question of whether a sum received by a taxpayer has the character of income or capital. As we have seen, this question can be (and is often) determinative of another question - whether the payment is a receipt of the taxpayer's business. This particular issue sometimes concerns the question whether the sum is really one that arises from the taxpayer's trade, or whether it derives from something else. In other words, it often raises the question of causation - for if a sum coming into a trader's hands is caused to come into his hands by something other than the business in which the trader is engaged, the sum, whatever its character, may not be a receipt of that business. As indicated earlier, this question is quite often linked inextricably with the question whether the sum is income or capital. However, for present purposes (and for convenience) we have herein treated these questions in different sections. In the remaining part of this chapter, we will examine the issue of causation, followed by an analysis of other factors that may fall to be taken into account in deciding whether a sum is a receipt of the taxpayer's trade.

Causation

Voluntary Receipts

This point concerns the issue of causation. Not only must sums alleged to be trading receipts be of an income or revenue nature, they must also be derived from the trade.[68] Thus, voluntary payments (even from present or past trading customers) are usually not trading receipts because there is often no causal link between the trade and the payment. For example, if a farmer meets a stranger on the road who then proceeds to give the farmer £20, this sum, regardless of whether it is considered to be income or capital,

---

68   See generally D. R. Davies (1979) BTR 212..

is not a receipt of the farmer's trade because of the absence of a causal link between the gift and the farming business. Now, supposing that the benefactor is not a stranger at all, but rather a former customer of the farmer. This would not change the character of the gift unless the money amounts to a late payment for goods or services already delivered. Now, supposing that the benefactor is not a former customer, but is rather a current customer. Again, unless the sum is remuneration for goods or services supplied by the farmer in the course of his farming business, there would still be no causal link which would turn the money into a receipt of the farming business. In other words, it is necessary to distinguish between a gift and a trading receipt.

The issue of voluntary payments has been addressed in a number of cases. First, *Walker v Carnaby Harrower et al.*[69] A firm of accountants had been auditors to a group of companies for some years. As a result of a group reorganization, the taxpayers were asked not to seek reappointment as auditors. The firm later received an unsolicited *ex gratia* payment of an amount equal to their last fees 'as solatium for the loss of the office of auditors'. That sum was not a gift to any individual partner. It was held that the sum was not a trading receipt. Pennycuick J explained the decision[70]

> At the end of their final term of office they had no legal claim of any description to receive any further payment from the companies. The companies then proceeded to make a wholly voluntary payment to the Respondent firm. It is, I think, irrelevant that the companies elected to make that payment in an amount identical to a penny with the fees paid to the firm during their last year of office. It seems to me that a gift of that kind made by a former client cannot reasonably be treated as a receipt of a business which consists in rendering professional services. The subject-matter of the assessment under Cases I and II is the full amount of the profits or gains of the trade or profession. Those profits have to be computed, it is well established, upon ordinary commercial principles. It does not seem to me that ordinary commercial principles require the bringing into account of this sort of voluntary payment, not made as the consideration for any services rendered by the firm, but by way of recognition of past services or by way of consolation for the termination of a contract. It is difficult to amplify the point any further.

[69]   [1970] 1 ALL ER 502; 46 TC 561.83
[70]   46 TC at 572-3.

A similar result was reached in *Simpson v John Reynolds and Co Insurance Ltd.*[71] The taxpayers were a firm of insurance brokers. When one of their longstanding clients was acquired by a public company, the client was required by the new owners to place all its insurance with one particular insurance group. The client then made a voluntary payment to the taxpayers, in recognition of the long period during which the taxpayers had acted as its broker and adviser on insurance matters. The Court of Appeal held that the payment was not a trading receipt. It was accepted by all three judges in the Court that that the mere fact that the payment was made voluntarily was not of itself decisive of the question. However, the fact that the payment was voluntary, coupled with the facts that it was made after the business relationship had terminated[72], that it was wholly unexpected, 'came out of the blue',[73] was not made by way of additional reward for any particular service rendered by the brokers or for their services generally,[74] was made in recognition of past services rendered to the client company over a long period, though not because those past services were considered to have been inadequately remunerated,[75] was made as a consolation for the fact that those remunerative services were no longer to be performed by the taxpayer for the donor, and the fact that there was no suggestion that at a future date the business connection might be renewed, all made it plain that this was not a trading receipt. Walton J captured the spirit of the decision[76].

> But when a payment is made purely voluntarily, on the termination of a trading relationship, that termination being so far as the parties can possibly foresee a permanent termination, and is made for no other reason than that the party making the payment is sorry that the relationship has had to terminate, and is grateful for the excellent service which the payee has given to it over a very long period of years, then it appears to me quite clear that the payment does not arise or accrue to the payee by reason of any trade carried on by it.[77]

In this case, the point was made that voluntariness does not stop a payment being a trading receipt. In *IRC v Falkirk Ice Rink Ltd.*[78] the Lord President (Emslie) said that the fact that a payment was voluntary is 'neutral'. In this case the taxpayer company operated an ice rink on a commercial basis and provided curling facilities to the public. The income from curling did not cover the cost of providing ice of the quality that was required. A members' club which made use of facilities provided by the taxpayers made a donation

---

[71]   (1975) 49 TC 693.
[72]   See Russell LJ at 712; Stamp LJ at 713.88
[73]   Per Stamp LJ at 713 89
[74]   Ibid.
[75]   Russell LJ at 712.
[76]   At 714.
[77]   See also *Murray v Goodhews* [1978] 2 All ER 40; (1977) 52 TC 86.
[78]   (1975) 51 TC 42 at 49; noted by P. Skitmore (1978) BTR 250.

to it in order to cover the additional cost of the curling and to enable it to continue to provide curling facilities in future. The payment was held to be a trading receipt. Lord Emslie said[79] that the payment was made in order that the taxpayer company might use it in its business, and that in substance and in form, it was a payment made to a trading company, artificially to supplement its trading revenue from curling, in the interests of the club and its members, to preserve the taxpayer company's ability to continue to provide curling facilities in the future. 'In its quality and nature this payment was of a business nature.'[80]

In *McGowan v Brown and Cousins*[81], another case in which a voluntary payment was held to be a trading receipt, Templeman J reviewed the authorities and put together some principles which we may be able to apply in reconciling the two lines of authority. The taxpayers in this case were estate agents who had acted for a company in connection with the acquisition of a site for development. The fee which they were paid for this work was acknowledged to be quite low for the work involved, but the taxpayers were prepared to accept the low fee because of a custom that the same agents would be engaged to sell the houses when they were eventually developed (this was a much more lucrative work). The site was eventually bought by another company which made an *ex gratia* payment to the taxpayers to compensate them for not using their services again. It was held that the sum was a trading receipt. It was a reward for services even though it was paid in pursuance of a moral rather than a legal obligation. In an enlightening passage Templeman J said[82]:

> [I]t seems to me that the broad line of distinction so far as taxability on this kind of voluntary gift is concerned, is a distinction which takes its origin in the question of whether the payment is attributable to specific work carried out by the recipient. If work is carried out then the payment, although voluntary, is made because payment has been earned. If the payment does not relate to specific past work then the payment is made, not because payment has been earned by work, but because the payment is intended for a deserving recipient. If the payment relates to work then, although the recipient may not be legally entitled, yet if he has a moral claim the payment is a receipt by him and a profit of his trade. When the payment is earned by work which has not been paid for or has not been adequately paid for then the payment has the quality of an income receipt liable to tax. On the other hand, if payment is not earned but is deserved, it is not income.

79   At 49-50.
80   At 50.
81   (1977) 52 TC 8.
82   At 15-16.

If the recipient has been paid in full for past work, but the person making the gift wishes to acknowledge the past conduct of the recipient or to give some token of regret at the termination of a business association and to acknowledge the fact that this termination of business association will not be entirely welcome to the recipient either for financial or other reasons, the payment is not earned but is deserved. It is not taxable ... In determining whether a gift is earned and therefore taxable, or deserved and therefore not taxable, the test seems to me to be to enquire whether the gift can be referred to the work of the recipient or whether it can be referred to the conduct of the recipient.

Unclaimed Balances and Deposits

Most people are probably familiar with the marketing strategy whereby traders try to extract a commitment from potential customers who appear to be interested to purchase certain goods or services, by requesting a 'deposit'. This type of sales strategy is common in the furniture and household goods, holiday, and travel industries. Typically, the potential customer is encouraged to 'reserve' the relevant goods or services by making a down payment, the full price to be paid later. The assumption is that, after making such a financial commitment, the customer is unlikely to want to lose the deposit by not completing the transaction. Also, most are familiar with the concept of appointing agents to sell goods and services. The agent takes a commission and pays the balance to the vendor. This practice is commonplace, indeed normal, in the property and auctioneering industries. The question then arises as to what happens if the potential customer fails to take delivery of the goods and does not bother to claim the deposit back, or, if a vendor fails to claim the proceeds of sale from the agent appointed to sell the goods or service. If the trader later appropriates the funds, are they trading receipts?

The authorities indicate that the matter is decided by the nature of the money at the time of receipt. This was the principle applied in *Morley v Tattersall*.[83] The taxpayers were a firm of horse auctioneers. Some of the sums which they received from sales of horses on behalf of vendors were never collected by the vendors and were subsequently distributed among the partners of the firm. The Court of Appeal held these sums were not trading receipts of the firm. According to Sir Wilfred Greene MR[84]:

---

[83]   (1938) 22 TC 51.
[84]   At 65.

The money which was received was money which had not got any profit-making quality about it; it was money which, in a business sense, was the client's money and nobody else's. It was money for which they were liable to account to the client, and the fact that they paid it into their own account, as they clearly did, and the fact that it remained among their assets until paid out do not alter that circumstance ... It seems to me that the quality and nature of a receipt for income tax purposes is fixed once and for all when it is received.

So the question is: 'whose money is the money at the time of receipt'? Obviously in the case of someone selling goods on behalf of another, the money belongs to the owner of the goods. However, this principle is not so easily applied to other situations. This is particularly so in the case of advances or deposits. This issue was confronted in *Smart v Lincolnshire Sugar Company Ltd*.[85] In this case, statutory advances were made by the government to some sugar manufacturing companies, subject to repayment in certain prescribed conditions. The taxpayer company was one of such companies, and the question was whether these advances were trading receipts. The House of Lords held that they were - and that they were trading receipts of the year of receipt and not of the year in which the contingency of repayment ceased. Lord Macmillan said[86] that the decisive factor was the fact that the payments were made to the taxpayer company, 'in order that the money might be used in their business.' They were intended artificially to supplement the company's trading receipts so as to enable them to maintain their trading solvency. According to him[87]:

> In the year with which your Lordships are concerned ... 'advances' were received by the Company which were intended to be used and could properly have been used to meet their current trading obligations, and in that year the contingency of possible repayment did not in fact arise.

It therefore seems that the relevant question in these cases concerns the purpose for which the payment was made. If the money was paid so that it would be used in the taxpayer's trade, then this would point to a trading receipt - even if it was repayable.

The principles of both cases were applied applied in *Elson v Prices Tailors Ltd*.[88] The taxpayers carried on business as tailors. They normally took

---

[85]   (1937) 20 TC 643.
[86]   At 670.
[87]   At 671.
[88]   At 679.

deposits from customers who ordered made-to-measure garments. These deposits would normally be returned to customers who were dissatisfied with the garments. However, the garments and deposits were sometimes not collected. In such cases, the deposits were transferred to a separate account. About five percent of the deposits were subsequently refunded to the customers, and the question was whether the ones that were never claimed at all were trading receipts. Ungoed-Thomas J held that the deposits on the facts were irrecoverable by the customers even if the taxpayers would normally refund them. He said[89] that the Lord Macmillan's statement in *Smart v Lincolnshire Sugar Company Ltd* applied, 'with the possible qualification that they were not in this case strictly paid in order to be used in the Company's business but subject to the consequence that they would be so used - but nothing turns on that distinction.' In this case, the deposits became the property of the taxpayer at the time of payment, and were therefore trading receipts.

It is well enough to say that sums paid so that they would be used in the taxpayer's trade thereby become trading receipts. Nothing is made of the point of what would be the position if the taxpayer subsequently pays the money back. Would this then be a trading expense or loss?[90] In *Morley v Tattersall Ltd*, Sir Wilfred Greene MR indicated that the nature and quality of a payment is 'fixed once and for all' when it is made. While this may be so under normal circumstances, it is important to note that the nature and quality may change subsequently by some event, or by operation of law. Sir Wilfred Greene MR himself contemplated this possibility, when, referring to some of the arguments of the Revenue in the case, he said[91]:

> It was essential, of course, for the argument, to discover some act of receipt within the Income Tax year for which the assessment was made, and, in order to get an act of receipt, the metaphorical expressions were used such as I have described, the holding in a new capacity of something which the partners had previously held in a different capacity, the turning into a trading asset of something which had previously not been a trading asset, and things of that kind, which, if they accurately represented the facts, might form some basis for an argument that, at the moment when they took place, a receipt had taken place.

An example of changes in the quality of a payment by operation of law can be seen in *Jay's the Jewellers v IRC*.[92] The taxpayers were jewellers and

---

88   [1963] 40 TC 671.
89   at 679.
90   Perhaps the best solution is to pay the money into a 'suspense account', and not bring them into the annual trading account, until such a time (if any) as the contingency of repayment ceases to exist (see Atkinson J in *Jay's the Jewellers v IRC*, (1947) 29 TC 274 at 286).
91   22 TC at 67.
92   (1947) 29 TC 274.

pawnbrokers. In the course of their pawnbroking business, they sold unredeemed pledges. Under the Pawn Brokers Act 1872, pledgers were entitled, within three years, to demand any surpluses of sale proceeds over the amounts due to the pawnbroker. For various reasons, in practice, the greater part of surpluses in respect of the sales of the unredeemed pledges were never demanded, and ultimately they became in fact the property of the pawnbroker. The question in the case was whether these unclaimed surpluses were trading receipts. Atkinson J held that the surpluses were not trading receipts in the year in which they were received, because that point was governed completely by *Morley v Tattersall*. According to him,[93] 'as a matter of law, these monies when received were not their monies at all; they belonged to their clients, and if a client came in the next day and demanded his money they would have to pay it away.' However, something important happened at the end of the three-year period specified in the 1872 Act.

> [A]t the end of three years, the money in question, the three-years-old surplus, did attain a totally different quality; a different quality was imprinted on surpluses three years old. I think there was then a definite trade receipt. At the end of the three years a new asset came into existence, an asset which had arisen out of a trade transaction...[94]

Thus, from that point, the sums, which were then irrecoverable by the pledgers, became the pawnbrokers' property, and thereby became trading receipts of the year.

Released Debts

This point relates to those situations in which a trader has claimed and received a tax relief in respect of a debt owed by the trade, and the debt is subsequently released in whole or part by the creditor. In such situations, the amount so released is treated by the statute as a trading receipt. The relevant provision is in TA 1988, Section 94(1), which provides:

> Where, in computing for tax purposes the profits or gains of a trade, profession or vocation, a deduction has been allowed for any debt incurred for the purpose of the trade, profession or vocation, then, if the whole or any part of the debt is thereafter released otherwise than as part of a relevant arrangement or compromise, the amount released shall be treated as a receipt of the trade, profession or

---

[93]   At 285.
[94]   At 287.

vocation arising in the period in which the release is affected.

For this purpose, 'relevant arrangement or compromise' has the same meaning as in TA 1988, Section 74[95].

Watson Brothers v Hornby

The case of *Watson Brothers v Hornby*[88] is one of the exceptions to the principle that a person cannot trade with himself or herself. It established the principle that, where one trader has two distinct trades and transfers goods from one trade to the other, that transfer must be treated as a sale and purchase at a 'reasonable price'. The taxpayers in the case had a farm from which they carried on the business of poultry dealers and breeders. They also ran a chicken hatchery for selling day-old chicks. They transferred some of the stock from the hatchery to the farm. The cost of producing saleable day-old chicks was more than the market value of the chicks at the time of the transfer. They succeeded in establishing a trading loss. MacNaghten J thus explained the decision[89]:

> The question now before the Court is: What is the price at which the chicks should be deemed to have been bought by the farm from the hatchery? The Appellants are the proprietors of both the hatchery and the farm and it is said that a person cannot trade with himself. That, no doubt, is quite true; but for the present purpose it is, I think, necessary to regard the hatchery and the farm as separate entities. Where one person buys goods from another but the contract of sale does not specify the price to be paid, the contract is, nevertheless, valid and enforceable. The law provided that the purchaser must pay a reasonable price ... The cost of the production of an article, whether it is a day-old chick or anything else, might no doubt happen to be its reasonable price, but there is no ground for saying that in the absence of any agreement it should be taken as the reasonable price. On the contrary, the market price would as a general rule be the reasonable price.

Sharkey v Wernher

The case of *Sharkey v Wernher*[98] presents another exception to the principle

[95] S.94(2). By s.74(2), the term refers to certain voluntary arrangements under the insolvency legislations, and to arrangements and compromises under the companies legislations.

[96] [1942] 2 All ER 506; 24 TC 506; approved by the House of Lords in *Sharkey v Wernher* [1955] 3 All ER 493; 36 TC 275.

[97] 24 TC at 509-510.

[98] [1955] 3 All ER 493; 36 TC 275.

that one cannot trade with oneself. The case establishes the principle that where a trader appropriates part of his or her trading stock for personal use, this must be brought into account at market value as a trading receipt. In the case, Lady Wernher transferred five horses from her business of a stud farm to her racing stables, which she kept for purely recreational purposes. The cost of breeding the horses had been debited in the stud farm accounts. In accordance with accounting practice, the transfer was entered into her accounts at cost price, thereby cancelling the initial entry of cost price of the stock-in-trade. The insertion of cost price would mean that the business would be in a no-gain, no-loss situation. The initial expense of cost would be offset by the credit of a transfer at cost. The Revenue successfully claimed that 'cost price' was not the correct figure for such a transfer, and that 'market value' was better economics and would present a fairer measure of assessable profits. Viscount Simonds confirmed the general proposition that one cannot trade with oneself, but said that this did not mean that 'a man cannot make a profit out of himself'[99]. According to Viscount Simonds,[100] once it is admitted or determined that an article forms part of the stock-in-trade of the trader, and that upon his parting with it so that it no longer forms part of his stock-in-trade, some sum must appear in his trading account as having been received in respect of it, the only logical way to treat it is to regard it as having been disposed of by way of trade, at its market value. Lord Radcliffe explained[101] that there were three possible methods of resolving the question. First, there might be no entry of a receipt at all. This method would be commended by the logic that nothing in fact is received in consideration of the transfer, and there is no general principle of taxation that assesses a person on the basis of business profits that he might have made but has not chosen to make. However, it would give an unfair advantage to the self-supplier. Secondly, a figure might be brought in at cost, and thirdly, a figure might be brought it at market value. His preference was thus expressed[102]:

> In a situation where everything is to some extent fictitious, I think that we should prefer the third alternative of entering as a receipt a figure equivalent to the current realisable value of the stock item transferred ... The realisable value figure is neither more nor less 'real' than the cost figure, and in my opinion it is to be preferred for two reasons. First, it gives a fairer measure of assessable trading profit as between one taxpayer and another, for it eliminates variations which are due to

---

[99]   36 TC at 296, 298.
[100]   At 299.
[101]   At 306.
[102]   at 307.

no other cause than any one taxpayer's decision as to what proportion of his total product he will supply to himself. A formula which achieves this makes for a more equitable distribution of the burden of tax, and is to be preferred on that account. Secondly, it seems to me better economics to credit the trading owner with the current realisable value of any stock which he has chosen to dispose of without commercial disposal than to credit him with an amount equivalent to the accumulated expenses in respect of that stock. In that sense, the trader's choice is itself the receipt, in that he appropriates value to himself or his donee direct, instead of adopting the alternative method of a commercial sale and subsequent appropriation of the proceeds.

Sharkey v Wernher has not been accepted without criticism. It has been suggested that the reasoning in the case conflicts with established principles of mutuality, with the existence of statutory transfer pricing rules, and with the principle that one should be taxed on what one receives not on what one could or might have received.[103]However, the rule is now well established. It also applies to all disposals of trading stock otherwise than in the course of trade, for example by gift to members of the trader's family, or friends. This was clearly established in *Petrotim Securities Ltd v Ayres.*[104] In this case, the taxpayer company, a dealer in securities, sold (in transactions described by Lord Denning MR as 'somewhat surprising') some securities to an associated company at a gross undervalue (this transaction was labelled the 'X' transactions in the case). The Court of Appeal held that these X transactions were not in the normal course of trade, that the figures should be disregarded for tax purposes, and that a market value should be substituted. Lord Denning MR referred[105] to *Sharkey v Wernher*, and said that it is not confined to cases where a person is a 'self-supplier'. According to him, 'it applies to any case where a trader may, for no reason, choose to give things away or throw them into the sea'. So, when a trader 'puts securities through his books at a derisory price, the figures are to be regarded as struck out for tax purposes; and in their place you must put in the market realisable value at the time.'[106]

Lord Denning MR subsequently explained fully the scope of this rule in *Mason v Innes*[107].

I start with the elementary principle of income tax law that a man cannot be taxed on profits that he might have, but has not, made ...

[103] See *Tiley and Collison's UK Tax Guide* 1997-98, para. 7:155. For further comment on the decision see Potter (1964) BTR 438.
[104] [1964] 1 WLR 190; (1963) 41 TC 389.
[105] 41 TC at 407
[106] Ibid. See also *Ridge Securities v IRC* [1964] 1 ALL ER 275; 44 TC 373; *Skinner v Berry Head Lands Ltd* (1960) 46 TC 377.
[107] [1967] 2 All ER 926; 44 TC 326.

in the case of a trader there is an exception to that principle. I take for simplicity the trade of a grocer. He makes out his accounts on an 'earnings basis'. He brings in the value of his stock-in-trade at the beginning and end of the year; he brings in his purchases and sales; the debts owed by him and to him; and so arrives at his profit or loss. If such a trader appropriates to himself part of his stock-in-trade, such as tins of beans, and uses them for his own purposes, he must bring them into his accounts at their market value. A trader who supplies himself is accountable for the market value. That is established by *Sharkey v Wernher* itself. Now, suppose that such a trader does not supply himself with tins of beans, but gives them away to a friend or relative. Again he has to bring them in at their market value.[108]

The rule in *Sharkey v Wernher*, itself being an exception to the principle that one cannot trade with oneself, is subject to exceptions. The exceptions or limits of the rule themselves raise questions. The first limit or exception to note is that the rule is limited to Schedule D, and, perhaps even to Case I of Schedule D. Thus it would be possible to confer benefits on oneself in relation to activities within other Schedules (perhaps rent free accommodation under Schedule A) without fear of *Sharkey v Wernher* attributing a market value to that transfer. The suggestion that the rule in *Sharkey v Wernher* might be confined to Case I of Schedule D arises out of *Mason v Innes* (above). In this case Hammond Innes, a famous author, had written a book called *The Doomed Oasis*, and had incurred and deducted travelling expenses to and from the Persian Gulf in obtaining background material used in the book. He then assigned the copyright to his father by way of a gift. The market value of the copyright was around £15,400. The Revenue claimed that, under the rule in *Sharkey v Wernher*, the market value of the copyright was a receipt of the taxpayer's profession. Their contention was that liability to tax does not, and should not, depend on the way in which a man keeps his accounts. Thus there is no difference in principle between a trader and a professional person. They argued that the appropriation of an asset, which has been produced in the ordinary course of a trade or profession, to the trader's or professional man's own purposes amounts to a realisation of that asset or the receipt of its value, and the taxpayer must bring it into account. It was held that the rule in *Sharkey v Wernher* did not apply. Lord Denning MR emphasised that the nature of a profession and the nature of a trade were very different, in that traders do

[108]   44 TC at 339.

have stock-in-trade but professional people normally do not.[109] He also emphasised that, in *Sharkey v Wernher* the accounts were presented on an earnings basis, whereas in *Mason v Innes* the accounts were presented on a cash basis. Lord Denning MR, rejecting the Revenue's arguments highlighted above, said[110]:

> Suppose an artist paints a picture of his mother and gives it to her. He does not receive a penny for it. Is he to pay tax on the value of it? It is unthinkable. Suppose be paints a picture which he does not like when he has finished it and destroys it. Is he liable to pay tax on the value of it? Clearly not. These instances - and they could be extended endlessly show that the proposition in *Sharkey v Wernher* does not apply to professional men. It is confined to the case of traders who keep stock-in-trade and whose accounts are, or should be, kept on an earnings basis, whereas a professional man comes within the general principle that when nothing is received there is nothing to be brought into account.

The result was that, at the end of the day, Hammond Innes was able to enjoy the benefits of the deductible expenses in relation to the production of *The Doomed Oasis*, and to confer the benefits of future sales to his father.

There are number of possible approaches to the interpretation of this decision. On one hand, one may focus on the distinctions, highlighted in the case, between trades and professions, and take view that the discussion on that point is sufficient to indicate that *Mason v Innes* clearly establishes that *Sharkey v Wernher* has no role to play in respect of professions. This approach is clear from the statement of Lord Denning MR, above. Another possible and closely linked interpretation is that the case simply highlights that *Sharkey v Wernher* is concerned only with goods - particularly, the value of the goods which it is a person's business to sell. Thus when a person is selling skills rather than goods, a principle developed in respect of the value of goods has no application. In this context it is useful to note the statement of Russell LJ that the copyright and other rights in the book in question in no sense formed stock-in-trade of Mr Innes, and that before the assignment to his father they had no part in any computation of profits and gains.[111] These two interpretations converge in the concept that traders sell their goods and professionals sell their skills.

An alternative interpretation of *Mason v Innes* is one that focuses on the

[109]   44 TC at 339.
[110]   Ibid.120
[111]   At 341.

manner and method of presentation of accounts. One could view *Sharkey v Wernher* as simply establishing that the correct manner of accounting for transfers 'other than for trading purposes', is, when accounts are presented on an earnings basis, to enter market values of the transferred items. Thus, the accounting practice employed by Lady Wernher was tested and declared to be wrong. On that interpretation, *Sharkey v Wernher* was not saying anything about the correct practice in relation to accounts presented on a cash basis (such as was the case in *Mason v Innes*). The court in *Mason v Innes* was correct therefore in refusing to regard itself bound by the decision in *Sharkey v Wernher.*[112]This approach can also be supported from the judgment of Lord Denning MR.[113] It would seem that a combination of the first two approaches is preferable to one which focuses on the accounting method.

A further limitation to the rule in *Sharkey v Wernher* is that it does not apply to a *bona fide* commercial transaction, even if that transaction represents a 'bad bargain' in terms of a sale at below market value. This principle emerges from *Jacgilden (Weston Hall) Ltd v Castle.*[114] Here, one Mr Rowe, a property developer, agreed to buy an hotel for £72,000. He later transferred the right to buy the hotel at this price to a company formed for that purpose, the shareholders of which were he and his wife. Accordingly, the hotel was conveyed by the vendors to the company, at Mr Rowe's direction, for the price of £72,000. At the time of the conveyance to the company, the hotel was worth £150,000. The company subsequently sold the hotel for £155,000, and was wound up. The Special Commissioners found that the deal between Mr Rowe and the vendors of the hotel was a genuine commercial deal. The question was the amount that should be entered into the company's books as the purchase price of the hotel. The company contended that, under *Sharkey v Wernher*, the market value at the time of the transfer of the right to buy the hotel (£150,000) should be used rather than the actual price paid (£72,000). This would have the effect of reducing the company's profits for tax purposes. Plowman J rejected the company's argument and held that the true purchase price should be entered. Plowman J[115] distinguished *Sharkey v Wernher*. First, in the first case, the court was concerned there with a disposal of property and not an acquisition, and therefore the question was what figure was to be credited, not debited, in the trading account. Also, in *Sharkey v Wernher*, there was a finding that the property in question was not sold or otherwise disposed of by way of trade, whereas in the present case there was a finding that the acquisition of the hotel was a commercial acquisition. Plowman J said[116] that the

[112] See generally, Potter (1964) BTR 483.
[113] Compare Davies LJ at 341; Russell LJ, ibid.
[114] [1969] 3 All ER 1110; 45 TC 685.
[115] 45 TC at 694-695.
[116] at 700.

Commissioners were entitled to conclude, as a matter of business common sense and notwithstanding any element of gift there may have been, that the transaction with which they were concerned was not a gift or a sale by Mr Rowe to the company at an undervalue, but a purchase by the company of trading stock at a price which had been fairly negotiated between Mr Rowe and the vendors. He also said that the *Sharkey v Wernher* line of authority has never been applied to a case where the price at which the property passed had been negotiated as a fair and proper price, and 'because it is an exceptional line of authority I think that the Court should be slow to extend it.'[117]

It is not clear from this case what point Plowman J was trying to make of the fact that *Sharkey v Wernher* involved a disposal, while this case involved an acquisition. Plowman J clearly indicated that this was a factor that distinguished the present case from *Sharkey v Wernher*. However, it is not entirely clear whether he was also trying to establish another exception to the *Sharkey v Wernher* principle. Such a rule, if introduced, would raise serious questions, and would also go against the decision of Pennycuick J in *Ridge Securities Ltd v IRC*[118] As Pennycuick J said in that case,[119] 'if a trader starts a business with stock provided gratuitously, it would not be right to charge him with tax on the basis that the value of his opening stock was nil'. Thus it cannot possibly be right that *Sharkey v Wernher* does not apply to acquisitions.

Also questionable is the conclusion that there was no gift by Mr Rowe to the taxpayer company. While the deal between Mr Rowe and the hotel vendors might have been a genuine commercial deal and the price fairly negotiated, the same cannot be said for the scenario whereby the company came to acquire the hotel. It is not clear how this could be said not to amount to a gift from Mr Rowe to the company. The company did not negotiate anything with the vendors and so was not a party to that original 'genuine commercial deal'. The facts do not show that the company paid a commercial price to Mr Rowe for the transfer to it of the right to buy the hotel at the price which Mr Rowe negotiated for his own purposes before the company was even formed. That Mr. Rowe and his wife were the only shareholders of the company is of no consequence. It would seem that this was a case where the Commissioners' findings could not be justified by the facts and in which the court would have been right to intervene. Be that as it may, the principle that *Sharkey v Wernher* does not apply to a genuine commercial transaction can be regarded as established.

---

[117]   Ibid. See also *Julius Bendit Ltd v IRC* (1945) 27 TC 44; *Craddock v Zevo Finance* (1946) 27 TC 267.
[118]   [1964] 1 All ER 275.
[119]   At 289.

There are other exceptions to the *Sharkey v Wernher* principle. The first relates to the valuation of trading stock on the discontinuance of a trade. By virtue of Section 100 TA 1988, if the stock is sold to another UK trader who is not connected with the seller, and the purchase price of the stock is deductible as an expense for the purchaser, the value of the stock will be the actual price for the sale. A similar rule applies to the valuation of work-in-progress at the discontinuance of a profession or vocation.[120]

A final exception can be seen in Section 84 TA 1988. This section applies to gifts of stock-in-trade to educational establishments, if that stock-in-trade would be plant or machinery in the hands of the educational institution. It also applies to gifts of capital assets for which capital allowance have been claimed by the donor. In the first case, the donor is not required to enter any amount into his books as consideration for the sale. In second case, there is a deemed disposal at nil value.

Transfer Pricing

The transfer pricing rules deal with dealings between associated persons, at an undervalue or overvalue.[121] Schedule 28AA(1) provides that, where provision has been made or imposed in a transaction or series of transactions between any two persons, and the provision is not such as would be made between independent enterprises, and the provision confers a potential UK tax advantage on one or both of the parties, the profits and losses of the persons so advantaged would be computed as if an arm's length provision had been made. This transfer pricing only applies where, at the time of the provision, one of the parties was directly or indirectly participating in the management, control or capital of the other, or the same person were so involved, in respect of each of the parties. For these purposes, 'transaction' includes arrangements, understandings and mutual practices, whether or not they are, or are intended to be, legally enforceable. (Sch. 28AA(3)). This rule is different from that in *Sharkey v Wernher* in that, in this case, the rule relates only to bodies corporate and partnerships (Sch. 28AA(4)) who are associated with each other. Such bodies are 'associated' for these purposes if one controls the other or both are controlled by the same third party. On the other hand, *Sharkey v Wernher* applies as much to individuals as it applies to bodies of persons, applies even where the parties are not 'associated', and even applies where the 'parties' to the transaction are one and the same person.

---

[120]   S.101, TA 1988.
[121]   See generally J. Elliot (1995) BTR 348.

Trading Stock

In addition to sums already received or earned, traders who operate their accounts on an earnings basis must also bring the value of their trading stock that remains unsold at the end of the accounting period into account as a trading receipt. If this not done, the result would be a distortion of the true state of the business. Similarly, the same trading stock would be entered as expense in the accounts in the following year, in order to avoid the danger of the same assets suffering double taxation. Subject to the provisions of section 100 TA 1988 (above) the trader may bring in each individual item at cost or market value, whichever is the lower, and may indeed pick and choose, bringing in some at cost, and others at market value.[122]

In this context, the market value refers to the best price available in the market in which the trader sells.[123] Thus a wholesaler would be applying the value of the stock in the wholesale market, while a retailer would be applying the value in the retail market. Where stock is purchased at different times and at different prices during the year leaving a residue that cannot be connected to any specific purchase, the normal method of valuing such stock is known as 'first in, first out' (FIFO), whereby the remaining stock is attributed to the latest purchases.

Work-in-Progress

At any point in time it is usual for traders and professional to have unfinished work. For example a furniture manufacturer may have any number of partly-completed chairs. These are referred to as work-in-progress, and the value thereof also has to be brought into account in ascertaining the trading receipts. So, how does one value work-in-progress? In a Joint Statement issued by the Inland Revenue and the Tax Faculty of the Institute of Chartered Accountants[124] it is claimed that work-in-progress, like stock, is an accounting concept - 'it is not for the Revenue to determine how to value it; it is solely a matter of the appropriate application of accountancy principles.' The purpose of valuation, according to the Statement, is to relate expenditure on such work to the period in which the income that it produces is earned,[125] such that if there is no expenditure, then there is no work-in-progress to be matched with income of later periods. The Statement also said that a sole trader or partnership with no fee-earning employees will have no work-in-progress,[126] and that there 'can be no work-in-progress in

---

[122] See *IRC v Cock, Russell and Co. Ltd.* [1949] 2 All ER 889; 29 TC 387.
[123] See *B.S.C. Footwear Ltd v Ridgeway* (1972) 47 TC 495.
[124] 'The new system for Taxing Professional Businesses: What is meant by"true and fair view"?', IR Tax Bulletin, December 1998, page 606 at 607.
[125] Para. 22.
[126] Para. 23

relation to a proprietors' labour'.[127] When work-in-progress is actually found, the 'basic principle' of valuation is said to be that it should be stated at the lower of cost and net realisable value.[128]

In ascertaining these, one may apply the direct-cost method, which values the work-in-progress by reference only to the costs of the materials and labour, or one may apply the on-cost method, which adds overheads to the direct costs. It has been held that neither of these methods is necessarily more correct than the other[129]. However, the Joint Statement by the Revenue and the ICA questions whether that view would be correct today.[130]

It points out that in *Duple Motor Bodies Ltd v Ostime* the Commissioners had found that the taxpayer's policy of applying the direct-cost method accorded with generally accepted accounting practice, but that such a policy would no longer accord with generally accepted accounting practice. It is clear that the Revenue and the ICA do not have the authority to question *Duple Motor Bodies Ltd v Ostime* in this way. However, their Statement in relation to that case may lead to an unwelcome re-opening of the debate on whether overheads must be included or whether the direct cost method is valid. That the issue is far from settled even among accountants is evident from later passages in the Joint Statement. It is stated (*inter alia*) that there are 'no rigid rules', and some of the passages then presented complicated rules to assist in deciding whether to add overheads of not. Since it seems that it is the policy of the taxpayer in *Duple Motor Bodies Ltd v Ostime* rather than the direct-cost method itself that the Joint Statement takes issue with, it would seem that the direct-cost method itself might still be valid. If so, the remaining passages of the Joint Statement as to the issue of overheads can only lead one to the conclusion that the taxpayer in *Duple Motor Bodies Ltd v Ostime* was right to have steered clear of that issue.

Profits from Land: 'Schedule A Businesses'

This section deals briefly with the principles governing the taxation of rents and other income derived from land under Schedule A. It may seem odd that this topic is being covered in a discussion on the taxation of trading income but, as we shall soon see, similar principles apply to income from Schedule

[127]   Para. 29.
[128]   Para. 29.
[129]   See *Duple Motor Bodies Ltd. v Ostime* [1961] 2 ALL ER 167; 39 TC 537.
[130]   Para. 25.

A businesses and other types of business under Schedule D Cases I and II.

This area of law has undergone significant change in recent times. First, Section 39 and Schedule 6 FA 1995 introduced a new Schedule A with respect to income tax only, effective from the year 1995-96. This meant that there were two versions of Schedule A - the 'old' version, which applied to corporation tax, and the 'new' version, which applied to income tax only. Section 38 and Schedule 5 FA 1998 introduced yet another Schedule A, with effect for income tax purposes for the 1998-99 and future years of assessment, and with effect for corporation tax from 1 April 1998 (subject to some transitional provisions). By this amendment, the profits of companies under Schedule A fall to be calculated on the same basis as that for income tax.

The Charge

Section 15(1)(1) TA 1998 charges tax under Schedule A on 'the annual profits arising from a business carried on for the exploitation, as a source of rents or other receipts of any estate, interest or rights in or over land in the United Kingdom'.[131]

The words 'arising from a business' in this provision are misleading and are not as limiting as they might first appear to be. This is because the statute clearly indicates that any transaction entered into for the exploitation, as a source of rents or other receipts of interests, estates or rights in land is deemed to be entered into in the course of such a business. (15(1)(2)) This means that an isolated transaction of letting, without any business structure, is caught by Schedule. A. For these purposes, all businesses and activities of a particular person that are chargeable under Schedule A are (with some qualifications or exceptions in the cases of foreign companies and insurance companies) treated as one single business. (s.15(1)(3))

The Schedule A charge includes profits arising from the right to use a caravan as defined under Section 29(1) of the Caravan Sites and Control of Development Act 1960, or houseboat defined as 'a boat or similar structure designed or adapted for use as a place of human habitation' (s.15(3)(2)) at a single location in the UK (s.15(3)(1)) It also covers sums payable for the use of furniture in cases of furnished lettings (in which case the sums paid for the use of the furniture are treated in the same way as rents) (s.15(4)(1)). In respect of leases for terms not exceeding 50 years, in respect of which the payment of a premium is required, a certain proportion of the premium is

---

[131] For the meaning of 'other receipts ...' see *Lowe v Ashmore* (1970) 46 TC 597. This term includes payments in respect of licenses to occupy, use, or exercise any rights over land, and rent charges, ground annual and feu duties and other annual payments in respect of land (s.15(1)(4))

treated as rent received when the lease was granted (s.34(1)). Exceptions to the charge include profits arising from the occupation of land (s.15(2)(1)), profits charged under Case I of Schedule D under Section 53(1) or Section 55 (s.15(2)(2)(a)), receipts treated as trading receipts in respect of tied premises (s.15(2)(2)(b)), or rent charged under Schedule D under Section119 or Section 120(1) (s.15(2)(2)(c)).

As under Schedule D Cases I and II, income tax is charged under Schedule A on the persons receiving or entitled to the income (s.21(1)), and is charged on current year basis, that is 'the full amount of the profits arising in the year of assessment' (s.21(2)). Generally, the profits of a 'Schedule A business' are computed in the same way as trading profits under Schedule D Case I Section 21A(1), thus a large number of provisions applying to trades under Schedule D Case I also apply to Schedule A (e.g., rules relating to deductible expenses, the rules relating to business entertainment, repairs of premises, post-cessation receipts and expenses, changes in partnerships, commencement and cessation of trades, etc) Section 21A and Section 21B.[132]

In spite of this similarity of treatment, Section 21C makes exception in the case of mutual trading. Transactions and relationships involved in 'mutual business' are treated by Section 21C(2) as if they took place between persons with no relationship of mutuality. By that token, surpluses or deficits are regarded as profits and losses if they would be so regarded if the business were not mutual (s.21C(3)).

---

[131]   See generally also the Inland Revenue Statement of Practice, 'Taxation of Rents', IR50, para. 119 *et seq.*

chapter seven
Schedule D Cases I and II - Trading Expenditure

Introduction

We have seen in the preceding chapters that the computation of trading profit involves the deduction of allowable expenditure from trading receipts. This chapter is concerned with the question of the types of expenses and losses which can be set against trading receipts in order to arrive at a profit figure. There are three qualifications for an item of expense to be allowable against trading receipts:

(i)   the expense must be of an income and not capital nature[1];

(ii) the expense must be incurred wholly and exclusively for the purposes of the taxpayer's trade, profession or vocation[2];

(iii) the particular expense must not be prohibited by statute[3].

The discussion that follows addresses these issues in turn.

Income or Capital?

It stands to reason that a tax on income which only takes into account receipts of an income nature will not allow expenses of a capital nature to be set against those income receipts. This principle was recognised by the Barons of the Exchequer as far back as the late 19th century[4].

Therefore, the requirement that an item of expenditure be income in nature invites the same distinction and discussion that took place when considering the need to take into account only income receipts and not capital receipts. We have seen in the previous chapter the difficulties inherent in the classification of payments received by a trader. Similar

---

[1]   See generally Lord Templeman in *Lawson v Johnson Matthey plc* [1992] BTC 324 at 327.
[2]   See TA 1988, s.74(1).
[3]   TA 1988, s.74(1).
[4]   See for example, Huddleston B in *Forder v Andrew Handyside and Co Ltd* (1876) 1 TC 65 at 70; compare Pollock B at page 69.

difficulties exist in the classification of the trader's outgoings. As with trading receipts, there have been a range of approaches or tests. The distinction between the 'tree' (eg, the machinery) and the 'fruit' (eg, the products that come out of the machinery) also comes into play here - expenses incurred on the tree will be capital, but those incurred on the fruit will be income. Then there is the dichotomy between fixed capital and circulating capital. The dichotomy has been variously described. One such description is by Lord Hanworth MR in *Mallet v Staveley Coal and Iron Company Ltd.*[5]: 'in dealing with any business, there are two kinds of capital, one fixed capital which is laid out in fixed plant, and the other circulating capital, which is turned over and over in the course of the business which is carried on.' Lord Haldane in *John Smith v Moore*[6] preferred to refer to the economist Adam Smith: 'Adam Smith described fixed capital as what the owner turns to profit by keeping it in his possession and circulating capital as what he makes profit of by parting with it and letting it change masters. The latter capital circulates in this sense.' The application of the dichotomy in this context is to the effect that the cost of purchasing circulating capital assets will be income and may then qualify for relief[7].

On the other hand, the cost of purchasing fixed capital assets (eg, permanent or semi-permanent investment items, such as plant and machinery) would normally be treated as capital expenditure which will not generally (excluding any Capital Allowances) be deductible. However, the term 'fixed capital', which conjures an image of fixed plant and machinery, is deceptive, for it does not follow that fixed plant and machinery are always items of fixed capital. Consider these words of Romer LJ in *Golden Horse Shoe (New) Ltd v Thurgood*[8].

> Land may in certain circumstances be circulating capital. A chattel or a chose in action may in certain circumstances be fixed capital. The determining factor must be the nature of the trade in which the asset is employed. The land upon which a manufacturer carries on his business is part of his fixed capital. The land with which a dealer in real estate carries on his business is part of his circulating capital. The machinery with which a manufacturer makes the articles which he sells is part of his fixed capital. The machinery that a dealer in machinery buys and sells is part of his circulating capital, as is the coal that a coal merchant buys and sells in the course of his trade.

Another test for capital expenditure is the so-called 'enduring benefit' test.

---

[5]   [1928] 2 KB 405 at 413.
[6]   [1912] 2 AC 13 at 19.
[7]   See for example, *Ammonia Soda Co. v Chamberlain* [1918] 1 Ch 266; *Golden Horseshoe (New) Ltd. v Thurgood* [1934] 1 KB 548; 18 TC 280.
[8]   [1934] 1 KB 548 at 563.

This was propounded by Viscount Cave LC in *British Insulated and Helsby Cables Ltd v Atherton*[9]:

> When an expenditure is made not only once and for all, but with the view to bringing into existence an asset or advantage for the enduring benefit of a trade, I think there is very good reason ... for treating such an expenditure as being properly attributable not to revenue but to capital.

To the natural question 'what is an enduring benefit?' Rowlatt J provides an answer in *Anglo-Persian Oil Co Ltd v Dale*[10].

> What Lord Cave is quite clearly speaking of is a benefit which endures, in the way that fixed capital endures; not a benefit that endures in the sense that for a good number of years it relieves you of a revenue payment. It means a thing which endures in the way that fixed capital endures. It is not always an actual asset, but it endures in the way that getting rid of a lease or getting rid of onerous capital assets or something of that sort as we have had in the cases, endures. I think that the Commissioners, with great respect, have been misled by the way in which they have taken 'enduring' to mean merely something that extends over a number of years.[11]

Viscount Cave LC was talking in the case of *Atherton* about expenditure incurred 'with a view' to bringing into existence an asset or advantage. However, the courts have often considered, not the 'view' of the person who incurred the expenditure, but rather, the questions, whether any asset was actually brought into existence by the expenditure, or whether the expenditure actually conferred an enduring benefit on the trade.[12]

Thus the enduring benefit test enables the court to consider the nature and effects of the expenditure and of the asset, outside the traditional accountancy practice of categorisation and balance sheet representation of fixed and current assets. It also enables the court to deal with the actual effects of the expenditure.

The enduring benefit test is not without criticism. For one, it is clear that 'money spent on income account, for example on durable repairs, may often yield an enduring advantage.'[13] It is also not clear what the correct approach is to the difference between a 'view' to create an asset or advantage on one

---

[9]   [1926] AC 205 at 213-214.
[10] (1932) 16 TC 253 at 262.
[11] Approved by Romer LJ in the same case, at page 274.
[12] See for example Lawrence LJ in *Anglo-Persian Oil Co.Ltd v Dale*, at page 271; Lord Macmillan in *Rhodesia Railways Ltd v Bechuanaland Protectorate IT Collector* [1933] AC 368 at 374; Lord Reid in *IRC v Carron Company* (1968) 45 TC 18 at 68; Lord Templeman in *Lawson v Johnson Matthey plc* [1992] BTC at 328.
[13] See Lord Reid in *IRC v Carron Company* 45 TC at page 68. According to Lord Reid (ibid), what matters in a case of this kind is the nature of the advantage for which the money was spent.

hand, and, on the other hand, whether such an asset or advantage was created successfully.

Yet another test is the 'identifiable asset' test. The test requires an examination of the nature and subject matter of the expenditure. The purpose of this examination is to ascertain whether an asset is identifiable as the subject of the expenditure. If such an asset can be identified, sums spent on the acquisition or improvement of that asset will be capital. This test was confirmed in *Tucker v Granada Motorway Services Ltd.*[14] In this case the taxpayer company paid a sum of £122,000 in order to secure a reduction in the rent paid by them under a 50-year lease of a motorway service area, for the unexpired term of 40 years. The House of Lords held that the payment was capital expenditure. Lord Wilberforce referred[15] to the observations of Rowlatt J about the enduring benefit test (above), and said that the fact that the benefit obtained was enduring, in the sense that it might last for over 40 years, was not sufficient to make the payment a capital payment. However, a payment to get rid of a lease or a disadvantage in a lease might be so sufficient. He proceeded to explain the principle:

> I think that the key to the present case is to be found in those cases which have sought to identify an asset. In them it seems reasonably logical to start with the assumption that the money spent on the acquisition of the asset should be regarded as capital expenditure. Extensions from this are, first, to regard the money spent on getting rid of a disadvantageous asset as capital expenditure and, secondly, to regard money spent on improving the asset, or making it more advantageous, as capital expenditure. In the latter type of case it will have to be considered whether the expenditure has the result stated or whether it should be regarded as expenditure on maintenance or upkeep, and some cases may pose difficult problems.

In this case, the payment was a once-for-all expenditure on a capital asset designed to make it more advantageous. Although the lease was non-assignable so that it had no balance sheet value before or after the modification, it was none the less an asset and a valuable one for the taxpayer's trade. If an asset, it was a capital asset.[16]

Thus the expenditure had been incurred on a capital asset (the lease), making it a more valuable asset for the taxpayer's trade[17]. Lord Salmon dissented, saying that while the lease was an asset of the company, he did not consider it to be a capital asset

14   [1979] 2 ALL ER 801; 53 TC 92.
15   53 TC at 107.
16   at 108.
17   Lord Salmon dissented, saying that while the lease was an asset of the company, he did not consider it to be a capital asset (at 109).
18   [1974] 3 All ER 146.

Similarly, in *Pitt v Castle Hill Warehousing Co Ltd*[18] expenditure on an asset, a road, was held to be capital expenditure. The particular expenditure on the road related to its construction. If the expenditure on the same asset had been for its maintenance and upkeep, such expenditure might conceivably have been classed as revenue expenditure and deductible.

With respect to the identifiable asset test, it seems that the word 'asset' is given a wide meaning, and is not restricted to tangible property. So, for example, goodwill is an asset, and a payment to protect or preserve goodwill is capital.[19] A credit agreement is also an asset, and a payment to secure release from onerous terms in such an agreement is capital.[20]

The whole basis of this test is that, unlike the fixed and circulating capital test, the item of expenditure is not categorised and fixed exclusively by the nature of the asset. For example, we have seen that in *Pitt v Castle Hill Warehousing Co Ltd*, expenditure on the same asset might be revenue or capital nature depending on the nature of the expenditure in relation to the asset. The same fixed asset might invite both capital and revenue expenditure. One might suggest that this test also has elements of a merging of some of the other tests. We need to identify the asset and its nature (fixed or circulating) and then we need to consider the nature of the expenditure on that asset, presumably also examining whether it brings into the business an enduring benefit or advantage. For example, the expenditure in *Pitt* on the construction of the road (to facilitate access to an industrial site without disturbing residents) brought in an enduring asset and a benefit and advantage in terms of public relations and goodwill.

Despite all these tests, it has been held that a payment to get rid of an employee, who it is not in the company's interest to retain, is income in nature.[21] Similarly, a payment to secure the termination of an agency contract which later proved burdensome (because unexpectedly high fees became payable to the agents) has been held to be income[22], as has a payment to remove 'insurmountable obstacles to the profitable development' of the taxpayer's business 'in contemporary economic and commercial conditions.'[23]

One might well regard an employee as an asset of the trade and therefore regard a payment to get rid of such an asset as a capital payment. One might also regard an agent as an asset of the business. Furthermore, one might arguably regard the departure of such an employee, or the freedom from such an agent, as conferring an enduring benefit (as defined).[24] So

[19] *Walker v Joint Credit Card Co Ltd* [1982] STC 427; 55 TC 617; *Associated Portland Cement Manufacturers Ltd v IRC* [1946] 1 All ER 68.

[20] *Whitehead v Tubbs* [1984] STC 1; 57 TC 472.

[21] *Mitchell v B W Noble Ltd.* [1927] 1 KB 719; compare Lord Keith of Kinkel in *Lawson v Johnson Matthey plc* [1992] BTC at 326 - '... a payment to get rid of an obstacle to successful trading is a revenue and not a capital payment ... This must be no less true of a payment made to save the whole of an existing business from collapse.'

[22] *Anglo-Persian Oil Co Ltd v Dale*, supra.

[23] *IRC v Carron Company* (1968) 45 TC 18 (HL), following *Anglo-Persian Oil Co Ltd v Dale*.

[24] The courts did not subscribe to this analysis - see for example Lawrence LJ in *Anglo-Persian Oil Co Ltd v Dale*, 16 TC at 271.

when the decisions are examined, we may be tempted to concur with Lord Greene's suggestion that the matter might as well be determined by a 'spin of a coin'. Equally, one might just consider that the matter is simply one of common sense and/or reality.

The Court of Appeal seemed to favour the common sense approach in *Lawson v Johnson Matthey plc*[25] while Lord Goff of Chieveley in the House of Lords[26] in the same case talked about 'the reality of the situation'.[27] However, in applying that common sense and reality the Court of Appeal and the House of Lords reached different conclusions as to the status of the expenditure in the case. The expenditure in this case consisted of a £50 million injection by a parent company (Johnson Matthey plc) into one of its wholly-owned subsidiaries, Johnson Matthey Bankers Limited (JMB). This cash injection was part of a scheme to facilitate the disposal of the wholly-owned subsidiary to the Bank of England. The Bank of England was not willing to buy the (worthless) shares of JMB unless, immediately prior to the purchase and transfer of the shares and the company, Johnson Matthey plc would inject the £50 million. Johnson Matthey plc was willing to do this in order to facilitate the disposal and avoid the insolvent liquidation of JMB. If Johnson Matthey plc had held onto JMB, JMB would have faced insolvency with severe ramifications for the goodwill and trade of the rest of the companies in the Johnson Matthey group. There was even a suggestion that it might lead to a closure of Johnson Matthey plc itself.

The General Commissioners took the view that the £50 million payment by Johnson Matthey plc was of a revenue and not capital nature because its purpose was 'to preserve the trade of Johnson Matthey plc from collapse.'[28]The Commissioners further noted that the link between the £50 million expenditure and the subsequent transfer of shares to the Bank of England did not operate to convert the £50 million into expenditure of a capital nature. On appeal, the High Court disagreed with the Commissioners, and declared that the nature of the expenditure must be determined objectively and that its determination must recognise the nature of what it could achieve.[29]

Such an analysis would facilitate the recognition of the achieved disposal of the shares and business of the subsidiary, JMB. That recognition would objectively indicate the expenditure to be of a capital nature, being part of the disposal of a capital asset. On further appeal to the Court of Appeal, the Court reviewed the long history of judicial comment in this area, noting that the 'enduring benefit' test of Viscount Cave has been undermined by

[25]   [1991] BTC 150.
[26]   [1992] BTC 324.
[27]   At 332.
[28]   [1990] STC 149.
[29]   [1990] STC 160.
[30]   See Fox LJ, [1991] BTC 150 at 156. The common sense approach was advocated by Lord Reid in *Strick (Inspector of Taxes) v Regent Oil Co. Ltd.* [1966] AC 295 at 313.
[31]   [1991] BTC at 156.

subsequent judicial comment.

The Court noted the absence of any definitive test for the determination of the income versus capital issue. Consequently the Court decided to follow the 'common sense' approach.[30] The position, according to Fox LJ[31], was as follows: JMB was a capital asset to the taxpayer company; the taxpayer company disposed of JMB to the Bank; the only terms on which the Bank was willing to acquire JMB was on payment of the £50m by the taxpayer company to JMB. Taking account of these factors, the situation, according to him was 'in reality, the same as if the Bank had said "We will take over JMB if you pay us £50m". Whichever way it was done, the payment seemed to be a payment by the taxpayer company to enable it to get rid of a capital asset the continued retention of which was harmful to the plc. Thus the 'common sense of the matter' was that the £50million was capital expenditure.

On further appeal to the House of Lords their Lordships differed from the conclusion reached by the Court of Appeal and held that the payment was revenue expenditure and deductible. The reality of the situation, according to Lord Goff of Chieveley, was that the payment was a contribution towards the rescue of JMB which the taxpayer knew that the Bank of England was going to mount immediately in the public interest.[32] Similarly, Lord Keith of Kinkel said that the payment was, 'on a proper analysis', not the payment of the price for getting rid of a burdensome asset, but a contribution required by the Bank of England towards its planned rescue operation.[33] Lord Templeman, who delivered the main speech, proceeded by drawing analogies from the authorities. According to him, the payment of £50million did not bring an asset into existence and did not procure an advantage for the enduring benefit of the trade.[34] The items of fixed capital which were disposed of (the shares in JMB) were not themselves of an onerous character, and the payment of £50million had no enduring effect on the capital of the taxpayer. The goodwill of the taxpayer was not improved, but was saved from extinction.[35] In this case, the payment was made solely to enable the taxpayer to continue in business.

One is hard pressed to find a neat categorisation for the approach of the House of Lords in this case. While the 'reality of the situation' is one theme, the speech of Lord Templeman seemed to contain an amalgam of a number of the available tests - particularly the enduring benefit and identifiable asset tests. Thus perhaps the real answer to the question 'how does one distinguish income expenditure from capital expenditure?' is now that one

---

[30]   See Fox LJ, [1991] BTC 150 at 156. The common sense approach was advocated by Lord Reid in *Strick (Inspector of Taxes) v Regent Oil Co Ltd* [1966] AC 295 at 313.

[31]   [1991] BTC at 156.

[32]   Lord Goff referred to the Court of Appeal's analysis as 'attractive', but on reflection came to the conclusion that it was too narrowly based, and ignored the reality of the situation. Compare Lord Emslie (at page 326), who also found the analysis of the Court of Appeal to be attractive, but too narrowly based.[1992] BTC at 332-333.

[33]   At 326.33

[34]   At 328; compare *Lord Reid in IRC v Carron Company,* 45 TC at 68.

[35]   At 329.

has to look at all the circumstances of the case and apply any mixture of the enduring benefit and identifiable asset tests that appears appropriate in the light of the reality the situation. This, it is submitted, does not advance the situation very much at all and is more or less tantamount to saying that the issue should be decided on a case-by-case basis. Perhaps that is as much as one is entitled to expect in these matters - as long as any case-by-case analysis takes account of established tests, particularly the two just referred to.

Statutory Provisions

Having examined the dichotomy between capital and income with respect to the characterisation of expenses, it remains to examine the other factors that are relevant to the determination of whether an item of expenditure is allowable as a deduction. The starting point for this discussion is Section 817(1) of the Taxes Act, which provides that, in arriving at the amount of profits or gains for tax purposes, no other deductions shall be made than such as are expressly enumerated in the Tax Acts. This is a misleading provision insofar as it purports that the allowable deductions are expressly enumerated in the statute. In actual fact, in most cases, the Taxes Act does not specifically provide for a deduction to be made. Rather, deductions are allowed by implication, first, because this is inherent in the concept that it is the 'profits', not the receipts of the trade that are charged to income tax, and, secondly, because the Taxes Act does contain an enumeration of the items which are disallowed. In this respect, the principle is that an item of expenditure that is not disallowed is allowed by implication. This principle can be found in the following passage in the judgment of Jenkins LJ in *Morgan v Tate and Lyle*[36].

> [The rule] does not provide that money wholly and exclusively laid out or expended for the purposes of the trade may be deducted, but that no sum shall be deducted in respect of any disbursements or expenses not being money wholly and exclusively laid out or expended for the purposes of the trade. It is, however, obvious that if no deduction at all of expenses from gross receipts was allowed, it would be impossible to arrive at the balance of the profits and gains of a trade upon which tax under Case I of Schedule D is to be assessed. Accordingly, it has long been well settled that the effect of

---

[36]   (1954) 35 TC 367 at 393-394.

these provisions as to deductions is that the balance of the profits and gains of a trade must be ascertained in accordance with the ordinary principles of commercial trading, by deducting from the gross receipts all expenditure properly deductible from them on those principles, save in so far as any amount so deducted falls within any of the statutory prohibitions contained in the relevant Rules, in which case it must be added backfor the purpose of arriving at the balance of profits and gains assessable to tax.

This passage, while explaining the reason why deductions can be made, also points to a very important principle with regard to the deductibility of expenditure - that which relates to the so-called principles of 'remoteness and duality' (wholly and exclusively). This was referred to at the beginning of this chapter. This issue is examined in the next section.

'Wholly and Exclusively'

The relevant statutory provision is in section 74(1)(a) which provides that no sum shall be deducted in respect of any disbursements of expenses, not being money wholly and exclusively laid out or expended for the purposes of the trade, profession, or vocation. This provision forms the backbone of the statutory deduction rules. Judicial responses to the provision result in the view that it incorporates the concepts of remoteness and duality.[37] Each item of expenditure must have been incurred for the purposes of the trade, etc. This is the principle of remoteness. The relevant item of expenditure must also have been incurred only for the purposes of the trade. This is the principle of duality (or perhaps more correctly, singularity - for the principle is that expenditure incurred for dual purposes is not allowable).

Let us examine the terminology employed within the provision. First, 'wholly'. In *Bentleys, Stokes and Lowless v Beeson*[38] Romer LJ, delivering the judgment of the Court of Appeal, said that the adverb 'wholly' refers to the quantum of the sums expended. This presumably means that the 'whole' of the amount claimed as an expense must have been expended for business purposes. Secondly, 'exclusively'. Romer LJ[39] said in the same case that this word concerns the 'motive or object in the mind' of the person making the expenditure. He said that this was a question of fact. Finally, what does the phrase 'for the purposes of the trade' mean? In *Bentleys, Stokes and Lowless v Beeson* Romer LJ seemed to link it with 'the object of

---

[37] For a general discussion see V Grout (1979) BTR 44, and 96.
[38] [1952] 2 All ER 82; 33 TC 491.
[39] At 503-504; approved by Lord Elwyn-Jones (dissenting) in *Mallalieu v Drummond* [1983] 2 All ER 1095 at 1097-1098.

promoting the business or its profit earning capacity'.[40]

However, in *Strong and Co of Romsey Ltd v Woodifield*[41] Lord Davey said[42] that these words mean 'for the purpose of enabling a person to carry on and earn profits in the trade'. According to him, it is not enough that the disbursement is made in the course of, or arises out of, or is connected with, the trade or is made out of the profits of the trade - it must be made for the purpose of earning the profits.[43]

It is not clear whether these two formulations will lead to different outcomes in practice, and if so, which should be preferred. Both Lord Davey and Romer LJ seem to be introducing their own glosses on the statutory words.[44] It is doubtful whether the statutory words justify or necessitate their formulations. When the statute speaks of the purposes of the trade, etc., it would seem that the attempt is to distinguish a business purpose from a personal purpose. The scheme of Section 74(1) itself proves this - for a large part of it seems to be preoccupied with the distinction between business and domestic or private purposes.[45]

Thus there is no reason to link the statutory provision with the purposes of earning profits or promoting the business. So, the provision could well be referring to expenses which are incurred in connection with the trade, profession or vocation. This would of course just amount to one introducing one's own gloss, as would any other attempt to define the phrase. Perhaps the best approach is that the phrase needs no interpretation at all, since it is plain enough for all to see. If anything requires interpretation at all, it would seem to be limited to the word 'for'. This may explain Lord Brightman's definition of the whole phrase as meaning 'expended to *serve the purposes* of the trade, profession or vocation', in *Mallalieu v Drummond.*[46]

The only difference between the statutory phrase and Lord Brightman's definition lies in the replacement of the word 'for' in the statute with the phrase 'to serve', and the definition therefore seems to involve no gloss on the statutory words. However, Lord Brightman then went on to approve Lord Davey's definition in *Strong and Co of Romsey Ltd v Woodifield* as an 'elaboration' of his definition - which then reintroduces the gloss initially avoided.

So what is the result of this analysis? From the judicial *dicta* on the issue, it seems to be this: an item of expenditure is prohibited by this subsection unless the whole of the amount claimed had been expended, either solely for the purpose of enabling the spender to carry on and earn profits in his or

---

[40]   at 504.
[41]   (1906) 5 TC 215
[42]   At 220. Referred to with approval by Lord Brightman in *Mallalieu v Drummond* [1983] 2 All ER 1095 at 1099; see also Romer LJ in *Newsom v Robertson* [1952] 2 All ER 728 at 732-733.
[43]   Ibid.
[44]   Lord Davey's gloss has been criticised by the Committee on the Taxation of Trading Profits (1951 Cmnd 8189), as being 'much too narrow' (para. 152), and 'unsatisfactory in its operation' (para. 153). The Radcliffe Commission was also highly critical of it (1955, Cmnd para. 127).
[45]   See for example, s.74(1)(b), (d), and (e).
[46]   [1983] 2 ALL ER at 1099 (emphasis supplied)

her business, or solely for the object of promoting the business or its profit-earning capacity. We might prefer to put it differently from the judicial *dicta* by saying that an item of expenditure is prohibited by this subsection unless the whole of the amount claimed had been expended solely for (or to serve) the purposes or interests of the business as opposed to any other private or domestic purpose or interest.

The most important word in the statutory test is 'exclusively'. This is what establishes the singularity concept - that there must only be a business purpose. In *Mallalieu v Drummond*[47] Lord Brightman said that the effect of the word is to preclude a deduction if it appears that the expenditure was not only to serve the purposes of the trade, profession or vocation of the taxpayer but also to serve some other purposes. According to him, such other purposes, if found to exist, will usually be the private purposes of the taxpayer. Thus if, at the time of incurring the expenditure, there existed, wholly or partly, some other purpose for the expenditure, such as a personal, private, or domestic purpose, then the whole of the expenditure will be incurred for a dual purpose and the whole of it will be disallowed - and it is immaterial that the business purposes are the predominant ones.[48]

The courts have taken a strict approach to the question whether the requirement for singularity of purpose is satisfied. In so doing, they have fastened onto the word 'purpose'. The relevant purposes are, in this respect, the purposes of the business, as opposed to the purposes of the taxpayer.[49]The two are different concepts, even though the purposes of the taxpayer (ie, his or her intentions or objects) are fundamental to the whole statutory test, in that, in order to ascertain whether the expenditure was incurred to serve the purposes of the taxpayer's business, it is necessary to discover the taxpayer's object in making the expenditure.[50] This might require the Commissioners to 'look into the taxpayer's mind at the moment when the expenditure is made'.[51]

In this analysis, it is clear that the purpose of the expenditure is a different concept from the issue of whether a personal benefit accrues to the taxpayer by virtue of the expenditure. It was Romer LJ who said in *Bentleys, Stokes and Lowless v Beeson*[52]:

> And it is quite clear that the purpose must be the sole purpose. The paragraph says so in clear terms. If the activity be undertaken with the object both of promoting business and also with some other purpose, for example, with the object of indulging an independent

47   [1983] 2 All ER at 1099.
48   Ibid.
49   Per Lord Brightman in *Mallalieu v Drummond*, at 1099.
50   Ibid.
51   Ibid. Compare Lord Elwyn-Jones (dissenting) at 1097 - Lord Elwyn-Jones concurred on this point.
52   33 TC at 504.

wish of entertaining a friend or stranger or of supporting a charitable or benevolent object, then the paragraph is not satisfied though in the mind of the actor the business motive may predominate. For the statute so prescribes. Per contra, if in truth the sole object is business promotion, the expenditure is not disqualified because the nature of the activity necessarily involves some other result, or the attainment or furtherance of some other objective, since the latter result or objective is necessarily inherent in the act.

Thus it appears that an inherent or unintended incidental personal or other benefit will not detract from the singularity of the business purpose and the deductibility of the expenditure. This approach was confirmed by the House of Lords in *Mallalieu v Drummond*. Lord Brightman said[53] that the object of the taxpayer in making the expenditure must be distinguished from the effect of the expenditure. He explained that expenditure made exclusively to serve the purpose of the business, may confer a private advantage but that that private advantage will 'not necessarily preclude the exclusivity of the business purpose'. He gave the example of a medical consultant flying to the South of France to attend to a patient. If a stay in the South of France was a reason, however subordinate, for the trip, no deduction was allowable, whereas if it were not a reason, but only an unavoidable effect, the deduction could be made.[54]

This apparently pragmatic (and sensible) approach was however not entirely apparent in the majority's decision in *Mallalieu v Drummond* itself. This case involved Ann Mallalieu, a barrister, who sought to deduct expenses on clothes bought for wear in court. The clothes were of a type demanded by court etiquette and it was clear that when the clothes were purchased the motive or object was exclusively the need to comply with court etiquette. The Commissioners found as a fact that she had ample other clothing for the purposes of warmth and decency and that the relevant clothes were used only in connection with her work. Nevertheless, they concluded that the expenditure had a dual purpose - the professional one of enabling her to earn profits and the personal one of enabling her to be properly clothed while working. They therefore disallowed her claim to deduct the expenses of cleaning and upkeep of the clothes. The House of Lords upheld this decision. While Lord Brightman admitted that Miss Mallalieu's only conscious motive when buying the clothes was her professional and business requirements,[55] he said that she however needed clothes to travel

---

[53]   [1983] 2 All ER at 1100.
[54]   Ibid. Compare Lord Elwyn-Jones (dissenting) at1098.
[55]   At 1103.

to work and clothes to wear at work. Therefore it was 'inescapable' that one object (although not a conscious motive) was the provision of clothing which she needed as a human being. Referring to the Court of Appeal's decision that the conscious motive was decisive, he rejected the notion that the object of a taxpayer is inevitably limited to the particular conscious motive in mind at the moment of expenditure.

Thus, while the motive of which the taxpayer is conscious of is of vital significance, it is not inevitably the only object which the Commissioners are entitled to find to exist. Thus for Miss Mallalieu, the conclusion was that one object was the provision of clothes which she needed as a human being, in the interests of warmth and decency, although this was not a conscious object. Thus there was a duality of purpose.

Lord Elwyn-Jones delivered a brief but sharp dissenting speech. It seems that the main bone of contention between him and the majority lay in the proper weight to be accorded to the taxpayer's conscious motives. Referring to Romer LJ in the *Bentleys* case, he explained that the test as to why the expenditure was incurred is subjective.[56] Applying this test, he was 'inevitably' led to the conclusion that the expenditure had been incurred wholly and exclusively for the purposes of the taxpayer's profession. According to him, the other benefits derived from the expenditure (that the clothes also provided her with warmth and decency) 'were purely incidental to the carrying on of her profession in the compulsory clothing she had to wear'[57]. The majority's decision in this case deserves the criticisms that it has attracted.[58]

The rather harsh application of the 'dual purpose' rule by the majority adds the possibility of the courts deciding on one's subconscious motives at the time of purchase. Added to the task of also deciding on one's conscious motives, this raises questions. Can one human being profess to know the conscious motives of another? If not, how can a human being proceed beyond that rather impossible task to an even more impossible one of discovering another's subconscious motives and intentions? The fact that such is considered to be subconscious indicates that not even the person who is alleged to have it is aware of it. This approach is astonishing[59].

It may of course be explained partly by the 'policy' considerations, which may actually have played more than a passing role in the outcome. This is obvious in the question posed by Lord Brightman[60] as to whether, if the deduction were allowed, it would also extend to 'other professional persons, such as solicitors accountants, medical practitioners, trades people and

---

[56] At 1103.62
[57] At 1097-1098.
[58] See J F Avery-Jones (1983) BTR 199. Kerridge ((1986) BTR 36) agrees with the outcome, but criticises 'the form of the decision'.
[59] Avery-Jones ((1983) BTR 199) rightly says that the taxpayer's unconscious motive is 'not a meaningful expression', and that all purposes must be conscious.
[60] At 1102.

persons in all other works of self-employed life, and if not why not'. With respect, this is nothing but the old 'floodgates' argument, which has been argued unconvincingly in other areas of law.[61] Issues of tax policy should perhaps be left in the hands of the those with the power to levy taxes and who are consequently accountable to the taxpayer at general elections.

To complicate things, the decision seems not to be all doom and gloom for those who must incur expenditure on business clothing. Lord Brightman went on to explain that the question is always one of fact and degree.[62] He cited the example of a self-employed waiter who would need to wear 'tails' as an essential part of the equipment of his trade. In such an instance Lord Brightman said that it would be open to the Commissioners to allow the expense of their upkeep on the basis that the money was spent exclusively to serve the purpose of the business. In this respect, it may well be that the statement of Templeman J in *Caillebotte v Quinn*[63] that 'the cost of protective clothing worn in the course of carrying on a trade will be deductible, because warmth and decency are incidental to the protection necessary to the carrying on of the trade' is still good law - the emphasis here being on the phrase 'protective clothing' - which is quite different from the barristers' regulated clothing involved in *Mallalieu v Drummond.*

In the event, the wisdom to be derived from this case is that the question whether an expense is incurred exclusively for the purposes of the taxpayer's business involves an examination of the state of the taxpayer's mind, both conscious and subconscious, at the time of the expenditure. A non-business conscious or subconscious object would negative a singularity of purpose, but an unavoidable effect would not. This may seem clear enough, but it is not clear why the fact that Miss Mallalieu was warm and decent while working in her regulated attire was not a mere unavoidable effect as opposed to an object of the expenditure.

Apportionment

The harshness of the 'wholly and exclusively' rule may be reduced in situations where apportionment is possible. If the expenditure incurred can clearly be divided to represent (i) expenditure that was wholly and exclusively incurred for business purposes, and (ii) expenditure that was incurred for, wholly or partly, a non-business purpose, the Revenue may

---

[61]   See generally, A. Olowofoyeku, *Suing Judges,* at 178-201 (1993, Clarendon Press, Oxford).
[62]   At 1103.
[63]   (1975) 50 TC 222 at 226.

accept apportionment of that expenditure. For example, the use of a room in one's home for business purposes may permit the apportionment of heating, lighting and other expenses of maintaining the house. The principle of apportionment seems to have been accepted by both the Revenue and the court in *Copeman v William Flood and Sons Ltd.*[64] In this case, William Flood was a pig dealer. A private company was formed to take over his pig business. The directors and shareholders of this company consisted of him, his wife, their two sons, and their daughter. In the relevant year, the daughter, aged 17, and one of the sons, aged 23, were each paid £2,600 as directors' fees. The daughter's duties involved answering telephone calls made to her father's residence by farmers, and the son's duties involved calling on farmers in order to purchase pigs. The company wanted to claim these directors' fees as deductions.

The Revenue argued that, having regard to the ages and duties of the children, the whole of the payments made to them could not be regarded as disbursements or expenses wholly and exclusively laid out or expended for the purposes of the company's trade. They argued that £78 would be an adequate sum to allow as a deduction in respect of remuneration for the daughter's services and £350 would be adequate in respect of the son's services. The company on the other hand argued that age was not a bar to earning capacity, that the directors' fees were expenses wholly and exclusively laid out for the purposes of their trade, and that it was for the company and not for the Inspector of Taxes to decide how much remuneration it would pay its officers.

The General Commissioners decided that they could not interfere with the prerogative of the company in paying such sums as remuneration to the directors as the company think fit. Lawrence J held that it did not follow that, because the sums of money were paid to the directors as remuneration, they were necessarily wholly and exclusively laid out for the purposes of trade.[65]He agreed that the Commissioners could not interfere with the prerogative of the company to pay to its directors whatever it thinks fit, but said that they could find 'in a proper case' that sums so paid are not wholly and exclusively laid out for the purposes of the trade. Since the Commissioners had not addressed their minds to answering the question whether the expenses were incurred wholly and exclusively for the company's trade, Lawrence J decided to remit the case to the Commissioners, 'to find as a fact whether the sums in question were wholly and exclusively laid out for the purpose of the Company's trade, and if they

[64] [1941] 1 KB 202; 24 TC 53.
[65] 24 TC at 56.

were not, to find how much of such sums was wholly and exclusively laid out for the purposes of the Company's trade'

It is clear that Lawrence J envisaged that at least part of the fees would have been incurred wholly and exclusively for the company's trade. The Revenue acknowledged this by suggesting what they felt were the 'adequate' sums to be allowed. It would seem that the principle of apportionment that was recognised in this case relates only to quantum (ie, the question whether the expenses were incurred 'wholly' for the purposes of the trade). It is clear that, generally, and objectively, staff salaries and directors' fees are business expenses. Very few businesses (if any) could get away with not paying their staff and directors for their services. Thus the question whether there is a duality of purpose in paying staff salaries will not arise. Salaries must be paid, and that is all there is to it. The labourer is worthy of his or her hire and there is no duality of purpose in paying for that hire.

What might raise questions is the amount paid as salaries and fees. This is what the Revenue were challenging in this case - the reason probably being the family relationship in the case. In cases wherein there is no family or other close relationship, it would be difficult for the Revenue to query the amount of directors' fees because that is purely a matter for the company concerned. However, where there is a close family connection and some of the fees may actually be more in the nature of pocket money than true fees for services, perhaps the Commissioners are entitled to scrutinise the transaction to see whether an apportionment should be made.

This approach may of course open up a can of worms - especially in respect of the so-called 'fat cat' directors, who earn such huge sums, the justifiability of which many would question. So it may well be that the principle of apportionment does not apply to issue of whether an expense was incurred exclusively for the purposes of the trade.[66] Indeed, a claim for apportionment may itself betray a duality of purpose.[67] Also, apportionment may not be possible at all in respect of some things (eg, the cost of a meal).[68]

Domestic Expenditure

Section 74(1)(b) provides that no sum may be deducted in respect of any disbursements or expenses of maintenance of the parties, their families or establishments, or any sums expended for any other domestic or private purposes distinct from the purposes of the trade, profession or vocation.

---

[66]   See especially the judgment of Templeman J in *Caillebotte v Quinn* (1975) 50 TC 222 - discussed below.
[67]   Templeman J, ibid, at 227. See also Plowman J in *Murgatroyd v Evans-Jackson*, (1966) 43 TC 581 at 589-590.
[68]   Ibid

This provision is closely linked with the 'wholly and exclusively' test just discussed. We have seen that, in respect of that test, Lord Brightman said in *Mallalieu v Drummond*[69] that if more than one purpose if found to exist for the expenditure, the other purposes will normally be the private purposes of the taxpayer. Thus it may be that this provision serves no useful purpose of its own, because it is clear that the presence of any of the purposes referred to in the provision would mean that the expense was not incurred 'exclusively' for business purposes. It may be argued that the usefulness of this provision lies in the way in which it will present a swift and decisive response in any case where the expenditure is clearly of a domestic nature. The answer to this argument would be that Section 74(1)(a) would also have provided the same swift and decisive response to such an expense - for it would be clearly not have been incurred for business purposes at all. Indeed, this much was stated by Pennycuick J in *Prince v Mapp*:[70] 'the second limb of [Section 74(1)(b)] is more or less automatically satisfied where [Section 74(1)(a)] is satisfied, that is to say, a sum which is expended in part for the purposes of a trade and in part for the purposes of a hobby is a sum expended for some other domestic or private purpose distinct from the purposes of the profession.' Thus perhaps the correct approach is to treat Section74(1)(a) and Section 74(1)(b) as being two aspects of the same principle. However, Section 74(1)(b) exists in the statute as a distinct provision in its own right and needs therefore be addressed. It is illustrated in practice in a number of areas, but it must be noted that most of the cases to which we shall refer here are as relevant to the question of exclusivity of purpose as they are to the question of whether they are domestic or personal expenses.

Food

One eats in order to live, not in order to work.[71] Thus the cost of feeding oneself will be a personal, not a business expense. In *Caillebotte v Quinn* the taxpayer was a self-employed carpenter, working on sites within a 40-mile radius of his home. He could not go home for lunch while away at work and so had to buy lunches. The cost of the lunches were much more than what it would have cost to have lunch at home. Ingeniously, he claimed that the additional cost of eating out was attributable to the need to eat a more substantial meal in order to maintain the energy expended in carrying out physical work, and to keep warm during the winter. The General Commissioners decided to allow a proportion of the costs of the lunches.

[69]   [1983] 2 All ER at1099.79
[70]   (1969) 46 TC 169 at 176.
[71]   Templeman J in *Caillebotte v Quinn* (1975) 50 TC 222 at 226.

Templeman J, considering both the exclusivity rule and the rule relating to domestic expenses, held that the Commissioners were wrong, that the cost of eating lunches was not apportionable, and that no part of the cost was deductible. Although this case was decided primarily on the exclusivity issue, it is clear from the first statement on this topic above, that it might very well (and arguably more appropriately) have been decided on the basis that the eating is purely a human thing and as such is an expense of maintaining the eater.

It is not clear, however, whether it is necessarily the case that the cost of food will not be deductible. Some types of expenditure on food may well not amount to expenditure of maintaining the eater as a living human being. For example, a Sumo wrestler may require a special diet, not to keep from starving and thereby staying alive, but in order to build or maintain his weight. The same goes for a heavyweight boxer who is considered 'small' and who therefore has to embark on a special diet to gain more weight and develop his strength. Would the expenditure on these special diets be considered to be over-and- above what these professionals need as human beings, and therefore wholly and exclusively incurred for the purposes of their professions? The answer is arguably 'yes'. The contention that they need to eat as human beings would appear too artificial in this type of context.

Medical expenses

Medical expenses constitute another example of domestic or personal expenses (or expenses of maintenance of the patient). They are incurred because the taxpayer is ill and the purpose is to cure that illness - they are not incurred because the taxpayer is a business person. The principle can be found in many cases. In *Norman v Golder*[72] the taxpayer, was a shorthand writer who had incurred medical expenses to cure an illness which he claimed to be a direct result of working in unfavourable circumstances. His claim to deduct the expenses failed. According to Lord Greene MR[73]:

> It is quite impossible to argue that doctors' bills represent money wholly and exclusively laid out for the purposes of a trade, profession, employment or vocation of the patient. True it is that if you do not get yourself well and so incur expenses to doctors you cannot carry on your trade or profession and if you do not carry on your trade or

[72]   (1944) 26 TC 293.
[73]   At 298

profession you will not earn an income, and if you do not earn an income the Revenue will not get any tax. The same thing applies to the food you eat and the clothes you wear. But expenses of that kind are not wholly and exclusively laid out for the purposes of the trade, profession or vocation. They are laid out in part for the advantage and benefit of the taxpayer as a living human being ... they are, in my opinion, expenses of maintenance of the party, his family, or a sum expended for a domestic or private purpose, distinct from the purpose of the trade or profession.

This case was followed in *Prince v Mapp*.[74] The taxpayer was an engineering draughtsman who played the guitar professionally and as a hobby. Due to an accident, he had to have an operation on his finger, in order to be able to continue to play the guitar. He is claim to deduct the cost of this operation was disallowed. Pennycuick J said that the expense in this case was not an expense of maintenance of the taxpayer - however, it was incurred at least partly for his private purposes.[75] He referred to the statement of Lord Greene MR (above), but seemed to qualify it somewhat[76]:

Lord Greene M.R. in that passage lays down in perfectly unqualified terms the proposition that expenses to doctors must always serve a dual purpose and accordingly can never be treated as representing money wholly and exclusively laid out for the purposes of a trade or profession. It may well be that in that passage Lord Greene did not have in mind the sort of medical care which an individual carrying on a trade or profession would not incur for any reason apart from the promotion of his trade or profession. It is quite easy to think of instances in which someone carrying on a trade or profession incurs some injury which is trivial in itself and in respect of which he would never otherwise expend money on medical care but which happens to be of vital importance for the purpose of that particular trade or profession. In such a case I am prepared to assume in favour of the taxpayer here that it would be possible for a taxpayer to incur expense which was wholly and exclusively for the purpose of his trade or profession. I say I am prepared to assume. I do not give any decision upon it because on the particular facts of this case it is not necessary for me to do so.

This raises the prospect of medical expenses being deductible, depending

---

[74] (1969) 46 TC 169.
[75] at 176.
[76] at 173-174.

on the circumstances and motives of the taxpayer in incurring those expenses. Pennycuick J made it clear that the crucial factor in this case was the fact that, while the doctor's evidence and the Commissioners' findings established that the taxpayer would not have had the operation if he had not wished to continue to play the guitar, the word 'professionally' was missing from both. Thus the inference must be that he wished to continue to play as he had done before (partly professionally and as partly a hobby).[77] This at the very least showed a dual purpose. Pennycuick J then said:

> I would mention in passing that if the finding had included the word 'professionally' (i.e. if it had read 'He would not have undergone it had he not wished to continue to play the guitar professionally') the result would I think have been otherwise. However, that word 'professionally' is not there.

In short, if the taxpayer had supplied the missing word in his discussions with his doctors, and had insisted that the word be included in their statement, then he would have been able to deduct the money, because this would have shown that it was not a private or domestic expense. With respect, this would seem to be a questionable approach to the issue, first, in the light of *Norman v Golder*, and also in the light of the judgment of Plowman J in *Murgatroyd v Evans-Jackson*.[78]

James Evans-Jackson was a trademark agent who was treated for an illness at a private nursing home. He had chosen private treatment because of the lack of a telephone, and the restricted facilities for visiting, that were involved in NHS hospital treatment. At the private nursing home, he was provided with a room and with all the necessary facilities for carrying on his business. He held conferences with clients there and saw members of his staff every day. He also dealt with correspondence. He claimed to deduct 60 per cent of his total expenses at the nursing home (ie, nursing home fees and charges for drugs and dressings, treatment, television and telephone) as a business expense in respect of the use of the room as an office. The Revenue claimed that the expenses were of a domestic or private nature and therefore were not allowable. The General Commissioners held that the taxpayer was entitled to the deduction, but they were reversed by the court. Plowman J said[79] that the case was indistinguishable from *Norman v Golder*. He said that even if the taxpayer had claimed the whole expense, it would not be a rational view of the situation to conclude that the whole of his expenses in the nursing home were incurred wholly and exclusively for the

77   At 176.
78   (1966) 43 TC 581.
79   At 588.
80   At 590.

purposes of his business.[80] According to Plowman J:

> The whole object of going into the nursing home in the first place was to receive treatment for the injury which he had sustained, and it seems to me that it would offend common sense to say that at any rate one of his motives or purposes for going into the nursing home was not to receive treatment for that injury - treatment that would be enure to his benefit, not merely during the time when he was carrying on his business, but as a living human being.

The implication of this case and *Norman v Golder* is that medical expenses will always have a private or domestic element, regardless of the taxpayer's motives or subjective intentions in seeking medical treatment. This seems to be the better approach to the issue, since it is difficult to see how, except in rare cases, one of the taxpayer's purposes for receiving treatment will not be to be cured of a human ailment. The fact that this will then enable the taxpayer to work in a particular occupation is not relevant, for, as Lord Greene MR said in *Norman v Golder*, the same point can be made about food, clothing, and perhaps, housing.

But as with food, perhaps there may be factual situations wherein medical expenses will be deductible. One example that springs to mind is cosmetic surgery. If a model or film star incurs medical expenses on cosmetic surgery such as silicone implants so as to increase his or her earning capacity, such expenses may well be deductible, for it may be argued that this is not an expense which he or she required as a human being. There would not be the purpose of receiving treatment for an injury which he or she had sustained, thereby introducing a duality of purpose. Whether the courts will accept this kind of analysis remains to be seen.

Travelling Expenses

The situation in respect of travelling expenses depends on the origin and destination of the journey. This will determine whether the travel is for private or domestic purposes, or whether it is for business purposes. Where the origin or destination of the journey is the taxpayer's home, this will point strongly to a domestic purpose, and it will be conclusive against the taxpayer in most cases. So, for example, the cost of travelling from home to

[73]   at 590.

work will not be deductible, because it is merely a living expense, incurred because a person chooses to live at a distance from where he or she works. Such expenses are not incurred because the traveller is a trader. One of the leading cases is *Newsom v Robertson*.[81]

Mr Newsom was a barrister who had his chambers at Lincoln's Inn in London, and his home in Whipsnade, Bedfordshire. He practiced his profession at his chambers, but often worked at home - particularly at evenings and weekends. During vacations he seldom went to London, but did most of the work at home. He claimed to deduct the expenses of travelling from his home to his chambers. The Special Commissioners held that the expenses were not deductible during term time, but were deductible during vacations. The Court of Appeal held that the expenses were not deductible at any time. Somervell LJ[82] doubted whether it was helpful to consider the journeys separately - rather, what had to be considered was 'the expenses of going to and fro', and it would be impossible to hold that one was deductible and the other not. According to him, Whipsnade as a location had nothing to do with Mr Newsom's practice - he could have had his home anywhere. The taxpayer's purpose in making the journeys was to get home in the evenings or at weekends, and the fact that he intended to and did do professional work when he got there did not even make this a subsidiary purpose of his profession.

Romer LJ concurring said[83] that it was 'almost impossible' to suggest that, when the taxpayer travelled to Whipsnade in the evenings or at weekends, he did so for the purpose of enabling him to carry on and earn profits in his profession how much more to say that he did it exclusively for that purpose. He said[84] that not even the journey to work in the morning can be said to be undertaken in order to enable the traveller to exercise his profession. Rather, such a journey is undertaken for the purpose of 'neutralising the effect of his departure from his place of business, for private purposes, on the previous evening'. Thus, the object of the journeys between home and work 'is not to enable man to do his work, but to live away from it'. It is however in the judgment of Denning LJ that the applicable test in such cases is to be found. Denning LJ said[85] that one must draw a distinction between living expenses and business expenses. In order to determine where to put a travelling expense, one must determine the base from which the trade, profession or vocation is carried on. According to Denning LJ, in the case of a tradesman, the base of his trading operation is his shop, but in the case of a barrister, it is his chambers.:

---

[81]   [1952] 2 ALL ER 728.
[82]   [1952] 2 ALL ER 728 at 730.
[83]   At 732-733.
[84]   At 732.
[85]   At 731.

Once he gets to his chambers, the cost of travelling to the various courts is incurred wholly and exclusively for the purposes of his profession. But it is different with the cost of travelling from his home to his chambers and back. That is incurred because he lives at a distance from his base. It is incurred for the purposes of his living there and not for the purposes of his profession, or at any rate not wholly or exclusively; and this is so, whether he has a choice in the matter or not. It is a living expense as distinct from a business expense.

This decision was followed in *Sargent v Barnes*.[86] The taxpayer, a dentist, travelled some 12 miles from home to his surgery. He had a laboratory about one mile from home, at which he called in the mornings (on the way to the surgery) to collect completed work and at evenings (on the way home) to deliver work. He claimed to have two bases of operation ie, the laboratory, and the surgery. His claim to deduct the cost of travelling between the laboratory and the surgery failed. Oliver J said[87] that what the court is concerned with is not simply why the traveller took a particular route (although that may be of the highest relevance in considering the deductibility of any additional expense caused by a deviation) but why he incurred the expense of the petrol, oil, wear and tear and depreciation in relation to this particular journey. In the present case, the expense was incurred, if not exclusively then at least in part, for the purpose of enabling the taxpayer to get from his private residence to the surgery where his profession was carried on, and the fact that it served the purpose also of enabling him to stop at an intermediate point to carry out there an activity exclusively referable to the business could not convert a dual purpose into a single purpose.

It is obvious that the question of what constitutes a trader's base of operations is a question of fact, and that, in some cases, a person's home can also be a base of operations. This would be the case in respect of doctors who have their surgeries in their residences, and would 'normally' be the case where the nature of the job is truly 'itinerant'.[88] It would also be the case in respect of a 'circuteer' - the barrister who has his home near London, but spends most of his time on the circuit, hardly ever appearing at his chambers in London.[89] Where a trader's home is clearly his or her base of operations, the principle propounded by Denning LJ in *Newsom v Robertson* comes into play, as was the case in *Horton v Young*,[90] where the taxpayer, a

---

[86]   (1978) 52 TC 335.
[87]   At 344.
[88]   See Brightman J in *Horton v Young* (1972) 47 TC 60 at 68.
[89]   See Lord Denning MR in *Horton v Young* 47 TC at 71.
[90]   47 TC 60.

self-employed bricklayer, was allowed to deduct the cost of travelling between his home and various building sites where he worked for short durations. In this case the taxpayer's home, where he kept his tools and did his office work, was held to be his base of operations. The Revenue claimed that his base of operations was the building sites where he worked, which meant that the base shifted as he moved from one site to the next. Lord Denning MR said[91] however that there was only one reasonable inference to draw from the primary facts - 'that Mr. Horton's house at Eastbourne was the locus in quo of the trade, from which it radiated as a centre. He went from it to the surrounding sites according as his work demanded.' Thus, when travelling between this base of operations to the various building sites he was travelling wholly and exclusively for business purposes and in the course of his business. His trade commenced at his base of operations and was continued at the various building sites.

It is interesting to note that Brightman J at first instance did suggest[92] a possible restriction in terms of ascertaining his 'normal area of work'. Should the taxpayer's home be situated outside that 'normal area', travel to and from that home would not be in the course of business and, consequently, would be disallowed.

Horton v Young raises more strongly the possibilities of categorising one's home as a base of operations and enabling travel from that base to other places of work to be deducted. It was even stated clearly there that a 'circuteer' barrister can have his home as his base of operations. So what befell Mr Newsom in his case? It seems that, despite the fact that Mr Newsom in *Newsom v Robertson* did complete some of his work at home, maintained a study at home for that purpose, and spent most of his time working at home during vacations, he did not do enough to convert his home into his base of operations. While this may have been true of term time, it is not clear why he could not have been regarded as having changed his base during vacations - unless the principle is that a person can only have one base of operations, and that this base can never change (which can hardly be correct).

Conference Attendance and Expenses

Attendance at a conference will normally involve travel, accommodation, subsistence and possibly conference fee expenses. Having examined the case law on food and travel expenses in general, what is the situation with

---

[91]   47 TC at 71.
[92]   (47 TC at 68)

respect to these types of expenses when incurred at conferences? Let us examine some of the cases relating to this specific point. In *Bowden v Russell and Russell*[93], a solicitor attended conferences in Washington and Ottawa. His wife accompanied him on these visits. Although he did put forward genuine business reasons to support his choice of conference, he also admitted an intention to enjoy, together with his wife, the social and holiday opportunities presented by the visits to Washington and Ottawa. The conference and travel expenses were disallowed on the grounds that the taxpayer had dual purposes, and as such the expenses were not incurred exclusively for business purposes. By contrast, in *Edwards v Warmsley, Henshall and Co*[94], a partner in a firm of accountants represented the practice at an international congress of accountants in New York. All the partners of the firm considered that information and contacts deriving from the visit were beneficial to the firm, that some useful contacts had been made, that methods of accounting had been seen which might be adopted by the firm, and that the firm's prestige had been increased. A claim to deduct the expenses in respect of the partner's return air fare, conference fee, and living expenses during the six days of the congress succeeded.

It is important to appreciate at this point the illustration of the medical consultant, provided by Lord Brightman in *Mallalieu v Drummond* (above) where Lord Brightman was careful to distinguish between object and effect. Thus, it appears that the taxpayer in *Edwards v Warmsley, Henshall and Co*, having incurred the expense with the proper business purpose, might seek on his arrival in New York to indulge in the personal benefits and opportunities of visiting New York. The latter might be regarded as an incidental effect of the exclusive business purpose.

Finally, the distinctions adopted in *Watkis v Ashford Sparkes and Harwood*[95] provide an interesting treatment of the costs of food, drink and accommodation. This case involved a firm of solicitors who wished to deduct (i) the costs of meals during business meetings held at lunchtime and in the evening during which times the solicitors would discuss the firm's business; and (ii) the cost of overnight accommodation, drinks and meals. These expenses were incurred as part of the attendance of the solicitors at the firm's annual conference. It was held that expenses in category (i) were not deductible, but all the expenses incurred in category (ii) were deductible. Nourse J, explained that the expenses of the meals in category (i) were expenses for a dual purpose; they served their private needs and purposes. Just as Miss Mallalieu needed to wear clothes not only when she was in

[93]   [1965] 2 All ER 258; 43 TC 301.
[94]   [1968] 1 All ER 1089; 44 TC 431.
[95]   [1985] STC 451
[96]   At 468.

court but also when she was not, so did the taxpayers need food and drink irrespective of whether they were engaged on a business activity or not.[96]

Nourse J further explained that the cost of food, drink and accommodation at the annual conference stood on a different footing. It could not necessarily be said to have been expenditure which met the needs of the partners as human beings. They did not need it, since they had their own homes where they could have spent the night. Thus the whole of the expenditure at the conference (food, drink and accommodation) was deductible as expenditure incurred wholly and exclusively for business purposes. It is interesting to note Nourse J's statement[97] that, with regard to the costs of the food and drink, 'reasonable amounts, are usually allowed in full. I have no reason to think that that practice does not correctly represent the law'.

Rent

Section 74(1)(c) prohibits the deduction of rent for 'the whole or any part of any dwelling-house or domestic offices', except where such part is used for the purposes of the trade, profession or vocation. Where any part is used for these purposes, the deduction allowable is restricted to two-thirds of the rent *bona fide* paid for any such dwelling-house or office, unless it appears in any particular case that, in the light of its circumstances, some greater sum ought to be allowed.

Repairs and Improvements

Section 74(1)(d) prohibits the deduction of 'any sum expended for repairs of premises occupied, or for the supply, repairs or alterations of any implements, utensils or articles employed, for the purposes of the trade, profession or vocation, beyond the sum actually expended for those purposes'. The effect of the last phrase in the provision is to limit the deduction to sums actually expended during the relevant year of assessment and to exclude apportionment of sums subsequently expended but attributable to repairs which may have accrued over a period.[98]Under this provision, the cost of purchasing and replacing tools can be deducted.[99]

The provision also covers such things as repairs of plant and machinery[100], and renewals of the same[101]. And, of course, as the subsection clearly shows, it also covers expenditure on the repairs of premises. The last point

[97]   At 469.
[98]   Vinelott J in *Brown v Burnley Football and Athletic Co. Ltd.* (1980) 53 TC 357 at 365.
[99]   See Pollock B in Forder v Andrew Handyside and Co. Ltd. (1876) 1 TC 65 at 69.
[100] See the Lord Justice-Clerk in *Caledonian Railway Co. v Banks* (1880) 1 TC 487 at 494.
[101] Ibid.See also Somervell LJ in *IRC v Great Wigston Gas Co.* (1946) 29 TC 197 at 207. Here, Somervell LJ rejected the Revenue's argument that their practice of allowing deductions in respect of renewals of plant and machinery was simply an extra-statutory concession. He said that such deductions were, in most cases, clearly authorised by the statute.

raises other issues, because Section 74(1)(g) prohibits the deduction of 'any capital employed in improvements of premises occupied for the purposes of the trade, profession or vocation'. The gist of these provisions is that expenditure on repairs of premises is income in nature, but expenditure on improvements is capital, which accordingly has to be disallowed. If this be so, it is not clear why there should be a specific provision to disallow what would in any case have been disallowed under general principles. Be that as it may, it becomes necessary to ascertain the difference between the repair of premises and the improvements thereof.

The distinction between repair and improvement is not always easy to explain. Traditionally, the question has often been asked whether what took place was a repair or a 'renewal' - a concept which is not in the statutory words but with which many cases have concerned themselves. A variety of approaches have been suggested and, at times, applied by the courts. One of the more attractive approaches is to consider whether the final result produces an increase in value of the asset. For example, expenditure on the same asset, a railway line, may result in an improvement (via an increase in its value) or may be merely a repair (ie, keeping the asset in proper working conditions, or maintaining its value or keeping it in its original state). Two cases serve as illustration. In *Rhodesia Railways Ltd v Bechuanaland Protectorate IT Collector*[102] the company had renewed some 74 miles of its railway track by putting down new rails and sleepers in place of ones which were worn, and it claimed the cost as a deduction. At first instance, it was held that the expenditure was of a capital nature, and was not the cost of a repair but of a reconstruction. However, the Privy Council reversed this decision and held that the periodical renewal of the rails and sleepers of a railway was in no sense a reconstruction of the whole railway. The track was simply restored to its previous unworn condition, without any element of improvement. Lord Macmillan said[103] that the expenditure did not result in the creation of any new asset, but that it was incurred to maintain the taxpayer's existing line in a state to earn revenue.

On the other hand, in *Highland Railway Co v IRC*[104] the replacement of old track and rail was not deductible because it represented an improvement: the new rail was of a superior kind and represented an increase in the value of the railway line. The Lord President[105] noted that what was involved was not a mere relaying of the line after the old fashion. It was not taking away rails that were worn out or partially worn out, and renewing them in whole or in part along with the whole line. According to him, that would neither alter

[102]   [1933] AC 368.
[103]   At 374.
[104]   [1889] 2 TC 485.
[105]   At 488.

the character of the line nor would it affect the nature of the heritable property possessed by the company. What was done was to substitute one kind of rail for another, steel rails for iron rails - this amounted to 'a material alteration and a very great improvement on the corpus of the heritable estate belonging to the Company' and thus the expenditure was incurred entirely 'for the permanent improvement of the property'.

Another approach, stems from the much quoted statement of Buckley LJ in *Lurcott v Wakely and Wheeler*[106] that:

> 'Repair' and 'Renew' are not words expressive of a clear contrast. Repair always involves renewal, renewal of a part; of a subordinate part...Repair is restoration by renewal or replacement of subsidiary parts of a whole. Renewal, as distinguished from repair, is reconstruction of the entirety, meaning by the entirety not necessarily the whole but substantially the whole subject matter under discussion.

In applying this *dictum*, Rowlatt J said in *O'Grady v Bullcroft Main Collieries Ltd*:[107]

> Of course, every repair is a replacement. You repair a roof by putting on new slates instead of the old ones, which you throw away. There is no doubt about that. But the critical matter is - as was pointed out in the passage read from Lord Justice Buckley's judgment in [*Lurcott v Wakely and Wheeler*] - what is the entirety? The slate is not the entirety in the roof. You are repairing the roof by putting in new slates. What is the entirety? If you replace an entirety, it is having a new one and it is not repairing an old one.

Since every repair is a replacement of something, and the replacement of an entirety is not repair, the courts then face the question of what is to be regarded as an 'entirety', and what is to be regarded as a 'part' of an entirety. The importance of this quest was pointed out by Lord Carmont in *Lawrie v IRC*[108] who said that the importance of considering an entirety is with a view to determining 'the character of the work done', because 'what might at first look like a renewal may when applying the matter to a larger unit, be shown to be only a repair.' It is also relevant to the question 'repair of what?'[109] - which then results in a quest to ascertain 'the whole which is said to have been repaired.'

106   [1911] 1 KB 905 at 923-924.
107   [1932] 17 TC 93 at 101.
108   [1952] 34 TC 20 at 26.
109   See Vinelott J in *Brown v Burnley Football and Athletic Co Ltd.* (1980) 53 TC 357 at 366.

The answer to these questions is not always clear. To the question 'repair of what?', we may answer 'repair of the factory', or 'repair of the factory's chimney', or 'repair of the waterworks' or 'repair of the railway line'. This would still raise the original question - 'what is the entirety here?'. In other words, does the thing which is presented as the answer to the question 'repair of what?' really amount to an entirety or does it amount to merely a part of an entirety?

In this analysis, the same thing can be an entirety in one case, and yet be a part of another entirety in another case. The difficulty inherent in such an analysis was presented by Donovan J in *Phillips v Whieldon Sanitary Potteries Ltd*[110]:

> In my judgment, the 'premises' for the purpose of [Section 74(1)(g)] may sometimes be the whole of the trader's business premises and may sometimes be a specific building forming part of those premises. Thus, if a factory window were blown out and had to be repaired, it would be obviously wrong to argue that as the entirety of the window had been restored it was not a repair to the premises. In such a case the "premises" would be the entire factory, in relation to which the window would be a repair and nothing else. But if, for example, a retort house in a gasworks was destroyed and had to be rebuilt, one would hardly call that a repair to the gasworks. The size of the retort house would compel one to regard that as the premises for the purpose of [Section 74(1)(g)]; and since it had been replaced in full it could not be said to have been repaired. These examples illustrate what I think is the truth, that there is no one line of approach to the problem which is exclusively correct. In some cases it will be right to regard the premises as the entire factory, and in others as some part of the factory. Whichever alternative is the right one to adopt will depend upon the facts of the particular case.

The decided cases offer further proof of the problems. *O'Grady v Bullcroft Main Collieries Ltd.* itself involved a factory chimney which had become unsafe, and which was replaced with a new one at an adjacent location. The new chimney was admitted to be an improvement on the old one. Rowlatt J held that the entirety in this case was the chimney itself, not the building to which it was attached. His reasoning was thus[111]:

---

[110]   (1952) 33 TC 213 at 219.
[111]   At 102.

What was this? This was a factory chimney to which the gases and fumes, and so on, were led by flues and then went up the chimney. It was unsafe and would not do any more. What they did was simply this: They built a new chimney at a little distance away in another place; they put flues to that chimney and then, when it was finished, they switched the gases from the old flues into the new flues and so up the new chimney. I do not think it is possible to regard that as repairing a subsidiary part of the factory. I think it is simply having a new one. And they had them both. Perhaps they pulled down the old one; perhaps they kept it, because they thought it was an artistic thing to look at. There is no accounting for tastes in manufacturing circles. Anyhow, they simply built a new chimney and started to use that one instead of the old one. I think the chimney is the entirety here and they simply renewed it,

By contrast, in *Samuel Jones and Co (Devonvale) Ltd v IRC*[112] the factory, not the chimney, was the entirety. In this case, the taxpayer company was involved in processing paper. A chimney of its factory was replaced because of its dangerous condition. However, the replacement chimney did not constitute an appreciable improvement over the original one. The company claimed to deduct the costs of removing the old chimney and building the new one. The Commissioners held that the cost of replacement of the chimney was capital expenditure but allowed the cost of removing the old chimney, but the court held that the whole cost of replacing the chimney (including the cost of removing the old chimney) was deductible. The Lord President (Cooper)[113] felt that *O'Grady* was distinguishable because in this case the facts demonstrated beyond a doubt that the chimney in the case was 'physically, commercially and functionally an inseparable part of an entirety, which is the factory.' He said that it was 'quite impossible' to describe this chimney as being the entirety, saying that it was 'doubtless an indispensable part of the factory, doubtless an integral part; but none the less a subsidiary part, and one of many subsidiary parts, of a single industrial profit-earning undertaking.' In spite of this explanation, it is not really clear why in this case the chimney was inseparable from the factory, but the one in *O'Grady* was.

In *Rhodesia Railways Ltd v Bechuanaland Protectorate IT Collector* the entirety was the whole of the railway, not the lines and the sleepers themselves. The lines and sleepers were merely subsidiary items of the

---

[112]   (1951) 32 TC 513.
[113]   At 518.

whole concern. This seems sensible enough. The decision in *Samuel Jones and Co (Devonvale) Ltd. v IRC* that the factory was the entirety and the chimney was just a part of that entirety also seems sensible enough. In *Margarett v The Lowestoft Water and Gas Co.*[114] a new reservoir, constructed some distance away from an older one which it replaced, was twice the capacity of the old one and, was, in several respects, an improvement on the old one. Finlay J held that this was not expenditure on repair but capital expenditure. According to him[115]:

> Now here the subject matter under discussion seems to me to be the reservoir, and I cannot think that it is material, though it is undoubtedly the fact, that the reservoir is part only of the Respondents' whole physical undertaking. It is a part perfectly clearly divisible from the rest, and it is the part with which we are dealing here.

The reservoir was the entirety because it was clearly 'divisible' from the rest of the property. Again, this concept of divisibility or separability appears. In *Lawrie v IRC*[116] the roof of the taxpayer's building fell into disrepair and reconstruction of the premises was undertaken involving the lengthening and heightening of the building and the construction of a new roof. The Special Commissioners held that the cost of the new roof was not deductible. They held that the expenditure was not on the repair of the premises or subsidiary or subordinate parts thereof, but on the reconstruction, alteration, extension and improvement of the building as a whole, involving in particular expenditure on an entirely new and enlarged roof. They also held that the roof was the entirety. Their decision that the expenses were not deductible was upheld by the court. However, the Lord President (Cooper) disagreed with their ruling that the roof was the entirety, holding that the 'entirety' to be considered was the building as a whole and not its roof. This was also the opinion of Lord Carmont.[117] In so deciding, both judges founded their conclusions on *Samuel Jones and Co. (Devonvale) Ltd v IRC*.

Finally, in *Brown v Burnley Football and Athletic Co Ltd.*[118] the erection of a new stand at a football ground was not a repair of any larger premises. Vinelott J said[119] that the question, 'what is the whole, the entirety, the entity which is said to have been repaired by replacement of part?', cannot be answered by any one yardstick or rule of thumb. Rather, it must 'be answered in the light of all the circumstances which it is reasonable to take

---

[114] (1935) 19 TC 481.
[115] At 488.
[116] (1952) 34 TC 20.
[117] At 25-26.
[118] (1980) 53 TC 357.132
[119] At 370.

into account'. Presumably in this case the new stand itself was the entirety. Vinelott J did not make clear what he considered to be the entirety, but since he clearly took the view that the entirety must be identified correctly, it can be presumed that the stand, and not some larger entity, was, in his judgment, the entirety. This again would be sensible. It is a decision that could be reached by the principle of separability or divisibility, because the seating stands can clearly be separated from the other structures in a football ground. So the cases seem to point to divisibility being a helpful criterion to decide the question 'what is the entirety with which we are concerned?'. Rowlatt J did not seem to consider this point in *O'Grady v Bullcroft Main Collieries Ltd* and, in the light of subsequent decisions, it is doubtful whether that decision can now be regarded as correct. However, in approaching this question, we must bear in mind that there is not infallible test, and the matter is a question of degree. Thus *O'Grady* may be seen as being correct in the light of its own facts.

Initial Repairs

One interesting application of the distinction between repairs and improvements can be seen in the judicial approach to reduced costs of purchase. Generally, if the acquisition costs of an asset are reduced to reflect the works that are needed to put the asset into a usable state, actual and subsequent costs of those works are not deductible. The works and costs represent capital expenditure - they are part of the costs of acquiring a 'usable' asset. This principle has been applied from early times[120]but the most celebrated case on the point is *Law Shipping Co. Ltd. v IRC*.[121] Here a shipping company bought a second-hand ship at a reduced price at a time when the ship's periodical Lloyd's survey was overdue. Substantial amounts were later spent on repairing the ship in order to to enable it to pass its Lloyd's survey and to be in a recognised usable condition. The company's claim to deduct the cost of repairing the ship failed. According to the Lord President (Clyde)[113]:

> It is obvious that a ship, on which repairs have been allowed to accumulate, is a less valuable capital asset with which to start business than a ship which has been regularly kept in repair. And it is a fair inference that the sellers would have demanded and obtained a higher price than they actually did, but for the immediate necessity of repairs to which the ship was subject when they put her in the market.

---

[120]   See *Highland Railway Co. v Balderston* (1889) 2 TC 485 - especially the Lord President at 487-488.
[121]   [1924] 12 TC 621.
[122]   At 626.

> The additional gains they had made by postponing repairs were thus counter-balanced by the diminished value of the ship on realisation

Lord Cullen said[123] that the repair costs were in substance equivalent to an addition to the price of the ship.

On the other hand, in *Odeon Associated Theatres Ltd v Jones*[124] a sum of money spent on completing repairs to a cinema that had recently been purchased was allowed as a deductible expense. The cinema was purchased in a state of disrepair because repairs had been impossible to complete owing to war-time restrictions. Salmon LJ[125]distinguished the Law Shipping case. First, in that case, the purchase price was substantially less than it would have been had the vessel been in a fit state of repair to pass the Lloyd's survey at the date of purchase. Here however, the purchase price paid by the taxpayers was in no way affected by the fact that the cinema was in disrepair at the date of its acquisition. Secondly, in the Law Shipping case the vessel was not in a state to pass survey at the time of purchase, and in order to obtain a Lloyd's certificate and turn it into a profit-earning asset it was necessary to spend a large sum on deferred repairs. Here, the cinema was a profit-earning asset at the date of its acquisition in spite of its state of disrepair. And, thirdly, in that case there had been no evidence that on established principles of sound commercial accounting the expenditure could properly be charged by the taxpayer as revenue expenditure. Here however, the Commissioners held, on ample evidence, that it was in accordance with the established principles of sound commercial accounting to charge the items to revenue expenditure, and these principles did not conflict with any statute. Thus the court was able to view the expenditure as merely repair costs of a capital asset rather than as part of the acquisition costs of a capital asset.

Damages and 'Losses'

Section 74(1)(e) prohibits the deduction of 'any loss not connected with or arising out of the trade, profession or vocation'. The first thing to note in respect of this provision is that the concept of 'loss' therein is not that which refers to overall trading loss computed in accordance with accountancy practice after taking account of the trader's receipts and expenses over the relevant period or year. The concept of 'loss' here refers to some liability or damage or other diminution in the trader's finances, which the trader then seeks to claim as a deduction. This could take the form of a payment of

---

[123]   At 628.
[124]   [1972] 2 WLR 331; (1971) 48 TC 257.
[125]   48 TC 257 at 283-284.

damages or other form of compensation, either in contract or in tort, or it could take the form of fraud or thefts by employees. The principle of this provision is that such a 'loss' can only be deducted if it is connected with the trade, or arises out of it - ie, it must be occasioned or suffered as a consequence of pursuing profits through the exercise of the trade, profession or vocation - it must fall on the trader in his or her professional or trade capacity and not in any other capacity. That causal link appears to be hard to establish, and the cases mostly go against the taxpayer. The leading case on this issue is *Strong and Co of Romsey Ltd v Woodifield*[126]. Here the taxpayers carried on the business of brewers and innkeepers. Part of their hotel (a chimney) collapsed and injured a guest. The taxpayers paid compensation to the injured guest and then sought to deduct that payment as a loss arising out of their trade. The House of Lords held that the loss was not deductible. It was held that the loss sustained by the taxpayers was not really incidental to their trade as innkeepers, but rather fell upon them in their character not of traders but of householders. According to the Lord Loreburn LC[127]:

> [I]t does not follow that if a loss is in any sense connected with the trade, it must always be allowed as a deduction for it may be only remotely connected with the trade or it may be connected with something else quite as much as or even more than with the trade. I think only such losses can be deducted as are connected with it in the sense that they are really incidental to the trade itself. They cannot be deducted if they are mainly incidental to some other vocation, or fall on the trader in some character other than that of trader. The nature of the trade is to be considered. To give an illustration, losses sustained by a railway company in compensating passengers for accident in travelling might be deducted. On the other hand, if a man kept a grocer's shop, for keeping which a house is necessary, and one of the window shutters fell upon and injured a man walking in the street, the loss arising thereby to the grocer ought not to be deducted.

The speech delivered by Lord Davey was unique (the rest of their Lordships agreed with the Lord Chancellor) in that it did not focus on the issue of 'loss'. Lord Davey appeared to support his conclusion by a consideration of the general requirement that the expense (loss, in this instance) must be wholly and exclusively incurred for the purpose of the business.

---

[126]   [1906] AC 448; 5 TC 215.
[127]   At 219.

In practice a wide range of losses have been allowed, even though it is not always possible to agree on or perceive the link between the loss and the carrying on of or capacity of the trade, profession or vocation. Examples include damages for libel published in the course of publishing a newspaper, damages for the wrongful dismissal of an employee, legal expenses, advertising expenses, and sponsorship expenses.

One thing that is clear is that the courts will often take a strict view of the question whether the necessary link with the trade exists. This can be seen from the cases involving fraud or thefts by employees. While fraud or theft by strangers may be difficult to link with the trade, if an employee of a trader defrauds the business or steals from the employers, one would have thought that this is a loss that is connected with the trade. It is unrealistic to say that the loss fell on the trader in the capacity of employer and not in the capacity of trader, for it is arguably the fact that the trader has employed the fraudster to help carry on the business and earn profits that has given the fraudster an opportunity which he would not have had otherwise - access to the trader's money. However the courts have not accepted this type of analysis.

In *Curtis v Oldfield*[128] the managing director of the taxpayer company, who had been in sole control of the company's business, had allowed to pass through the company's books some money matters relating to his private affairs. On his death, it was found that some money was owing to the company from his estate. The debt was valueless because his estate was insolvent, and it was written off as a bad debt in the company's account. Rowlatt J disallowed the claim because it was neither a trading debt (see below) nor a loss that had arisen out of the trade. He said[129] that, in point of law it was the profits of the company's trade, and not the company itself, that was being assessed to tax. In considering whether these losses arose out of the company's trade, the situation was that

> the assets of the Company, moneys which the Company had got and which had got home to the Company, got into the control of the Managing Director of the Company, and he took them out. It seems to me that what has happened is that he has made away with receipts of the Company dehors the trade altogether in virtue of his position as Managing Director in the office and being in a position to do exactly what he likes.

However, Rowlatt J suggested that petty thefts by employees may be

---

[128] (1925) 9 TC 319.
[129] At 330.
[130] At 330-331.

deductible[130].

> [I]f you have a business in the course of which you have to employ subordinates, and owing to the negligence or the dishonesty of the subordinates some of the receipts of the business do not find their way into the till, or some of the bills are not collected at all ... that may be an expense [or loss] connected with an arising out of the trade in the most complete sense of the word.

This decision was applied in *Bamford v ATA Advertising Ltd*[131] wherein a director of a company had misappropriated some £15,000, which the company claimed to deduct. Brightman J held that the money was not deductible because it was not a loss 'connected with or arising out of' the company's trade. In this case, counsel for the company had argued that there was no logical distinction between petty theft by a subordinate employee and massive defalcation by a director. Brightman J rejected that argument[132]:

> In my view there is a distinction. I can quite see that the commissioners might find as a fact that a £5 note taken from the till by a shop assistant is a loss to the trader which is connected with and arises out of the trade. A large shop has to use tills and to employ assistants with access to those tills. It could not trade in any other way. That, it seems to me, is quite a different case from a director with authority to sign cheques who helps himself to £15,000, which is then lost to the company. In the defaulting director type of case, there seems to me to be no relevant nexus between the loss of the money and the conduct of the company's trade. The loss is not, as in the case of the dishonest shop assistant an incident of the company's trading activities. It arises altogether outside such activities. That, I think, is the true distinction.[125]

With respect, this distinction between petty thefts and massive defalcations is not convincing. If the distinction lies in the amounts involved, that would seem illogical and arbitrary. For example, if a shop assistant takes £5,000 from the till, or if a bank cashier helps himself to huge sums of money from his till, is this a petty theft or a massive defalcation? If the true distinction lies in where the theft occurs, that still seems to be arbitrary. If a shop assistant

---

131   [1972] 3 All ьR 535; 48 TC 359.
132   48 TC at 368.
133   See also *Roebank Printing Co Ltd v IRC* (1928) 13 TC 864.

takes £5 from the till that would be a petty theft that arises out of the trade. What if the money was taken from the safe in the backroom - or from the money bag on the way to make a deposit at the bank? It would make no sense to say in the first case that the loss fell on the trader as a safe-owner, and, in the second case, as a bank depositor. So wherein lies the true distinction, if one does in fact exist? Does it lie in whether the loss was occurred when the employee was engaged in the activity of earning profits in the trade? This would cover the case of a check-out assistant or cashier taking money from the till. Would it cover the case of a finance director with the authority to write cheques who then fraudulently writes a cheque to himself? If not, why not?

By analogy with Brightman J's own example, a large business or company has to have a finance manager or director with access to the company's money. It could not trade in any other way. It is unconvincing to say that the finance director's duties are not connected with the company's trade. A trader does not just sell goods. He or she or it would need (if the business is successful) an organisation to provide the necessary infrastructure for the carrying on and management of the business. Lack of good management and infrastructure can quickly reduce a profitable business (or one with the potential to be profitable) to nothing, as customers vote with their feet.

Thus, the distinction being sought to be made here seems artificial. A better approach would be that all losses caused by the activities of the trader's employees due to opportunities presented to them by their employment arise out of or are connected with the trade.

Bad Debts

Section 74(1)(j) prohibits deductions in respect of any debts, except a bad debt proved to be such, a debt or part of a debt released by the creditor wholly and exclusively for the purposes of his trade, profession or vocation as part of a relevant arrangement or compromise, and a doubtful debt to the extent estimated to be bad. The last phrase means, in the case of the bankruptcy or insolvency of the debtor, the whole debt except to the extent that any amount may reasonably be expected to be received on the debt. Although not clearly specified in the subsection, it seems that, for a debt to be deductible, it must be a debt of the trade. According to Rowlatt J in *Curtis v Oldfield*[134]:

---

[134]   9 TC at 330.

When the rule speaks of a bad debt, it means a debt which is a debt that would have come into the balance sheet as a trading debt in the trade that is in question and that is bad. It does not really mean any bad debt which, when it was a good debt, would not have come in to swell the profits.

Business Entertainment

The statutory rules in respect of business entertainment constitute Parliament's reaction to cases such as *Bentley, Stokes and Lowless v Beeson*[135] Section 577(1) provides that no deduction is allowed in respect of expenses incurred in providing business entertainment. Section 577(3) includes in this prohibition an allowance given to an employee for business entertainment, except where the amount falls to be charged on the employee as an emolument under Schedule E. Section 577(5) defines 'business entertainment' to mean entertainment (including hospitality of any kind) provided by a trader or a member of his staff in connection with the trade. However, the definition excludes things provided for *bona fide* members of the trader's staff, unless its provision for them is also incidental to its provisions for others. Section 577(8) extends the prohibition to the provision of gifts, except where the article given incorporates a conspicuous advertisement for the donor and is not food, drink, tobacco, a token or voucher exchangeable for goods, and the cost to the donor together with the cost of other gifts to the same person in the same year does not exceed £10. This exception would cover things like calendars, diaries, pens and mugs. Section 577(9) allows the deduction of gifts made to charities, and section 577(10) allows deductions in respect of trading stock provided by the trader in the ordinary course of the trade for payment, or, with the object of advertising to the public generally, gratuitously. This will cover promotional or complimentary copies of items which the trader sells in his her trade.

Partnerships

Partnerships are not legal persons and so the profits and expenses of a partnership belong to the individual partners. The logical consequence of the partnership's lack of legal personality is that one must look to the

---

[135]   [1952] 2 All ER 82; 33 TC 491.

individual partners rather than the firm's intentions when considering the purpose of the expenditure incurred by the firm. For example, in *MacKinlay v Arthur Young McClelland Moores and Co*[136] a partnership (the 'firm') sought to deduct expenditure incurred in providing a substantial contribution toward the removal expenses of two of the partners. The partners had moved at the firm's request. The Court of Appeal had held that these expenses were deductible because they were incurred by the firm wholly and exclusively for business purposes,[137] Slade J suggesting that it was 'the collective purpose of this notionally distinct entity which has to be ascertained'. The House of Lords disagreed with the reasoning of the Court of Appeal. The House confirmed that, in ascertaining the purpose of the expenditure, one must look to the intentions and motives of the individual partners. In this particular case, the expenditure had a dual purpose, one of which was the provision of personal and private benefits to the partners as householders. Accordingly the expenditure was disallowed as not being incurred 'wholly and exclusively' for business purposes.

Trading Losses

A trading loss will arise if, in the relevant accounting period, the computation of profits reveals that expenditure and allowances (including adjustments to stock) exceed receipts. If a loss is computed the taxpayer will need to consider whether any relief is available.[138] That some relief should be available has long been acknowledged[139], but the form of the relief has caused some debate. The debate has focused on the issues of (i) whether relief should be confined to allowing the taxpayer to carry forward any loss to set against the future profits of the same trade or business only; (ii) whether the relief suggested in (i) should be limited in time, perhaps for six years only; (iii) whether the taxpayer should enjoy the ability to carry forward the loss to set against his future profits or income from whatever source; and (iv) whether the taxpayer ought to be able to roll back the loss suffered and set it off against previous years trading profits - with or without a time limit.

Following the enactment and development of earlier legislation, provisions now exist (TA 1988 Sections 380-401) to facilitate loss relief in the form of (i), (iii) and (iv) above. Loss relief started life as the ability to set-off trading loss

[136] [1989] STC 898.
[137] [1988] STC 116.
[138] Exceptionally, the Schedule E employee might suffer a loss. In such a case relief is also available under TA 1988, s.380.
[139] For example, see the Final Report of the Royal Commission on the Taxation of Profits and Income, Cmnd 9474 (1955) (at para 486), where the Commission said that any suggestion that a relief for loss should not be available was plainly unacceptable. The same Committee did however refer to the development of loss provisions under Schedule D as a comparatively recent growth. S. James and C. Nobes (*The Economics of Taxation*, page 61) give a number of arguments in favour of losses being allowed to be set against trading profits, the main thrust of which is that this would bring government into a sort of partnership with enterprise, sharing in the profits (through taxation) and losses (through loss-offsets) thereby reducing the risks associated with enterprise.

against current trading profit enjoyed by the same taxpayer in distinct and separate trades.[140] This was developed to allow a trader to set-off a trading loss against other income (from whatever source) of the same period. Eventually, the situation was reached where business or trade losses could be carried forward to be set-off against trade profits of the same business or trade[141]. This ability to carry forward was also developed and extended to set-off against general income from whatever source.

The issue of whether a taxpayer ought to be allowed to carry back loss caused some concern. In 1951 the Committee on the Taxation of Trading Profits stated that objections of principle can be raised against any suggestion of carrying losses back:

> It would introduce a novel proposition into Income Tax if tax admittedly due for a particular year and correctly representing the taxpayer's capacity to pay for that year could be reclaimed by reference to circumstances arising in a later year.[142]

In 1955 the Radcliffe Commission stated that it would be theoretically unreasonable to allow losses to be carried back and set-off against profits of past years.

Despite the theoretical objections, both Committees actually objected to any general ability to carry back losses on practical grounds. It was stated that complicated provisions would be necessary in order to facilitate and achieve 'carry back' and that it would cause additional work to the Inland Revenue and to the taxpayer and his advisers. However, one exception and permitted area of carry-back was deemed necessary to facilitate the circumstances where, during the last year of the business's operation, the business and the taxpayer suffer a substantial loss with no corresponding general income against which that loss might be set. There was therefore a need to provide an avenue of relief for such a loss. That avenue of relief is now to be found in Section 388, TA 1988.

Before we proceed to examine the details of the current provisions dealing with loss relief, it is important to appreciate that some of the provisions overlap, giving the taxpayer a choice as to the order in which the provisions and relief will apply.[143]

[140]   Income Tax Act 1805 and 1842.
[141]   This was originally subject to a six-year limitation period - until the limitation period was removed by the Income Tax Act 1952.
[142]   Report of the Committee on the Taxation of Trading Profits, Cmd 8189 (1951) at para 80.
[143]   See *Butt v Haxby* [1983] STC 239; 56 TC 547.

Statutory Provisions

Opening Losses

Section 381 allows the trader to make a claim for losses sustained in the first year of the business, or in any of the next three years of assessment, to be carried back and set-off against general income for the three years before that in which the loss was sustained. The loss must be first set against the income of earlier years before later years. Section 381 is available to individuals (eg, partners and sole traders) but not to limited companies.

Terminal Losses

Section 388 allows a trader to claim for 'terminal' losses in his or her trade to be carried back and set-off against the profits of that trade for a period of three years preceding the one in which the trade ended. As the phrase 'terminal loss' indicates, carry-back under section 388 only applies where the trade, profession or vocation has been permanently discontinued.

Set-off against General Income

Section 380 allows the taxpayer to carry across losses from his trading activities to be set-off against his general income in that year of assessment, and against general income from the preceding year. Losses must first be set against income of the current year before any unrelieved excess can be set against income of the preceding year. There is also the possibility to elect to set any unrelieved losses against any chargeable gains tax realised in that year. In making such an election, the taxpayer will not enjoy any Capital Gains Tax annual exemption.[144]

Two main restrictions apply to the use of s.380. First, the taxpayer has to make a claim for the relief, within a specified 12-month period (S.380(1))., and secondly, relief is only available if the business was genuine, i.e., the loss-making business was run on a commercial basis with a reasonable expectation of profit.[145]

Carry Forward against Subsequent Profits

Section 385 allows the taxpayer to carry forward any unrelieved loss of his

[144] FA 1991 s.72.
[145] TA 1988 s.384.

trade, profession or vocation and set that loss against the first available profits of the same trade, profession or vocation without time limit. Where the loss cannot be relieved wholly in this way, the trader can set it against any income received by the business which has already been taxed at source, such as dividend or interest payments (S.385(4)).

In doing so, a repayment claim may be made. The overriding restriction imposed on section 385 is the requirement that the taxpayer carries on the trade, profession or vocation. Any discontinuance of the activity will remove the relief, except:

> any technical discontinuance of a partnership through the retirement of one of the partners shall be ignored. The continuing partners will be entitled to carry forward a share of the loss and:[146]

> if the taxpayer transfers his business to a company in return for a transfer of shares, the taxpayer can carry forward the loss to set off against income derived by him from the company - for example, earned income from a service contract with the company, or unearned income in the form of a return on his shares (dividends).[147]

Relief under section 385 will apply automatically unless the taxpayer makes a claim under section 380. If the latter option is chosen, then any unrelieved loss remaining after the application of section 380 will be dealt with, automatically, under section 385.

Carry Forward on Transfer of Business to Company

If a business, a sole trader or partnership, is sold (either through incorporation or takeover) to a limited company, any loss sustained by the business in its final year cannot be carried forward into the company. Instead, section 386 allows the former proprietor of the business to set-off any loss against any future income that he or she receives from the company (salary, dividends, etc.) provided that, in the relevant year of assessment, he or she owns shares in the company, and the company continues to trade. As an alternative to section 386, the proprietor could use the carry-back provisions of section 388. In more complex situations, section 386 will assist in providing relief for any unabsorbed losses under section 388.

---

[146]   TA 1988 s.113.
[147]   TA 1988 s.386.

Schedule D Case VI

Schedule D Case VI is delcared to apply to 'any annual profits of gains not falling under any other case of schedule D and not charged by virtue of Schedule A or E'[148] This is the general or sweeping-up provision of the Schedular system (see earlier discussion of the doctrine of source). Case VI also catches matters specifically declared by statute to be placed within Case VI - these include profit and gains from furnished lettings; securities transactions, post-cessation receipts and the transfers of assets abroad.

It is the general (or sweeping-up) aspects of Case VI that are of interest. An examination of judicial comments and application of Case VI reveals that it is not as wide or as all-embracing as it initially appears. The first restriction on Case VI is that it applies to income receipts only and (not capital gains or profits). Thus in *Scott v Ricketts*[149] the Court of Appeal declared that a payment to an estate agent for the agent agreeing to forgo claims in a development scheme was a capital sum and therefore not caught nor taxable under Case VI. Similarly in *Earl Haig's Trustee v IRC*[150] a trustee owned some diaries and the copyright attached to those diaries. The trustees permitted the use of the diaries in the production of a bibliography and received a sum of money for doing so. The Court of Appeal held that the sum of money received was as a consequence of a realisation (in part) of a capital asset (the diaries and copyright). The money was not income and was not therefore assessable under Case VI.

A second limitation on the scope of Case VI emanates from the words 'profit or gains'.[151] The term 'profits or gains' is used elsewnere in Schedule D and the implication is that the words must be consistent in their meaning and application and that the activities that present or create the profit or gain must be analogous. Technically the requirement is that the 'profit and gains' are of the same kind (*ejusdem generis*) as 'profit and gains' taxed elsewhere under Schedule D. This requirement has invited the conclusion that the profit or gain must be derived from an activity analogous to an 'adventure in the nature of a trade, or a profession[152]. This means that the Case VI will usually apply to casual earnings (normally from the performance of services) but not gifts[153] nor betting winnings and receipts. For example, in *Hobbs v Hussey*[154]a solicitor's clerk wrote and published his memoirs in the *People* newspaper. This was not the clerk's profession or trade, merely a 'casual' activity. The clerk also assigned the copyright of the article to the newspaper. The court held that the payment received by the clerk was in

[148] TA 1988, s18 (It is also a residual provision to those sums not caught by Schedule F, TA 1988 s20)
[137] [1967]2 All ER 1009
[150] [1939] 22 TC 725
[151] The term 'annual' does not imply that the profit or gain must recur, simply that the 'profit or gain' must fall within and be assessed in a year of assessment.
[152] This analogy is necessary because 'profits and gains' are related in Schedule D Cases I and II to 'adventures in the nature of a trade or proffesion'. The *ejusdem generis* approach demands such an analogy and application
[153] In *Scott V Ricketts* [1967] 2 All ER 1009, Lord Denning MR confirmed that 'profits and gains does not include garatuitous payments.
[154] (1942) 1KB 491

return for the performance of 'casual' services and therefore assessable under Case VI. Although the performance of the services also involved the sale of property (the copyright). Lawrence J emphasised that the essence of the performance was the revenue nature of the receipt which was ' the fruit of the individuals capacity' derived from but was not 'the capital itself'.

In some instances the distinction between an 'adventure in the nature of trade' (Schedule D Case I) and an analogous activity (Schedule D Case VI) is difficult to determine. For example, in *Jones v Leeming*[155] the taxpayer was party to a scheme whereby he participated in the acquisition and sale of rubber estates for a profit. The House of Lords concluded that the profit was not assessable under Case VI because it was not a profit within Schedule D. At an earlier stage the Court of Appeal had pointed out the difficulty (if not illogical approach) of the *ejusdem generis* application. Lawrence LJ suggested that if an isolated transaction such as this is not an adventure in the nature of a trade (Case I) then it is difficult to conclude that it is a transaction *ejusdem generis* with such a transaction (Case VI): '...All the elements which would go to make such a transaction an adventure in the nature of trade in my opinion would be required to make it a transaction *ejusdem generis* with such an adventure.'

The logical conclusion would be that the Case VI is redundant in that *ejusdem generis* activities must demonstrate the characteristics of trade and would therefore be 'trade' and assessable under Case I. Perhaps a more generous approach to the interpretation of Case VI is required - especially if it is to adequately perform a role as a 'sweeping-up' or anti-avoidance provision for casual earnings.

Finally, it should be noted that there are no rules for allowable deductions under Schedule D, Case VI; and if expenses exceed a receipt, the loss can be deducted only from other Schedule D, Case VI income of the same tax period or of subsequent tax periods.

[155]   (1930) AC 415

chapter eight
Capital Allowances

Introduction

In the post-war period in particular, businesses have received tax incentives in an attempt to encourage the acquisition of and investment in capital assets such as plant, machinery and industrial buildings. The tax incentive have taken the form of an allowance to be set-off against the annual profits of the business. Normally, the acquisition costs of the capital asset would only be taken into account on the assets 'disposal' under the Capital Gains Tax regime - a large and unnecessary wait. Relying on the Capital Gains Tax regime to accommodate the costs of expenditure would probably result in a disincentive effect with little investment taking place in the development and updating of business machinery and premises. A lack of investment would have consequent adverse effects on the economy.[1]

The 'allowance' received under the capital allowances scheme has varied from a 100 per cent initial allowance to a reduced percentage writing down allowance only. The latter demanded more patience and planning from the businesses and would not offer immediate tax consequences and benefits.

It became increasingly apparent that the capital allowance system was subject to abuse : businesses would invest in unnecessary or unproductive capital simply to enjoy the tax deductions attributable to those investments. This abuse (and suspected abuse) caused the Government to review the system and announce a three-stage reform of the capital allowances system. The (then) Chancellor of the Exchequer, Mr Nigel Lawson, explained that 'too much of British investment had been made because the tax allowances made it look profitable rather than because it would be truly productive'.

In order to encourage 'investment decisions based on future market assessments, not future tax assessments', Mr Lawson announced a three

[1] It is important to note that capital allowances postpone tax rather than permanently reduce it . Such a postponement is useful in the early years when the money can be used for other purposes or in times of inflation when the real value of the eventual payment falls.

stage reform as follows :

> In the case of plant and machinery ... the first year allowance will be reduced from 100 per cent to 75 per cent for all such expenditure incurred after today [13 March 1984], and to 50 per cent for expenditure incurred after 31 March next year. After 31 March 1986 there will be no first year allowances, and all expenditure on plant and machinery will qualify for annual allowances on a 25 per cent reducing balance basis. For industrial building, I propose that the initial allowance should fall from 75 per cent to 50 per cent from tonight, and be further reduced to 25 per cent from 31 March next year. After 31 March 1986 the initial allowance will be abolished, and expenditure will be written off on an annual 4 per cent straight line basis[2].

Since that statement there does appear to have been a change in attitude. For example, first year allowances became available on expenditure on qualifying assets between the period of 1st November 1992 to 31st October 1993 at a rate of 40 per cent. The relief was then increased to 50 per cent for expenditure incurred between 2nd July 1997 and 1st July 1998.

The full details of these changes can be found in the Capital Allowances Act, 1990. Before we look at those details, we must first consider the meaning of industrial building and plant and machinery.

Industrial Buildings

Industrial buildings are defined in the 1990 Act.[3] The definition is complex but worthy of discussion. In essence the definition attempts to equate 'industrial' with manufacture and production, but not distribution activities. However, if the storage and distribution of goods is for the purpose of the business, then the building and its use will be classed as 'industrial'.[4]

Also excluded from the definition of 'industrial' is the use of a building as a dwelling, retail shop, hotel, office or showroom.[5]

Apportionment is allowed to facilitate part qualifying and part non-qualifying use. Apportionment is subject to a very generous allowance of total costs where the non-qualifying use is insignificant - representing not more than 25 per cent of the total construction costs of the building.[6]

[3]   March 13, 1984. Hansard, HC, Vol 56, Cols 295-296. Mr Lawson still believed that the much amended and reduced capital allowance system would still be more generous than a system of commercial depreciation.Note that an initial allowance has been retained in respect of industrial buildings in particular circumstances, such as Capital expenditure on the construction of a building in an enterprise zone where expenditure on commercial buildings or structures may qualify for a full 100% first year allowance..
[3]   See s18, CAA 1990.
[4]   See *Saxone Lilley and Skinner (Holdings) Ltd v IRC* [1967] 1 All ER 756.
[5]   CAA 1990, s18 (4) and *Satsfield v Dixons Group plc* [1998] STC 938.
[6]   Ibid, at s18(7).

Finally, it is important to appreciate that where an initial allowance still remains, it is only available to the person who incurs the cost of the building; writing down and balancing allowances are available to those who enjoy a relevant interest. A relevant interest means that the person who incurs the expenditure must have an interest in the property at the time of the expenditure.[7] For example, a leaseholder or freeholder who incurs capital expenditure on improvement would be able to enjoy the allowance. Their position as freeholder or leaseholder represents an interest in the property.

Plant and Machinery

'Plant' and 'machinery' are not defined by legislation. Their meanings must be determined by the courts and must depend on the particular facts of the case. Judicial guidance on this matter contains many contradictions and difficulties. The best advice is to focus on the facts of the case and to consider '... whether it can really be supposed that Parliament desired to encourage a particular expenditure out of, in effect, taxpayers' money and ... ultimately, in extreme cases, to say that this is too much to stomach ...'.[8]

The real difficulty in understanding and distinguishing 'plant' involves the need to distinguish 'premises and setting' from 'plant', in a manner that facilitates the recognition of plant as an integral part of the carrying-on of the business. Such a recognition of the integral nature of plant has appeared in judicial comments as the 'functional', 'business' or 'amenity' test[9]. Some even refer to a very broad 'premises' test to support the need for a distinction. The *dicta* of Lindley LJ in *Yarmouth v France* is often cited as the basis for the adopted distinctions :

> '... in its ordinary sense [plant] ... includes whatever apparatus is used by a business man for carrying on his business - not his stock-in-trade which he buys or makes for sale; but all goods and chattels, fixed or moveable, live or dead, which he keeps for permanent employment in his business.'[10]

It appears that we ought to accept (with some caution) that 'plant' is not stock-in-trade nor business premises - unless those business premises perform the function of and represent 'plant' (integral to the business). The following cases might be of interest in illustrating the distinctions and the

---

[7]   Ibid at s20.
[8]   Per Lord Wilberforce in *IRC v Scottish and Newcastle Breweries Ltd* [1982] STC 296. It was suggested that this was destined to become known as the 'nausea test'. See [1983] BTR 54 at 55.
[9]   For an interesting debate on the conflict between the functional and the business test see the debate in *Gray v Seymours Garden Centre* [1993] 2 All ER 809 (noted 1994 BLR 5)
[10]   [1887] 19 QBD 647 at 658.

difficulties in this area.

IRC v Scottish and Newcastle Breweries Ltd[11] - included a claim for costs of metal structures (seagulls in flight) incurred by the owners of an hotel. The purpose of the purchase and erection of these metal structures was to contribute to the creation of an 'ambience' or 'atmosphere' in the hotel. The court accepted that the metal structures were plant. The court emphasised that the seagulls performed a functional role in that the 'creation of ambience or atmosphere was an important function of the trade of successful hoteliers and publicans.' It was also stated that the metal structures were not part of the 'setting in which they did their business - but, the setting offered to customers for them to resort to and enjoy, and hence plant.'[12]

In *IRC v Barclay Curle and Co Ltd*[13], expenditure was incurred on the excavation and concrete work in the construction of a dry dock. The House of Lords accepted that this represented expenditure on plant. Lord Reid explained that although the dry dock was a structure or premises, it was also plant : 'The only reason why a structure should also be plant ... is that it fulfils the function of plant in the trader's operations ...'.[14]

Similarly in *Cooke (Inspector of Taxes) v Beach Station Caravans Ltd*[15], the 'structures' of a swimming pool and a paddling pool in a caravan park were held to be plant. Megarry J emphasised that they were not premises in the sense of 'where it's at' (the location of the business activity). They were apparatus in that they were part of the means whereby the trade of a caravan park was carried on.

In *J Lyons and Co Ltd v A-G*[16], the purchase and erection of lamps in a tea shop were not plant in that they performed a general function of the provision of light and not a specific trade function in relation to the particular needs and conduct of that trade.

In *Wimpy International Ltd v Warland*[17], Wimpy failed in its claim that expenditure on such items as shop fronts, floors, suspended ceilings, lights and wall finishes represented expenditure on plant. The court emphasised that 'the fact that different things might perform the same functions of creating atmosphere was irrelevant: what matters is that one thing may function as part of the premises and the other as plant.' Thus it was concluded that '... something which becomes part of the premises instead of merely embellishing them, was not plant, except in the rare case where the premises are themselves plant.'[18]

---

[11] Supra n8.
[12] This case inspired the advice that one should "always re-decorate one's walls and ceilings with loose chattels". [1983] BTR 54 at 56.
[13] [1969] 1 WLR 675.
[14] Ibid at 679.
[15] [1974] STC 402.
[16] [1944] Ch 281.
[17] [1989] STC 273.
[18] Supra at 279, per Fox LJ.

Capital Allowances : The Details

A consolidated Act, the Capital Allowances Act 1990, provides the details of the allowances and charges for the chargeable periods ending after 5 April 1990.

Plant and Machinery[19]

The details allow this capital allowance to be claimed by Schedule D Case I and II taxpayers and Schedule E taxpayers. It is also available in relation to furnished holiday lettings under Schedule D Case VI and, where the plant and machinery is used in the maintenance or management or premises, to a general landlord under Schedule A or Schedule D Case VI.

In respect of the Schedule D taxpayer, the expenditure must be incurred wholly and exclusively for the purposes of the trade, although apportionment is expressly stated as available in circumstances of dual purpose.[20] The Schedule E taxpayer is required to establish that the expenditure on the plant and machinery took place because its provision was 'necessary' in the performance of the duties of the Schedule E taxpayer.[21] This additional requirement of the Schedule E taxpayer can, once again, prove excessively onerous.[22]

To accord with accountancy practice, there have been some major changes in relation to the determination of the date when the expenditure is deemed to have been incurred. The expenditure is now deemed to have been incurred on the date on which the obligation to pay becomes unconditional.[23] It is important to appreciate that this change will recognise the situation where an obligation to pay becomes unconditional even though the sum does not have to be paid until a later date. Exceptions apply if the date of payment falls four months after the obligation to pay has become unconditional - the due date of payment will then be used in this instance.

Having determined the date of incurrence, we need to consider next the tax period in which the allowance may be claimed.[24] For the Corporation Tax payer, the relevant period is the incurrence within the appropriate Accounting year. Similarly, the Schedule E taxpayer's relevant period is the year of assessment. For those who adopt a preceding year basis under Schedule D, it normally means a delay in the enjoyment of the allowance or claim in accordance with the application of this basis of assessment.

[19] It should be noted that Schedule AA1 to the CAA was introduced in November 1993 with the intention of seeking to make it clear that land, buildings and structures do not generally qualify as plant.

[20] CAA 1990, s79. It is interesting to note here that in Munby v Furlong (1977) the Court of Appeal accepted that law textbooks and reports were plant wholly and exclusively used by a barrister for the purposes of his profession!

[21] CAA, 1990, s27(2)(a) - although this requirement is not to apply in relation to the purchase of a motor vehicle (s27(2A) - (2E)).

[22] See White v Higginbotham [1983] STC 143 - where the provision of a projector to a vicar was not 'necessarily' incurred for the performance of his duties.

[23] CAA 1990, 159(3). The previous rule used the 'date' when the expenditure became payable (CAA 1968, s82).

[24] CAA 1990, s160.

If, having applied the allowance or change to the annual profits of the trade, profession or employment, there remains a surplus of allowance or charge, the surplus can be rolled forward to be set against future profits[25] or against general income.[26]

The Allowance

Previously a first year allowance together with a writing-down allowance was permitted. We noted in the introduction the concern that was caused by the possible abuse of, in particular, the first year allowance. First year allowances are not available for expenditure incurred after 31 March 1986, but allowances were reintroduced for expenditure incurred on qualifying assets between 1 November 1992 and 31 October 1993 at 40 per cent of the costs of the qualifying asset.

First year allowances next became available at 50 per cent for expenditure incurred between 2 July 1997 and 1 July 1998 for small and medium-sized companies. The Finance Act 1998 extended the period to 1 July 1999, whilst reducing the first year allowance to 40 per cent except for capital expenditure on British qualifying films where the first year allowance is 100 per cent. In March 1999 the Chancellor announced that the 40 per cent first year capital allowances would be extended for a further year and that the British Film Industry would continue to qualify for greater relief.

The writing-down allowance has been retained and this allows the taxpayer to progressively write-off the cost of the plant and machinery. The details are below.

The Basic Allowance

This consists of an allowance of 25 per cent (on a reducing balance basis) of the 'qualifying expenditure' (expenditure minus any other allowances) on the plant and machinery. The allowance will apply once the expenditure has been incurred, irrespective of whether the asset is in use, on assets wholly and exclusively purchased for the purposes of the trade, profession or vocation. Apportionment of the allowance on terms that are just and reasonable is permitted to recognise non-business purpose and use.[27]

There is an exception to the 25 per cent writing-down allowance in the case of long-life assets (machinery and plant with a working life of 25 years or

[25]   CAA 1990, s140.
[26]   TA 1988, ss382, 383.
[27]   CAA 1990, s.79.

more). Here the writing-down allowance is six per cent where a person incurs expenditure of more than £100,000 on such assets and they were acquired on or after 26 November 1996 (CAA, ss.38A - 38H).

Pooling

It is normal for a trade to acquire a number of items of plant and machinery. It then becomes convenient, and possible, to create a 'pool' of plant and machinery. The writing-down allowance of 25 per cent will then be applied to the value of the 'pool' rather than the value of individual items.[28]

Disposal

If an item of plant or machinery is disposed of, provision must be made to ensure that the disposal consideration or value is taken into account.[29] It is most important that the allowance enjoyed by the business equate with the actual cost to the business of that item of plant or machinery. 'Disposal' is given a wide meaning to include a disposal by sale; a disposal by extinction (destruction) and a disposal through the loss of possession ('loss' or theft).[30] Sale consideration, insurance monies or deemed market value will represent the sum that must be taken into account.

Balancing Allowances and Charges

No writing-down allowance is available in the year that the business ceases or terminates. Proceeds from the sale of the plant and machinery are deducted from the qualifying expenditure in the pool (or individual items if non-pooled). If a surplus of 'qualifying expenditure' remains, that surplus will be converted into a 'balancing allowance' to be deducted from the taxpayer's profits and income. Conversely, if the proceeds of sale of the plant and machinery exceed the qualifying expenditure, the excess is treated as a balancing charge and becomes a taxable receipt of the business - this process is known as the 'clawback' of capital allowances.

Short-life Assets[31]

It is possible for the taxpayer to elect that certain short-life assets should not join a general pool of plant and machinery. It is also possible to enjoy a pool of short-life assets. A short life asset is one that is expected to be disposed

---

[28] CAA 1990, s.24. Note that more detailed rules demand that certain assets must be pooled separately or that certain assets may not be pooled. For example, see CAA 1990, ss.31, 34, 37 and 41.

[29] CAA 1990, s.26.

[30] CAA 1990, s.24.

[31] See details in CAA 1990, s.37.

of within five years. Any election in relation to those assets must be made within two years from the date of their acquisition. The purpose of this permitted de-pooling election is to enable the taxpayer to realise the balancing allowance on short-life assets at an earlier time than would normally be available. If those assets were part of a general pool, it normally results in 80 per cent of the cost being written-off over eight years.

Industrial Buildings

Capital allowances are available for the construction or purchase of an industrial building. The base allowance is a writing-down allowance at a rate of four per cent of the cost price of the industrial building.[32] This four per cent allowance is available for each year the taxpayer uses the building for industrial purposes up to a maximum of 25 years. The entire expenditure is deemed to have been written-off after 25 years.   Note that only the expenditure on the building or structure qualifies, the cost of buying the land on which the building or structure stands is specifically excluded (s.21 (i)).

A balancing allowance or charge will arise if the building or interest in the building is sold (or demolished, destroyed or relevant use ceases) within the 25-year period.[33] The balancing allowance or charge is computed involving a comparison of the disposal expenditure with the outstanding qualifying expenditure. It is important to appreciate that a balancing charge will not recover more than the allowances given, thus an excessive disposal consideration will give rise to the potential of Capital Gains Tax. This represents an attempt to ensure that the capital allowances given correspond to the actual depreciation suffered by the taxpayer.

The purchaser of a secondhand industrial building may also be entitled to a writing-down allowance.[34] This entitlement depends on the sale to the purchaser falling within the 25-year period. That purchaser will then be entitled to an allowance (not confined to the 4% rate) based upon the residue of expenditure.   The residue of expenditure represents any unrelieved expenditure of the vendor plus any balancing charge (or minus a balancing allowance).

Special rules apply to (1) hotel buildings and extensions[35] and (2) enterprise zones[36]. Although hotels do not technically fall within the definition of industrial buildings, specific provisions have been introduced to permit expenditure on the construction or improvement of 'qualifying hotels' to be

[32]   CAA 1990, s.3.
[33]   CAA 1990, s.4.
[34]   CAA 1990, s10.
[35]   CAA 1990, s7.
[36]   CAA 1990, ss1 and 6.

written-off on an annual writing-down allowance of 4 per cent.

In order to stimulate development in declared enterprise zones, 100 per cent initial allowances are available for capital expenditure on industrial buildings, hotels and commercial buildings. The 100 per cent initial allowance is not mandatory : an election can be made to enjoy a reduced percentage initial allowance with the balance being written-off annually at 25 per cent of the cost on a straight line method of provision.

Other Allowances

Other specific items and areas of expenditure are eligible for capital allowances and charges.   These include expenditure incurred on the construction, wholly or partly, of agricultural or forestry buildings[37]; expenditure incurred on the construction of property for letting as assured tenancies[38]; capital expenditure on scientific research[39]; and expenditure incurred in the acquisition of patents and 'know-how'[40].   In March 1999, the Chancellor announced that in an attempt to encourage innovation, the Government is introducing in 2000 a tax credit on research and development for small and medium-sized companies.

Assessment of the Changes and Reform

We mentioned at the beginning of this chapter, that Mr Nigel Lawson sought reform of the capital allowance system in a direction that would encourage a balanced approach to investment. He, and others, were concerned that the 'old' system of capital allowance was far too generous and had resulted in low-yielding, and even loss-making, investment at the expense of jobs. Following the changes introduced there was some concern that the reforms may have swung the pendulum too far: that there was no longer sufficient encouragement for investment.   During the 1990s there have been various campaigns seeking a more generous treatment of investment.   These have included campaigns by the CBI, and by employer's federations in engineering, motor manufacturing and in metal trades.   They have been supported in their campaigning by the results of academic papers and

34   CAA 1990, Part V.
35   CAA 1990, Part III.
36   CAA 1990, Part VII.
37   TA 1988, ss 520-528.

research. For example, Devereux concluded that the new system of capital allowances acts as a disincentive to real investment.[41]

It is certainly a difficult task to develop and arrange a system of capital allowances that provides the required balance of sufficient incentives for good investment. Although, in the March Budget of 1993, the Chancellor did provide some good news for businesses, the issue of capital allowances and incentives for investment was once again a cause of criticism. The Chancellor announced a number of peripheral and limited changes to capital allowance details.[42] The failure to directly address or consider the possible extension and increase of capital allowances was described as 'one by omission'.[43]

It also drew the following comments from industry : 'We were disappointed that little emphasis was placed on improving investment in high technology. This Budget fell short of directly encouraging UK companies to invest and to meet the anticipated recovery'[44] and, 'This Budget does nothing to bring about the massive switch from consumption to investment which is essential for lasting recovery.'[45]

The debate is certain to continue. The temporary re-introduction of a first year allowance rate of 40 per cent in 1992-93 and 50 per cent for small and medium-sized companies and unincorporated associations in 1997-98 provides some encouragement to those calling for greater assistance to businesses, particularly the small and medium sized enterprises. Even greater support is available to those involved in the British Film Industry!

Finally, it should be noted that some hope is given to those who find the case law confusing in this area. The 'Tax Law Rewrite' is to include capital allowances in an attempt to make the law 'clearer and easier' to use whilst reflecting the relevant case law (IR Press Release 142/98).

---

41   M. Devereux. "Corporation Tax : The Effect of 1984 Reforms on the Incentive to Invest", (1988) Fiscal Studies, 9 (1), 62.
42   These changes relate to the ability of a connected person to elect to treat the sale of industrial buildings as having taken place at their tax written-down value.
43   *Financial Times*, March 17, 1993.
44   Spokesperson for the Machine Tool Technologies Association (*Financial Times*, March 17, 1993).
45   N. Johnson, DG of the Engineering Employers'Federation. *Financial Times*, March 17, 1993.

chapter nine
The Taxation of Pure Income Profit

Introduction

The uncertainties of life in modern societies often lead the astute to endeavour to lay aside some money, either to save for the proverbial 'rainy day' or, to provide some security in respect of the inevitable retirement. In such cases it often makes sense to keep the money, not in current banking accounts which return no profit but rather attract charges, but, for the security conscious, in interest-yielding building society or bank accounts, or Government Treasury Bills; or, for the more adventurous and daring, in various high-profit investments. Whichever way the money is kept, it will or may yield some financial return. This will normally be pure profit (in the sense that the financial return is, in its entirety, a profit), or investment income, and, inevitably, there will be income tax implications. This chapter is concerned with the principles that govern the taxation of such 'pure profit', or investment income.

The principal charging provision for income tax purposes is section 18(3) of the ICTA 1988 which charges tax under Case III of Schedule D in respect of:

(a) any interest of money, whether yearly or otherwise, or any annuity or other annual payment, whether such payment is payable within or out of the United Kingdom ... but not including any payment chargeable under Schedule A;

(b) all discounts; and

(c) income from securities which is payable out of the public revenue of the United Kingdom or Northern Ireland.

For the purposes of corporation tax, section 18(3A) provides for a different charge under Case III. In this respect, the subsection charges tax under Case III in respect of the following.

   (a) Profits and gains which, as profits and gains arising from loan relationships, are to be treated as chargeable under this Case by virtue of Chapter II of Part IV of the FA 1996[1].

   (b) Any annuity or other annual payment which

      (i) is payable ... in respect of anything other than a loan relationship;

      (ii) is not a payment chargeable under Schedule A.

   (c) Any discount arising otherwise than in respect of a loan relationship.

The discussions in this chapter will focus mainly on annuities and other annual payments, while interest and discounts are examined in outline only.

Interest of Money

The question whether a particular sum of money amounts to 'interest of money' is a question of law.[2] The answer is not dependent on the form of words used by the parties to a transaction - rather, 'the question must always be one of the true nature of the payment'. However, as is typical of the Taxes Act, the statutory definition of 'interest' is not particularly illuminating. Section 832(1) of the ICTA 1988 provides that interest 'means both annual or yearly interest and interest other than annual or yearly interest'. This strange definition, which at least one judge has found himself reading 'with disappointment'[3], by simply saying that 'interest', in short, means 'interest' begs the question 'what is interest?'. It seems that, while this is a question of law, there is no special or technical meaning to be attributed for income tax purposes to the word 'interest'. In *Re Euro Hotel (Belgravia) Ltd*[4], Megarry J commenced his analysis of the word with a reference to the Shorter Oxford Dictionary definition which defined interest as 'money paid for the use of money lent (the principal), or for forbearance of a debt, according to a fixed ratio (rate per cent)'.

Rowlatt J presented a similar answer to this question in *Bennett v Ogston*[5],

---

[1]   Case V of Schedule D does not include tax in respect of any income falling under this provision.
[2]   Megarry J in *Re Euro Hotel (Belgravia) Ltd.* [1975] 3 All ER 1075 at 1083.
[3]   Ibid at 10813
[4]   [1975] 3 All ER at 1083.
[5]   (1930) 15 TC 374 at 379.

saying that interest is a 'payment by time for the use of money'.[6]

In *Re Euro Hotel (Belgravia) Ltd.*[7], Megarry J referred with approval to a definition given by Rand J of the Supreme Court of Canada in *Reference Re Saskatchewan Farm Security Act* 1944, Section 6[8], that, 'interest is, in general terms, the return or consideration or compensation for the use or retention by one person of a sum of money belonging to, in a colloquial sense, or owed to, another'.

Thus the essence of interest is that it is a payment which becomes due because the creditor has not had his money at the due date.[9] It may be regarded either as representing the profit which the creditor might have made if he had had the use of his money, or the loss that he suffered because he did not have that use. The general idea is that the creditor is entitled to compensation for the deprivation.[10]

It seems that, as a general rule, two specific requirements must be satisfied for a payment to amount to 'interest of money'. These were outlined by Megarry J in *Re Euro Hotel (Belgravia) Ltd.*[11]

> First, there must be a sum of money by reference to which the payment which is said to be interest is to be ascertained ... Secondly, those sums of money must be sums that are due to the person entitled to the alleged interest.

According to Megarry J, these two requirements are not exhaustive in every case, nor are they inescapable. Thus for example, a payment does not cease to be interest of money 'if A lends money to B and stipulates that the interest should be paid not to him but to X'.[12]

From the above authorities, we may derive a number of propositions. First, there must be a principal sum by reference to which the interest is calculated. In this respect, Rand J of the Supreme Court of Canada said in *Reference Re Saskatchewan*[13] that 'the definition' and 'the obligation' of interest assumes that it is referable to 'a principal in money or an obligation to pay money.' According to him, without this 'relational structure' in fact, no obligation to pay money can be an obligation to pay interest - regardless of the basis of calculating the amount. In the same case, Kellock J said that there can be no such thing as interest 'on principal which is non-existent'.[14]

Secondly, the principal sum must be owed, or 'belong' (in the colloquial

---

6. Compare Farwell J in the non-tax case of *Bond v Barrow Haematite Steel Co.* [1902] 1 Ch 353 at 363: 'Interest is compensation for delay in payment'.
7. [1975] 3 All ER 1075 at 1084.
8. [1947] 3 DLR 689 at 703.
9. Lord Wright in *Riches v Westminster Bank Ltd.* [1947] 1 All ER 469 at 472
10. Lord Wright, ibid.
11. [1975] 3 All ER 1075 at 1084.
12. Ibid.
13. [1947] 3 DLR 689 at 703.
14. Ibid at 707.

sense) to a creditor.[15]Thirdly, the payment alleged to be interest must be for the use of that principal sum[16] as compensation calculated by time[17], for delay in payment. Fourthly, the payment must be due to the creditor or the creditor's nominee.[18]

It had once been thought that, in cases of an award of damages with interest by a court, that 'interest' is really 'damages' and therefore does not fall within the charge to income tax. This was the approach taken by Wright J in *Re National Bank of Wales Ltd.*[19]

This approach was rejected by the House of Lords in *Riches v Westminster Bank Ltd.*[20] The appellant in this case had entered into an agreement with R under which he introduced R to a transaction involving the purchase of certain shares. The agreement provided for R to pay to the appellant 50 per cent of any profit which R might make on resale of the shares. R bought the shares and sold them at a profit, but fraudulently understated the amount of profits made on the sale. On the death of R, the appellant discovered the true extent of the profits, and commenced an action against the respondents as judicial trustee of R's will, claiming an account of the profits of the resale of the said shares, and payment of the difference between the amount already paid by R and the amount due on the true profits. The judge gave judgment for the appellant in the sum of £36,225 (the correct amount due to the appellant from R on the resale of the shares), and added a sum of £10,028 in exercise of his discretion to award interest under section 3 of the Law Reform (Miscellaneous Provisions) Act 1934. The respondent paid the amount due under the judgment, but deducted £5,014, representing income tax due on the interest payment of £10,028 awarded by the judge. The appellant claimed that the tax was not due, because although the £10,028 was called 'interest' in the judgment, it was, in reality, damages. The House of Lords upheld decisions of the lower courts in favour of the respondent.

According to Viscount Simon, there is no essential incompatibility between the two conceptions (interest and damages).[21]He said that the observations of Wright J in *Re National Bank of Wales* (above) were wrong[22], and that if damages are increased by adding interest to a principal sum, that does not prove that such interest is not liable to tax[23]. Viscount Simon then referred to the argument of counsel for the appellant that the added sum was not in the nature of interest as used in the Income Tax Acts because that added sum only came into existence when th~ judgment was given, and that, from that

---

[15]   Rand J in *Reference Re Saskatchewan* [1947] 3 DLR 689 at 703; Megarry J in *Re Euro Hotel (Belgravia) Ltd.* [1975] 3 All ER 1075 at 1084-1085.
[16]   Rowlatt J in *Bennett v Ogston* (15 TC 374 at 379); Megarry J in *Re Euro Hotel (Belgravia) Ltd.* [1975] 3 All ER 1075 At 1085).
[17]   Megarry J in *RE Euro HOtel (Belgravia) Ltd* [1975] 3 All ER 1075 at 1085.
[18]   Megarry J in *Re Euro Hotel (Belgravia) Ltd* [1975] 3 All ER 1075 at 1084.
[19]   [1899] 2 Ch 629.
[20]   [1947] 1 All ER 469
[21]   At 470. Compare Lord Wright at 473 - 'there is no incompatibility ... between interest proper and interest by way of damages'.
[22]   At 471. Compare Lord Wright at 473.
[23]   At 471.

moment, it had no accretions under the order awarding it. His response was thus:

> I see no reason why, when the Judge orders payment of interest from a past date on the amount of the main sum awarded (or on a part of it), this supplemental payment, the size of which grows from day to day by taking a fraction of so much per cent, per annum of the amount of which interest is ordered, and by the payment of which further growth is stopped, should not be treated as interest attracting Income Tax. It is not capital. It is rather the accumulated fruit of a tree which the tree produces regularly until payment.

Lord Wright described as 'artificial' the contention that money awarded as damages for the detention of money is not interest and has not the quality of interest.[24] Such a contention was also erroneous because interest was in essence a payment that was due because the creditor did not get his money when it was due. From that point of view, it was immaterial whether the money was due under a contract, or under a statutory provision, or whether it was due for any other reason in law.[25] According to Lord Wright:

> In either case the money was due to him and was not paid or, in other words, was withheld from him by the debtor after the time when payment should have been made, in breach of his legal rights, and interest was a compensation, whether the compensation was liquidated under an agreement or statute, as for instance under Section 57 of the Bills of Exchange Act, 1882, or was unliquidated and claimable under the Act as in the present case. The essential quality of the claim for compensation is the same, and the compensation is properly described as interest.

In rejecting the argument that the sum in question 'could not be interest at all because interest implies a recurrence of periodical accretions, whereas this sum came into existence *uno flatu* by the judgment of the court and was fixed once for all', Lord Wright said that the payment in truth represented the 'total of the periodical accretions of interest during the whole time in which the payment of the debt was withheld'.[26]

Lord Simonds for his part also viewed the alleged distinction between interest and damages as fallacious, because it assumes an incompatibility between the ideas of interest and damages, for which there was no

[24]   At 472.
[25]   Ibid.6
[26]   at 474.

justification.[27]According to him, this confuses the character of the payment with the authority under which it is paid. In fact, its 'essential character' may be the same regardless of whether it is paid under a contract, a statute, or a court's judgment. Regardless of whether it is called 'interest' or 'damages in the nature of interest' or even just 'damages', the real question remains the same - 'what is its intrinsic character?'. In Lord Simonds' view, one may well be misled in the consideration of this question by a description due to the authority by which the payment is made. The result then is that a payment does not cease to be 'interest' merely because it emerges and is fixed in one instant by a court, or, because the principal sum by reference to which it is calculated is due, not in contract, but under statute, or, because the liability to pay the interest itself is not contractual but is based on a court order.

Tax on Interest

The general scheme of Schedule D Case III is the deduction of income tax at source by the payer under ICTA 1988 section 348 and section 349 (concerning which we shall say more later), so that the payee or recipient receives the sums net of tax. However, by virtue of section 348(1) and section 349(1), payments of interest are excluded from these deduction rules. Thus the general rule is that interest is to be paid gross, and the recipient will be assessed directly under Case III[28].

There are exceptions however. Section 349(2) requires the payer to deduct income tax at the lower rate[29] from any payment of yearly interest, and account for such deduction to the Revenue, where the payment is chargeable under Schedule D Case III and is paid:

(a) by a company (excluding building societies) or local authority, otherwise than in a fiduciary or representative capacity (ie, paid on their own behalf);

(b) by or on behalf of a mixed partnership (ie, one having a company in it); or,

(c) to any person whose usual place of abode is not in the United Kingdom.

Section 349(3) provides exceptions to the deduction requirements of section 349(2). This would mean in some cases that the payment of interest is to be

---

[27]   At 476.
[28]   It has been said that the tax on interest leads to a 'double taxation of savings' (the income is taxed when earned, and then the interest gained from saving it is taxed again) - see S. James and C. Nobes, 'The Economics of Taxation', page 56 *et seq*.
[29]   See TA 1988, sections 1A, 3, and 4.

gross, and, in some other cases, special deduction rules apply. The exceptions apply in the following situations.

(a) Interest payable on an advance from a bank, if at the time when the interest is paid the person beneficially entitled to the interest is within the charge to corporation tax as respects the interest (ie, interest which is paid to a bank by a customer who has borrowed money from the bank, if the bank would be liable to corporation tax in respect of the interest). This type of interest is always paid gross.

(b) Interest paid by a bank in the ordinary course of its business. Note in this respect section 480A which applies to interest paid by a 'deposit taker' requiring a deduction of tax at source in certain situations (eg, if the payee is an individual who is resident in the United Kingdom)[30].

(c) A payment to which section 124 applies (interest on quoted Eurobonds);

(d) A payment to which section 369 applies (mortgage interest payable under deduction of tax).

(e) Payments which are 'relevant payments' for the purposes of Chapter VIIA of Part IV (paying and collecting agents).

(f) Cases to which the deduction rules under section 480A apply.

(g) Cases to which the deduction rules under section 480A would apply, but for section 480B.

(h) Cases to which the deduction rules under section 480A would apply, but for section 481(5)(k).

Because the deduction requirement under Section 349(2) applies to yearly interest, a distinction is drawn between short interest which is always paid gross, and yearly interest. This issue was addressed by the Court of Appeal in *Cairns v McDiarmid*, where Kerr LJ said[31]:

[T]he authorities show that the answer depends on the true intention of the parties. A bank loan for a fixed period of less than a year does not carry 'yearly' (or annual) interest merely because the rate of

---

[30] See section 481 for definitions and requirements.
[31] (1982) 56 TC 556 at 582.

interest is expressed as a percentage by reference to the period of a year ... On the other hand, a loan on a mortgage which is nominally repayable after six months and which carries interest at a rate per annum will qualify as carrying annual interest because the true intention of the parties is that it should be a long-term loan, beyond a year and indeed probably over many years.

Sir John Donaldson MR concurred, saying[32]:

It is well settled that the difference between what is annual and what is short interest depends upon the intention of the parties ... because it is possible to have a short term and indeed a very short term investment, e.g. over-night deposits, and such an investment does not involve any annual interest, regardless of whether the interest is calculated at an annual rate. On the facts found by the Commissioners, the loan to Mr. Cairns was never intended to last for more than a few days, albeit the was entitled to postpone repayment for two years. In fact, as was always intended, his liability was discharged within the week ...

Discounts

Most people who have shopped for goods at some time have been given a 'discount' - in the form of reduced prices - by their vendors. This is a common usage of the word 'discount' but this, and other popular usages of the term, are not necessarily the type of discount taxable under Schedule D Case III. As Rowlatt J said in *Brown v National Provident Institution*[33]:

[I]t is clear that it is not every difference in amount between a sum payable in future of the same sum represented by cash down which is an annual profit or gain by way of discount even though popularly the word 'discount' may be used to describe it ... [T]he difference between the cash and the credit prices of an article bought is commonly described as discount for ready money allowed by the seller but it is not taxable as income under case 3.

For the purposes of Schedule D Case III, Fox LJ in *Ditchfield v Sharp*[34] referred with approval to the dictionary definition of 'discount' as: '[A] deduction ... made for payment before it is due, of a bill of account ... the

32   56 TC at 581.
33   [1919] 2 KB 497 at 506.
34   [1983] STC 590 at 593.

deduction made from the amount of a bill of exchange or promissory note by one who gives value for it before it is due.'

The receiver of the bill is the one who gives the discount. According to Lord Sumner in *Brown v National Provident Institution*[35] there are two economic elements present in discounts 'one the value of the usufruct forgone, as measured by interim interest, and the other the risk that the money will never be repaid at all'.

One of the most common forms of discount is Government Treasury Bills, where the public purchase Bills for less than the redemption value (in effect lending the government money for a period) and redeem the Bill on maturity for its redemption value. What is taxed is the difference between what was given for the Bill and what was finally received on the Bill's maturity.

In cases of loans, since there is no general rule that any sum which a lender receives over and above the amount which he lends ought to be treated as income,[36] the question often arises whether an amount received by a lender in excess of the loan represents a discount, or a premium, ie, a sum payable on the return of money lent, in excess of the loan, but which is not interest because it is not paid by reference to time (eg, a fixed sum of £500 payable on any loan above £25,000)[37].

In *Lomax v Peter Dixon*[38], it was held that where no interest is payable as such, the transaction will normally, if not always, be a discount (this will also apply where the interest is inadequate).[39] Where a proper rate of interest is charged, the extra sum demanded in addition will be a premium. The point was made in this case that the true nature of the 'discount' or the premium, as the case may be, is to be ascertained from all the circumstances of the case and that, apart from any matter of law which may bear upon the question (such as the interpretation of the contract), the question will fall to be determined as a matter of fact by Commissioners. Lord Greene MR identified the matters which ought to be considered in deciding the true nature of the 'discount' or premium (in so far as it is not conclusively determined by the contract). First, the terms of the loan and the rate of interest expressly stipulated for it, and, secondly, the nature of the capital risk and the extent to which, if at all, the parties expressly took or may reasonably be supposed to have taken the capital risk into account in fixing the terms of the contract.[40]

---

[35]   (1921) 8 TC 57 at 96.
[36]   Per Lord Greene MR in *Lomax v Peter Dixon* (1943) 25 TC 353 at 363.
[37]   (1943) 25 TC 353.
[38]   Premiums are normally capital in nature.
[39]   See Lord Greene MR at 367.
[40]   Ibid.

Annuities and Other Annual Payments

The term 'annuity' generally refers to income which is payable year-by-year. It was more particularly described by Watson B in *Foley v Fletcher*[41] when he said that an annuity exists 'where an income is purchased with a sum of money, and the capital has gone and has ceased to exist, the principal having been converted into an annuity'. A similar idea was expressed by Matthew LJ in *Secretary of State for India v Scoble* when he said[42]:

> 'Annuity,' in the ordinary sense of the expression, means the purchase of an income. It generally involves the conversion of capital into income, and, reasonably enough, where the buyer places himself in that position, the Act of Parliament taxes him; he is taken at his word, he has got an income secured in the way I have mentioned.

These statements obviously refer to one common kind of annuity - purchased annuities. It should however be noted that not all annuities are purchased (eg, annuities under a will or trust). These do not cease to be annuities simply because they are not purchased.

A number of points need to be noted at this stage of the discussion. First, the precise boundary between annuities and what is described in the statute as 'other annual payments' is yet to be fixed, but this of itself is of no serious consequence as similar principles apply to both types of payment. Secondly, the category of what constitutes an 'other annual payment' is 'quite a limited one'.[43] Thirdly, neither the Taxes Act nor the courts have attempted to define the term 'other annual payment', for the simple reason that, 'apart from some broad principles', a precise definition is not possible.[44] Hence we must examine the characteristics which a payment must have in order to fall into this category.

Characteristics of 'Annual Payments'

The characteristics of an annual payment were listed by Jenkins LJ in *IRC v Whitworth Park Coal Co. Ltd.*[45]

---

[41]   (1858) 157 E.R. 678 at 684
[42]   (1903) 4 TC 618 at 622.
[43]   Sir Wilfred Greene MR in *Re Hanbury (deceased); Comiskey v Hanbury* (1939) 38 TC 588 at 590; compare Lord Radcliffe in *Whitworth Park Coal Co. v IRC* [1959] 3 All ER 703 at 715.
[44]   Lord Upjohn in *Campbell V IRC* [1968] 3 All ER at 602.
[45]   [1958] 2 All ER 91 at 102-104.

The *Ejusdem Generis* Rule Applies

Not all recurrent payments are annual payments for the purposes of Schedule D Case III. For a payment to qualify as an annual payment, it must be *ejusdem generis* with (ie, of the same type as) the specific instances given in the shape of interest of money and annuities.[46] Most of the other characteristics to be discussed are actually reflections of this requirement.

A Binding Obligation is Required

Voluntary payments cannot be annual payments. At best, they will be gifts. In order to be an annual payment, a payment must fall to be made under a legally enforceable obligation, as distinct from mere voluntary payments.[47]The essence of annual payments is that the payer is thereby alienating a slice of his income. According to Lord Upjohn in *Campbell v IRC*, 'the payer is regarded as having parted with that part of his income which ... he pays away. The income that he pays away is that of the payee'.[48]

Thus, if the payments are not made under a binding legal obligation, the payer can hardly be said to have alienated or 'parted with' any part of his income. The income is still his, to do with it as he likes, and if he chooses to give it away to someone else on a periodical basis, that is entirely a matter for him. Thus for example, dividends paid by a company are not annual payments since there is no obligation to pay them and their distribution depends in every instance upon a declaration by the company.[49]

For the purposes of the required obligation, a will, a contract, or a deed of covenant will suffice. Furthermore, according to Jenkins LJ, the fact that the obligation to pay is imposed by an order of court and does not arise by virtue of a contract does not exclude the payment from Case III. Thus a court order will also suffice.

Recurrence

Like interest and annuities, the payment must possess the essential quality of recurrence implied by the description 'annual'[50]. In this respect, the word 'annual' does not admit of any significant interpretation.[51]To the courts, it simply means 'recurrent' - a necessary but inconclusive factor.

In other words, 'annual' means that the payment must be 'of a recurring character'.[52] This requirement has been given a broad interpretation in the authorities. Thus Warrington LJ said in *Smith v Smith*[53] that the fact that a

---

[46]   Jenkins LJ, referring to Hamilton J in Hill v Gregory (1912) 6 TC 39 at 47; see also Watson B in Foley v Fletcher (1858) 157 E.R. at 685; Scrutton LJ in Howe v IRC, (1919) 7 TC 289 at 303.
[47]   Jenkins LJ, referring to Lord Sterndale MR in Smith v Smith [1923] P. 191 at 197.
[48]   [1968] 3 All ER at 603.0   [1990] STC 55 at 62.
[49]   Per Viscount Simon, LC in *Canadian Eagle Oil Co Ltd v R* [1945] 2 All ER 499 at 504.
[50]   See Lord Maugham in *Moss Empires Ltd v IRC* [1937] 3 All ER 381 at 386.
[51]   Lord Radcliffe in *Whitworth Park Coal Co v IRC* [1959] 3 All ER 703 at 715
[52]   Viscount Simonds in *Whitworth Park Coal Co v IRC* [1959] 3 All ER 703 at 712.
[53]   [1923] P. 191 at 201.Gri2es'. Iservices (per Megarry J in Pritchard v Arundale (1972) 47 TC 680 at 686). Megarry J clearly and correctly emphasised that there does not exist a range of categories :

payment is to be made weekly does not prevent it from being annual, provided that the weekly payments may continue beyond the year.[54]

Furthermore, according to Lord Macmillan in *Moss Empires Ltd v IRC*[55]the fact that payments are contingent and variable in amount does not affect the character of the payments as annual payments. Therefore the element of recurrence is satisfied if the payment is capable of being recurrent[56], even if it never recurs in fact.[57]

In *Moss Empires*, the taxpayer company, by agreement, undertook to another company, to make available to that company a sufficient sum to enable it to pay, for each of the next five years, a fixed rate of dividends less income tax at the current rate, if its profits fell below a certain level. In each of the five years covered by the agreement, the taxpayers were called upon to make payments under their obligation. The payments thus made by the taxpayer varied significantly from year-to-year. It was argued for the taxpayers that the payments were not annual payments because they were casual, independent, not necessarily recurrent, and throughout subject to a contingency. While this argument had commended itself to Lord Moncrieff (dissenting) in the Court of Session, the House of Lords did not accept it. Lord Macmillan said[58] that there was a continuing obligation, extending over each and all of the five years, to make the payments. Thus the payments were still annual payments even though they were contingent and variable.

Pure Income Profit

It is necessary for the payments to be pure income profit in the hands of the recipient. Viscount Simonds said in *Whitworth Park Coal Co v IRC*[59] that this requirement exists because no deductions are permitted under Case III. Lord Radcliffe explained in *Whitworth Park Coal Co v IRC*[60], that it is inconsistent with the scheme of deduction of source that Case III of Schedule D should contain payments that are gross in the hands of the recipient and which are not his pure income. Lord Upjohn further explained in *Campbell v IRC*[61] that it is well settled that tax cannot be deducted by the payer in respect of payments which in the hands of the recipients are gross receipts for advice or services or goods supplied which merely form an element in discovering what the profits of the recipients are. The sum of these statements seems to be that, in order for a payment to be an annual payment for the purposes of Case III, it must be of such a nature that it is taxable in its entirety in the hands of the recipient.

54   Compare Lord Sterndale MR (at 196) - an obligation which cannot exceed twelve months cannot create an annual payment.
55   [1937] 3 All ER 381 at 385.
56   Lord Maugham in *Moss Empires* ([1937] 3 All ER, at 386).
57   See Lord Greene MR in *Asher v London Film Productions Ltd.* [1944] KB 133 at 140 - 'You can have an annual payment ... even though it happens by some accident or other to fall due in one year only. The question is, has it the necessary periodical or recurrent quality?'.
58   [1937] 3 All ER at 385.
59   [1959] 3 All ER 703 at 712
60   [1959] 3 All ER at 715.
61   [1968] 3 All ER at 602.[1968] 3 All ER at 602.

It is obvious that there are some 'annual' payments which, by their very nature and quality, cannot possibly be treated as the pure profit income of the recipient (the proper response to them being to treat them as an element to be taken into account in discovering what the profits of the recipient are), or, which themselves contain payments of such nature. Such payments will not fall within Case III.[62]

This then raises questions as to the proper distinction between those 'annual payments' which are the pure income profit of the recipient, and those which are not. Lord Donovan provided an answer in *Campbell v IRC*[63]:

> One must determine, in the light of all the relevant facts, whether the payment is a taxable receipt in the hands of the recipient without any deduction for expense or the like. Whether it is, in other words, 'pure income' or 'pure profit income' in his hands, as these expressions have been used in the decided cases. If so it will be an annual payment under Case III. If, on the other hand, it is simply gross revenue in the recipient's hands, out of which a taxable income will emerge only after his outgoings have been deducted, then the payment is not such an annual payment.

This test shows for example that a trading receipt will not be an annual payment. The point is illustrated by *Howe v IRC*[64]. The taxpayer had paid the premiums due in respect of his life insurance policies by the means of payments made under a deed of covenant to pay the same. He claimed to deduct the premiums so paid in computing his total income for super tax purposes, on the grounds that they were annual payments. It was held that such deduction was not allowable. Warrington LJ pointed out[65] that although the payments would go to swell the profits and gains arising or accruing to the insurance company on which income tax is chargeable, the tax is not charged on the premiums themselves. Thus, it was clear that the payments were not pure income in the hands of the insurance company, since they would only be trading receipts, to be taxed in its hands only after deducting allowable expenditure. And, according to Scrutton LJ[66]:

> It is not all payments made every year from which income tax can be deducted. For instance, if a man agrees to pay a motor garage £500 a year for five years for the hire of and upkeep of a car, no one suggests that the person paying can deduct income tax from each yearly payment. So also, if he contracted with a butcher for an annual

62   n See generally, Sir Wilfred Greene MR in *re Hanbury (deceased)*; *Comiskey v Hanbury* (1939) 38 TC 588 at 590.
63   [1968] 3 All ER 588 at 606.
64   (1919) 7 TC 289.
65   At 300.
66   At 303.

sum to supply all his meat for a year. The annual instalment would not be subject to tax as a whole in the hands of the payee, but only that part of it which was profits.

For the same reason that trading receipts cannot be annual payments within Case III (the need to deduct expenses before arriving at a profit figure) receipts of an individual's profession will not be annual payments. In *Jones v Wright*[67] the taxpayer was a solicitor, who as trustee of certain trusts was entitled under relevant charging clauses to be paid all the usual professional and other charges for any business done for the trusts. He subsequently arranged with his fellow trustees and with the beneficiaries to retain a percentage of the trust income *per annum*, as an alternative to charging the usual professional fees. The question was whether these retained profits were annual payments, or whether they were receipts of the taxpayer's profession chargeable under Schedule D Case II. Rowlatt J held that they were receipts of the tax payer's profession. Referring to *Howe v IRC*, Rowlatt J said[68] that, for a payment out of profits or gains to fall within the principles of Case III, it had to have been paid 'by way of a division of profits' (ie, a payment whereby the payer was alienating a slice of his or her profits, the 'divided' part of those profits then becoming the income of the recipient)[69]. According to Rowlatt J, if the relevant payment

> is a payment by way of a spending of profits, as in the case put by Lord Justice Scrutton, of a lump sum per annum, say for the use of a motor garage, or something of that sort, it is not division of those profits, but it is a spending which creates a new profit, which is taxable in the hands of the recipient.

The implication is that a payment which is a division of profits is pure profit in the hands of the recipient and will fall within Case III (not being receipts of the profession). On the other hand, a payment which is not a division of an existing profit but is rather the spending of that profit in return for goods or services (the owner's prerogative), results in a new profit being created. That new profit would have had a cost borne by the recipient, in respect of which the recipient might be entitled to a deduction or allowance, before arriving at a taxable figure. This therefore could not be an annual payment since it is not, in its entirety, a profit.

The principle with respect to trading and professional receipts is clear

---

[67]   (1927) 13 TC 221.
[68]   13 TC at 226.
[69]   It does not seem that the 'division of profits' principle is seeking to create a new criterion for annual payments. Rather, it seems to be linked with the concept of 'pure income profit'.

enough. What is not so straightforward is the response to the proposition that, when a payment is made subject to a counter-stipulation, or in return for consideration, or is not 'pure bounty', then it is not pure profit in the hands of the person who is subject to the counter-stipulation or who has to give the consideration. This proposition apparently has some support in the cases. One of the cases often referred to in support of the proposition is *IRC v National Book League*.[70]

The League was a charitable company limited by guarantee, which had the object of promoting and encouraging by all suitable means the habit of reading and the wider distribution of books. It provided certain facilities to its members, including a reading room, a drawing room, and a licensed bar and restaurant. It proposed to increase the subscriptions paid by members from a certain date, but invited members renewing their subscriptions to enter into deeds of covenant with the league 'to remain members and to pay their annual subscription at the existing rates for at least seven years'. The advantage of such a covenant to members was that they would escape any increases in subscription rates during the seven years. About 2,800 members entered into the covenants. The League claimed to recover tax on the gross sums named in the deeds, on the basis that the sums were annual payments. The Court of Appeal rejected the claim. In deciding whether the covenanted payments were, in these circumstances, pure income profit in the League's hands, Lord Evershed MR said[71] that the question was, 'looking at the substance and reality of the matter can it be said that those who entered into these covenants have paid the sums covenanted without conditions or counter stipulations'? He answered this question in the negative. In this case, there was 'in a real sense', a condition or counter-stipulation on the part of the league against which the covenant was entered into. It therefore followed that the payments under the covenants were not pure income profit. Morris LJ, concurring, proffered the following analysis of the issue[72]:

> The question arises whether the payments can be said to be pure gifts to the charity. In the terms of a phrase which has been used, can the payments be said to be pure income profit in the hands of the charity? If the payments were made in such circumstances that the League was obliged to afford to the covenantors such amenities and such benefits of membership as would at any particular time be offered to all members, and if those amenities and benefits were

---

[70]   [1957] 2 All ER 644.
[71]   [1957] 2 All ER 644 at 650.
[72]   At 652.

appreciable and not negligible, then I do not think that the payments were pure income profit in the hands of the charity.

While this case is often referred to as laying down a rule that anything given in return for the payments would be fatal to their being annual payments, it should be noted that this case may not have been trying to lay down such a general principle at all. Morris LJ in the statement above seemed to imply that a payment could still be a 'pure gift' if the benefit given in return was not 'appreciable' or if it was 'negligible'. Lord Evershed MR[73] specifically disclaimed laying down any general principle that, 'whenever a covenantor in favour of a charity is allowed certain privileges, it therefore follows that he can no longer say that he has paid without conditions or counter stipulations.' The proper test, according to him, is whether in all the circumstances, and looking at 'the substance and reality of the matter', the covenantor can be treated as being a 'donor of the covenanted sums' to the charity.

It is noteworthy also that Lord Evershed MR did indicate that the question 'whether particular advantages or promises can be dismissed on the principle of *de minimis non curat lex*' was relevant.[74] This particular question is a question of law. Although Morris LJ seemed to focus on the facilities offered by the League to its members in general, Lord Evershed MR seemed to be more concerned with the peculiar advantages enjoyed by those who paid their subscriptions by way of the covenant, rather than by any other means. He pointed out[75] that, first, they would be able to continue to be members at the lower subscription rates, and they had a promise or assurance that, whatever may happen to other persons' subscription rates, their own rates would not be raised for seven years. Secondly, they would have the advantage that, while paying the lower, pre-existing rates, they would still continue to enjoy, like other members who paid the higher rates, the full range of club amenities. Given these factors, it is easy to see why it was decided that the covenanted subscriptions were not pure income profit (or 'pure gifts') in the hands of the League.

Another case applying the 'counter-stipulation' principle is *Taw and Torridge Festival Society Ltd v IRC*.[76] Like *IRC v National Book League*, this case involved a company limited by guarantee, established for charitable purposes. Its main object was the management of the North Devon Festival of the Arts. The society had received payments under deeds of covenant, offering seats at reduced rates for all concerts, recitals, ballets and plays, as

[73]   at 650.
[74]   at 651.
[75]   ibid.
[76]   (1959) 38 TC 603.

a privilege to the covenantors. The Commissioners held that the sums were not annual payments. On appeal to the High Court, Wynn-Parry J said[77], following *IRC v National Book League*, that the question was whether the payments 'are properly to be regarded as annual payments within the Income Tax Acts or whether, upon the true view, they have been made subject to conditions and counter-stipulations, in which case they would be robbed of the character of being annual payments.' He felt that the case fell squarely within the *IRC v National Book League* decision, and he was, on the facts of this case, unable to apply the *de minimis* rule to ignore the counter stipulation.[69]

According to him, while the offer of one seat at a reduced rate for every concert, recital or ballet or play may at first appear insubstantial, Morris LJ had indicated in *IRC v National Book League* that what he had to consider was the benefit to members. In considering this, he would then find that 'an enthusiastic member choosing to attend the ballets and plays over a year' would be able to obtain a rebate amounting to about 25 per cent of the covenanted subscription. Thus, while he had 'a very great sympathy' with the society, he could not apply the *de minimis* rule. Wynn-Parry J agreed that the *de minimis* issue was a question of law, but added that, in applying it, one must use common sense. This indicated that he could not shut his eyes to the circumstance that experienced Special Commissioners, in considering this very question, had come to the same view[79]. In the event, the payments under the covenants were not pure income profit.

A more recent example is *Essex County Council v Ellam*.[80] The council arranged for S's son to attend a special school. The school normally looked to local authorities to pay the fees of any child on the usual termly basis, leaving it to the authorities to make any appropriate arrangements for the child's parents to reimburse or contribute to the fees for the child's terms. S then signed an agreement to reimburse the council any amount paid in respect of the fees of his son. Later S executed a deed of covenant to make payments to the council in respect of the said fees. A claim that the payments under the covenant were pure income profit was rejected. Dillon LJ said[81] that it was impossible to regard the payments by S under the deed as pure income of the council without regard to the obligation which the council undertook to pay the fees of S's son. One goes to cancel the other. He said however[82] that the payments would clearly have been the pure income of the council if they had not been earmarked as they were for the particular purpose for which they were earmarked.

---

[77]   At 608.
[78]   At 609.
[79]   Ibid.
[80]   [1989] STC 317.
[81]   At 322.
[82]   At 325.

In spite of cases like this however, it can be regarded as established that the question whether or not there existed some counter-stipulation or whether consideration was given, is not decisive. This point was made quite clearly in *Campbell v IRC* where the House of Lords disapproved of certain statements of Lord Greene MR in *IRC v National Book League* (above). Viscount Dilhorne described as wrong any notion that any sum paid subject to a condition or counter-stipulation will not qualify as an annual payment within Case III[83] while Lord Guest said that this would be a construction of 'annual payments' which was too narrow and for which there was 'no ground or reason or authority.'[84]

Viscount Dilhorne was of the opinion that the decision in *IRC v National Book League* could not be justified on the ground that there was a condition or counter-stipulation that, during the period of the covenants, the covenantors would be exempt from any increase of subscription.[85] He pointed out that the charge under Case III itself[86] indicated that the amounts charged may be payable as an 'obligation by virtue of any contract'.[87]

Thus, if an annual payment payable by virtue of a contract comes within the relevant statutory provisions, it must follow that the fact that there is consideration for the promise to pay, whether or not in the form of a condition or counter-stipulation, does not necessarily exclude the annual payments from the scope of Case III.[88]

Lord Hodson took the view that the decision in *IRC v National Book League* could be supported on the broad grounds that the payments in that case were in the nature of annual subscriptions to a club.[89] He however said that Lord Evershed MR, in taking the point about 'conditions and counter stipulations', used language which went too far. He rejected the Crown's argument that payments are disqualified unless they are made as 'pure bounty'.[90]

With regard to what might be considered the correct test, Lord Donovan said that[91]:

> [O]ne cannot resolve the problem whether a payment is an annual payment within Case III simply by asking the questions 'Must the payee give or do something in return?' or 'Did the payer make some counter stipulation or receive some counter benefit?'; or 'Was it pure bounty on his part?'

83   [1968] 3 All ER at 593.
84   Ibid, at 600.
85   Ibid, at 594.
86   See ICTA 1988, s.18(3).
87   Lord Donovan said that the statements about counter stipulations contradict the charging words of Case III of Sch. D itself which envisage that an annual payment may be payable 'by virtue of any contract' and that, therefore, the recipient may have to give or do something in return for the payment, which will not in such circumstances be 'pure bounty' in his hands.
88   [1968] 3 All ER at 594.
89   At 599.
90   Ibid; compare Lord Upjohn at 602.
91   [1968] 3 All ER 588 at 606.

The question is not whether there was a counter-stipulation in respect of a payment but simply whether any sum can be claimed as an expense of earning the payment. Viscount Dilhorne explainer further[92]:

> [T]he fact that there is consideration for the promise to pay, whether or not in the form of a condition or counter-stipulation, does not necessarily exclude the annual payment from the scope of [Case III]. If however, the consideration or counter-stipulation relates to the provision of goods or services and so deprives the payments of the character of 'pure income profit', it will have that effect.

Thus, the real question (although there may be exceptions) is whether the payment is being made in return for goods and services.[93] The test makes it necessary to decide each case on its own facts[94].

Apart from the *dicta* in *Campbell v IRC*, the proposition that the presence of consideration or counter-stipulations is not necessarily fatal to a payment being pure income also has support in direct decisions. In *Delage v Nugget Polish Co Ltd*[95] the defendants became entitled, by virtue of an agreement with the plaintiffs, to use a trade secret for the making of 'blacking'. This was to be in return for payments, for a period of 40 years, of an annual sum of money calculated as a percentage of the gross receipts on the sale of the said blacking, and brown polish. It was held that the payments under the agreement were annual payments.[96]

Furthermore, annuitants under purchased annuity schemes do give consideration (cash) for the annuities that they receive, but these are still within Case III. Nevertheless, the effect of a counter-stipulation or the provision of consideration cannot always be predicted with certainty. This creates problems for bodies which need to attract funding by donations/deeds of covenant, and which may need to provide some incentive (in the form of benefits) to attract such funds. In this respect statute has now stepped in to assist certain charities in this situation. If the sole or main purpose of a charity is the preservation of property, or the conservation of wildlife, for the public benefit, such a charity is permitted by Section 59 FA 1989 to provide consideration (in the form of viewing rights) to persons from whom it receives annual payments.

In addition to the aforementioned characteristics of annual payments outlined by Jenkins LJ in *IRC v Whitworth Park Coal Co Ltd* two other factors emerge from the cases.

---

[92]   at 594.
[93]   Lord Donovan, at 605, and 607.
[94]   Lord Donovan at 607.
[95]   (1905) 92 LT 682.
[96]   See also *Asher v London Film Productions Ltd.* [1944] KB 133.

The payment must 'have the character of income in the hands of the recipient'. What this means is that the payment must be of an income (and not capital) nature.[97] This is clear from the requirement that payments have to be the recipient's pure 'income' profit. This requirement formed one of the grounds of the decision in *Campbell v IRC* itself. Here, a charitable trust which had been established for the purpose of acquiring a business, received sums under a deed of covenant from the company ('Tutors') which owned the business. The payments under the covenant were subject to an understanding (held by the courts to involve a legally enforceable obligation) that the trustees would use the sums received under the covenant for the purpose of purchasing Tutors' business. The payments under the covenant were held not to be annual payments. Viscount Dilhorne said[98] that the payments had not the quality and nature of income in the hands of the trustees and Lord Hodson said that the payments were 'instalments of capital'[99] but it was Lord Donovan's analysis that was most illuminating. According to him[100]:

> The covenant itself is simply to pay an annual sum to the trustees, the amount of which is measured by Tutors' profits. Familiarity with deeds of covenant of this sort fosters an initial assumption, perhaps, that what is being provided is an annual income; but if Tutors had specifically desired to provide the trustees with a capital sum payable by seven yearly instalments the deed of covenant as drafted would have served that purpose equally well ... Tutors wanted the trustees to buy Tutors' business and to do so with money which Tutors would themselves provide. They came to a clear understanding with the trustees that the trustees would use the money so provided for this purpose and for no other; and I agree with your Lordships that in the circumstances of this case the understanding would have been enforceable in contract. One therefore has a case where a person wishing to sell an asset provides the prospective purchaser with the purchase price. That seems to me as clear a case of a gift of capital as one could want.

Thus, in spite of the recurrent nature of the payments, and in spite of the method whereby they were calculated (measured by profits) the payments, being linked by an obligation to purchase assets, had the character of capital in the hands of the recipient. The House of Lords was not in this case

---

[97]   Per Viscount Dilhorne in *Campbell v IRC* [1968] 3 All ER 588 at 592; compare Warrington LJ in *Howe v IRC*, 7 TC at 300.

[98]   At 595.

[99]   At 598.

[100]   At 604-605.

attempting to lay down any general principle that payments applied to the purchase of assets are necessarily therefore capital payments. Lord Donovan himself expressly disclaimed any such notion[101] and Lord Upjohn[102] was careful to avoid laying down any general principle. However, in spite of these disclaimers, it can be taken as established that where recurrent payments clearly represent instalments of the purchase price of a capital asset they will be capital instalments and not annual payments.[103]

This is illustrated by *IRC v Ramsay*.[104] The taxpayer agreed to buy a dental practice for £15,000, of which £5000 was to be paid at once, the balance being paid by ten yearly instalments of a sum equal to 25 per cent of the net profits of the practice for each year. If the amounts so paid over during the ten years were, in the aggregate, more or less than the balance of the primary purchase price, that price was to be treated as correspondingly increased or diminished. No interest was payable on any outstanding balance. The taxpayer claimed that the practice was sold, not for a fixed capital sum, but for a down payment and further annual sums of the nature of income payments. He argued that the description given to such payments in the agreement was immaterial, and therefore claimed to deduct the instalments in computing his income for surtax purposes. It was held that the instalments were capital payments, and not annual payments, and therefore the deductions sought were not permissible. According to Lord Wright MR[105]:

> [T]his is not the case of an annuity, or a series of annual payments. It is a case in which a capital lump sum has been stipulated as the price of a piece of property, and it is none the less so because the payment of that sum is to be made by instalments, instalments at certain specific periods, no doubt, but not instalments of a fixed price. It is none the less, in my judgment, a capital sum because in the working out of the transaction, and in the discharge of that capital sum, the Vendor according to the terms of the agreement may have to be content with a lesser amount than the £15,000. The £15,000 is not an otiose figure; it is a figure which permeates the whole of the contract, and upon which the whole contract depends. That being so, I think that the [instalment] in question was a sum in the nature of capital ...

This case highlights some of the problems of determining whether periodic

---

[101]   At 605.
[102]   At 603
[103]   See for example Channell B in *Foley v Fletcher* - 'I am of opinion that the words ... annual payments do not include those payments which are in respect of the purchase money of an estate, and are in the nature of capital and not of income.' (1858) 157 E.R. at 686.
[104]   (1935) 20 TC 79.
[105]   20 TC at 98.

payments linked to disposals of property are capital or income. The arguments proceeded on an 'all or nothing' basis - ie, either the whole of the relevant instalment was an annual payment (income), or the whole of it was an instalment of the purchase price of an asset (capital). This wholistic approach to the question is bound to lead to difficulties in some situations. Happily, it is not a universal principle and can give way when necessary. Thus, if a payment is part income and part capital it can be dissected for income tax purposes. Authority for this proposition can be found in *Secretary of State for India v Scoble*.[106]

In this case, the East India Company contracted with the Great India Peninsular Railway Company to purchase the railway and works. The agreement gave the East India Company the option, instead of paying the purchase price by a lump sum, to pay by 'an annuity to be reckoned' from a certain date. In such a case, the rate of interest which was to be used for calculating the 'annuity' was prescribed. The British Government, which succeeded to the obligations of the East India Company, gave notice to exercise the option of paying an annuity. The Secretary of State deducted income tax from the first two instalments, and the plaintiffs, as the annuity trustees, brought an action to recover the tax deducted from so much of the payments as represented capital. Phillimore J decided in favour of the Secretary of State. The Court of Appeal (in a judgment which was upheld by the House of Lords) reversed that judgment. It was held that the payments under the contract were not pure 'annuities', but contained a capital element - *viz*, part of the purchase price of the railway and works. It was common ground that the parts of the payments which represented interest were taxable. The real question in the case, according to Vaughan Williams LJ[107] was: 'is Income Tax payable upon that portion of the annual payment which you can discover from the very terms of the contract is a mere payment of an instalment necessary to complete the payment of an existing debt?' The question was answered in the negative. Stirling LJ[108], referring with approval to the judgment of the Divisional Court in *Nizam Guaranteed Stock Railway Company v Wyatt*[109] said that the mere fact that a sum is designated as an annuity is not conclusive, but that 'the real nature of the transaction' must be looked at. According to him, the real nature of the transaction in this case was that the so called 'annuities' were simply annual payments of equal amount, being instalments of a debt, and were made up partly of principal, partly of interest.[110] Following *Foley v Fletcher*[111] , the word 'annuity,' under these circumstances, is not to be read in such a way as to make capital taxable.

[106]   4 TC 618 at 619.
[107]   At 621.
[108]   (1890) 2 TC 584.
[1090]   4 TC at 621.
[110]   157 E.R. 678.
[111]   [1903] AC 299; 4 TC 618.

The Secretary of State had argued against this type of dissection on the grounds that, if that dissection was to be permitted in this type of case, then in the case of every terminable annuity which has been purchased for value, each annual payment of that annuity would have to be dissected into capital and interest and only the portion which represents interest ought to be taxed. Stirling LJ in response to this argument said[112]:

> Those are cases of purchase of annuities, where investment has been made in that form of property, and the legislature in so many words has said that that is to be taxed; and it is recognised in this very case throughout that an annuity of that kind is taxable. And I in no way depart from that. ... it is a different matter where it appears, on the face of the transaction, that the so-called annuity is not a thing of that kind, but simply represents instalments of an existing debt. It matters not, it appears to me, whether the debt be one which is a purchase arising from a sale, or be in the case of the repayment of a loan.

So two main principles come out of *Secretary of State for India v Scoble*. First, the terminology employed by the parties is not conclusive (rather, the court has to examine the real nature of the transaction), and, secondly, a payment which, when properly analysed, partly represents income and partly represents capital will be dissected for income tax purposes. Both issues came up again in *Vestey v IRC*.[113]

Here, a block of shares were estimated by accountants to be worth £2 million. This price assumed an immediate payment in full by the purchaser. However, the parties were contemplating a sale of the shares on the term that the taxpayer should receive an annual sum over a long period of years. In this wise, the accountants considered that, in respect of this 'unusual arrangement', allowance must be made for 'the interest factor'. Assuming a net interest rate of two per cent, it was recommended that the shares be sold in return for 'an annual payment of £44,000 extending over 125 years'. Consequently, the shares were sold 'in consideration of the sum of £5.5 millions payable by instalments of £44,000 per annum over 125 years'. The sale was expressed to be 'without interest'.

The Revenue claimed that, since the payments of £44,000 were annuities, they were taxable as the taxpayer's income. The taxpayer on the other hand contended that the payments were capital sums, being instalments of the price payable for the shares. The Special Commissioners held that the

[112]   4 TC at 622
[113]   [1961] 3 All ER 978.

payments of £44,000 (other than the first) contained an interest element which was taxable. The taxpayer appealed, and the Revenue cross-appealed. Cross J, after reviewing the existing case law, including *Secretary of State for India v Scoble*, held that the amounts of the instalments should be dissected into capital and interest. Reiterating that the use of terminology by the parties is inconclusive, he said that 'if the Crown cannot say that there is any magic in the use of the word "annuity", why should the taxpayer be able to say that there is any magic in the use of the words "purchase price"?'.[114] Cross J was of the opinion in this case that the authorities on the point were in 'a somewhat confused state'.[115]

However, *Secretary of State for India v Scoble* seemed to have been clear enough, so where did the confusion lie? The apparent confusion lay in *dicta*. In *Foley v Fletcher*[116], Pollock CB had said that 'if the plaintiff had sold her estate for an annuity, so calling it, the annuity would have been liable to Income Tax. But she sold it for a sum which is payable by instalments, which, is therefore, not chargeable.' There is nothing wrong with the second part of the statement. However, the first part might have been problematic if it had not been disregarded by the Court of Appeal in *Secretary of State for India v Scoble*. If that part of the the statement was purporting to state that the label attached to the transactions by the parties is conclusive, then it is clear that such a view can no longer be sustained.

More troublesome are *dicta* from the Court of Appeal in more recent cases. First, a statement in the judgment of Romer LJ in *IRC v Ramsay*[117]:

> If a man had some property which he wishes to sell on terms which will result in his receiving for the next twenty years an annual sum of £500, he can do it in either of two methods. He can either sell his property in consideration of a payment by the purchaser to him of an annuity of £500 for the next twenty years, or he can sell his property to the purchaser for £10,000, the £10,000 to be paid by equal instalments of £500 over the next twenty years. If he adopts the former of thetwo methods, then the sums of £500 received by him each year are exigible to Income Tax. If he adopts the second method, then the sums of £500 received by him in each year are not liable to Income Tax, and they do not become liable to Income Tax by it being said that in substance the transaction is the same as though he had sold for an annuity. The vendor has the power of choosing which of the two methods he will adopt, and he can adopt the second method if he thinks fit, for the purpose of avoiding having to pay

114   [1961] 3 All ER 978 at 986.
115   At 982
116   157 E.R. 678.
117   20 TC at 98.

Income Tax on the £500 a year. The question which method has been adopted must be a question of the proper construction to be placed upon the documents by which the transaction is carried out.

Secondly, a statement in the judgment of Lord Greene MR in *IRC v Wesleyan and General Assurance Society*[118]:

> In dealing with Income Tax questions it frequently happens that there are two methods at least of achieving a particular financial result. If one of those methods is adopted, tax will be payable. If the other method is adopted, tax will not be payable. It is sufficient to refer to the quite common case where property is sold for a lump sum payable by instalments. If a piece of property is sold for £1,000 and the purchase price is to be paid in ten instalments of £100 each, no tax is payable. If, on the other hand, the property is sold in consideration of an annuity of £100 a year for ten years, tax is payable. The net result from the financial point of view is precisely the same in each case, but one method of achieving it attracts tax and the other method does not.

As indicated earlier, Cross J in *Vestey v IRC* took the view that the authorities were in a confused state. According to him[119], if Romer LJ was right in *IRC v Ramsay*, it would follow that the whole of the £5.5 million of the *Vestey v IRC* transaction could properly be regarded as the purchase price of the shares. With respect to Cross J, that conclusion does not follow at all. Romer LJ's statement can be seen as dealing only with a situation where there was clearly no element of interest in the instalments of £500. If the facts establish that the parties contemplated a real element of interest (as they quite clearly did not in *IRC v Ramsay*, but they quite clearly did in *Vestey v IRC*), the court would have to accept that as evidence of the real intention of the parties. It is arguable that the statement of Romer LJ does not deal with this type of situation at all, and that therefore it is correct in what it purports to deal with. Cross J said in *Vestey v IRC*[120] that the £10,000 in Romer LJ's example must clearly have been far more than the value of the property at the date of the supposed sale, and that if it had been worth £10,000, the annuity would have been far more than £500 a year. With respect, this seems to be nothing more than conjecture and there is nothing to indicate that this will be the case (other than an assumption that people will always desire to receive interest on instalmental payments). Modern commerce (eg, the 'zero per

---

[118]   [1946] 2 All ER 749 at 751.
[119]   [1961] 3 All ER at 985.
[120]   Ibid.

cent interest for two years' often offered by dealers in furniture and other household goods) proves that such an assumption is often false, even in the context of pure commercial transactions. In short, if the statement of Romer LJ is restricted to its proper context, there is nothing wrong with it or confusing about it. Viewed in any other context, it is merely *obiter* and can admit of exceptions.

Much the same can be said of the statement of Lord Greene MR in *IRC v Wesleyan and General Assurance Society*. It is clear that this statement was also *obiter*, and was made in a different context. The context was that of a discussion of the doctrine of 'form and substance' in which the court was invited to convert, by judicial construction, transactions which were actually loans, into payments of an annuity, so that the Revenue could charge tax on the payments. This invitation was rejected by Lord Greene MR[121] on the basis that this was not the function of the court, especially since the principle of the 'substance of the transaction' had been 'exploded' in *IRC v Duke of Westminster.*[122] Thus, again, the statement under discussion seems to be correct when viewed in its proper context, and again, it clearly can admit of exceptions.

In sum, the state of the authorities seems to be that the courts will examine the true nature of the parties' transactions to determine whether periodical payments connected to a sale of an asset are really payments of instalments of the purchase price (in which case they are capital and not liable to tax under Case III); or whether there really has been a purchase of an annuity (in which case the payments are income and liable to tax under Case III); or, whether they contain a mixture of instalments of purchase price and sums representing interest on the purchase price (in which case the payments are dissected).

The Payment Must 'form part of the income of the recipient'[123]

This, although related to the income/capital discussion above, concerns a different issue. It is concerned with the question whether a payment is really the income of the recipient or whether it is the income of someone else (ie, who 'owns' the income?). This was another ground for the decision in *Campbell v IRC*.

Viscount Dilhorne raised (without answering) the question 'whether the payments made by Tutors to the trustees on the clear understanding that

---

121   [1946] 2 All ER at 751.
122   [1936] AC 1.
123   Viscount Dilhorne in *Campbell v IRC* [1968] 3 All ER at 588 at 592; compare Lord Upjohn at 603.

they would be used to buy Tutors' business and so returned to Tutors can properly be regarded as ever belonging to the trustees in a real sense at all'.[124]

Lord Guest answered this question in the negative. Approving the Crown's argument that 'there must be a transfer of title to the income', Lord Guest said[125]: 'If *unico contextu* with the alleged transfer there is a contract to pay it back on the purchase of the business, then there is no transfer of title to the income and, therefore, no annual payment.'

Conclusion

In sum, the words 'other annual payments' under Schedule D Case III can be said to refer to payments similar in character to interest of money and annuities, made under a binding legal obligation, having the quality of recurrence, which are the income of the recipient, and which constitute pure profit in his or her hands. Having examined the meanings of the different types of income charged under Case III, we will now proceed to examine the machinery of collection under the Case.

Deduction of Tax at Source

As has been noted earlier, the scheme of Schedule D Case III is the deduction of income tax by the payer before making the payment. The rationale for such deductions was given by Lord Upjohn in *Campbell v IRC*[126]:

> For the purposes of income tax the payer is regarded as having parted with that part of his income which by covenant or contract he pays away. The income that he pays away is that of the payee and so he is entitled to deduct tax on paying it.

The machinery for the deduction is contained within sections 348 and 349 ICTA 1988. Both sections apply to different types of payment and the consequences attendant upon their application are significantly different - all we will say about this now is that section 348 is far more beneficial to the taxpayer than section 349.

First, we need to identify the types of payment to which each of the sections applies. Section 348 applies 'where any annuity or other annual payment

---

[124]   At 595.
[125]   At 601.
[126]   [1968] 3 All ER 603.

charged with tax under Case III of Schedule D, not being interest, is paid wholly out of profits or gains brought into charge to income tax'.[127] The section extends to royalties and other sums paid in respect of the user of a patent (S.348(2).) On the other hand section 349 applies where the payments are 'not payable or not wholly payable out of profits or gains brought into charge to income tax' (See s.349(1)).

Hereafter, we will refer to the phrase 'profits or gains brought into charge to income tax' as 'taxed income', and to profits or gains which do not fall within that description as 'untaxed income'. If section 348 applies only in respect of payments made wholly out of taxed income and section 349 applies in respect of payments not so made, the question then arises as to how the source of any particular payment is to be decided. The first point to note here is that the mere fact that accounts are kept in some particular way ought not to alter the rights of the Revenue, and ought not to militate against the rights of the taxpayer,[128] i.e., the particular form adopted by a taxpayer in his accounts should neither assist nor injure him. The question of how the source of a payment is to be determined was answered by Lord Wilberforce in *IRC v Plummer*[129]:

> The general rule, in the case of an individual at least, is that what is significant when one is considering the application of the statutory rule, is not the actual source out of which the money is paid, nor even the way in which the taxpayer for his own purposes keeps his accounts, if indeed he keeps any, but the status of a notional account between himself and the revenue. He is entitled, in respect of any tax year, to set down on one side his taxed income and on the other the amount of the annual payments he has made and if the latter is equal to or less than the former, to claim the benefit of [s.348].

What this statement means is simply that if the payer has income out of which the annual payment could have been made, section 348 applies rather than section 349, even if the payment is actually made out of capital. All that we are concerned with is whether the payer had sufficient taxed income to cover the payment, and not, for example, whether he made the payment straight out of his salary or out of funds borrowed from Australia.

---

[127]   See s.348(1). For a critical view of this provision see J Tiley (1981) BTR 263.
[128]   Per Lord Hanworth MR in *Central London Railway Co. v IRC* (1934) 20 TC 102 at 134.
[129]   [1980] AC 896 at 909.

Example

> Launcelot is a barrister who earns at least £100,000 every year from his profession. He has an obligation under a covenant to make payments of £2,000 every month to his favourite charity for the next six years. Last year, he made a cash purchase of some farmland at an auction, and so was a little short of cash. He had to sell some of his shares on the stock market in order to meet his obligations under the covenant.
>
> Although Launcelot's payments for last year were actually made out of the proceeds of the sale of the shares, and not out of his earnings as a barrister, they will still be covered by section 348. He earned enough from his profession (at least £100,000) to cover his obligations under the covenant (£24,000) and the fact that the payment was in real life made from another source is irrelevant.

If, however, the payer has deliberately restricted himself for other legal reasons to pay out of capital, then the general rule stated by Lord Wilberforce is overridden and section 349 will apply. The point was made by Romer LJ in *Central London Railway Co. v IRC*[130] that although the form in which accounts are kept is not conclusive, yet it may be that a particular form has been adopted for the purpose of definitely deciding and recording the fact that a decision has been made, that a certain payment is to be made out of capital. Such a form of account, which debits the payment to capital, may have been adopted for the purpose of making it clear that revenue is set free for other purposes. According to Romer LJ[131]

> [W]here, not for the purposes of convenience or for the purposes of giving effect to the payer's own notions of account keeping, but for the purpose of definitely deciding and of recording the fact that a decision has been come to that a certain payment of interest is to be paid out of capital and not out of interest, then the account is not only of great importance but, in the absence of evidence to the contrary, is conclusive upon the matter.

This principle was applied in *Chancery Lane Safe Deposit and Officers Co. Ltd v IRC*.[132] The company borrowed some money to finance building works. On the advice of its auditors, the company, in order to give a fair view of its

---

[130] (1934) 20 TC 102 at 141.
[131] Ibid.
[132] (1965) 43 TC 83.

affairs, charged part of the interest payments on the loans to capital (the company's taxable profits exceeded the amount of the interest payments and so it could have paid out of taxable profits). The Revenue claimed that the interest payments were paid out of capital and not out of profits or gains brought into charge to income tax. The company on the other hand claimed that the allocations to capital were mere bookkeeping entries irrelevant for tax purposes, and that the interest payments were made out of profits brought into charge to income tax.

It was held by a majority of the House of Lords (Lords Reid and Upjohn dissenting) that the payments must be treated as having been made out of capital. There was a deliberate choosing of attribution to capital rather than to revenue. It was not a matter of method of domestic bookkeeping. The accounts merely evidenced the fact that a decision was taken, was acted upon, and was maintained. The company's definite attribution precluded an entirely inconsistent attribution for tax purposes. Lord Morris of Borth-y-Gest said[133]

> If a company makes and adheres to a decision that a payment should be out of capital and orders all its affairs on that basis, it would be strange if it could assert that the payment should be deemed to be one payable out of profits or gains. An attribution of a yearly payment to profits or gains brought into charge to tax can only be in reference to the year in which the payment is made. If a payment is attributed to capital, the practical result follows that the sum available or carried forward as available for distribution by way of dividends is increased. If a sum is so carried forward it does not, of course, follow that distribution by way of dividends will take place, nor does it follow that, if there are dividends, there will be deductions of tax. It would seem incongruous, however, if a company, having decided (which means the same as 'definitely' decided) to charge a payment to capital and having regulated its proceedings on that basis, could say that the payment was not to be deemed to be charged to capital. This does not mean that in any ordinary case a company, in seeking vis-a-vis the Revenue to make an attribution of an annual payment, is fettered merely because of some form of entry that it has made in books or accounts. It merely means that what was in fact and in reality a payment out of capital cannot be paraded in the guise of a payment out of revenue. That would be more than departing from documents or accounts: it would be departing from fact: it would be a distortion of history.

[133]   At 115.

The gist of this decision is that a deliberate decision to pay out of capital, which has practical consequences in the real world, or which affects the interests of persons other than the decision-maker, cannot thereafter be interpreted differently. If Mr X decides to make a particular payment out of his savings, or from proceeds of the sale of his car, that is his own business (as long as his taxed income is sufficient to cover his liability to make annual payments in the relevant year). The method so chosen may just have been the most convenient means of making the payment at that particular time - a case of simple domestic bookkeeping, and he has not committed himself, for any defined period, to continue making the payments in that fashion.

The same result will ensue if the Managing Director of X Ltd decides to make this month's royalty payment from the proceeds of a sale of equipment, simply because the cash was available there and then. That is again a case of domestic bookkeeping. If however the same X Ltd passed a resolution to make all future payments of particular royalties by realising investments, this, because of all the consequences that will invariably flow therefrom, may lead to a different result, and X Ltd may not be able to claim that the payments are from income. As Lord Morris noted in the *Chancery Lane* case[134], a payment cannot in one and the same year be debited to capital, with the result that the dividend fund is enhanced, and also notionally be treated as debited to revenue so as to enable tax which is deducted to be retained. 'That would require the sum in one year to render two incompatible and inconsistent services. The money must speak either as a payment out of capital or as a payment out of income'.

We will now examine the effects of the application, first, of section 348, and secondly, that of section 349.

Payments under Section 348

When Section 348 applies, the payer is entitled (but not obliged) to deduct (and retain) a sum representing the amount of income tax on the payment[135], the recipient shall allow such deduction to be made[136], and the payer shall be discharged of his obligation to make the payment (S.348(1)(c)).

This in effect means that the payment is deductible in the hands of the payer. As has been noted earlier, the payment is an alienated slice of the payer's income, and since it represents the income of someone else (ie, the recipient) and not of the payer, it follows that the payer is not liable to tax on that slice of income.

---

[134]   43 TC at 117.

[135]   S.348(1)(b). The deduction will normally be at the basic rate, except in the case of interest, where the deduction will be at the lower rate (see s.4 and s.1A ICTA 1988).

[136]   S.106(1) TMA 1970 imposes a penalty for refusing to permit deduction.

Example

> Natalia covenants to pay a gross sum of £1,000 every year to 'Save the Elephant', a registered charity. Assuming a basic rate of 23 per cent, if section 348 applies, Natalia is entitled to deduct tax of £230 and to pay the balance of £770 to the charity.
>
> The annual payment is part of the recipient's total income in the year when the payment becomes due and, if the deduction is made, the recipient is treated as having received the gross sum, and as having paid tax on it at basic rate (s.348(1)(d)). Thus in this example, 'Save the Elephant' will be treated as having received £1,000, and having paid tax of £230 on that sum.

If the recipient is only a basic-rate tax payer then there is nothing more to be done in respect of the payment. If, on the other hand, the recipient is a higher-rate tax payer then he or she has to pay the difference between the tax paid at basic rate and that which would have been due at the higher rate. If the recipient's marginal rate is zero (eg, charities, and individuals who either have no income or whose income fall below the personal allowance) then a refund of tax can be claimed from the Revenue.

Payments under Section 349

When section 349 applies, the payer is obliged to deduct the amount of income tax from the payment (s.349(1)). Where only part of the payment was not made out of taxed income, the tax, in effect, only has to be deducted from that part. Furthermore, the person by or through whom the payment was made is obliged to deliver an account of the payment to the inspector, and is liable to tax at the applicable rate on the whole of the payment, or on so much of it as is not made out of taxed income (s.350(1)).

Payments without Deduction of Tax

We have just discussed the requirement for deduction of tax under section 349. What if the parties wish to dispense with the deduction of tax? This section examines the various ways in which such a wish may possibly be achieved.

Agreements for Non-deduction

One obvious method of implementing a wish to dispense with the deduction of tax is for the parties to enter into an agreement to that effect. However, an obstacle to this course of action exists in section106(2) TMA 1970, which provides that every agreement for the payment of interest, rent or other annual payment in full without allowing deduction of income tax shall be void. A number of points should be noted with respect to this provision. First, the provision applies only to agreements. It does not for example apply to trustees. In *Re Goodson's* settlement[137] the settlor directed trustees to pay annuities to his wife, and directed that the annuities should be enjoyed free of income tax. It was held that the settlor did not by the settlement create any agreement with the trustees or anybody else. Thus the provisions of (what is now) section 106(2) TMA 1970 did not apply (see below, however, for the effect of a 'free of tax' stipulation). Secondly, the provision invalidates only the part of the agreement relating to non-deduction of tax and not the whole agreement. It follows that where there is such a provision in an agreement, the payer is still entitled, or obliged, to deduct tax depending on whether section 348 or section 349 applies.[138]

The Use of Formulae

The provisions of section 106(2) TMA 1970 can be circumvented by the use of certain formulae. If the parties wish to ensure that a fixed sum is paid each year to the recipient irrespective of fluctuations in tax rates, such a wish can be implemented by the means of the common formula - to pay such sum as after the deduction of income tax at the basic rate for the time being in force will leave x amount. Such a formula was approved in *Booth v Booth*[139] as not being contrary to section 106(2). All that it means is that the amount so specified is net of income tax. The payer is thus left with the responsibility for handling the tax affairs in respect of the gross sum. However, while circumventing section 106(2) TMA 1970, this is only a partial solution to the problem of non-deduction of tax. The recipient is relieved of the responsibility of bothering about tax deductions, but the payer is not. In fact, the payer is in a situation which is not much different from what it would have been if the formula had not been used at all.

---

[137]   [1943] Ch 101.
[138]   See Scrutton J in *Blount v Blount*[1916] 1 KB 230 at 237-238.
[139]   [1922] 1 KB 66.

Payments 'free of tax'

It is actually possible to stipulate that a payment be made 'free of tax'. A provision to pay £x 'free of tax' does not fall foul of section 106(2) because of the decision of the House of Lords in *Ferguson v IRC*[140] that the effect of such a provision is an undertaking to pay such sum as after deduction of income tax leaves £x. In *Ferguson*, a husband and wife entered into a deed of separation whereby the husband agreed to pay the wife the sum of £35 free of income tax. During the relevant periods, the husband lived abroad and had no UK income and thus the Revenue sought to tax the wife on the £35. It was held that the sum had already borne tax because the agreement was to pay a gross sum which, after deduction of tax, leaves £35, and that therefore the tax sought was not claimable.

A 'free of tax' stipulation attracts a number of consequences. Generally, it operates to ensure that the recipient in any event ends up with the specified amount, no more and no less. Thus if the recipient obtains any repayment of tax from the Revenue, he is obliged to return such repayment to the payer. This is the rule in *Re Pettit*.[141]

In this case a testator provided an annuity 'free of tax' by his will. The sums were paid wholly out of taxed income, and the annuitant received some repayment from the Revenue. It was held that the annuitant must return a proportion of that repayment to the trustees as the annuity bore to the annuitant's total income. A further consequence is that if the recipient is liable to higher rate tax, the payer is obliged to satisfy this liability too. This is the rule in *Re Reckitt*.[142]

The result is that the obligation of the payer varies with the marginal rate of the payee and this can present some accounting problems. Apart from this fact, just as with the case of the use of formulae (above), a 'free of tax' stipulation does not actually provide a solution to the non-deduction problem. While it relieves the recipient of all responsibility for tax, it imposes on the payer a far higher burden than he would normally have had to bear. As such, except this is precisely what the parties want, such a provision is counter-productive. The inevitable conclusion therefore is that there is no practical way of implementing a non-deduction of tax.

---

[140]   [1970] AC 412.
[141]   [1902] 2 Ch 765.
[142]   [1932] 2 Ch 144.

Failure to Deduct Tax

The Payer and the Recipient

In cases of a failure by the payer to deduct the tax which he is entitled or obliged to deduct there is no obligation on the recipient to refund the over-payment - at least as long as the payer failed to make the deduction under a mistake of law (eg, thinking that no deduction is necessary because the recipient is a charity). An action will not lie against the recipient for recovery of the sum, and the payer is not entitled to withhold later payments.[143]

Where the payment is one of a series within the same tax year, and some instalments remain to be paid, the payer may not make good his loss by making the deduction from one of the later payments.[144]

Exception may be made, where the failure to deduct was due to a mistake fact, in which case recovery is possible[145](eg, where the mistake is one of calculation); and where the applicable rate of tax increases after the payment, the excess can be recovered (s.821 ICTA 1988).

The Parties and the Revenue

The first point to note here is that there is no penalty for non-deduction. If the payment is made under section 348, failure to deduct tax will not generally be of any concern to the Revenue, since they will have got the tax already, or will still get it (in both cases, from the payer). However, since any deduction which is made is to be treated as income tax paid by the recipient (s.348(1)(d)), it follows that, in cases of non-deduction, no tax can be treated as having been paid. The Revenue take the view that the recipient cannot make a repayment claim, but give concessionary relief in respect of maintenance payments.[146]

If the payment is made under section 349 the Revenue will simply assess the payer, who in any case is liable under section 350(1), to the appropriate rate of tax on the payment. The result is that the payer has nothing to gain by not deducting the tax.

---

[143] *Re Hatch* [1919] 1 Ch 351; *Warren v Warren* (1895) 72 LT 628.
[144] *Johnson v Johnson* [1946] 1 All ER 573 (explaining *Taylor v Taylor,* [1937] 3 All ER 571).
[145] *Turvey v Dentons* [1953] 1 QB 218.
[146] Under ESC A52. This concession is classified obsolescent.

Changes under Finance Act 1988

The Finance Act 1988 introduced certain rules in respect of the income tax treatment of annual payments, the effect of which was to take most of them out of the tax system. The relevant provision is now in section 347A, ICTA 1988, which provides that any annual payment made after 14 March 1988 by an individual, which would otherwise have fallen within Case III of Schedule D, shall not be a charge on the payer's income, that no deduction can be made on account of the payment, and that the payment is not the income of the recipient or of any other person. This means that, as a general rule, new arrangements for annual payments (eg, covenants) by individuals have no income tax consequences whatsoever. Thus, for example, the covenants which parents used to make in favour of their children who were attending university will no longer be effective as a means of getting the Revenue to 'subsidise' university education.

This is the general rule, but section 347A(2) provides exceptions for payments of interest, covenanted payments to charity, payments made for *bona fide* commercial reasons in connection with an individual's trade, profession or vocation, etc. (eg, partnership retirement annuities), and payments which fall within section 125(1) (ie, purchased annuities paid wholly or partly out of capital). Payments made in pursuance of an existing obligation were exempted from this rule by section 36(3) FA 1988. 'Existing obligation' for these purposes is defined by section 36(4), and generally refers to obligations incurred before 15 March 1988. However, Schedule 17, para. 4(1), FA 1995 provides:

> Section 347A of the Taxes Act 1988 (annual payments not a charge on the income of the payer) applies to a payment which is treated by virtue of Chapter IA of Part XV of the Taxes Act 1988 as income of the payer notwithstanding that it is made in pursuance of an obligation which is an existing obligation within the meaning of section 36(3) of the Finance Act 1988.

What this means is that payments which are treated as the income of the settlor under the anti-avoidance rules of part XV (see below) now fall within the exclusions in section 347A. Generally, an annual payment will be ineffective for tax purposes under part XV, and the payments will be treated as the income of the payer (s.660A) unless the income arises from property in which the settlor has no interest (see exceptions in s.660A(8) and s.660A

(9)). By this token, even covenants entered into before 15 March 1988 would seem now to be ineffective unless they fall within an exception to the section 660A provisions. The result is that the only exceptions now are those within section 347A itself, and those excluded from the operation of s.660A - basically, covenanted payments to charities, etc., and, perhaps, capital settlements.

Note that section 347A applies only to payments made by individuals (references to an individual in s.347A(2) include references to a Scottish partnership in which at least one partner is an individual. See s.347A(6).). Thus payments made by other entities, such as companies or trusts, and payments under wills, are not affected, and are still subject to the normal Case III provisions.

Anti-avoidance Provisions

A discussion of the taxation of pure income profit will not be complete without a mention of the anti-avoidance provisions contained in Part XV ICTA 1988, and which generally apply in respect of 'settlements'. Annual payments within Case III will generally come within the scope of these provisions because of the wide meaning given to 'settlement'. Section 660(G)(1) defines a settlement as including any disposition, trust, covenant, agreement or arrangement, or transfer of assets. Most annual payments are made under trusts, covenants, or agreements, and any payment not made under these will definitely be made under an 'arrangement' or a 'disposition'. The Part XV provisions are discussed in more detail in the next chapter. However, it is useful to note here the general principle in section 660A(1) to the effect that (with certain exceptions) any income arising under a settlement during the life of the settlor will be treated as the income of the settlor unless the settlor has no interest in the property from which the income arises.

chapter ten
The Taxation of Trusts and Settlements

Introduction

Individuals, partnerships, and corporations are generally taxable on their income, whether arising from employments, trades, or investments. The taxation of the income arising or accruing to these persons or entities is covered in various sections of this book. There remains however yet another entity which is capable of making profits and receiving income. This entity is the trust.

Trusts can often serve as convenient mechanisms for splitting, accumulating, or distributing income. The planning opportunities inherent in this method of handling income are evident. For example, a taxpayer with income-yielding properties may settle the property with a direction to the trustees to accumulate the income arising therefrom. On one view of the matter, without more, tax could be saved - the income accrues to the trustees and therefore the settlor will not be liable to tax on it. Since it does not 'really' belong to the trustees, they might also not be liable to tax on it. The income will accumulate tax-free, until one day, when it has been capitalised, it will be distributed free of income tax to one or more beneficiaries. In another scenario, an individual with a high marginal rate may settle income or income-producing assets on trust for beneficiaries who are not taxpayers or who have lower marginal rates. This would not only take advantage of the beneficiaries' lower rates, it would also take advantage of their personal reliefs.

Not surprisingly, this state of affairs is largely a dream because, under the UK tax system, trustees are 'persons', trusts are taxable entities in their own right, just like individuals and corporations, and the income accruing to trustees is taxable in their hands. Lest this be seen as presenting another opportunity for total avoidance of UK tax (eg, by appointing foreign trustees), although any income arising from the trust property would normally accrue to the trustees only, it is not the rule that the trustees alone are to attract the attention of the tax collector. According to Viscount Cave LC in *Williams v Singer*[1], such a principle would lead to 'strange' results. Rejecting it, he said[2]:

> If the legal ownership alone is to be considered, a beneficial owner in moderate circumstances may lose his right to exemption or abatement by reason of the fact that he has wealthy trustees, or a wealthy beneficiary may escape Super-tax by appointing a number of trustees in less affluent circumstances. Indeed ... a beneficiary domiciled in this country may altogether avoid the tax on his foreign income spent abroad by the simple expedient of appointing one or more foreign trustees.

Thus, the taxation of trust income falls into a three-tier system. In some cases, income tax is charged on the trustee. In cases where a trustee is made chargeable with the tax, the statutes recognise the fact that he is a trustee for others, and he is taxed on behalf of his beneficiaries, who will accordingly be entitled to any exemption or abatement which the income tax statutes allow.[3] In other instances, the tax is charged on the beneficiary, who will normally be given credit for any tax already borne by the trustees in respect of the income that is to be taxed. Finally, in certain situations (see the anti-avoidance rules in respect of 'settlements' below), tax is charged on the settlor.

The question why we should tax trusts is easy enough to answer. As seen above, the tax planning opportunities that would be created if trusts were not taxed would be enormous. This factor has been seen to be inherent in the history of trusts. For example, according to Mayson[4]:

> The lineal ancestor of the trust, the use, was itself developed in order to avoid taxation - the feudal dues of the Crown. It is a tribute to the ingenuity of many that some 450 years after the enactment of the Statute of Uses the trust is still an appropriate vehicle for the avoidance of one's fiscal burden.

Thus we should tax trusts in order to avoid the shortfall in tax revenue that

[1] [1921] 1 AC 65; (1920) 7 TC 387.
[2] 7 TC at 411.
[3] See Viscount Cave LC in *Williams v Singer* 7 TC at 411 - 412.
[4] *Mayson on Revenue Law* (1993) 14th ed., page 431.

would be the inevitable result of not taxing them. If an anti-avoidance motive is thought to be insufficient justification, then there is the added justification that if trusts, like other legal entities, can trade, invest, and otherwise earn income, then there is no reason why, unlike other legal entities, they should escape tax on those activities. That trusts are administered solely for the benefit of others (the beneficiaries) does not lead to a different result, since on one view of the matter, companies can also be said to be run solely for the benefit of others (the shareholders) - but this has never been seen as a reason why companies should not be taxed.

The question of how we should tax trusts is more involved. For one, we could simply treat them like individuals and tax them accordingly. This would apparently present a simple and straightforward solution. The 'rate applicable to trusts' (chargeable generally in respect of accumulation or discretionary trusts) would go. Trusts would suffer tax on trust income at the starting/lower, basic, and higher rates, just like individuals, and that would be it. This would remove the distortions in fiscal matters caused by trusts and discourage the use of trusts solely for tax-planning purposes. However attractive this solution may seem, a closer examination reveals problems.

First, it is obvious that trusts are not individuals and therefore there is no analogy that can be drawn between the two. Any attempt to treat them on an equal basis can be said to rest on shaky foundations which will quickly crumble. For example, if we are to treat trusts as we treat individuals, do we allocate 'personal reliefs' to them as well? If not, why not? It may be argued that since personal reliefs are only allocated to 'individuals', trustees should not receive them. This begs the question why personal reliefs should be allocated only to individuals, but it also undermines the principle of treating trusts like individuals. In this respect, it is useful to note that, while under the ICTA 1988 trustees do not enjoy the 'personal allowance' given to individuals under section 257, the Capital Gains Tax legislation generally allows trustees to claim half of the annual exemption available to individuals.[5]

In respect of certain types of trust, the trustees can claim the full exemption.[6] The allocation of this exemption (or part of it) to trustees is not due to the fact trustees are taxed like individuals under the Capital Gains Tax legislation. The legislation recognises the difference between trusts and individuals quite clearly, and there are specific provisions for taxing trustees. However, the annual exemption allocated to trustees can be defended by pointing out that the exemption is simply referred to in the statute as an

5   TCGA 1992, Sch. 1 para. 2.
6   TCGA 1992, Sch. 1, para. 1.
7   TCGA 1992, s 3.

'annual exempt amount'[7] - which is not as clearly linked to individuals as the 'personal allowance' of the income tax legislation. This answer itself raises a number of other questions but, at the least, it would be supportive of the argument that to treat trustees like individuals for income tax purposes should involve allocating personal reliefs to them too. However, this might lead to distortions if beneficiaries are to receive credit for the tax paid by the trustees (see below). In any event, if it is thought that trustees should also be entitled to personal reliefs, then at what level should this be? Should the trustees' 'personal allowance' be the same as that of an individual[8], or should it be less, or indeed, more? Any number of arguments can be advanced in favour of each.

Secondly, this solution does not address the issue of income-splitting. A high earner with income-yielding assets could still save a considerable amount of tax by settling those assets on trust for others. The effect of this would still be as described above - the settlor would then be taking advantage of the trustees' marginal rates (from the starting/lower, to basic to higher rates) instead of paying higher-rate tax on the whole. If trusts had personal reliefs, the settlor (who would have exhausted his or hers) would also be taking advantage of these. Thus, unless other rules are in place to combat avoidance, trusts would still be valuable devices for tax planning.

Thirdly, what would be done with the beneficiaries when they finally receive distributions from the trustees? Would they still be taxable on the distributions, or would the trustees have exhausted all the tax liabilities? If the beneficiaries are to receive a tax credit in respect of tax paid by the trustees, what would the tax credit amount to? Would the beneficiaries then be entitled to refunds of tax if they are non-taxpayers and,if so, at what rate would the refunds be calculated? If beneficiaries are basic-rate tax payers would they be entitled to a refund in respect of any higher-rate tax paid by the trustees? If the trustees had claimed any 'personal reliefs', how would this be reflected in the tax credits given to beneficiaries?

Thus this approach to taxing trusts raises difficult questions and would be extremely problematic to implement. In order to recognise fully the nature of trusts, it would need to be underpinned by intricate provisions relating to settlors and beneficiaries and, perhaps, some provisions dealing with undistributed income. The result would be a situation which is as complicated as the present one.

A second possible approach to the issue of how we should tax trusts would be to recognise the differences between trusts and individuals, charge trusts

[7]   TCGA 1992, s 3.
[8]   See ICTA 1988, s. 257.

only at a flat rate (eg, the basic rate) and give tax credits to beneficiaries in respect of the tax already paid by trustees. The beneficiaries would then resolve any remaining tax liabilities or any tax refunds with the Revenue. This approach would also however raise the planning opportunities already referred to - and provision would need to be made in respect of undistributed income.

A third possible approach would be to ignore trusts completely for tax purposes, and treat any income accruing to trustees as income accruing to the settlor. This would arguably be the simplest and most effective approach of all. All trusts would be ineffective for tax purposes and, for these purposes only, the settled property and the income thereof would be deemed to still belong to the settlor. There would be no tax on trustees or beneficiaries, and whether trust income is accumulated or distributed would be inconsequential. The problem with this approach would be in respect of cases where the settlor is dead and the settlor's death has not terminated the trust. In such cases, income received by the trustees after the settlor's estate has been administered may escape tax altogether.

The current approach adopted by the ICTA 1988 to taxing trusts is a curious caricature involving a blend of aspects of the second and third approaches just discussed. Trust law is generally thought to be complex, and the law relating to the taxation of income from trusts and settlements is no less complex. The complexity arises out of the problems inherent in different approaches to taxing trusts, some of which have been highlighted above. These problems and the need to avoid a loss of tax revenue have led to intricate provisions which have the effect of reducing (but not eliminating) the attractiveness of trusts as devices for tax planning. Recent years have witnessed moves to simplify the applicable rules (particularly those relating to the taxation of 'settlements'), but these have probably not gone far enough. The discussion that follows attempts to present the principles in a clear and accessible way.

Trust

The first question that we address our minds to is what the tax legislation means when it refers to a trust. Not surprisingly, we find that the word 'trust' is not defined in the Taxes Act. This omission (which is typical of the Act) may be due to the fact that 'trust' does not appear to have any special meaning for tax purposes. As is inevitably the case in such situations, it would appear that its plain and ordinary meaning under the general law would suffice. Trust law texts are often shy of giving a definition and perhaps it is impossible to produce a universally acceptable and all-encompassing definition. Thus, we will not attempt to give such a definition here. We can however take as a starting point one of the definitions in the *Concise Oxford English Dictionary*, which defines trust as (*inter alia*): 'A confidence placed in a person by making that person the nominal owner of property to be used for another's benefit'.[9]

This is one aspect of the matter. In another respect, the trust could be seen as the entity in which the property is placed, or the vehicle whereby the person in whom the confidence is placed is able to become the nominal owner of the property in question. The Inland Revenue in one of their booklets ('Trusts, An Introduction') give this definition; 'A trust is an obligation binding a person or a company (a trustee) to deal with property in a particular way, for the benefit of one or more beneficiaries'.[10]

These are all different angles of the same thing. In terms of the taxation of trust income, the term 'trust' is often used in the sense of the entity itself in which the confidence is reposed or on which the obligation to deal with property is imposed. Obviously the entity is unable manifest itself in the real world and therefore has to be represented by others. It also has to carry out its functions and discharge its obligations through those representatives. Normally, those representatives would be the trustees. One of their first duties in respect of taxes would be to inform the Revenue of the fact that a trust has been created and that they are the trustees thereof.[11] This then raises the question 'who is a trustee'?

Trustee

Again, there is no specific definition of 'trustee' for income tax purposes - and again, this word is not a term of art and does not generally have any special meaning or tax purposes.[12] The *Concise Oxford English Dictionary* defines 'trustee' as;

'A person or member of a board given control or powers of administration of property in trust with a legal obligation to administer it solely for the

---

[9] 9th Ed., 1995, page 1498.
[10] IR booklet IR152, page 1
[11] See IR152, page 3.
[12] See however Section 69(1) TCGA 1992 which provides that the trustees of a settlement shall be treated as being '... a single and continuing body of persons (distinct from the persons who may from time to time be the trustees) ...'

298 The Law and Theory of Income Tax

purposes specified'.[13]

The relevant statements in the Revenue booklet IR152[14] confirm that there is no special or technical meaning to be attributed for tax purposes to 'trustee', since they simply repeat the position under the general law:

> The trustees are the legal owners of the trust property. They are under a legally binding obligation to handle the property of the trust in a particular way and for a particular purpose ... The trust can continue even though there may be changes in the people who are its trustees, but there must normally be at least one trustee.

Finally, in *Williams v Singer*[15] Lord Phillimore said:

> The very essence of the position of a trustee is that he is a person who at law has all the rights of an owner, but who has nevertheless the obligation, which he has undertaken by accepting the trust, of using his powers as legal owner for the benefit of some person not himself or some object not his own.

The Charge on Trustees

There is no specific provision in the Taxes Act which charges trustees, *qua* trustees, to tax on income accruing to them. However, the Act does contain specific provisions charging people who receive income. Thus, section 21(1) ICTA 1988 provides that income tax under Schedule A shall be charged on and paid by the persons receiving or entitled to the income. Section 59(1) charges income tax under Schedule D on the persons receiving or entitled to the income. Section 231(1) gives a tax credit in respect of qualifying distributions under Schedule F to the persons receiving the distributions. Since it is the trustees who are normally in receipt of trust income, such provisions apply to charge them to income tax in respect of the income which they have received. The principle that trustees are charged by virtue of the fact that they receive income is exemplified in the speech of Viscount Cave LC in *Williams v Singer*, where he said[16]:

> [I]f the Income Tax Acts are examined, it will be found that the person charged with the tax is neither the trustee nor the beneficiary as such,

---

[13]   9th Ed., 1995, page 1498. Compare IR152, page 2.
[14]   IR152, page 2.
[15]   7 TC 387 at 416.
[16]   7 TC at 411.

but the person in actual receipt and control of the income which it is sought to reach. The object of the Acts is to secure for the State a proportion of the profits chargeable, and this end is attained (speaking generally) by the simple and effective expedient of taxing the profits where they are found. If the beneficiary receives them he is liable to be assessed upon them. If the trustee receives and controls them he is primarily so liable.

The point was reiterated in *Reid's Trustees v IRC*[17] where trustees were held assessable under Schedule D because they received the income. The Lord President (Clyde) rejected the argument that the only 'person' to whom income could arise or accrue within the meaning of the Act is a person who is beneficially entitled to the income in his own right. In his view, trustees are the proper persons to be assessed in all cases in which the income of the trust estate received by them, or to which they are entitled, is not tax-deducted at source. And, in the case of trust income which is tax-deducted at source, they could not be heard to ask repayment of the tax on the plea that the income did not arise or accrue to them but to others, whether such others were income-beneficiaries or capital-beneficiaries.[19]

The Scope of the Charge

Trust income accrues to trustees jointly, and they are liable to tax on it jointly, not jointly and severally.[20] It has already been seen in a statement referred to at the beginning of this chapter that trustees are charged on behalf of their beneficiaries.[21] This means that their personal circumstances are not relevant to the charges imposed on them in their capacities as trustees. There are a number of points to note in this respect, which are discussed immediately below.

Individuals

Although trustees in their official capacities are 'persons', they are not 'individuals'.[22] This has certain consequences. First, because personal reliefs are generally available only to individuals, the trustees cannot claim any personal reliefs. For example Lord Johnston in *Fry v Shiels* said[23]:

---

[17]   (1929) 14 TC 512.
[18]   at 523.
[19]   At 524.
[20]   *Dawson v IRC* [1989] STC 473; [1989] BTC 200 (HL); note that the effect of this particular decision (as far as the residence of trustees is concerned) has been reversed by FA 1989, s.110.
[21]   Viscount Cave LC in *Williams v Singer* (7 TC at 411-412.
[22]   See for example Viscount Sumner in *Baker v Archer-Shee*, (1927) 11 TC 749 at 767.
[23]   (1914) 6 TC 583 at 588

I think that the question before us is solved at once when one observes that Section 19, which gives this relief commences not with the usual words, 'Any person' which may be held to include not merely a plurality of persons but a body, whether trustees or a corporation, regular or irregular, but that the word 'individual' is used; and I think it is used with a clear intention, and that intention is one which squares with the object of the provision. That object I conceive to be to relieve a man who by his own exertions and his own daily work makes an Income.

However trustees may claim reliefs available to 'persons', (eg loss relief) and, they may claim deductible expenses in respect of a trade carried on by the trust. Secondly, the trustees are not charged at rates lower than the basic rate because these apply only to individuals.[24] Thirdly, the trustees are not liable to higher rate tax because, by virtue of section 1(2)(b) ICTA 1988, this rate of tax is charged only on individuals. This particular point makes trusts still appear to be profitable devices for tax planning by high-income earners whereby they may dump their income-producing assets in trusts, and leave the income thereof to accumulate. The attractiveness of this has been reduced by the introduction of a different rate of tax (the 'rate applicable to trusts') in respect of certain types of trust (see below).

Trust Expenses

In calculating the taxable income of the trust for basic rate tax purposes, no deduction can be made for trust expenses of administration. In *Aikin v MacDonald's Trustees*[25] the trustees had an interest in certain tea estates in India. They received remittances representing profits from those estates. This income was subject to charge under Schedule D Case V and the trustees sought to deduct certain expenses incurred in this country in connection with the management of the trust. The Lord President, rejecting the claim, said[26]:

It seems to me that all the authorised deductions and charges occur at an earlier stage than that at which these expenses have been incurred. When the net sum was placed in the hands of the trustees, it had passed through all the vicissitudes which entitled anyone to make deductions. It had come home, and was in their hands for them to apply to their uses. The fact that their uses are trust uses does not

---

[24]   See s.1(2)(aa) ICTA 1988.
[25]   (1894) 3 TC 306.
[26]   At 308.

seem to me to make any difference in the present question ... It seems to me that the expenses which are authorised to be deducted are expenses excluded by the terms of the present claim, because the words of the present claim are quite explicit that these expenses have been incurred in this country in connexion with the management of the trust, and they are not expenses at all specifically relating to the investment in question, except in this sense, that the income of the investment in question constitutes the bulk of the trust estate.

The *ratio* of this decision is that, the deduction sought was not permissible under Schedule D because it had not (as required by the Schedule D deduction rules) been incurred wholly and exclusively in earning the profit in question, but had rather been incurred after the income was earned. According to Lord Adam[27], the expenses looked very much like sums 'expended in any domestic or private purposes, as distinct from the purposes of the manufacture, adventure, or concern'. Lord McLaren said that the only kind of deductions allowed is expenditure incurred in earning the profits, and, 'that there is no deduction under any circumstances allowable for expenditure incurred in managing profits which have been already earned and reduced into money pounds, shillings, and pence'. Lord Kinnear said[28] that this was not a deduction of money laid out or expended for the purpose of the trade or concern at all, but merely a deduction from the cost of distributing net income after it had come into this country.

However, even though the case did not purport to lay down any general principle in respect of trust expenses of administration generally, its practical effect is that such expenses will not ever be deductible for basic rate tax purposes, simply because they could never be expenses of earning the relevant income.

Trustees not Receiving Income

The principle that trustees are charged to tax because they receive income may have a corollary - that, if the trustees do not receive the income, but the income rather 'accrues directly' to a beneficiary, the trustees are not liable to tax on the income. Some authority for this proposition can be found in *Williams v Singer*[29]. The trustees in the case were resident in the United

---

[27]   at 308-309. Compare Lord Mclaren at 309.
[28]   at 310.
[27]   [1921] 1 AC 65; 7 TC 387.

Kingdom but the trust income in question was derived from shares in an American company. The trustees were the registered owners of the shares, and they gave instructions to the Bank of British North America, in New York, to collect and receive the dividends on the shares and to credit them to the account of the beneficiary at the said bank in New York. No part of the dividends was at any time remitted to, or received, in this country and the beneficiary was at all material times resident and domiciled outside the United Kingdom. Since the beneficiary (being non-domiciled and not having remitted any income to the United Kingdom) could not be taxed on the income, the Revenue sought to tax the trustees. The Revenue relied on the first general rule in section 100 of the Income Tax Act 1842 which, like s.21(1) of the ICTA 1988, charged tax on the persons 'receiving or entitled unto' such profits, and argued that, since the income in the case 'accrued' to the trustees as the legal holders of the investments, and the trustees were the persons legally entitled 'to receive' the income, they were the persons chargeable under the Act. The Revenue claimed that they were entitled to look to those trustees for the tax and were neither bound nor entitled to look beyond the legal ownership. It was held that the trustees were not liable to tax on the income, because they had received no part of it. Viscount Cave LC said[30] that the trustees, who had directed the trust income to be paid to the beneficiaries, and who had themselves received no part of it, were not assessable to tax in respect of such income. Lord Phillimore said[31] that, the trustees in this case merely existed in order to preserve the settlement. Their duty so long as the beneficiary remained alive was to see that the dividends reached her. Although they in law were entitled to the dividends, the person 'entitled' within the meaning of the relevant statutory provisions, and the person to whom they 'belonged' within the meaning of the provisions was, the beneficiary.

This case indicates that the person 'entitled' to receive income is not necessarily the person in whom the legal title vests. In cases in which a trustee has directed income to be forwarded directly to a beneficiary or to an agent of the beneficiary, the trustee has the duty under section 76(1) TMA 1970 to make a return of the name, address and profits of the person to whom the payment was directed to be made.

---

[30]   7 TC, at 412.
[31]   At 418.

The Extent of Trustees' Liability

Much has been said about the correct interpretation of the authorities (especially *Williams v Singer* and some cases referring to it) in the context of the extent of the liability of trustees to income tax. Whiteman and Wheatcroft took *Williams v Singer* to establish the principle that 'income of a trust which is paid directly to a beneficiary without passing through the hands of a trustee is not assessable on the trustee.'[32] They also stated that the fact that income accrues to a beneficiary in whose hands it is not liable to tax may constitute a good answer to an assessment on the trustees. The authors then referred to *dicta* in *Baker v Archer-Shee*[33] suggesting that a trustee may not be assessable in respect of income to which a beneficiary is absolutely entitled, even if not paid to the beneficiary, and stated that these *dicta* were 'disregarded' in *Reid's Trustees v IRC* (above). Their conclusion was that, in view of this, and of the wordings of the relevant statutory provisions, their interpretation was correct. Mayson, referring to *Williams v Singer* (*supra*) and *Corbett v IRC*[34], states that 'income which is not received by [the trustees] but is paid directly to a beneficiary, or which they do receive but which they have a duty to pay to a beneficiary is not their income for income tax purposes'.[35]

Tiley and Collison, referring to *Williams v Singer*, state that 'since the trustee is assessable simply because income accrues to him, it follows that where income accrues not to him but directly to the beneficiary, the trustee is not assessable.'[36] They further state (referring to *Reid's Trustees v IRC*) that where trustees receive income they may not be assessable if the income accrues beneficially to a *cestui que* trust in whose hands it is not liable to income tax.[37] According to them, this is a 'second interpretation' of *Williams v Singer*, which can only apply where 'the link between the income and the beneficiary is established'[38].

Finally, Shipwright and Keeling[39] list three possible bases on which trustees may be assessed to income tax. First, trustees are liable in respect of trust income except where they have not received it, but it has rather gone directly to the beneficiary; secondly, trustees are liable except in cases where the beneficiary entitled to the trust income is not a UK taxpayer; thirdly, trustees are liable except in cases where a beneficiary is absolutely entitled to the income (in this case, entitlement is determined according to trust law principles). They prefer the third approach, saying that this is an

---

[32] Whiteman and Wheatcroft on Income Tax, 2nd ed. para 17-02.
[33] [1927] AC 844; 11 TC 749.
[34] [1937] 4 All ER 700; [1931] 1 KB 567
[35] *Mayson on Revenue Law*, 14th ed., page 454.
[36] Tiley and Collison's *UK Tax Guide*, 1997-98, para 11:03 (Butterworths).
[37] ibid, para 11:04.
[38] Ibid.
[39] A. Shipwright and E. Keeling, *Textbook on Revenue Law*, 1997, 402-403.(referring to *Williams v Singer, Reid's Trustees v IRC* and *Dawson v IRC* [1988] 3 All ER 573; [1988] STC 684 (CA).)
[40] [1937] 4 All ER 700 at 705.

extension of the 'actual receipt and control' test. Let us examine the relevant *dicta* in the cases.

In *Corbett v IRC*[40] Sir Wilfred Greene MR said:

> [W]here trustees are in receipt of income which it is their duty to pay over to beneficiaries, either with or without deduction of something for the trustees' expenses on the way, that income is, at its very inception, the beneficiaries' income. It is perfectly true that for assessment purposes the trustees may fall to be assessed, but the income is the beneficiaries' income from the very first ...

Later in the same case, Sir Wilfred Greene MR said that, although the trustees hands were the hands to receive the income, and although the trustees, after receiving the income, might have to pay expenses out of it with the effect that the beneficiaries only received a net sum, the income when it came into the hands of the trustees was the beneficiaries' income and any tax which it had borne before reaching the trustees was the beneficiaries' tax.[41]

In *Baker v Archer-Shee* Lord Carson[42] approved the statement of Lord Hanworth MR in the Court of Appeal that, in respect of sums placed in the hands of trustees for the purpose of paying them over to beneficiaries, one may eliminate the trustees for income tax purposes, since the income is that of the beneficiaries, not the trustees. In the same case, Viscount Sumner[43] said that the court had to consider whether the income of a trust fund 'belongs' to the beneficiary 'so that the beneficiary is chargeable as if it arose to him directly as his'.

These *dicta* seem clear enough. However, as noted above, *Reid's Trustees v IRC*[44] seemed to throw a spanner in the works. The facts of this case are relevant. The testator held some five per cent War Loans the interest on which was payable without deduction of income tax. According to the testator's settlement his wife and daughter were each to have the life rent of £20,000, and his son was to have another sum of £20,000 absolutely. If the daughter died leaving children they were to have her £20,000 among them; if she died leaving no children her £20,000 was to go to the testator's son or his heirs. The residue of the estate was to be divided into three equal shares, of which one was to go to the son absolutely and the other two were to be held for the wife and daughter in the same way as the respective provisions of £20,000 each. Shortly after the testator's death, the trustees received

41   [1937] 4 All ER 700 at 707.
42   11 TC 749 at 782.
43   11 TC 749 at 766.
44   (1929) 14 TC 512.

some interest in respect of the War Loans, and were assessed to income tax thereupon. The trustees argued that, on the basis of *Williams v Singer* and *Baker v Archer-Shee*, they were not liable to the tax and that they would be liable only when acting for incapacitated or non-resident beneficiaries. It was also their argument that the only 'person' to whom income could 'accrue' under the Income Tax Acts was a person beneficially entitled to the income in his or her own right.

The General Commissioners held that the trustees were liable in respect of two-thirds of the income (ie, the part referable to the testator's wife and daughter), but that they were not liable in respect of the one-third which was referable to the testator's son, since their sole duty was to pay the amount to him as his income. The Court of Session held that the trustees were liable in respect of the whole of the interest, because they were the persons 'receiving or entitled to' the income.

Much was said in the judgments about the effects of *Williams v Singer* and *Baker v Archer-Shee*. The Lord President (Clyde) said[45] that, notwithstanding the apparently imperative terms of the relevant statutory provision, the decision in *Williams v Singer* negatived the view that trustees receiving or entitled to the income under Case V of Schedule D are necessarily the persons liable to income tax in respect of such income. He said that, in both *Williams v Singer* and *Baker v Archer-Shee*, there were *dicta* 'enunciated without apparent qualification, which point to the complete elimination of trustees in the matter of assessability to Income Tax',[46] but he felt that such a consequence was not 'really contemplated by the decisions pronounced nor in the judgments by which those decisions were supported.' According to him, it was recognised that there are many cases in which trustees are assessable, 'albeit as trustees having no beneficial right of their own to the income.' Lord Clyde said that trustees are the proper persons to be assessed 'in all cases in which the income of the trust estate received by them, or to which they are entitled, is not tax-deducted at source'. Where the tax has been deducted at source, the trustees cannot request a repayment on the plea that the income did not arise or accrue to them but to others. The effect of the two cases is, according to him, that while trustees who receive or are entitled to income cannot now be regarded as 'assessable and liable *prima instantia* for the tax in all cases', they would be so liable in 'a great many' cases.[47] Thus the conclusion:

[T]rustees, albeit only the representatives of ulterior beneficial

---

[45]   14 TC at 522.
[46]   At 524.
[47]   At 524-525.

interests, are assessable generally in respect of the trust income ... but that - just because they represent those beneficial interests - they may have a good answer to a particular assessment, as regards some share or part of the income assessed, on the ground that such share or part arises or accrues beneficially to a cestui que trust in whose hands it is not liable to Income Tax, e.g., a foreigner under Case V, Rules 1 and 3.

Lord Sands was able to distinguish both *Williams v Singer* and *Baker v Archer-Shee*. First, none of the beneficiaries had any interest or claim to the specific sum of interest, other than as part of the general estate in which they were interested. Thus, the trustees were the persons entitled to or receiving the income represented by the interest in question and were liable to tax in respect thereof.[48] Secondly, the two cases were not really applicable. *Williams v Singer* simply involved the question whether substance was to be preferred to theory.[49]

The substance was that the income never came into the coffers of the trustees, and they never touched or handled it. The theory was that, since they were the owners of the securities, and it was by their own mandate, which presumably they might have recalled, that payment was made directly to the beneficiary, it was open to argument that theoretically the income must be held to have been received by them. In this respect:

> [I]t was found that the substance of the matter and not any mere theory was to be regarded. That was all that was determined by the judgment in *Williams v Singer*. It was not held, and the decision does · not involve, that when a body of trustees receive income of the trust estate not taxed at the source and proceed to distribute it among beneficiaries, they are not assessable to Income Tax and are bound to pay over the income to the beneficiaries without deduction, leaving it to the Revenue to pursue the beneficiaries.[50]

As far as *Baker v Archer-Shee* was concerned, Lord Sands felt that the question was simply whether substance was to be preferred to form. His interpretation of the case was as follows. There was a life interest in a foreign trust estate, consisting partly of stocks and shares. The matter turned upon the question whether the trust income arose from 'stocks, shares or rents', or from 'other possessions'. The substance of the matter was that the thing

48   14 TC at 526.
49   At 527.
50   Ibid.
51   at 528.
52   14 TC at 531.

from which the income arose was dividends on stocks and shares. The form of the matter was that, technically, the source of the income was not stocks and shares but a beneficial interest in a trust estate. The House of Lords decided in favour of the substance, and 'this was the sole subject matter of decision in the case.'[51]

Lord Morison said[52] that neither *Williams v Singer* nor *Baker v Archer-Shee* raised any question as to the person chargeable to tax. Rather, they related solely to the ascertainment of the income from foreign investments chargeable under Cases IV and V of Schedule D. Both Lord Morison[53] and Lord Blackburn[54] said that the trustees were the ones 'entitled' to the income - a view concurred in by Lord Clyde[55] and Lord Sands.[56]

Can all these *dicta* and decisions be reconciled? One thing to be noted from the statements of Sir Wilfred Greene MR in *Corbett v IRC* is that, although he was clear that income which trustees are obliged to hand over to a beneficiary (ie, income to which a beneficiary is absolutely entitled) 'belongs' to the beneficiary, it does appear from the statements that, in such cases, the trustees are not necessarily not liable to income tax on such income. On the contrary, he made it clear that the trustees 'may fall to be assessed'. On the other hand, clearly, the statements of both Lord Carson and Viscount Sumner in *Baker v Archer-Shee* imply that, in cases wherein a beneficiary is absolutely entitled to the trust income, only the beneficiary is liable to tax thereon.

A connecting thread in all these disparate statements may be *Dawson v IRC*.[57] Dillon LJ pointed out[58] that it was the beneficiary in *Williams v Singer* who was 'in receipt and control' of the trust income. In the same case, Nicholls LJ said[59] that, in cases where the beneficiary has 'an absolute, vested interest' in trust income, 'nice questions' might arise as to whether there was any income accruing to the trustees, as distinct from, or in addition to, the beneficiary, and in respect of whether the trustees, as distinct from, or in addition to the beneficiary, received or were entitled to the income.

The connecting thread seems to lie in the concepts of receipt (and control), and entitlement. Therefore it may be argued that the real distinction between *Reid's Trustees v IRC* and the combination of *Williams v Singer and Baker v Archer-Shee* lies in the fact that, while in *Reid's Trustees v IRC* the trustees were the ones who *in fact* received the income and who also were the ones held by the court to be 'entitled to' the income (ie, both elements of receipt and entitlement were satisfied), in *Williams v Singer and Baker v Archer-*

[52]   14 TC at 531.
[53]   At 530.
[54]   At 529.
[55]   At 522
[56]   At 526
[57]   [1988] 3 All ER 753.
[58]   At 759.
[59]   At 757.

Shee, the beneficiaries were the ones who in fact received the income, and who were held by the court to be 'entitled to' the income. *Baker v Archer-Shee* was not even about the liability of trustees at all. The 'nice questions' referred to by Nicholls LJ in *Dawson v IRC* still remain. These revolve around the meanings of 'receive' and 'entitled to'. First, 'receive'. This can refer either to actual (ie, *de facto*) receipt of income, or to constructive (theoretical) receipt of income. This distinction was referred to by Lord Sands in *Reid's Trustees v IRC* (above) when he said that:

> [t]he income never came into the coffers of the trustees, they never touched or handled it. But they were the owners of the securities, and it was by their own mandate, which presumably they might have recalled, that payment was made directly to the beneficiary. It was, therefore, open to argument that theoretically the income must be held to have been received by them.'

As Lord Sands pointed out, the constructive receipt option was rejected by the House of Lords in *Williams v Singer*. Thus, 'receive' for these purposes must mean 'receive in fact', or 'actually receive'. The issue of entitlement (ie, who is 'entitled to' income) is not as easily settled. It may be related to the question of who the income 'belongs' to, but even that is not without its difficulties. In *Williams v Singer*, the Revenue argued for a construction of entitlement which was based solely on legal title. If such an argument were to succeed, the question who is entitled to trust income would attract a swift and decisive response - the trustees - since legal title in the trust property, and thus the trust income, resides in them. However, this argument was not accepted in the case. As indicated earlier, the approach of Lord Phillimore[60]to the issue was that the trustees in the case merely existed in order to preserve the settlement, and their duty so long as the beneficiary remained alive was to see that the dividends reached her. Thus, although they in law were entitled to the dividends, the person 'entitled' within the meaning of the relevant statutory provisions, and the person to whom they 'belonged' within the meaning of the provisions was the beneficiary. This indicates that entitlement in equity may be more important than entitlement in law. This view is also evident in the speeches in *Baker v Archer-Shee*.[61] On this view of the matter, the beneficiary who is absolutely entitled to trust income would always be the person 'entitled to' the trust income under the tax statutes, and trustees would only be 'entitled to' trust income if there is no beneficiary with an absolute entitlement.

[60]   7 TC 387, at 418.
[61]   See for example Lord Wrenbury, 11 TC 749 at 779.
[62]   See for example Lord President Clyde at 522.

However, the Court of Session in *Reid's Trustees v IRC*[62] seemed to define entitlement to mean entitlement in law (which would support the Revenue's argument in *Williams v Singer*). This may indicate that the Court of Session, in taking this approach, was wrong in this aspect of its decision in *Reid's Trustees v IRC*. However, since the trustees in that case had actually been in receipt of the income, the decision itself (that they were assessable in respect of the whole of it) may have been correct on the basis that the person receiving the income was liable to tax on it. It may also be that the decision that the trustees were entitled to the income may be supported on an alternative basis - Lord Sand's view that none of the beneficiaries (under the terms of the settlement) had 'any interest or claim to the specific sum of interest' - in which case the trustees would be the only ones who could have been entitled to the income.

The final issue that arises from these cases involves those situations wherein the person receiving the income is different from the person 'entitled to' it. In *Williams v Singer* and *Baker v Archer-Shee*, the persons receiving the income (the beneficiaries) were also the persons entitled to it. The same was true (on one interpretation - the one that looks to the terms of the settlement rather than legal entitlement) of *Reid's Trustees v IRC*. It may thus be said that all these cases were correctly decided. As seen earlier, one interpretation of the *dicta* in some of the cases is that, in cases where the receiver of the income is different from the person entitled to it, the receiver (i.e., the trustees in most cases) would not be liable to tax. This is just another way of saying that, where a beneficiary is absolutely entitled to the trust income, the trustees will not be liable to tax on that income, whether or not the trustees receive it. This approach was not accepted by the Court of Session in *Reid's Trustees v IRC*, but seems to be accepted in other cases. If it is agreed that the receiver of the income was also the person entitled to it in the three cases just referred to, the result would be that anything said about this present point in all of those cases was *obiter dicta*. If this is so, then it does not matter whether or not the Court of Session in *Reid's Trustee v IRC* 'disregarded' the dicta in *Baker v Archer-Shee*. Presumably, *obiter dicta* from the House of Lords is to be preferred to conflicting *obiter dicta* from the Court of Session. Therefore we may say that the following principles are established:

[a] where trustees do not in fact receive income, they are not liable to tax on it;

[b] if someone other than the trustees is entitled to the trust income,

then, that person, rather than the trustees, is liable to tax on it - and this regardless of who is in actual receipt of the income.

These propositions more or less sum up the academic comment referred to at the beginning of this section. They however still raise questions. First, in respect of proposition [a], what would be the case if the trustees are entitled to the trust income (for example in the case of a discretionary trust), but yet direct trust income to be paid directly to a discretionary beneficiary? Would *Williams v Singer* and the *dicta* in *Baker v Archer-Shee* apply? That is arguably the case, but it is not the inevitable conclusion because both *Williams v Singer* and *Baker v Archer-Shee* involved cases where the beneficiary had a vested interest and it could be argued that they did not contemplate this type of scenario at all. If the trustees were to escape tax in these circumstances, might this be an effective way to avoid 'the rate applicable to trusts' in respect of discretionary trusts? (see below). In respect of proposition [b], where the trustees receive the income, but the person entitled to it is a beneficiary, is there a rule that the liability of the beneficiary is exclusive? The *dicta* of Lord Carson and Viscount Sumner in *Baker v Archer-Shee* (above) indicate that this would be the case. However, in the context of statutory provisions charging the persons 'receiving or entitled to' income, why should not the Revenue be able to assess either?

In sum, although the extent of the liability of trustees may be summarised in the two propositions above, it is clear that this area of the law is not free from uncertainty. This is an area where the law is in dire need of some clarification.

The 'Rate Applicable to Trusts'

As seen earlier, because trustees (not being individuals) are not liable to higher rate tax, trusts provide planning opportunities for those in higher income brackets, whereby income-yielding assets could be settled, the income taxed at the trustee's (basic) rate, left to accumulate, and finally be distributed as capital. The attraction of such planning has been reduced (but not eliminated) by the imposition of a special tax rate on the income of certain trusts. This special rate is known as the 'rate applicable to trusts'. Section 686(1A) of the ICTA 1988 (as amended by s.54(3) of the FA 1997) provides that the rate applicable to trusts, in relation to any year of assessment for which income tax is charged, shall be 34 per cent or such other rate as Parliament may determine. The rate applicable to trusts currently in force still amounts to a few per cent below the higher rate of tax. This means that it may still be profitable for people with high incomes who possess income-yielding properties to settle such properties on trusts which will attract the rate applicable to trusts.

Section 686(2) specifies the situation in which the rate applicable to trusts applies. The first condition is that the trust income is income which is to be accumulated or which is payable at the discretion of the trustees or any other person (whether or not the trustees have the power to accumulate the income). (S.686(2)(a)).

The second condition is that the income is not, before being distributed, either the income of any person other than the trustees, or treated as the income of a settlor for any of the purposes of the Income Tax Acts. (S.686(2)(b)).

In short, the rate applicable to trusts applies to accumulation and discretionary trusts in circumstances wherein the income, while remaining with the trustees, is treated only as that of the trustees. Exception is made in respect of income arising under trusts established for charitable purposes only, and to income from investments, deposits or other property held for the purposes of certain specified retirement benefit schemes and personal pension schemes (S.686(2)(c)).

With respect to the latter exemption, although the word 'property' can have a wide meaning, it has been held that it is to be construed in this context *ejusdem generis* with the words that precede it ('investments' and 'deposits').[63] Thus construed, it 'connotes some asset held by the trustees which (like investments and deposits) produces income'. Thus, the exemption is restricted to the 'fruits of ownership', and does not extend to the fruits of other activities. By this token, income derived by trustees from an activity which was subsequently held to be a trading activity was not exempt under this provision.[64]

It has been seen that one of the conditions for the rate applicable to trusts is that the trust income is income which is to be accumulated or which is payable at the discretion of the trustees. For these purposes, it is not necessary for the trustees to be under a duty to accumulate. It suffices that they have a power to accumulate the income. This is illustrated by *IRC v Berrill*[65] in which the trustees of a settlement were directed to hold the

---

[63]   Lightman J in *Clarke (HMIT) v British Telecom Pension-Scheme Trustees* [1998] BTC 362 at 404.
[64]   Ibid.
[65]   (1981) 55 TC 429; [1981] STC 784.

income for the settlor's son. The trustees had an overriding power, during the beneficiary's life, or for 21 years, whichever was the shorter, to accumulate the whole or part of the trust income and to hold such accumulations as an accretion to capital. The trustees having exercised the power to accumulate, the Revenue assessed them to tax at the additional rate (now the rate applicable to trusts).

The taxpayers argued that the language of section 686(2), which describes the income arising to trustees which is to be subject to additional rate tax, is wholly inapt to include income arising to trustees to which a beneficiary is entitled subject to a power of accumulation. This is because the opening words of section 686(2)(a), 'income which is to be accumulated', are apt to describe only income which trustees are under a positive duty to accumulate. They also argued that the words 'before being distributed' in section 686(2)(b) were apt to exclude and must have been intended to exclude from subsection (2) a trust under which income when it arises to trustees is income to which a beneficiary is entitled subject to the exercise of a power to accumulate it. They contended that the relevant contrast was between income which, when it arises, is income to which a beneficiary is entitled (albeit subject to a power to accumulate it) and income which will become the income of a beneficiary only when it is distributed in pursuance of some discretion vested in the trustees or in some other person.

Vinelott J, whilst of the view that the argument was 'formidable'[66] held that the trustees were indeed assessable at the additional rate. According to him,[67] the words 'income ... which is payable at the discretion of the trustees' were as easily applied to income which trustees have power to withhold from a beneficiary entitled in default of the exercise of the power, as they were to income which they have power to apply or which they are bound to apply pursuant to a mandatory discretionary trust. He said that, while it is true that the words 'whether or not the trustees have power to accumulate it' do not fit naturally the case where the discretion consists of a power to withhold income by accumulating it, that inelegance of expression did not afford a ground for departing from what appeared to be the plain intention of the legislature. He accepted the Revenue's argument that the purpose of section 686 (2)(a) is to describe in general terms the income to which subsection (2) is intended to apply, and that the rest of the subsection contain particular savings or exceptions from that general description.

The rate applicable to trusts also applies in situations where infant beneficiaries have contingent interests and section 31 Trustee Act 1925

[66]   55 TC at 441.
[67]   At 443.

applies, whereby the trustees may apply the income for their maintenance. Finally, the trustees of a discretionary trust may be subject to a further charge to tax under section 687 when they make a distribution of income to a beneficiary. This charge will arise where the rate of income tax is higher in the year of distribution than it was in the year when the income arose to the trustees. The section applies where in any year of assessment trustees make a payment to any person 'in the exercise of a discretion' (whether the discretion is exercisable by them or by another person) in circumstances wherein the income is, by virtue of the payment only, the income of the recipient for all the purposes of the Income Tax Acts, or, is treated as the income of the settlor by section 660B (s.687(1)).

By virtue of section 687(2), the amount paid will be treated as a net amount corresponding to a gross amount from which tax has been deducted at the rate applicable to trusts for the year in which the payment is made. The tax which is deemed to have been deducted will be treated as tax paid by the recipient (or where appropriate, by the settlor), and will be treated as income tax assessable on the trustees. The trustees will be entitled to credit for the tax already borne by them at the time when the income arose, and to some other specified deductions (See generally, s.687(3)).

Obviously, if there is no difference between the tax rates applicable in the year in which the income arose and those applicable in the year in which the payment was made, the section would have no real bite. Thus it is only of real importance when tax rates are increasing.

The Charge on Beneficiaries

Trust income which has accrued to trustees would normally have suffered tax either by deduction at source before payment to the trustees, or in the hands of the trustees. Thereafter, either there will be beneficiaries entitled to the income, or the trustees will exercise a discretion to accumulate, or distribute the income among beneficiaries. The taxability of a beneficiary depends on whether or not he or she has a vested right in the trust income.

---

[66]   (1927) 11 TC 749.

Vested Rights

As has been pointed out in the discussion on the extent of the liability of trustees, income to which a beneficiary is entitled forms part of his total income, whether or not he receives it from the trustee. This is because the income 'belongs' to the beneficiary, not to the trustee. The leading case is *Baker v Archer-Shee*.[68] In this case, Lady Archer-Shee had a life interest, under her father's will, in a trust estate held by trustees in the United States. The trust fund consisted of foreign stocks and shares. The dividends, as they accrued, were placed to the credit of Lady Archer-Shee's bank account in New York and were not remitted to this country. The question was whether these dividends fell to be assessed as part of the income of her husband, who was resident in the United Kingdom.

The House of Lords held (Viscount Sumner and Lord Blanesburgh dissenting) that Lady Archer-Shee was entitled to the stocks and shares which formed the trust fund, and to the income thereof, during her life. Therefore her husband was rightly assessed whether the income was remitted here or not. According to Lord Wrenbury[69], the question was not what the trustees had thought proper to hand over and had handed over (which is a question of fact) but what, under her father's will, Lady Archer-Shee was entitled to (which is a question of law). Even though the trustees had a first charge upon the trust funds for their costs, charges and expenses, the fund still belonged to the beneficiary. Lord Carson concurring, said[70]:

> In my opinion upon the construction of the will of [Lady Archer-Shee's father] once the residue had become specifically ascertained, the Respondent's wife was sole beneficial owner of the interest and dividends of all the securities, stocks and shares forming part of the trust fund therein settled and was entitled to receive and did receive such interest and dividends. This, I think, follows from the decision of this House in Williams v Singer ... and in my opinion the Master of the Rolls correctly stated the law when he said 'that when you are considering sums which are placed in the hands of trustees for the purpose of paying income to beneficiaries, for the purposes of the Income Tax Acts you may eliminate the trustees. The income is the income of the beneficiaries; the income does not belong to the trustees'.

[68]   At 778-779.
[70]   At 782.
[71]   [1931] AC 212; 15 TC 693 (HL).

The decision of the majority in this case was based on the assumption that American law on the rights of Lady Archer-Shee under the trust was the same as English law. Subsequently, in *Garland v Archer-Shee*,[71] expert evidence on American law showed that it was different from English law, and that the assumption of the majority in *Baker v Archer-Shee* was incorrect. The case was finally resolved in favour of the taxpayers (to the extent that liability was based on amounts actually remitted to the UK). In spite of this development (ie, a determination based on expert evidence as to the differences between English and American law), the main principle in *Baker v Archer-Shee* remains valid. The principle therein established is that, when a beneficiary is entitled to trust income as it arises, such a beneficiary is taxable on that income as it arises, because it is his income. Thus there is liability even on undistributed income. As seen earlier, *dicta* by Lord Carson and Viscount Sumner in the case seem to indicate that the beneficiary's liability is exclusive in such cases. The rate applicable to trusts will not apply even if the income is accumulated because the income 'before distribution' belongs to someone other than the trustees, ie, the beneficiary.

This principle can apply only where certain conditions are fulfilled. First, it is necessary that the beneficiary has a vested interest, and, secondly, it is necessary that the beneficiary's vested interest is not liable to be divested, ie it is indefeasible. Thus for example the rule will not apply where the beneficiary's interest is contingent, or where the interest can be divested. This latter point is illustrated by *Cornwell v Barry*[72] in which funds were held in trust for settlor's grandchildren then living, or born during the eight year life of the settlement, for their, his or her absolute use and benefit. During the period, there was only one child. A claim was made in respect of personal reliefs and allowances on behalf of the child, on the ground that, as he was the only child living, the trustee was required during those years to hold the income as and when received upon trust for the child absolutely. It was held that, the child's interest, if vested, was liable to be divested. His interest was defeasible because more children could have been born during those eight years, and thus the claim failed. Harman J said[73] that any child either in existence when the deed was made or coming into existence during the eight years thereafter was an object of the trust. He rejected the argument of the taxpayer that, so long as there is only one child who fulfills any of those qualifications, he is entitled to the whole income as and when received, and it is indefeasibly his. This, according to Harman J, would be an entirely mistaken view of the trust, because:

---

[72]   (1955) 36 TC 268.
[73]   At 274.

[T]he Trustee is to look not only at the child in existence but any child who may come into existence, and during the eight years he is not bound, as I see it, to make any application of the money at all. He would if he were a reasonable man, but he is not bound to. It is quite true that the trust is for the absolute use and benefit of these children, but it is in such shares and in such manner as the Trustee thinks fit. Consequently, he has the eight years in which to make up his mind. He may during that time divide it into shares or give it all to one or other of the objects of the trust, and even if at any time during the eight years there were no object of the trust, he would still, in my view, have to hold the money in case, before the end of the period, an object should come into being. Consequently, though it may well be, and I think is, the fact that [the child] being in existence had got a vested interest in this money, it was an interest which was liable to be divested if another object of the trust came into existence during the eight years. It is not until the end of this time that you could say: The class is closed; the object is achieved; and the money, if there be any unapplied, vests absolutely in any of the persons who were objects of the trust, and whether then dead or then living matters not.[74]

Grossing Up

The income to which the beneficiary is entitled would have suffered tax in the trustee's hands. In order to ascertain the amount which will enter into computation for the beneficiary's total income, the income would fall to be grossed up in order to reflect basic rate tax paid by the trustees. Depending on the beneficiary's circumstances, he may either be liable to higher rate tax on the trust income, or be entitled to a refund. The formula for grossing up the income is as follows:

$$Z = Y \times \frac{100}{100 - R}$$

where:

R = the rate of tax

Y = the amount of the payment

Z = the gross sum.

It should be noted that the gross amount so calculated will not necessarily be the same as the income accruing to the trustees. This is due to the decision of the Court of Session in *Macfarlane v IRC*[75] where it was held that,

[74]   Ibid. See also *Stanley v IRC*, 26 TC 12; [1944] 1 All ER 230.
[75]   (1929) 14 TC 532.

although trust expenses are not deductible in the trustees' hands in computing the trustee's income, they are deductible in the trustees' hands in computing the beneficiary's income. In this case the taxpayer had made a claim to the Revenue for repayment of income tax on the basis that the whole of the income of the trust estates was his income, without any deduction in either case in respect of the expenses of management of the estates (ie, that he was liable to income tax in respect of the part of the income of the trust estate which was expended upon the administration of the trust, so as to yield a higher repayment of tax). The Revenue argued that the taxpayer's income was only the net income remaining after deduction of the expenses of management of the trust estates. The Revenue's argument was upheld. Lord Sands said[76] that the primary aspect of the matter was not one of abatement or exemption but of initial liability. He said that the argument of the taxpayer involved the contention that he was liable to income tax in respect of income which he did not handle and could not under any arrangement handle, which was not expended under any authority conferred by him, and over the expenditure of which he had no control. Lord Blackburn said that, on the true construction of the trust deed, the income to which the beneficiary was entitled was no more than the amount of the income of the trust funds which may be available after the expenses of the trust had been paid.[77] Thus a beneficiary is worse off and ends up with a lower tax credit, as the following example shows.

> The trustees receive income amounting to £100. They incur £20 expenses in managing the trust. Since this £20 is not deductible in their hands in computing their own tax liability, they pay tax on the full £100. Assuming a basic rate of 23 per cent, they pay £23 in tax, and have £77 left for distribution. Because the £20 is deductible in their hands in computing the beneficiary's income, they deduct it, and have £57 left for distribution to the beneficiary. This amount is grossed up at the basic rate:
>
> $57 \times {}^{100}\!/_{77} = £74.02$

The tax credit is: £74.02 - £57 = £17.02. Since the total income coming into the trust has suffered £23 in tax, a tax credit of just £17.02 leaves the taxpayer out of pocket.

---

[76] At 540.113

[77] Ibid. See also *Elizabeth Murray v IRC* (1926) 11 TC 133.

Annuities

Where the beneficiary is entitled to an annuity under a trust, he is not entitled to the trust income as it arises, and the rule in *Baker v Archer-Shee* does not apply. The annuity will fall to be taxed under Case III of Schedule D. The Finance Act 1988 provisions, which render annual payments by individuals ineffective, do not apply to take the payments out of the tax scheme because the trustees are not 'individuals'.

No Vested Rights

Typical cases in which beneficiaries do not have vested interests in trust income involve discretionary and accumulation trusts. A beneficiary under a discretionary or accumulation trust cannot be taxed unless he receives the income, since he is not entitled to anything. If and when a payment is made to the beneficiary, the income would fall to be classified as an annual payment under Schedule D Case III.

Contingent Rights: Trustees Act 1925, Section 31

Where beneficiaries have contingent rights to income, the rule in *Baker v Archer-Shee* cannot apply simply because the contingency which will entitle them to income may never happen. This will be the case where section 31 of the Trustee Act 1925 applies. Section 31 relates to trusts for infant beneficiaries. In subsection (1), it provides that, where any property is held by trustees in trust for any person, whether that person's interest is vested or contingent, the trustees may (at their sole discretion), during the infancy of such person, pay or apply the whole or part of the income produced by the trust property for his maintenance, education or benefit. The trustees have the discretion regardless of whether any other fund exists for the same purpose, and regardless of whether there is any person bound by law to provide for the infant beneficiary's maintenance or education.[78]

The trustees are obliged by section 31(2) to accumulate the residue of the income during the beneficiary's infancy. The power to apply the income for the infant's education, maintenance or benefit is subject to any prior interests or charges affecting the settled property (S.31(1)). The effect of section 31 of the Trustee Act 1925 is to convert all trusts in which an infant

[78]   Trustee Act 1925, s.31(1)(a) and s.31(1)(b).

has an interest (which interest is not dependent on that of an adult) into an accumulation and maintenance trust in the sense that any income which is not spent on the maintenance or education of the infant must be accumulated.

If the beneficiary, on attaining the age of 18, does not have a vested interest in the income, the trustees are directed to pay the income from the trust property and the income from any accretions thereto to the beneficiary, until he dies, or his interest fails, or he attains a vested interest in the income (S.31(1)(ii)).

This means that if a beneficiary only had a contingent interest during his infancy, he will, on attaining the age of 18, be entitled only to the income from the accretions and not to the accretions themselves. On the other hand, if the beneficiary attains the age of 18 years or marries under that age, and the beneficiary had a vested interest in the income until either event, then the trustees are to hold all accumulations in trust for that beneficiary absolutely (S.31(2)(i)(a)).

The same principle applies where, on attaining the age of 18 or on marriage below that age, the beneficiary becomes entitled to the settled property from which the income arises (S.31(2)(i)(b)).

In any other case (for example where a beneficiary dies below 18 years), the trustees must hold the accumulations as an accretion to the capital of the settled property. A number of things follow from these provisions. First, even in cases where an infant beneficiary has a vested interest in trust income, he will not be liable to income tax on any undistributed income. The income is not his own because, although he has a vested interest, his right to receive income is contingent or subject to being divested if he fails to attain majority. This is because by virtue of section 31(2) the accumulations will be added to capital in that event, and will not go to his estate. If he eventually reaches 18 and the accumulations are paid to him, they will by then have become capital in nature. The leading case is *Stanley v IRC*.[79]

In this case an infant had vested interests in certain estates under his father's will. The trustees accumulated the surplus income which was not applied for his maintenance and, when he attained majority, he became absolutely entitled to those accumulations. The Revenue sought to tax him for the years of his infancy. The real question concerned the precise interest in surplus income which an infant having a vested interest enjoys during his infancy by virtue of the provisions in section 31. The Revenue's contention

---

[79]   (1944) 26 TC 12; [1944] 1 All ER 230.

was that the infant had a vested interest in the surplus income as it accrued and that there was nothing in section 31 which deprived him of that interest during infancy. Rather, all that the section did was to divest him of his title to the accumulations of surplus income if he died before attaining his majority. In other words, an infant has a vested interest in the accumulations, which interest is defeasible in the event of his dying before majority. The Court of Appeal rejected these arguments and held that the income was not the infant's income at the time that he should have been assessed to tax on it. The reason for this was that, section 31 of the Trustee Act 1925, if he had not attained majority, the accumulations would never have been his, but would have been added to capital which would go to the remainderman. Lord Greene MR said[80]:

> The infant does not during infancy enjoy the surplus income. It is not his in any real sense. The title to it is held in suspense to await the event and if he dies under [the age of 18] his interest in it (whether or not it be truly described as a vested interest) is destroyed. He is in fact for all practical purposes in precisely the same position if his interest in surplus income were contingent. If he attains [the age of 18] he takes the accumulations, if he dies under [the age of 18] he does not ... We are disposed to think that the effect of the Section is better described not as leaving the interest of the infant as a vested interest subject to defeasance, but as engrafting upon the vested interest originally conferred on the infant by the settlement or other disposition a qualifying trust of a special nature which confers on the infant a title to the accumulations if and only if he attains [the age of 18] or marries. The words in Sub-section (2)(i)(a), if 'his interest ... during his infancy or until his marriage is a vested interest', and the corresponding words in Subsection (2)(ii), 'notwithstanding that such person had a vested interest in such income', appear to us to refer to the nature of the interest conferred upon the infant by the settlement or other disposition, and not to affirm that the interest of the infant in the surplus income remains a vested interest notwithstanding the alteration in his rights effected by the Section. If this view is right, the interest of the Appellant in the surplus income during his minority was a contingent.

Thus, the effect of section 31 of the Trustee Act 1925 is to make the infant's interest in the surplus income accruing during his infancy a contingent interest only - it prevents an infant from having an indefeasible vested interest in the income of the trust fund (ie, until something is paid, nothing is an infant's income, no matter what his interest is in the trust property). However, if an infant who does not have a vested interest in the settled property receives income from the trustees, or if amounts are applied for his education, maintenance or benefit, then the infant becomes liable to tax on those payments. Section 687 will apply, and the amount of the payment (grossed up at the rate applicable to trusts) will enter into the computation of his total income.

In cases wherein a beneficiary has an interest in income which interest is contingent upon his attaining an age in excess of 18, (e.g., 'to S when he is 30 years old'), section 31(1)(ii) provides that the trustees should pay the income (from the trust fund and from the accretions to the fund) to him on attaining 18. This means that, on attaining majority, the beneficiary obtains an indefeasible vested right in the income and he will be liable to tax in respect of that income whether or not he receives it. This is illustrated by *IRC v Hamilton-Russell*.[81]

The trustees in this case were directed to hold funds and income for the beneficiary upon his attaining 21. The beneficiary attained 21 in 1928, became the sole beneficiary under the settlement, and thereupon became entitled to call for the transfer of all the trust funds and the accumulations thereof to himself. He did not do so, but allowed the trustees to receive the income from the trust fund and the accumulation fund, and to continue investing the income, until early in 1939. The beneficiary's executors argued that, although as the sole beneficiary under those trusts, he could have legally determined them, he did not in fact do so. Consequently the income did not become his, but was accumulated under the trusts, and turned into capital before the trusts were determined.

The Court of Appeal however held that the income belonged to the beneficiary as from the time when he attained 21 and was assessable to income tax. Luxmoore LJ said[82] that the trust became unenforceable as soon as the specified event occurred. The trustees could at any time after the happening of that event, even though asked by the beneficiary to continue the accumulations, have refused to do so, and, in the same way, the beneficiary could, contrary to the wishes of the trustees, have insisted on a transfer to himself of the whole of the trust funds. According to Luxmoore LJ, the reason why the trusts then became unenforceable and ineffective was because the funds were 'at home' and belonged solely to the

[81]   (1943) 25 TC 200; [1943] 1 All ER 474.
[82]   25 TC at 208.

beneficiary for his own absolute use and benefit. The capital and income were his and no one else was interested in them: if the income was left in the hands of the trustees, and they invested it, they only did so by the sufferance of the beneficiary whose income it was.

Payments out of Capital

The general rule in respect of payments out of capital is that, when trust income has been capitalised, it retains that character when paid out to the beneficiaries, and is not liable to income tax. However, where the trustees have to pay an annuity, with power to supplement the payments with payment out of capital, the situation may be different, and payments made out of capital in such cases may be income in the recipient's hands. The principle is that the situation depends on the rights of the recipient, not the source of the payments.

In *Brodie's Will Trustees v IRC*[83] the testator directed the trustees to pay the income from certain trust property to his widow during her life. He wished that the payments would not be less than £4,000 per annum and therefore directed that, should trust income be deficient in any year to pay this sum, recourse should be had to capital to make up the deficiency. During a number of tax years, the trustees made payments to the widow of varying amounts out of the capital of the estate, in order to make up that sum each year. It was held that the payments were income in the hands of the widow and were taxable under Case III of Schedule D, even though they were paid out of capital. Finlay J. said[84]:

> [I]f payments out of capital are made, and made in such a form that they come into the hands of the beneficiaries as income, it seems to me that they are income, and not the less income because the source from which they came was in the hand, not of the person receiving them, but in the hands of somebody else, capital.

According to Finlay J,[85] if the capital belonged to the beneficiary, or if he was beneficially entitled to both the income and capital of the trust, then the payments out of capital would have been capital in his hands.

Another relevant case is *Cunard's Trustees v IRC.*[86] Trustees held a fund on trust to pay the income thereof to the testatrix's sister. The will further provided that, if in any year the income of the trust fund was insufficient to

83   17 TC 432.
84   At 439.
85   17 TC 432 at 439.
86   (1945) 27 TC 122; [1946] 1 All ER 159.
87   27 TC at 132.

enable the sister to live at the testatrix's residence in the same degree of comfort as during the testatrix's lifetime, the trustees were empowered to resort to the capital of the testatrix's residuary estate to make up any deficiency in the trust income. The trustees paid sums out of capital to the sister in two years of assessment. The Court of Appeal held that the payments were income in the hands of the beneficiary. Lord Green MR said[87]that the sister's title to the income arose when the trustees exercised their discretion in her favour and not before, and that, at that moment a new source of income came into existence. The fact that they were made out of capital was irrelevant. The payments were to be made 'by way of addition to the income' in order to enable the sister to live in the same degree of comfort as before. The testatrix was in fact providing for a defined standard of life for her sister, that provision being made in part out of income and in part (at the discretion of the trustees) out of capital. According to Lord Greene MR, the purpose of the payments was an income purpose and nothing else and the payments were therefore income.

This type of reasoning led the Revenue to argue in *Stevenson v Wishart*[88] that any payment out of capital, which is made for an income purpose, is income in the beneficiary's hands. In this case, properties were transferred by the settlor into discretionary trusts on behalf of (*inter alia*) his mother-in-law (Mrs H). The trustees made a series of payments totalling £109,000 out of the capital of the fund to meet Mrs H's medical and nursing home expenses before her death. The Revenue claimed that the payments, being recurrent sums paid out of capital for the maintenance of a beneficiary, were for an 'income purpose' and therefore constituted the income of the beneficiary for tax purposes. The argument was rejected. The Court of Appeal held that, although payments by trustees out of capital could be income in the beneficiary's hands, it was not sufficient that the payments were either periodic, for educational purposes, or for personal maintenance. The payments involved in this case, although recurrent, were of substantial amounts that were outside normal income resources, did not create an income interest, and were of capital nature. Fox LJ said[89]:

> [T]here is nothing in the present case which indicates that the payments were of an income nature except their recurrence. I do not think that is sufficient. The trustees were disposing of capital in exercise of a power over capital. They did not create a recurring interest in property. If, in exercise of a power over capital, they chose to make at their discretion regular payments of capital to deal with the

88   (1987) 59 TC 720; [1987] STC 266; [1987] 1 WLR 1204.
89   At 765.

specific problems of [Mrs H's] last years rather than release a single sum to her of a large amount that does not seem to me to create an income interest. Their power was to capital what they appointed remained capital.

It is thus clear that neither regularity nor recurrence is a conclusive factor, and the courts have to look at the whole set of circumstances.

Settlements

We have seen earlier in our discussions the planning opportunities which are presented by trusts. A person who wishes or who is obliged to provide another person with an income, or with a source of income may do so in one of many ways. First he may simply transfer the sum of money, either in a lump sum or periodically, and without any legal formalities. This is a simple transfer of assets. Each such transfer is entirely voluntary and is in law nothing more than a mere gift. Secondly, he may execute a deed or other type of legal instrument transferring part of his income. This may be referred to as an income settlement - it enables the donor to retain the source from which the income flows (the tree), while giving away the income itself (the fruit). While the execution of the instrument transferring the money may have been voluntary, a legal obligation may arise under the instrument, and the payments thereunder may be legally due. Thirdly, he may transfer income-producing capital assets to trustees to pay the income generated thereby for the benefit of the objects. This is known as a capital settlement, because the donor gives away the capital out of which the income is to be made (the tree - and by the same token, the fruit which it produces).

The first method (voluntary gifts) would not normally be tax efficient, and would in most cases attract no income tax consequences. Little planning can be achieved in this way. On the other hand, income and capital settlements inherently contain tax-planning opportunities, especially for those in large income brackets. Income or capital may be settled for one's spouse, children or grandchildren (who one would normally be obliged to maintain) to take advantage of their personal reliefs and/or low tax rates, and to reduce one's total income from high tax brackets to lower ones.

The tax system's response to the planning opportunities has been two-fold. First, to introduce a different rate of tax (the rate applicable to trusts) for certain types of trusts (see above), and, secondly, to introduce anti-avoidance legislation in Part XV of the ICTA 1988, in respect of arrangements described as 'settlements'. All the three methods of parting with one's income or property described above may well fall within the scope of these anti-avoidance provisions. The Finance Act 1988 rendered income settlements largely ineffective by disallowing the deduction of annual payments made by individuals, and so the real choice now for new arrangements is whether or not to settle capital. The discussion that follows analyses the anti-avoidance provisions relating to the taxation of settlements.

Definition of 'Settlement'

Section 660(G)(1) ICTA 1988 defines settlement to include any disposition, trust, covenant, agreement, arrangement, or transfer of assets. This is a very wide definition, which would cover almost all types of transaction that a person may engage in - including the type of voluntary gifts referred to above.

A number of cases provide illustrations. In *Thomas v Marshall*[90] a father opened Post Office Savings Bank accounts for his children, and transferred certain sums into those accounts by way of absolute and unconditional gifts. He also gave each child £1,000 in three per cent Defence Bonds. The interest on the bank accounts and on the bonds were treated by the Revenue as his income for tax purposes. The taxpayer, while conceding that each of the relevant gifts might be described as a transfer of assets, if the phrase were to be given its ordinary meaning, argued that, since the word 'settlement' was the only word used in the charging provision, it was 'the dominant word', and a transaction does not come within the provision unless it was 'something in the nature of a settlement'. Thus, a transaction which might ordinarily be described as a transfer of assets did not come within the section unless, either it was accompanied by some restraint on alienation, such as would subject the transferee to some action at law or in equity if be attempted to alienate the subject of the gift, or, the income and the capital of the subject of the gift were given to different persons, or, the legal title and the equitable interest in the subject of the gift were conferred on different persons.

The House of Lords however held that there was nothing in the context which should lead the courts to give the words 'transfer of assets' any

---

[90] (1953) 34 TC 178; [1953] AC 543.
[91] See Lord Morton of Henryton at 202
[92] 27 TC 385.

leaning other than that which they ordinarily bore, or to infuse into them some flavour of the meaning ordinarily given to the word 'settlement'.[91] Thus, the absolute gifts to the children were settlements. Similarly, in *Hoods-Barrs v IRC*[92] the taxpayer transferred a block of shares to each of his two infant and unmarried daughters. It was held that these as transfers of assets were settlements and that he was liable to tax on the dividends. The argument that the phrase 'transfer of assets' cannot include an absolute gift by a parent to a child was rejected by the Court of Appeal.

These cases illustrate the width of the definition given to the word 'settlement' and the willingness of the courts to give certain words in the definition (particularly, 'transfer of assets') their ordinary (and wide) meanings. It has even been held that transfers of money can be settlements if made under compulsion (eg, under a court order).[93]

However, according to Nourse J in *IRC v Levy*[94], it has long been recognised that Parliament cannot have intended the definition of 'settlement' to extend as widely as a literal reading of it might suggest. Thus, the courts have imposed a limitation on the meaning of settlement. This judicial gloss on the statutory words takes the form of a requirement of 'bounty' in a transaction in order for it to constitute a settlement. This requirement seems to have developed from a principle that, in order for a transaction to be excluded from the ambit of the settlement provisions, it must be a *bona fide* commercial transaction.[95] This concept was then extended by Plowman J in *IRC v Leiner*[96] into a statement that some element of bounty is necessary and that a *bona fide* commercial transaction is excluded. This analysis was accepted by Lawrence J in *Bulmer v IRC*.[97]

The definitive statement of the bounty principle is however to be found in the decision of the House of Lords in *IRC v Plummer*[98]. In this case, a charity paid £2,480 to the taxpayer in return for a covenant by the taxpayer to pay it a sum of £500 each year for five years. The purpose of the scheme was to enable the taxpayer to deduct the payments and so reduce his total income for surtax purposes. The Revenue claimed that, far from being annual payments, the scheme was a settlement and the payments remained the income of the taxpayer. It was held that, because the transaction contained no element of bounty, it was not a settlement[99]. According to Lord Wilberforce[100]:

> [I]t can, I think, fairly be seen that all of these provisions [in Part XV], have a common character. They ، re designed to bring within the net

93   See *Yates v Starkey* (1950) 32 TC 38; *Harvey v Sivyer* [1985] 2 All ER 1054; (1985) 58 TC 569.
94   (1982) 56 TC 68 at 86.
95   See *Copeman v Coleman* [1939] 3 All ER 224.
96   (1964) 41 TC 589 at 596.
97   [1966] 3 All ER 801 at 809-811.
98   (1979) 54 TC 1; [1980] AC 896.
99   Note that the effect of this decision has now been reversed with respect to reverse annuity schemes (see ICTA 1988 s.125).
100 54 TC at 43.

of taxation dispositions of various kinds, in favour of a settlor's spouse, or children, or of charities, cases, in popular terminology, in which a taxpayer gives away a portion of his income, or of his assets, to such persons, or for such periods, or subject to such conditions, that Parliament considers it right to continue to treat such income, or income of the assets, as still the settlor's income. These sections, in other words, though drafted in wide, and increasingly wider language, are nevertheless dealing with a limited field - one far narrower than the field of the totality of dispositions, or arrangements, or agreements, which a man may make in the course of his life. Is there then any common description which can be applied to this? The courts which, inevitably, have had to face this problem, have selected the element of 'bounty' as a necessary common characteristic of all the 'settlements' which Parliament has in mind. The decisions are tentative, but all point in this direction.

The requirement of bounty is said not to be a word of definition-- rather, it is a judicial gloss on the statute which is 'descriptive of those classes of cases which are caught by the section in contrast to those which are not'.[101]

Although it is 'a conception admittedly not without its difficulty'[102] it has been applied consistently by the courts. However, Lord Roskill has warned that, because it is a judicial gloss on the statutory words, the courts must be extremely careful not to interpret this descriptive word too rigidly. Lord Roskill then went to state the sense behind the requirement of bounty[1030]:

What the cases have sought to do is to distinguish between those cases where the recipient has in return for that benefit which he has received accepted some obligation which he has to perform, either before receiving the benefit or at some stated time thereafter, and those cases where the recipient benefits without any assumption by him of any correlative obligation.

This indicates that the idea of bounty is closely linked to the presence or otherwise of a correlative obligation (or consideration) of the part of the recipient. However, it seems that this is not conclusive and that the principle of the exclusion of *bona fide* commercial transactions may be more determinative of the bounty issue than the mere presence or absence of a correlative obligation. Thus, in *IRC v Levy*,[104] where the taxpayer made an

---

[101]   Lord Roskill in *Chinn v Collins* [1981] 1 All ER 189 at 200.
[102]   See Lord Wilberforce in *Chinn v Collins* [1981] 1 All ER 189 at 194.
[103]   [1981] 1 All ER at 200.
[104]   (1982) 56 TC 68; [1982] STC 442.
[105]   56 TC at 87.

interest-free loan to a company of which he was the sole beneficial shareholder, it was held that there was no settlement as there was no element of bounty (even though the company got something - the use of the money - for nothing). Nourse J said[105]:

> Before a disposition, trust, covenant, agreement or arrangement can be a settlement within [s.660(G)(1)] it must contain an element of bounty. For that purpose a derivative bounty of the kind conferred by the exercise of a special power of appointment may be enough. On the other hand, a commercial transaction devoid of any element of bounty is not within the definition. The absence of any correlative obligation on the part of him who is on the receiving end of the transaction may be material, but is not conclusive in determining whether it contains an element of bounty or not.

The decisions on 'bounty' are not necessarily inconsistent with those which held payments made under compulsion to be settlements. Cases such as *Yates v Starkey* (*supra*) and *Harvey v Sivyer* (*supra*) involved payments by parents to their own children under court orders. Nourse J suggested in *Harvey v Sivyer*[1106] that it may well be that the natural relationship between parent and young child is one of such deep affection and concern that there must always be an element of bounty by the parent, even where the provision is on the face of things made under compulsion.

Settlor

Section 660(G)(1) provides that a settlor is any person by whom the settlement was made. Section 660(G)(2) further provides that a person shall be deemed to have made a settlement if he has made or entered into it directly or indirectly and, in particular, if he has provided or undertaken to provide funds directly or indirectly for the purpose of the settlement or has made with any person a reciprocal arrangement for that other person to make or enter into the settlement. The word 'purpose' in this definition does not import any mental element, as *IRC v Mills*[107] shows. The taxpayer in this case was an actress. When she was 14 years old, her father, in order to make sure that her earnings were 'legally protected', incorporated a company and settled the shares on trust for her absolutely on attaining the age of 25. She then signed a service contract with the company giving it the right to her exclusive services for five years at a salary of £400 a year. The

---

[106]   58 TC at 577.
[107]   (1975) 49 TC 367; [1975] AC 38.
[108]   at 408.

bulk of the company's profits in respect of her films was distributed to the trustees as dividends. The trustees accumulated the income. It was held that the incorporation of the company, the issue and settlement of the shares therein, and the service agreement, were an arrangement which constituted a settlement. The taxpayer was the settlor, since it was her services that provided the company with funds from which to pay dividends to the trust - she had thereby indirectly provided income for the purposes of the settlement. Viscount Dilhorne said[108]:

> I do not agree with Lord Denning M.R. that the word 'purpose' in this section connotes a mental element or with Buckley L.J. that there must be a motivating intention. I do not myself think that it assists to consider whether the question he posed is to be answered objectively or subjectively. I do not consider it incumbent, in order to establish that a person is a settlor as having provided funds for the purpose of a settlement, to show that there was any element of mens rea. Where it is shown that funds have been provided for a settlement a very strong inference is to be drawn that they were provided for that purpose, an inference which will be rebutted if it is established that they were provided for another purpose.

It is possible to have more than one settlor for a settlement. For example, in *IRC v Mills* the taxpayer's father was also a settlor because he had made the settlement.[109] However, where there is more than one settlor, then section 660E(1) provides that the provisions shall apply to each settlor as if he were the only settlor, whereby references to property comprised in a settlement would only include property originating from that settlor (s.660E(2)(a).), and references to income arising under the settlement would include only income originating from that settlor (s.660E(2)(b)).

The Basic Charge

Section 660A(1) provides that income arising under a settlement during the life of the settlor shall be treated for all purposes of the Income Tax Acts as the income of the settlor and not as the income of any other person, unless the income arises from property in which the settlor has no interest.[110]

From this basic charge, section 660A(9) excludes income consisting of

---

[109] See Viscount Dilhorne at 409.
[110] For a discussion on a predecessor of this charge, see R Burgess (1971) BTR 278.

330 The Law and Theory of Income Tax

annual payments made by an individual for *bona fide* commercial reasons in connection with his trade, profession or vocation, and covenanted payments to charity (as defined by s.347A(7)). By virtue of section 660C(1), the tax charged under this Chapter will be charged under Schedule D Case VI. The settlor is entitled to the same deductions and reliefs as he would have if the income taxed here had been received by him (s.660C(2)). The income is treated (subject to s.833(3)) as the highest part of the settlor's income (s.660C(3)). The settlor is entitled to reclaim tax paid under this provision from the trustee or any other person to whom the income is payable (s.660D(1)). Where there are two or more settlors, section 660E provides for apportionments to be made.

Retaining Interest

We have seen that the general charge under Part XV does not apply in respect of income arising from property in which the settlor has no interest. In what circumstances does a person retain an interest in property for these purposes? Section 660A(2) provides (subject to the rest of the section) that, a settlor shall be regarded as having interest in property, if that property, or any derived property is, or will, or may become payable to or applicable for the benefit of the settlor or the settlor's spouse in any circumstances whatsoever. 'Derived property' is defined by section 660A(10) as being, in relation to any property, income from that property or any other property directly or indirectly representing proceeds of, or of income from, that property or income therefrom.

However, there are some permitted interests and, by virtue of section 660A(4), the settlor will not be regarded as having an interest in property if the property can only be payable to or applied for the benefit of the settlor or the settlor's spouse in the event of:

[1] the bankruptcy of any person who is or may become beneficially entitled to the property or any derived property, or

[2] an assignment of or charge on the property or any derived property being made or given by some such person, or

[3] in the case of a marriage settlement, the death of both parties to the marriage and of all or any of the children of the marriage, or

[4] the death of a child of the settlor who had become beneficially entitled to the property or any derived property at an age not exceeding 25.

Section 660A(5) also provides another exception - that, a settlor will not be regarded as having an interest in property if and so long as some person is alive and under the age of 25, during whose life the property concerned or any derived property cannot be payable to the settlor or the settlor's spouse, except in the event of that person becoming bankrupt or assigning or charging his interest in the property or any derived property.

For these purposes, the 'spouse' of the settlor does not include a person to whom the settlor is not married but who he may later marry. (S. 660(3)(a)). The term also does not include a spouse from whom the settlor is separated, under a court order, or under a separation agreement, or in such circumstances that the separation is likely to be permanent. (S. 660(3)(b)). Finally, it does not include the widow or widower of the settlor. (S. 660(3)(c)).

Gifts between Spouses

We have referred earlier to the suggestion of Nourse J in *Harvey v Sivyer* that the natural relationship between parent and young child is one of such deep affection and concern that there must always be an element of bounty by the parent. It may well be thought that the same goes for the natural relationship between spouses (at least, those who are not estranged). In order to prevent the situation which may otherwise arise that gifts between spouses will invariably be treated as settlements, these anti-avoidance provisions provide some relief for transfers of property between married couples. Section 660A(6) provides that the reference in section 660A(1) to a settlement does not include an outright gift by one spouse to the other, of the property from which the income arises, unless either the gift does not carry a right to the whole of that income, or the property given is wholly or substantially a right to income. 'Outright gift' is defined by exclusion. For these purposes, a gift is not an outright gift if it is subject to conditions, or if the property given or any derived property is or will or may become payable to or applicable for the benefit of the donor in any circumstances whatsoever. Some of these terms were examined in the case of *Scrutton v Young*.[111]

---

[111] [1996] BTC 322.

In this case, a company, of which the taxpayers were the only shareholders and directors, resolved at an extraordinary meeting to create some preference shares which were eventually allotted to the taxpayers' wives. The preference shares carried the right to 30 per cent of the net profits of the company in any year in which the company resolved to distribute profits. They also carried the right to attend and speak but not to vote at general meetings of the company. The preference shareholders were only entitled on liquidation of the company to repayment of the sums subscribed for their shares. Subsequently, the company resolved to distribute some profits, and paid substantial sums as dividends on the preference shares for three successive years of assessment. It appears that the transactions were entered into in order to take advantage of new rules on the separate assessment of wives.

The questions arose whether the creation of a new class of preference shareholder and the allotment of shares to the taxpayers' wives constituted an 'arrangement' and were therefore 'settlements', and, if so, whether income arising under the settlements was to be treated as the income of the settlors. The question also arose whether the preference shares taken by each wife were gifts wholly, or substantially a right to income. These questions were all answered in the affirmative. The allotment of preference shares was within the definition of settlement 'as being an arrangement or disposition containing the necessary element of bounty'.[102]With respect to the question whether the preference shares were wholly or substantially a right to income, Sir John Vinelott said:[113]

> It seems to me that the answer to that question must be in the affirmative. The preference shares entitled the holders to a preferential dividend if the taxpayers (the only directors and the holders of all the ordinary shares) determined to distribute the whole or part of the profits arising in any given year. Apart from that right to income, the only rights conferred on the preference shareholders were the right to repayment of the nominal sum paid on the allotment of the shares and the right to attend and be heard, but not to vote at, general meetings of the company. As a matter of strict legal principle, the preference shares were assets distinct from the income derived from them, but in reality they could never have been realised. The income was dependent upon the taxpayers determining to distribute part of the profits of the company.

[112]   Sir John Vinelott at 333.
[113]   Ibid.

Section 660A(7) excludes from the scope of the meaning of settlement an irrevocable allocation of pension rights by one spouse to another in accordance with the terms of a relevant statutory scheme. Section 660A(8) also excludes income arising under a settlement made by one party to a marriage by way of provision for the other, either after the dissolution of the marriage, or while they are separated under an order of a court, or under a separation agreement or in such circumstances that the separation is likely to be permanent.

Unmarried Minor Children of the Settlor

The lenient treatment given to spouses does not extend to unmarried young children of the settlor. Thus, there is a residual charge in respect of income paid to an unmarried minor child of the settlor during the settlor's life. Where income arising under a settlement has not been treated as the settlor's income under section 660A, and it is then paid to an unmarried minor child of the settlor or otherwise falls to be treated as income of an unmarried child of the settlor during the settlor's life, such income is treated for all the purposes of the Income Tax Acts as the income of the settlor and not as the income of any other person (s.660B(1)).

An exemption is provided in section 660B(5) in respect of income paid to a child in a year in which the aggregate amount paid to that child does not exceed £100. For the purposes of this residual charge, 'child' is defined to include a step child and an illegitimate child (s.660B(6)(a)).

'Minor' means a person under the age of 18, and references to 'payments' include payments in money or money's worth (s.660B(6)(c)).

The provision is widened to cover possible payments out of capital (in cases where trust income has been accumulated), for which purpose section 660B(2) provides that, where income arising under a settlement is retained or accumulated by the trustees, any payment whatsoever made thereafter by virtue or in consequence of the settlement to an unmarried minor child of the settlor shall be treated as a payment of income to the extent that there is available retained or accumulated income. For this purpose section 660B(3) deems that there is available retained or accumulated income if the aggregate of the income which has arisen under the settlement since it was made is more than the aggregate of any income so arising, which has been:

[1] treated as the income of the settlor, or

[2] paid (whether as income or capital) to or for the benefit of, or otherwise treated as the income of, a beneficiary other than an unmarried minor child of the settlor, or

[3] treated as the income of an unmarried minor child of the settlor, and subject to tax in any of the years 1995-96, 1996-97, or 1997-98, or

[4] applied in defraying any of the trustees' expenses which were properly chargeable to income, or would have so been but for any express provision of the trust.

Capital Sums Paid to the Settlor

Section 677(1) provides that any capital sum paid to the settlor by the trustees of a settlement shall be treated as the settlor's income, to the extent that it falls within the amount of available income of the year of payment and up to the next ten years. Any sum which is treated as the settlor's income under this section is grossed up at the rate applicable to trusts (s.677(6)) in order to ascertain the amount that would enter into the calculation of his total income. Tax is charged under Schedule D Case VI, and credit is given for tax at the rate applicable to trusts, or the tax charged on the grossed up sum, which ever is less (s.677(7)).

The provisions apply equally to capital sums received by the settlor from a body corporate connected with the settlement (s.678). By s.677(9), 'capital sum' means any sum paid by way of loan or repayment of a loan, and any other sum paid otherwise than as income, which is not paid for full consideration in money or money's worth. The definition excludes sums which could not have become payable except in one of the events mentioned in section 673(3), but, a sum paid to the settlor includes sums paid to the settlor's spouse, or to the settlor or the settlor's spouse jointly with another person (s.677(9)(b)).

Also included within the scope of sums paid to the settlor are sums paid by the trustees to a third party at the settlor's direction, or by virtue of assignment by the settlor of his right to receive it, if the assignment was on or after April 6 1981; and, any sum which is otherwise paid or applied by the trustees for the benefit of the settlor.

For the purposes of section 677(1), section 677(2) provides that, 'available income', in respect of a capital sum paid in a year, is the aggregate of the income arising in the year and the income of previous years, to the extent that such income has not been distributed. Thus the concept is linked to income which the trustees have accumulated. Certain deductions from these sums are available in arriving at the amount of available income, for example sums which have already been treated as the income of the settlor for tax purposes, and an amount equal to tax at the rate applicable to trusts on the aggregate of undistributed income which has already been treated as the settlor's income (see generally, s.677(2)).

Where the capital sum paid to the settlor was paid to by way of a loan, and he repays the whole of the loan, no part of it shall be treated as his income for any year subsequent to the year of repayment (s.677(4)).

The moral of the anti-avoidance provisions is that the settlor should create a capital settlement in which he has completely divested himself of all interest in the settled property. He should also ensure that neither himself, nor his spouse, nor any of his unmarried infant children can or do receive any money from the trustees of that settlement.

chapter eleven
Tax Planning

'Whenever one activity is taxed more highly than others there is a *ceteris paribus* argument that people will switch to the lightly taxed (or untaxed) activity'.[1] Tax planning normally involves a deliberate arrangement of the taxpayer's financial affairs to take advantage of the fiscal opportunities presented by relieving provisions and/or loopholes in tax legislation. During times of high rates of tax, the tax avoidance and planning industries thrive through their ability to present the taxpayer (for an appropriate fee) with 'off the peg' tax planning schemes.[2]

Early judicial responses to these planning endeavours were informed and coloured by peculiar rules developed by the courts specifically in relation to the interpretation of taxing statutes. By virtue of the Bill of Rights 1688, taxes can only be levied by Parliamentary legislation. The Act provides that 'the levying of money for or to the use of the Crown by pretence of prerogative without grant of Parliament for longer time or in other manner than the same is or shall be granted is illegal'.

The imposition of income taxes in the beginning (to finance the Napoleonic wars)[3] was seen as a mischief and an infringement of privacy and other civil liberties,[4] which had to be kept within within its due bounds. Hence the emergence of the principles that the subject is not to be taxed 'unless the words of statute unambiguously impose the tax on him';[5] that where a statutory provision is ambiguous, the taxpayer must be given the benefit of any doubt;[6] and that the onus is on the Revenue to show that a taxing statute imposes a charge on the taxpayer. As Lord Cairns explained in *Partington v AG*:[7]

> If the person sought to be taxed comes within the letter of the law, he

---

[1]   C. V. Brown and P. M. Jackson, 'Public Sector Economics', page 425 (4th edn, Blackwell, 1990).

[2]   See *IRC v Plummer* [1979] STC 793. See also *Vestey v IRC* [1980] STC 10 (reviewed by A. Sumption (1980) BTR 4) for an insight into the success of these schemes.

[3]   See generally S. Dowell, 'A History of Taxation and Taxes in England', Vol II, page 225 (3rd edn, Frank Cass & Co. Ltd., 1965); S. James and C. Nobes, 'The Economics of Taxation', page 125 (4th edn, Prentice Hall, 1992).

[4]   See S. James and C. Nobes, op. cit

[5]   Per Lord Simonds in *Russell v Scott* [1948] AC 422 at 423; compare Lord Normand in *Ayrshire Employers Mutual Ins.Assoc. v IRC.* 27 TC 331 at 344.

[6]   Lord Thankerton in *IRC v Ross and Coulter* [1948] 1 All ER 616.

[7]   [1869] LR 4 HL 100 at 122.

must be taxed, however great the hardship may appear to the judicial mind to be. On the other hand, if the crown, seeking to recover the tax, cannot bring the subject within the letter of the law, the subject is free, however apparently within the spirit of the law the case might otherwise appear to be. In other words, if there be admissible, in any statute, what is called an equitable construction, certainly such a construction is not admissible in a taxing statute, where you can simply adhere to the words of the statute.

This statement of Lord Cairns is echoed more dramatically by Rowlatt J in *Cape Brandy Syndicate v IRC*[8] when Rowlatt J was explaining the principles of construction of taxing statutes:

[I]n taxation you have to look simply at what is clearly said. There is no room for any intendment; there is no equity about a tax: there is no presumption as to a tax; you read nothing in; you imply nothing, but you look fairly at what is said and at what is said clearly and that is the tax.

To this literalist approach to interpreting tax statutes, and the concomitant judicial responses to tax planning, has been attributed the initial successes of the tax avoidance industry - a success which has been described as being 'to the detriment of the general body of taxpayers'.[9] According to Lord Steyn, the result was that the court appeared to be relegated to the role of a spectator concentrating on the individual moves in a highly-skilled game, wherein the court was mesmerised by the moves in the game and paid no regard to the end result, or the strategy of the participants.

Some in the House of Lords inevitably have come to the conclusion that this literalist approach to the construction of taxing statutes is no longer tenable. In *IRC v McGuckian* Lord Steyn[10] referred to the advances in the law of interpretation of statutes wherein there was a shift away from literalist to purposive methods of construction. However, 'tax law remained remarkably resistant to the new non-formalist methods of interpretation', and was 'by and large left behind as some island of literal interpretation'. He then proceeded along the lines that the literalist approach has been discarded even in this area of law. Referring to the landmark decision of the House of Lords in *IRC v Ramsay*[11] Lord Steyn said that in that case,

Lord Wilberforce restated the principle of statutory construction that

---

8   [1921] 1 KB 64; 12 TC 358 at 366;
9   Per Lord Steyn in *IRC v McGuckian* [1997] 3 All ER 817 at 824.
10   [1997] 3 All ER at 824.
11   [1981] 1 All ER 865.

a subject is only to be taxed upon clear words. To the question 'what are clear words'? he gave the answer that the court is not confined to a literal interpretation. He added 'There may, indeed should, be considered the context and scheme of the relevant Act as a whole, and its purpose may, indeed should, be regarded'. This sentence was critical. It marked the rejection by the House of pure literalism in the interpretation of tax statutes.[12]

Whether or not one agrees with the conclusions of Lord Steyn in respect of the role now played by literalism in statutory construction, the nail in the coffin of literalism in tax legislation presented by him in *IRC v McGuckian* is significant. It represents the latest shot in the seemingly relentless onslaught of the House of Lords on artificial tax planning schemes. This onslaught is part of a 'new approach' to tax avoidance schemes. The 'old approach' was an approach that is alleged to have unduly favoured the taxpayer. That approach lay in the recognition by the House of Lords in *IRC v Duke of Westminster* that, every man is entitled if he can to order his affairs so as that the tax attaching under the appropriate Acts is less than it would otherwise be,[13] and had its high watermark in *IRC v Plummer*.[14]

This seemingly blanket permission of all activities that can reduce one's taxes was however subject to the constraints of legality. This constraint had earlier been alluded to by Lord Clyde in *Ayrshire Pullman Motor Service v IRC*[15] when he said:

No man in this country is under the smallest obligation, moral or other, so as to arrange his legal relations to his business or to his property so as to enable the Revenue to put the largest possible shovel into his shares. The Inland Revenue is not slow - and quite rightly - to take every advantage which is open to it under the taxing statutes for the purpose of depleting the taxpayers pocket. And the taxpayer is, in the like manner entitled to prevent, so far as he honestly can, the depletion of his means by the Revenue.

The phrase 'so far as he honestly can' in this statement is crucial, for lack of honesty in one's dealings with the Revenue is a sure recipe for trouble. Thus, there was and still is a need to distinguish between tax avoidance and tax evasion[16] - the former being perfectly lawful, while the latter is not.[17] The distinction between tax avoidance and tax evasion was considered by the

12   [1997] 3 All ER at 824.
13   (1936) 19 TC at 520 (per Lord Tomlin).
14   [1979] STC 793.
15   (1929) 14 TC 754 at 763-764.
16   There is growing recognition of a concept of 'tax mitigation'. This is an imported concept which we shall discuss later.
17   For a general discussion on the various descriptions of tax planning, see A.J. Sawyer (1996) BTR 483.

Royal Commission on the Taxation of Profits and Income in 1955. In its Final Report, the Commission stated that tax evasion:

> denotes all those activities which are responsible for a person not paying the tax that the existing law charges upon his income. Ex hypothesi, he is in the wrong, though his wrongdoing may range from the making of a deliberately fraudulent return to a mere failure to make his return or to pay his tax at the proper time.[18]

In Commissioner of *Inland Revenue v Challenge Corporation Ltd*[19] Lord Templeman said that tax evasion occurs when the Commissioner is not informed of all the facts relevant to an assessment to tax. We may also add to this those cases in which the Commissioner or Inspector is actually deceived or deliberately misled as to the relevant facts. Thus any action which amounts to tax evasion is as such an illegal act and does not fall within the permitted 'ordering of affairs' referred to by Lord Tomlin in the *Westminster* case.

On the other hand, tax avoidance is generally permitted, although the effectiveness of a tax avoidance plan will often be a contentious issue between the Revenue and the taxpayer. According to the Royal Commission on the Taxation of Profits and Income, tax avoidance consists of 'some act by which a person so arranges his affairs that he is liable to pay less tax than he would have paid but for the arrangement. Thus the situation which he brings about is one in which he is legally in the right'.[20]

The word 'arrangement' is a crucial concept in this context. In *Commissioner of Inland Revenue v Challenge Corporation Ltd*[21] Lord Templeman said that income tax is avoided and a tax advantage derived from an arrangement when the taxpayer reduces his liability to tax without involving him in the loss or expenditure entitling him to that reduction. According to him, the taxpayer who is engaged in tax avoidance does not reduce his income or suffer a loss or incur expenditure but, nevertheless, obtains a reduction in his liability to tax as if he had. Thus most tax avoidance involves a pretence, because the reality of the situation is normally that 'in an arrangement of tax avoidance the financial position of the taxpayer is unaffected (save for the costs of devising and implementing the arrangement)'.[22]

Lord Goff of Chieveley waxed lyrical in in *Ensign Tankers (Leasing) Ltd v Stokes*,[23] saying:

> Unacceptable tax avoidance typically involves the creation of

---

[18]   Cmnd 9474, para 1016.
[19]   [1987] 1 AC 155 at 167.
[20]   Cmnd 9474, para 1016.
[21]   [1987] 1 AC at 168.
[22]   At 169.
[23]   [1992] BTC 110 at 128.

complex artificial structures by which, as though by the wave of a magic wand, the taxpayer conjures out of the air a loss, or a gain, or expenditure, or whatever it may be, which otherwise would never have existed. These structures are designed to achieve an adventitious tax benefit for the taxpayer, and are in truth no more than raids on the public funds at the expense of the general body of taxpayers, and as such are unacceptable.

Tax planning is often equated with tax avoidance because tax evasion cannot even come into the equation. However, as we have just seen from the speeches of two Law Lords, tax avoidance is hardly regarded as a virtue. While tax avoiders and their advisers would naturally view tax avoidance as, at worst, morally and ethically neutral[24] (they may even see it as being a commendable exercise[25]), some elements of tax avoidance can conjure images of inequity and unacceptability. Tax planning and avoidance schemes often introduce artificial 'losses' or 'gains' that would not have existed in straightforward transactions, and often lack genuine business and commercial intent other than the intent to avoid one's fair share of the tax burden. Often, only the rich can afford the type of specialist advice needed to secure a successful scheme, and so, tax planning can be seen as an instrument of the rich employed brazenly in their bid to cast their tax burden, which they clearly can bear, onto the shoulders of others. Such considerations would then lead naturally to a perception that such behaviour is 'unacceptable' and ought not to be permitted. It is this type of unacceptable tax avoidance that has been the focus of judicial debate and consideration in recent years. At times judicial attempts to grapple with the situation and/or to articulate the unacceptability of the taxpayer's activities has resulted in some apparent confusion over the concepts of 'evasion' and 'avoidance'.

Most strikingly this was seen in *Furniss v Dawson*[26], when Lord Scarman appeared to refer to unacceptable 'tax avoidance' schemes as 'tax evasion'. This drew a comment from Lord Goff that '... unacceptable tax avoidance schemes which Lord Scarman described as "tax evasion" - a label which is perhaps better kept for those transactions which are traditionally so described ...'.

Before we examine the judicial approaches to tax planning, there are a number of matters that we should note. First, accurate information about the level and practice of evasion and avoidance is difficult to obtain.[27] The Inland

24   For a general discussion on the ethical issues raised by tax planning see P. F. Vineberg (1969) BTR 31.
25   Contrast the view expressed about tax avoiders by Viscount Simon LC in *Latilla v IRC* [1943] AC 377 at 381: 'There is, of course, no doubt that they are within their legal rights, but that is no reason why their efforts, or or those of the professional gentleman who assist them in the matter, should be regarded as a commendable exercise of ingenuity or as a discharge of the duties of good citizenship.'
26   [1984] AC 474 at 513.
27   See generally, M. O'Higgins (1981) BTR 286 and 367; P. Dean et. al. (1980) BTR 28.

Revenue have indicated that it is 'not implausible' that incomes not declared for tax purposes could amount to 7.5 per cent of gross domestic product. Academic researchers have confirmed that tax evasion might be high and that professionals are keen to advise on tax avoidance schemes - albeit that there was some resistance to the consideration of complex artificial tax avoidance schemes.[28]

Secondly, just as accurate information on the extent of avoidance and evasion is difficult to obtain, accurate information on the causes of evasion and avoidance is just as difficult to obtain. High tax rates[29], imprecise and incomprehensible legislation, weak investigatory and legal penalties[30] might all contribute to the encouragement of tax avoidance and evasion. Some of these points are encapsulated by Kay in a statement which also highlights causes of tax avoidance[31]:

> The incidence of evasion is a function of the mechanisms by which tax is assessed and collected, and the extent to which they can be controlled and monitored; the incidence of avoidance is a function of the tax base and depends on the extent to which legislation is successful in expressing the underlying economic concepts. Avoidance depends on the base: evasion on assessment procedures. There is an area which lies in between the two, and this is mainly where the tax treatment of some transaction depends on the reason for undertaking the transaction. This is bound to prove difficult to police and offers scope for distorting and misrepresenting activities which gradually shade from tax avoidance into tax evasion.

Social attitudes are also important. In some countries tax evasion is perceived as a national sport or even a moral duty. In the United Kingdom the social penalties of evasion are probably high (as they also appear to be in relation to complex artificial tax avoidance schemes) - although we can all sympathise with the unintended evasion of the example of an elderly neighbour making and selling her home-made jam to a few close friends without any appreciation of the tax liability that should have attached to her 'profits'. Thirdly, one might question why we should be concerned with the practice of tax evasion and avoidance. The answer extends beyond the social unacceptability and inequity of evasion and avoidance.[32]

Included in the answer must be a consideration of the economic costs of the activity. These costs include the resource costs of the time and effort

---

[28]   See M. W. Spicer (1975) BTR 152; Sandford, 'Hidden Costs of Taxation',   Institute for Fiscal Studies (1973).24
[29]   Brown and Jackson ('Public Sector Economics', page 424) note that the 'incentives' for illegal evasion are likely to rise as marginal tax rates rise.
[30]   See Brown and Jackson, op. cit., 429.
[31]   J. A. Kay, 'The Economics of Tax Avoidance' (1979) BTR 354.
[32]   ibid at 355-356.Kay points out that the opportunities for avoidance are not evenly distributed between individuals or across activities.

devoted to the development of evasion and avoidance schemes; the 'loss' to any wealth redistribution and planning schemes; and the costs of policing and responding to evasion and avoidance developments. These costs might be seen as providing sufficient reason to pursue and regulate evasion and artificial avoidance schemes and their creators.

Judicial Responses - the Old and the New

We begin our journey through the changing and developing judicial responses to tax planning by examining what is often regarded as the 'traditional approach' - one which was put forward by the House of Lords in *IRC v Duke of Westminster*[33]

The traditional or *Westminster* approach demands that the authorities impose a tax on the individual in accordance with the legal effects of his arrangements, and rejects the notion that one must ignore the form of a transaction to look for 'the substance' of the matter. This approach demands recognition of the legal and tax result of the taxpayer's arrangements.[34]

> ... it has to be recognised that the subject, whether poor and humble or wealthy and noble, has the legal right so to dispose of his capital and income as to attract upon himself the least amount of tax. The only function of a Court of Law is to determine the legal result of his dispositions so far as they affect tax ....

These arrangements and their legal effects are not to be undone or ignored - except in very rare circumstances, and certainly not for the sole purpose of imposing a greater tax burden on the taxpayer. In *IRC v Duke of Westminster* itself the Duke entered into a covenant to pay his gardener a yearly sum by weekly payments (£1.90 per week) for a period of seven years or during their joint lives. The covenant was expressed to be without prejudice to the gardener's normal weekly wage (£3.00), although there was an understanding that the gardener would only take the balance of £1.10 per week as his wage. The purpose of the scheme was to enable the Duke to deduct the covenanted sum in computing his total income for surtax purposes. The Revenue claimed that the covenanted sum represented the

---

[33]   (1936) 19 TC 490.
[34]   See Lord Atkin at 511

gardener's wages and could not therefore be deducted for surtax purposes. The House of Lords disagreed and held (Lord Atkin dissenting) that the covenanted sums were annual payments under Schedule D Case III and thus were deductible for surtax purposes.

The Revenue had argued that, in accordance with the doctrine that the court may ignore the legal position and have regard to 'the substance of the matter', here the substance of the matter was that the gardener was serving the Duke for something equal to his former salary or wages and that, therefore, while he was so serving, the annuity must be treated as salary or wages. Lord Tomlin said[35] that this argument was based on misunderstanding of language used in some earlier cases. He said that the doctrine seemed to involve substituting 'the uncertain and crooked cord of discretion' for 'the golden and straight mete wand of the law'. Lord Tomlin emphasised the taxpayer's freedom to enjoy the benefits of the tax consequences of his affairs. The courts must recognise and tax the legal status and effects of the taxpayer's arrangements. In a famous passage, he declared[36]:

> Every man is entitled if he can to order his affairs so that the tax attaching under the appropriate acts is less than it otherwise would be. If he succeeds in ordering them so as to secure this result, then however unappreciative the Commissioners of Inland Revenue or his fellow taxpayers may be of his ingenuity, he cannot be compelled to pay an increased tax. This so-called doctrine of 'the substance' seems to to be nothing more than an attempt to make a man pay notwithstanding that he has ordered his affairs that the amount sought from him is not legally claimable.

Lord Wright said[37] that he did not understand the Revenue's arguments on the expression 'payments for continuing service ejusdem generis with wages or salaries'. He said that the payments must be one thing or the other - either annual payments or wages - and that there was no room for anything intermediate or in the nature of *cy pres*. According to him, once it is admitted that the deed is a genuine document, there is no room for the phrase 'in substance' - or, more correctly, the true nature of the legal obligation and nothing else is 'the substance'.

In this case, the legal effect and substance of the transaction were both that the Duke had entered into a legally binding and enforceable deed of covenant, the private understanding with the gardener notwithstanding. In this respect, Lord Macmillan[38] referred to the risk to which the Duke left himself exposed, 'namely, that his servants may quit his employment and take their services elsewhere and yet continue to exact the covenanted weekly payments from him.' This obviously would have been sufficient to indicate that payments under the covenants were not wages, because they were still payable as such even if the gardener left the Duke's employment.

In *Ensign Tankers (Leasing) Ltd v Stokes*[39], Lord Templeman pointed out that, on the basis that the gardener was enjoying his annuity to the full, but worked voluntarily for the Duke for half wages, the embarrassments would not all be on the Duke's side. The gardener would incur liability to income tax for wages to which he was entitled but voluntarily omitted to draw. He thus preferred Lord Atkin's dissenting analysis that the gardener worked full time for full wages, and volunteered that he would not take his annuity until he had retired - 'gardeners do not work for Dukes on half-wages'. With respect, this analysis is as problematic as Lord Templeman thinks that the first analysis is. For one, it does not seem to accord with the actual facts of the case.

The *Westminster* doctrine invites the taxpayer to arrange his affairs so as to enjoy maximum tax benefits and invites the courts to recognise the status of those arrangements and apply any tax benefits or tax rules accordingly. Some take the view that this is a recognition of form over substance. Although this might be a convenient way of explaining the *Westminster* case, it is not entirely accurate. The courts have always been willing to look beyond the presented 'form' to ascertain the true status of the taxpayer's arrangements. This is formally apparent when the courts declare the form or label to be a 'sham'. Less formally it is apparent when the courts find that the substance dictates the form. In the determinant of legal status and in the attaching of the appropriate tax consequence, the process demands recognition of both substance and form. For example, in the *Westminster* case Lord Tomlin referred[40] to the statement of Warrington LJ in *In Re Hinckes, Dashwood v Hinckes*[41] that the court does look at the substance, but that in order to ascertain the substance, the court must look at the legal effect of the bargain which the parties have entered into. Lord Tomlin thus concluded[42]:

> [H]ere the substance is that which results from the legal rights and obligations of the parties ascertained upon ordinary legal principles,

---

[38]   At 527.
[39]   [1992] BTC 110 at 118-119
[40]   At 521.
[41]   [1921] 1 Ch 475 at 489.
[42]   19 TC at 521.

and, ... the conclusion must be that each annuitant is entitled to an annuity which, as between himself and the payer is liable to deduction of income tax by the payer and which the payer is entitled to treat as a deduction from his total income for surtax purposes.

Many principles have been derived from the approach exemplified by the *Westminster* case. First, a transaction which on its true construction is of a kind that would escape tax, is not taxable on the ground that the same outcome could have been produced by entering into a transaction in another form which would have attracted tax. What this simply means is that a person ought to be taxed by reference to the transactions into which he has actually entered, and not by reference to transactions into which he might have entered to achieve the same object or result. Thus, if the object is to make a donation to a favourite charity, there are a number of possible methods of achieving this object. One method, which is not tax efficient, is to send the funds to the charity, without any ceremony. Another method is to complete the necessary formalities and give the money as a lump sum through the 'gift aid' scheme. This is tax efficient and attracts tax relief. Yet another (tax efficient) method is to divide the sum into periodic payments made under a four-year deed of covenant. Having chosen either of the tax efficient methods, one cannot be treated 'as if' one had chosen the first (and tax inefficient) method. To relate this to *Westminster*, if the Duke wished to make regular payments to his gardener, and chose to do so by a deed of covenant rather than by a pay rise or a regular wage payment, he cannot be treated as if he did the latter. The difficulty here lies in the private 'understanding' between the Duke and his gardener.

Another principle that emerges from the 'old' or 'traditional' approach is that it is not the function of the court to stretch statutory provisions so as to 'catch' a person who is involved in a tax avoidance scheme. It was Lord Simon of Glaisdale who said in *Ransom v Higgs*[43]:

> It may seem hard that a cunningly advised taxpayer should be able to avoid what appears to be his equitable share of the general fiscal burden and cast it on the shoulders of his fellow citizens. But for the courts to try and stretch the law to meet hard cases (whether the hardship appears to bear on the individual taxpayer or on the general body of taxpayers as represented by the Inland Revenue) is not merely to make bad law but to run the risk of subverting the rule of law itself. Disagreeable as it may seem that some taxpayers should

[43]   (1974) 50 TC 1 at 94.

escape what might appear to be their fair share of the general burden of national expenditure, it would be far more disagreeable to substitute the rule of caprice for that of law.

It is also clear that, unless statute otherwise provides, the fact that the taxpayer had fiscal motives for entering into the transactions does not invalidate the transactions.[44]

These principles are eminently sensible and probably unassailable. Yet their application led to a thriving tax avoidance industry involving schemes of the kind which were probably never envisaged by their Lordships in *Westminster*. But is the traditional approach really so porous as to allow taxpayers to get away with almost anything? It seems not. The traditional approach does not envisage a blinkered or blind approach to the taxpayer's activities. Although a genuine transaction may not be ignored and has to be treated as such, the court will not necessarily accept the parties' description of their own transactions as conclusive. Thus, 'sham' transactions or documents will be disregarded. Lord Tomlin recognised this in the *Westminster* case, when he said that there may be cases where documents are not *bona fide* or intended to be acted upon, but are only used as a cloak to conceal a different transaction.[45]

However, he said that no such case was made or even suggested in the case. While Lord Tomlin did not use the word 'sham' to describe the types of transaction or document that he was referring to, the term has been attributed thereto in subsequent cases. The concept is still very much alive today, and the principle, even under the new approach, is that shams will be disregarded.

Diplock LJ addressed the issue of sham documents in *Snook v London and West Riding Investments Ltd.*[46] referring to them as those which are:

> executed by the parties to the 'sham' which are intended by them to give to third parties or to the court the appearance of creating between the parties legal rights or obligations different from the actual legal rights and obligations (if any) which the parties intended to create... All parties thereto must have a common intention that the acts or documents are not to create the legal rights and obligations which they give the appearance of creating. No unexpressed intentions of a 'shammer' affect the rights of a party whom he has deceived.

---

[44]   See for example Lord Wilberforce in *Ramsay v IRC* [1982] AC 300, at 323; (1981) 54 TC 101 at 184; Viscount Dilhorne in *Lupton v FA and AB Ltd.* [1972] AC 635 at 655; Lord Morris in *Finsbury Securities Ltd. v IRC* [1966] 1 WLR 1402 at 1417.

[45]   19 TC at 521.

[46]   [1967] 2 ALL ER 518 at 520.

Lord Wilberforce in *Ramsay v IRC*[47] preferred to define 'sham' as referring to documents or transactions, which, while professing to be one thing, are in fact something different, while 'genuine' transactions or documents are described as those which are, in law, what they profess to be. However it is important to note that the concept of 'sham' appears to enjoy a rather limited scope in that it may have become too technical in its requirements. In essence it demands evidence of an intention to conceal or deceive - a fact that may make it more appropriate to be linked to tax evasion than tax avoidance. In *IRC v McGuckian*[48] Lord Steyn made it clear that tax avoidance does not necessarily mean that a transaction is a sham, and in *Stone v Executors of Hitch (dec'd)*[49] Jonathan Parker J said that the artificiality (in the sense of a lack of commercial purpose) of a particular transaction does not in itself suggest sham. The following words of Jonathan Parker J are poignant in summing up the narrowness of the concept[50]:

> In a case involving a complex and artificial tax avoidance scheme, where the scheme and documentation is sloppily executed, where the evidence of the taxpayer and of his legal adviser (the deviser of the scheme) is found to be unreliable, and where their dealings with the Revenue have been less than straightforward, there must be a strong temptation for any tribunal to, in effect, throw up its hands and cry 'Sham!'. But ... so long as the Snook definition of sham remains the accepted definition - that temptation has, to my judgment, to be resisted.

The New Approach

The limitations of the traditional *Westminster* approach soon became obvious - particularly, in the context of 'off the peg', artificial tax avoidance schemes. The purchasers of these 'off the peg' schemes (or even tailor-made schemes) would seek to enjoy the tax consequences of each transaction in a multi-transaction scheme, examined in isolation from the whole. They would insist, relying on the *Westminster* case, that the courts should recognise the status and effects of each isolated transaction, and that such recognition should result in the application of appropriate, and often isolated, tax principles and concessions. This was in reality an

[47]   54 TC at 184.
[48]   [1997] 3 All ER 817 at 826.
[49]   [1999] BTC 103 at 134.
[50]   [1999] BTC at 136.

invitation to ignore the fiscal reality of the overall effects of the whole scheme, but rather to concentrate on each isolated step in the scheme. It soon became apparent that the courts would need to react to the artificiality of this situation - but that they must react in a manner which would not undermine the taxpayer's freedom (strongly supported in the *Westminster* case) to organise his or her affairs so as to enjoy the maximum possible tax benefits.

Ramsay v IRC (*supra*) is considered to be the starting point for the development of a 'new approach' to tax avoidance schemes. It seems however that the earliest incidences of what is now the new approach can be traced back to Lord Mansfield in the 18th century in a case where he seemed to look to the substance of a transaction that had been devised to circumvent a statutory charge, to the effect that the scheme was unsuccessful.[51]

This approach seems to have been lost during the heyday of the *Westminster* approach. After *Westminster*, evidence of a changing judicial attitude can be found in the case of *Floor v Davis*[52]. This case involved the disposal of shares from X to Y. In order to avoid capital gains tax, X set up a subsidiary company, and transferred shares to that company in consideration of the issue of shares. The subsidiary would then transfer those shares to Y. Subsequently, the subsidiary was dissolved and all its assets transferred to X. Thus, X had, indirectly, achieved the disposal of shares to Y through this subsidiary. On the issue of whether the 'disposal' ought to be treated as one from X to Y, thus removing the Capital Gains Tax advantages, or simply whether each step should be examined in isolation from the whole, the court erred on the side of the latter. The decision was perceived as being in keeping and consistent with the decision in *IRC v Duke of Westminster*. The dissenting judgment of Eveleigh LJ provided an insight into changing attitudes. Eveleigh LJ suggested[53] that the courts were not required to consider each step in isolation. The real issue was whether in reality they were faced with a disposal of shares from X to Y. If so, they should treat it as a transfer from X to Y and not a transfer by the subsidiary to Y - at least for tax purposes.

This suggestion was later confirmed as principle in *Ramsay v IRC*. This case involved a complex series of transactions designed to create an 'allowable loss' for Capital Gains Tax purposes. The true state of affairs was that, at the end of the series of transactions, the taxpayer's financial position was in reality just the same as it was at the beginning. Although the scheme

[51]   See I. Ferrier (1981) BTR 303.
[52]   (1979) 52 TC 609.
[53]   At 633-634.

produced a 'loss', the taxpayer had not suffered any real or actual loss. The House of Lords decided that such artificial schemes should be looked at as a whole for the purpose of determining their tax consequences. The courts should not look to each isolated transaction but to the fiscal reality of the series of related transactions, comparing the taxpayer's position at the beginning and at the end of the scheme. Lord Wilberforce, responding to the argument that the court could not go behind a genuine document or transaction to look for some supposed underlying substance, said[54]:

> This is a cardinal principle but it must not be overstated or overextended. While obliging the court to accept documents or transactions, found to be genuine, as such, it does not compel the court to look at a document or a transaction in blinkers, isolated from any context to which it properly belongs. If it can be seen that a document or transaction was intended to have effect as part of a nexus or series of transactions, or as an ingredient of a wider transaction intended as a whole, there is nothing in the doctrine to prevent it being so regarded: to do so is not to prefer form to substance, or substance to form. It is the task of the court to ascertain the legal nature of any transaction to which it is sought to attach a tax or a tax consequence and if that emerges from a series or combination of transactions, intended to operate as such, it is that series or combination which may be regarded.

This is the new approach to tax avoidance schemes. It is an approach in which one must look for the real loss or the real gain.[55]

In *Ramsay v IRC*, although the scheme produced a 'loss', it was not a real loss (since the taxpayer had incurred no loss in the real world), and therefore was not allowable. The principle was followed and applied in *IRC v Burmah Oil Co Ltd*.[56]

Here, a series of transactions were designed to create an 'allowable loss' for Capital Gains Tax purposes. Lord Fraser of Tullybelton, referring to *Ramsay*, said[57] that the question was whether the scheme, when completely carried out, did or did not result in a loss such as the legislation in question is dealing with, that is, a 'real loss'. In the case, although the transactions involved in the scheme were real, the loss which was the end result of them was not real, and so the scheme failed.

It is interesting to note that in *Burmah Oil*, Lord Diplock was careful to stress

---

[54]   54 TC at 185.
[55]   See Parker LJ in *Craven v White* [1987] 3 WLR 660 at 704.
[56]   (1981) 54 TC 200.
[57]   At 220.

the differences between the tax avoidance scheme found as acceptable in the *Westminster* case, and the tax avoidance schemes declared unacceptable in *Ramsay* and *Burmah Oil*. The former consisted of simple arrangements between two consenting (real) persons, whereas the later involved inter-connected transactions between artificial persons (limited companies) without minds of their own but directed by a single mastermind.[58] One appeared to be an acceptable arrangement of one's affairs whereas the other appeared to be an unacceptable artificial tax avoidance scheme. Lord Diplock made it clear that the new approach had not overruled the *Westminster* case. However, he also made it clear that the new approach involved recognising that the famous *dictum* of Lord Tomlin in the *Westminster* case tells us little or nothing as to the methods of ordering one's affairs that will be recognised by the courts as effective to lessen the tax that would attach to them if business transactions were conducted in a straight forward way.

Thus while the true state of the law is still that a man is entitled if he can to arrange his affairs so as to pay less tax than he would otherwise have done, it seems that a further truth is that, in many cases, a man cannot do so, no matter how hard he tries.[59] This is because he may be treated under *Ramsay* as having made a different arrangement from that which he believed himself to have made. Lord Diplock clearly stated that *Ramsay* marked a 'significant' change in the approach adopted by the House of Lords with respect to preordained series of transactions.[60]

The real problem is that of trying to ascertain when and in what circumstances the courts would adopt this new approach. *Furniss v Dawson*[61] provided some insight into judicial thinking in this area. The case involved a scheme to defer liability to Capital Gains Tax. The Dawsons wished to sell some shares to Wood Bastow. An outright sale would give rise to immediate tax liability under Capital Gains Tax rules. The scheme to defer tax involved the taxpayers transferring the shares (through a share exchange) to a newly incorporated Manx company, Greenjacket Investments Ltd. Greenjacket Investments Ltd then sold its acquisition of the taxpayer's shares to Wood Bastow. The eventual sale price equated with the originally planned sale price of £152,000. The Revenue claimed that the reality of the scheme was a chargeable disposal from the taxpayer to Wood Bastow for £152,000. Applying the new approach, the House of Lords agreed with the Revenue's assessment. The transaction was a disposal of the taxpayer's shares to Wood Bastow, and had immediate (as opposed to

---

[58]   54 TC at 214.
[59]   See McNeill J in *R v Inspector of Taxes, ex p Fulford-Dobson* [1987] 3 WLR at 289-290.
[60]   54 TC at 214.
[61]   [1984] STC 153; 55 TC 324. For comment, see C. N. Beattie (1984) BTR 109.

deferred) tax implications.

Furniss v Dawson has been referred to as the 'high water mark' of the new approach. It certainly took the tax avoidance industry by surprise, since the new approach had hitherto only been applied to 'circular' or self-cancelling transactions. *Furniss v Dawson* involved what has been termed a 'linear' transaction, yet the House of Lords applied the new approach to that transaction. Two distinct approaches were apparent in the House of Lord's analysis of the new approach. The first approach is to be found in the speech of Lord Brightman, although Lord Brightman was careful to stress that he was adopting and following a formulation proposed by Lord Diplock in *Burmah Oil*. According to Lord Brightman[62]:

> First, there must be a pre-ordained series of transactions; or, if one likes, one single composite transaction. This composite transaction may or may not include the achievement of a legitimate commercial (i.e. business) end ... Secondly, there must be steps inserted which have no commercial (business) purpose apart from the avoidance of a liability to tax - not 'no business effect'. If those two ingredients exist, the inserted steps are to be disregarded for fiscal purposes. The court must then look at the end result. Precisely how the end result will be taxed will depend on the terms of the taxing statute sought to be applied.

The second approach is to be found in the speech of Lord Bridge. Lord Bridge took strength from the experiences of United States Federal Courts, and suggested that, in cases of composite transactions, it was perfectly legitimate for the court to draw a distinction between the substance and the form of the composite arrangement, without in any way suggesting that any of the single transactions which make up the whole are other than genuine.[63] Under either approach, the scheme in *Furniss v Dawson* would fail.

After *Furniss v Dawson*, there was some concern over the way in which the new approach would develop - would it confine its area of application to the rather mechanistic and legalistic requirements of Lords Brightman and Diplock, or would it follow the US approach of enjoying a wide application in searching for the substance and fiscal reality of the composite arrangement? The latter (which has been described as analogous to the search for the Holy Grail) would provide a wider scope for judicial discretion but would suffer from uncertainty and imprecision of application. In *Furniss*

---

[62] 55 TC at 401.
[63] 55 TC at 392.

v Dawson, Lord Bridge resisted[64] any attempt to provide an exposition of all the criteria by which form and substance are to be distinguished. According to him, once a basic doctrine of form and substance is accepted, the drawing of precise boundaries will need to be worked out on a case-by-case basis. Perhaps if criteria were propounded, the 'substance over form' approach would face the danger of becoming as mechanistic and restrictive as Lord Brightman's approach.

In any event, it is difficult to see how this 'substance over form' could be adopted without overruling the *Westminster* case, which was definite in its rejection of the 'substance of the matter'. It would seem that the two-point approach of Lord Brightman is preferable. This is the approach that was adopted by the House of Lords in a decision which developed further the principles of the new approach - the decision in three conjoined appeals: *Craven v White*; *IRC v Bowater Property Developments Ltd*; and *Baylis v Gregory*.[65]

Both *Craven v White* and *Baylis v Gregory* involved the *Furniss v Dawson* type of share transfer schemes. In *Baylis v Gregory* it was originally intended that a sale to X would take place by the taxpayer transferring shares to a Manx company, followed by the Manx company then transferring those shares to X (as in *Furniss v Dawson*). However, following the transfer of the shares by the taxpayer to the Manx, X withdrew from the scheme. Eventually (some 20 months later) another buyer (Z) was found, and the sale to Z took place. The House of Lords unanimously held that the new approach did not apply - the sale was not one by the taxpayer to Z, but rather one by the Manx to Z. In *Craven v White*, the taxpayer company was considering either a merger with X or a sale of its shares to Z. In preparation for the proposed merger with X, the taxpayer transferred (in a share exchange as in *Furniss v Dawson*) its shares to a Manx company. Before the merger was completed, negotiations with Z were resumed, the outcome of which was the sale of the relevant shares by the Manx company to Z. Once again, the House of Lords held (Lords Templeman and Goff dissenting) that the new approach did not apply - the sale was by the Manx company to Z, not one by the taxpayer to Z. In *IRC v Bowater Property Developments Ltd*, a scheme was devised to provide the maximum tax benefits in a sale of land. Bowater Property Developments Ltd divided land into five parts and transferred each part to a separate company within its group. Each company then sold their part of the land to Z Ltd. The tax benefits of this arrangement enabled the five companies to enjoy individual statutory allowances under the Development

---

64　Ibid.
65　[1988] 3 All ER 495; STC 476. For comment, see R. K. Ashton (1988) BTR 482; G. Mansfield (1989) BTR 5.

Land Tax regime. If Bowater had directly sold the land to Z Ltd, Bowater only would have enjoyed statutory allowances. The House of Lords unanimously held that the new approach did not apply, and that the transfers of land were transfer by the five individual companies; not a transfer from Bowater to Z Ltd.

The importance of these three joined appeals (hereafter referred to as *Craven v White*) is reflected in how they interpreted *Furniss v Dawson* and applied the new approach. As indicated earlier, the House of Lords favoured the Brightman and Diplock approach to the question of when the new approach would apply. Lord Oliver, in a speech which seemed quite critical of *Furniss v Dawson*[66], was careful to emphasise that *Furniss v Dawson* simply brought forth the principles of statutory construction established in *Ramsay*. *Furniss v Dawson* was not an authority for any wider proposition such as

> a general proposition that any transaction which is effected for the purpose of avoiding tax on a contemplated subsequent transaction and is therefore 'planned' is, for that reason, necessarily to be treated as one with that subsequent transaction and as having no independent effect even where that is realistically and logically impossible.[67]

According to Lord Oliver, the question which fell to be determined in *Furniss* was (as it in the present case)

> whether an intermediate transfer was, at the time when it was effected, so closely interconnected with the ultimate disposition that it was properly to be described as not, in itself, a real transaction at all but merely an element in some different and larger whole without independent effect.

He said that this was a question of fact - but one which had to be approached within the bounds of what is logically defensible. As far as *Ramsay* itself was concerned, Lord Oliver asserted that it was no authority for any proposition wider than that 'where it can be shown that successive transactions are so indissolubly linked together, both in fact and in intention, as to be properly and realistically viewed as a composite whole, the court is both bound and entitled so to regard them.' This theme of the tight binding

---

[66]   See for example, Lord Oliver's query ([1988] 3 All ER at 517) as to whether, apart from the tripartite contract on which reliance was placed in *Furniss v Dawson*, the reconstitution of the parties activities in that case was 'rationally and logically possible within the accepted principles of construction provided by *Ramsay* or, indeed, any other principle'.

[67]   [1988] 3 All ER at 523.

of the transactions flowed through the whole of Lord Oliver's speech. For example, he later again explained the principles to be derived from *Ramsay* as being that one has to look at the transactions as a whole, and ask whether 'realistically they constitute a single and indivisible whole and whether it is intellectually possible so to treat them'.[68]

We shall examine this theme again when we look at the concept of 'preordained'. It suffices to say here that this theme eventually led Lord Oliver to reformulate the prerequisites for the application of the new approach. Lord Brightman's two-stage test in *Furniss v Dawson* was to the effect that, first, there must be a preordained series of transactions, making one composite transaction, which may or may not include the achievement of a legitimate commercial or business effect or end, and, secondly, that there must be steps inserted into those transactions which have no commercial or business purpose apart from the avoidance of liability to tax. This test was redefined by Lord Oliver as a four-fold test[69]:

1. that the series of transactions was, at the time when an intermediate transaction was entered into, preordained in order to produce a given result;

2. that the intermediate transaction had no other purpose than tax mitigation;

3. that there was at that time no practical likelihood that the pre-planned events would not take place in the order ordained, so that the intermediate transaction was not even contemplated practically as having an independent life; and

4. that the preordained events did in fact take place.

According to Lord Oliver, the court can, in these circumstances, be justified in linking the beginning with the end so as to make a single composite whole to which the fiscal results of the single composite whole are to be applied.

The majority's decision in *Craven v White* was described by Lord Templeman (dissenting) as distorting the effect of *Furniss v Dawson*, with the potential to 'revive a surprised tax avoidance industry and cost the general body of taxpayers hundreds of millions of pounds by enabling artificial tax avoidance schemes to alter the incidence of taxation'.[70]

However, while it may indeed have had the result of distorting the effect of

---

[68]   Ibid at 525.
[69]   At 527.
[70]   At 509.
[71]   For example, Lord Keith went to the extent of saying that *Furniss v Dawson* must be restricted to its own facts (at 501).

Furniss v Dawson,[71] it is arguably more principle-based than *Furniss v Dawson* itself, and, in seeking to formulate clear guidelines, it can be said to have placed the law on a clearer footing. The majority were right to reject the notion that the mere presence of an 'artificial tax avoidance scheme' permits the court to intervene, and Lord Oliver's four-fold test seems to be a sensible and clear approach to the question. This test employs a number of important terms, which we shall now examine.

'Preordained'

Craven v White and previous cases talked of a 'preordained' series of transactions. It is clear that the 'preordained' here relates to the whole series of transactions (or the whole scheme) and not to a subset of it.[72] But what does 'preordained' mean? Much of Lord Oliver's speech in *Craven v White*, in pursuing the theme of tight binding of transactions, was in reality concerned with this issue. According to Lord Oliver[73], 'preordained' means more than simply 'planned or thought out in advance.' Rather, it involves a degree of certainty and control over the end result at the time when the intermediate steps are taken. This however does not require absolute certainty (in the sense that every single term of the transaction which ultimately takes place must then be finally settled and agreed). It means at least that the principal terms should be agreed to the point at which it can be said that there is no practical likelihood that the transaction which actually takes place will not take place.

Lord Oliver was of the view that it was insufficient that the ultimate transaction which finally takes place, although not envisaged at the intermediate stage as a concrete reality, is simply a transaction of the kind that was then envisaged. On the contrary, it must, on the facts:

> be possible to analyse the sequence as one single identifiable transaction and if, at the completion of the intermediate disposition, it is not even known to whom or upon what terms any ultimate disposition will be made, I simply do not see how such an analysis is intellectually possible.

Lord Oliver was careful to emphasise that the court had no business reconstructing the parties' transactions in the quest to ascertain whether a

---

[72] See *Fitzwilliam v IRC* [1993] BTC 8003. See especially Lord Browne-Wilkinson at 8036.
[73] At 528.

transaction was preordained. That decision had to be made solely on the basis of the facts and events, all of which must clearly establish a 'cut and dried' deal - and nothing less would suffice. This approach is linked to *Ramsay* itself. Explaining the link, Lord Oliver said[74]:

> A transaction does not change its nature because of an event, then uncertain, which subsequently occurs and *Ramsay* is concerned not with reforming transactions but with ascertaining their reality. There is a real and not merely a metaphysical distinction between something that is done as a preparatory step towards a possible but uncertain contemplated future action and something which is done as an integral and interdependent part of a transaction already agreed and, effectively, predestined to take place. In the latter case, to link the end to the beginning involves no more than recognising the reality of what is effectively a single operation ab initio. In the former it involves quite a different process, viz. that of imputing to the parties, ex post facto, an obligation (either contractual or quasi contractual) which did not exist at the material time but which is to be attributed from the occurrence or juxtaposition of events which subsequently took place. That cannot be extracted from *Furniss v Dawson* as it stands nor can it be justified by any rational extension of the *Ramsay* approach. It involves the invocation of a different principle altogether, that is to say, the reconstruction of events into something that they were not, either in fact or in intention, not because they in fact constituted a single composite whole but because, and only because, one or more of them was motivated by a desire to avoid or minimise tax. That may be a very beneficial objective but it has to be recognised that the rational basis of *Ramsay* and *Furniss v Dawson* then becomes irrelevant and is replaced by a principle of nullifying a tax advantage derived from any 'associated operation.'

Applying these principles in the case itself, in *Craven v White*, the final step was not practically certain or likely at the time of the intermediate step, because the taxpayer had at that time genuinely believed that a sale to Z would not take place. The taxpayer believed that a merger with X was the more probable outcome. Similarly, in *Baylis v Gregory*, the breakdown of negotiations and the subsequent sale to a different purchaser some 22 months later indicated the absence of 'certainty'. Likewise, in *IRC v Bowater Property Developments Ltd*, no 'certainty' or preordained event was present.

---

[74]   At 527.

At the time of entering into the fragmentation of the land, the ultimate purchaser was not a party to the fragmentation arrangements.

While Lord Oliver concentrated on the practical likelihood of all the pre-planned transactions taking place as planned, Lord Keith took a different approach to the question of 'preordained'. He said[75] that, in ascertaining the true legal effect of a series of transactions, it is relevant to take into account that all the steps in it were contractually agreed in advance, or that they had been determined in advance by a guiding will (normally the taxpayer) which was in a position, for all practical purposes, to secure that all of them were carried through to completion. This is obviously a different test from the 'practical likelihood' test. The latter is focused on probability, while Lord Keith's test is focused on contract, or, the ability of the taxpayer to secure the completion of the scheme. Both tests when applied to the same set of facts, may well produce different results in some cases. The 'no practical likelihood test' is a 'double negative' test which requires a high degree of probability, does not require certainty,[76] but possibly requires a 'near certainty'.[77]

However, it might be more uncertain in application than Lord Keith's test, because while with the benefit of hindsight one might feel confident to answer the question whether there was no practical likelihood that the scheme would not be carried through, it would be difficult to answer this question at the time that is material - when the intermediate steps were being taken. Invariably, it might involve 'second-guessing' - something which would seem far removed from the proper judicial function. Lord Keith's test is however not without its difficulties. How does one assess the ability of the taxpayer to secure completion? This might be easy enough in the context of corporations which are under the control of one or more of the parties to the transaction. But what about natural persons, or corporations which are not under the control of any of the parties?

Perhaps the best approach is to merge both tests, so that a series of transactions would be preordained if:

(a) there is a contractual obligation to carry them through, or

(b) there is a master-mind or guiding will who or which can secure their completion, or

---

[75]   At 500.
[76]   Per Knox J in *Pigott v Staines Investments Ltd* [1995] BTC 90 at 113.
[77]   Knox J, ibid, at 108.

(c) they are pre-planned, and there is no practical likelihood that they will not be carried through as planned.

Thus it may be that there is no need to adopt an 'either, or' approach to the tests. This approach to the question may have been later adopted by Lord Keith himself. In deciding in *Fitzwilliam v IRC*[78] that the scheme in that case was preordained, Lord Keith seemed to apply Lord's Oliver's approach in *Craven v White*, saying that the transactions 'all formed part of a pre-planned tax avoidance scheme and that there was no reasonable possibility that they would not all be carried out.'

Both the Keith and Oliver tests were criticised (naturally) by Lord Templeman in his dissenting speech in *Craven v White*. First, he said[79]:

Two transactions can form part of a scheme even though it is wholly uncertain when the first transaction is carried out whether the taxpayer who is responsible for the scheme will succeed in procuring the second transaction to be carried out at all.

And then he later added[80]

If the shadowy, undefined and indefinable expressions 'practically certain', 'practical likelihood', and 'practical contemplation' possess any meanings, those expressions and those meanings are not to be derived from *Dawson*.

On that basis, Lord Templeman was able to conclude that the intentions in *Craven v White* were eventually fulfilled as part of the planned arrangements. With respect, an approach which allows the court to intervene on the basis that there is a planned tax avoidance scheme (as defined) seems to be more objectionable in principle than the approach which restricts the court's intervention to cases which can realistically and intellectually be described as pre-ordained - especially one that also gives a clear definition of 'preordained'.

---

[78]   [1993] BTC 8003 at 8015.
[79]   At 506.
[80]   At 508.

'Commercial Purpose'

We have examined the concept of 'preordained' as one of the prerequisites of the new approach. Preordainment is however not necessarily fatal to a scheme's success. One other essential characteristic of a composite transaction for the purposes of the new approach centres around the question of the purposes of the individual transactions in a composite scheme. Lord Keith said in *Fitzwilliam v IRC*[81] that the fact of preordainment is not sufficient in itself, to negative the application of an exemption from a tax liability which the series of transactions is intended to create, unless the series is capable of being construed in a manner inconsistent with the application of the exemption. For example, preordainment cannot be used as an excuse to re-characterise a 'perfectly normal and straightforward commercial transaction into a thoroughly abnormal and unusual transaction whose only merit ... is that it attracts a tax advantage'.[82]

Lord Brightman in *Furniss v Dawson* and Lord Oliver in *Craven v White* both pointed to a second criterion - that there are steps inserted into the preordained series of transactions, for no commercial purpose, other than the avoidance of liability to tax. Such a step was treated as a 'fiscal nullity' (a concept which is not without difficulty - see below) in *Furniss v Dawson*. The position was explained by Vinelott J in *Shepherd v Lyntress Ltd*[83]:

> It is a necessary but not sufficient condition for the application of the Dawson principle that there should be a finding that the intermediate step which it is sought to disregard as having no fiscal consequence was inserted for no purpose except that of saving tax. The intermediate step is disregarded because if a composite transaction is treated as a single transaction it is evident that it falls outside the purpose of the exemption or the relief of the allowance which the taxpayer seeks to avail himself of.

According to Lord Keith in *Fitzwilliam v IRC*[84] the reference to the insertion of steps which have no commercial purpose apart from the avoidance of liability to tax indicates that this is a feature that demonstrates the artificiality of the whole scheme. This of course raises the question whether the presence of any commercial purpose demonstrates the non-artificiality of the scheme. The answer to this might be affirmative. Browne-Wilkinson VC said in *Overseas Containers (Finance) Ltd v Stoker*[85] that if essentially the transaction is of a commercial nature and there is a genuine commercial

---

purpose, the presence of a collateral purpose to obtain a tax advantage does not 'denature' what is essentially a commercial transaction. On the other hand, if the sole purpose of a transaction is to obtain a fiscal advantage, it is logically impossible to postulate the existence of any commercial purpose.

He went on to say[86] that a finding that the dominant purpose (as opposed to the sole purpose) was a fiscal advantage does not by itself inevitably lead to a finding in law that the taxpayer's transactions were not normal trading transactions. This seems to indicate that as soon as any commercial purpose is found it is impossible to describe the transactions as amount to an 'artificial' tax avoidance scheme.

The problem, when the second prerequisite is found to exist lies in the correct analysis of what happens to the steps that were inserted for no commercial purposes. As indicated earlier, in *Furniss v Dawson*, such a step was treated as a 'fiscal nullity' (meaning perhaps that it is treated as generating neither a gain nor a loss). In practical terms, it seems that the inserted step was simply disregarded in *Furniss v Dawson*, and then the tax consequences of the whole scheme were determined without reference to that step. This meant that the 'end result' in that case (a sale by the Dawsons of their shares to Wood Bastow) was an edited version of what really happened - arguably amounting not to a construction of the parties activities, but to a reconstruction thereof. It is not difficult to see why Lord Oliver was so critical in *Craven v White* of *Furniss v Dawson*, and why Lord Keith suggested that it should be restricted to its own facts. In Ensign *Tankers (Leasing) Ltd v Stokes*[87] Lord Templeman said:

> The task of the courts is to construe documents and analyse facts and to ensure the taxpayer does not pay too little tax or too much tax but the amount of tax which is consistent with the true effect in law of the taxpayer's activities. Neither the taxpayer nor the Revenue should be deprived of the fiscal consequences of the taxpayer's activities properly analysed.

In the light of statements like this, how can the disregarding of the intermediate steps in *Furniss v Dawson* be justified? It seems that the courts are not always sure how to approach the matter. In *Fitzwilliam v IRC* Lord Keith[88] preferred to explain the *Furniss v Dawson* decision by saying that, in that case, the intellectual basis upon which the House was able to disregard

---

[86]   At 161.
[87]   [1992] BTC at 120.
[88]   [1993] BTC at 8012.

the fiscal consequences of the interposition of Greenjacket was that all the parties involved had formally agreed upon what was to happen, but they were not formally bound to bring it about. Thus the *Ramsay* principle 'made it possible to hold that the final result for fiscal purposes was the same as it would have been if the parties had been so formally bound'. He subsequently suggested that it was not legitimate 'to alter the character of a particular transaction in a series or to pick bits out of it and reject other bits'.[89]

In *Ensign Tankers (Leasing) Ltd v Stokes*[90] Millet J (as he then was) said that the principles of *Ramsay* and *Furniss v Dawson* do not entitle the court to 'disregard' the component elements of a composite transaction by treating them as if they never happened. According to him, the real question is whether some step in a preordained series of transactions is so closely connected with the rest that it is to be treated not as having an independent effect but as merely an element in a different and larger whole. His rationalisation of what happened in *Furniss v Dawson* is that the transfer to Greenjacket was not disregarded, but was rather treated for what it was - a step in the disposal to the ultimate purchaser. Then the question was whether that step fell within the words of a statutory exemption.

These explanations of *Furniss v Dawson* seem to be trying hard to establish that that case did not really involve the disregarding of anything. On that basis, the decision can be supported, and does not contravene any established principle. It would also be able to escape the criticisms rightly directed at any judicial attempt to attribute to the parties something which they had not done. On the other hand, other judicial comment seems to accept that the reality of the situation is that transactions are being disregarded. We have already referred to Vinelott J's statement in *Shepherd v Lyntress Ltd.* That was not a lone voice. In *Fitzwilliam v IRC* Lord Browne-Wilkinson said[91] that the Commissioners or the court must identify the real transaction carried out by the taxpayers and apply the words of the taxing provisions to the real transaction - and if this real transaction is carried through by a series of artificial steps, then they must disregard for fiscal purposes the steps artificially inserted. According to him the provisions of the taxing statute are to be construed as applying to the actual transaction that the parties were effecting in the real world, 'not to the artificial forms in which the parties chose to clothe it in the surrealist world of tax advisers'.

Lord Browne-Wilkinson took the same line again in *IRC v McGuckian*,[92] saying that the approach pioneered in the *Ramsay* case and later decisions

---

[89]   At 8015.
[90]   [1989] BTC 410 at 478.
[91]   [1993] BTC at 8035.
[92]   [1997] 3 All ER 817.

is an approach to construction, to the effect that[93] in construing tax legislation, the statutory provisions are to be applied to the substance of the transaction, disregarding artificial steps in the composite transaction or series of transactions inserted only for the purpose of seeking to obtain a tax advantage.

There is no doubt that the latter analysis is the correct interpretation of the principles of and decision in *Furniss v Dawson*. The case did involve the disregarding of the interposed transactions involving Greenjacket, and this is precisely what Lord Brightman himself quite clearly said that he was doing, and what he thought that the court should do when the new approach applies. In so doing, *Furniss v Dawson* extended *Ramsay* perhaps quite unnecessarily, and also created a number of problems, which the courts have since been grappling with. The attempts of other judges and Law Lords thereafter to rationalise the decision in other ways shows the amount of disquiet that it has raised. It could perhaps rightly be described as an extreme and unwarranted form of judicial intervention.[94]

The principle of disregarding certain activities, or treating them as fiscal nullities, is not only suspect, but it is also bound to be nonsensical in some cases. (We will say more about this later). In *Furniss v Dawson*, the Dawsons were left at the end with shares in Greenjacket, but with no cash. Greenjacket was left with money for the sale of its property, but no Capital Gains Tax liability. The Dawsons had a Capital Gains Tax liability in respect of a disposal made by Greenjacket, of property belonging to Greenjacket. If the facts had been exactly the same, save that Greenjacket had been a United Kingdom as opposed to a Manx company, it is doubtful whether the decision would have been the same. However, if the true principle is that the court is seeking to ascertain the true nature of the taxpayer's activities, then it must be that that 'true nature' itself cannot vary depending on whether the intermediate transactions involved United Kingdom or foreign persons. The result is, it is submitted, that the only ways in which *Furniss v Dawson* can be defended are either to say as Lord Keith in *Craven v White* that it depended on its own facts (another way of saying that it was wrongly decided) or to explain it on the same basis as Lord Keith in *Fitzwilliam* or Millet J in *Ensign*. Although the concept of 'disregarding' transactions has often featured in speeches in the House of Lords, it can hardly be said that the House is unanimous in its approach to that issue, or that such a concept has been wholeheartedly endorsed by the whole House. As long as some of their Lordships continue to toe the 'disregarding' line, while some are

---

[93]   At 823; compare Lord Steyn at 827.
[94]   This description was not accepted by Lord Steyn in *IRC v McGuckian* ([1997] 3 All ER 817 at 823–824).

apparently averse to that form of analysis or approach, it might be argued that the debate is still open. This, coupled with the justified criticisms of judicial attempts to so reconstruct the transactions which the parties have entered into, would seem to raise serious questions about the defensibility of the 'disregarding' approach. That being so, it may be that the proper approach to steps inserted for no commercial purpose is not to disregard them or treat them as fiscal nullities, but to treat them as indistinguishable parts of the whole transaction, with no independent existence or effect of their own. And this will only be possible where it is possible in respect of such intermediate steps to say that 'realistically they constituted a single and indivisible whole in which one or more of them was simply an element without independent effect', and where it is 'intellectually possible so to treat them'.[95]

The New Approach: Fixing the Limits

The next question that arises relates to the proper scope of the new approach. It obviously applies to Income Tax and Capital Gains Tax. Is this the correct scope? Interestingly, there has been an attempt in the Court of Appeal to apply the principles of the new approach to a dispute under the Agricultural Holdings Act 1948 which had no tax connotations whatsoever. In *Gisborne v Burton*[96] Dillon LJ referred to the principles established in *Ramsay* and *Furniss v Dawson* and said:

> It seems to be that a similar principle must be applicable wherever there is a preordained series of transactions which is intended to avoid some mandatory statutory provision, even if not of a fiscal nature. You must look at the effect of the scheme as a whole, instead of concentrating on each preordained step individually, and you do not, as it were, blow the whistle at half-time.

Russell LJ, concurring with Dillon LJ, said[97] that he had not derived 'a lot of assistance' from the tax avoidance cases. However, he 'gratefully' acknowledged their theme - 'that where there are a number of transactions creating a composite whole the court should be astute not to consider the

[95]   Per Lord Keith in *Fitzwilliam v IRC* [1993] BTC at 8014; compare his Lordship at 8016.
[96]   [1988] 3 All ER 760 at 765; distinguished in *Hilton v Plustitle Ltd.* [1988] 3 All ER 1051 (CA).
[97]   [1988] 3 All ER 760 at 774.

individual transactions in isolation but should look at the overall result of what is achieved.'

It is rather astonishing that a principle which was developed in response to a specific problem - off-the-shelf artificial tax avoidance schemes - can be extended in this way.[98] If this were to be followed, it would amount to a dangerous and unwarranted escalation of judicial activism. Apart from the fact that it is not legitimate to take principles developed in response to one thing and then bolt those principles onto other unrelated areas, the *Ramsay/Dawson* principle bears no analogy with non-tax cases unless certain parts of it are to be taken out of context. It is well enough to refer to a preordained series of transactions which should then be considered as a whole. This however is only half of the cake. The analysis abandons the second limb of the new approach - that there should be steps inserted for no commercial purpose other than to avoid tax, in which case the inserted steps are treated as fiscal nullities. This is where the analogy breaks down. The second limb of the new approach only makes sense in the context of tax cases and therefore it is not clear how the *Ramsay/Dawson* principle can correctly be applied to non-tax cases. It is difficult to fault the approach of Ralph Gibson LJ (dissenting) in *Gisborne v Burton* whereby he was unconvinced that the principles of the tax avoidance cases are applicable to 'the construction and enforcement of a transaction in private law between private citizens'.[99]

In any event, the House of Lords seems not to be too keen to extend the new approach beyond Income and Capital Gains Tax. In *Fitzwilliam v IRC*[100] Lord Browne-Wilkinson referred to the provisions in the Capital Transfer (now Inheritance) Tax legislation which render taxable dispositions effected by associated operations. He said that the provisions amounted to a statutory enactment, 'in much wider terms', of the *Ramsay* principle, and that, accordingly, it could be argued 'that there is no room for the court to adopt the *Ramsay* approach in construing an Act which expressly provides for the circumstances and occasions on which transfers carried through by 'associated operations' are to be taxed'. He however felt that it was not necessary to express any concluded view on the point at this time.[101]

The point raised by Lord Browne-Wilkinson is pertinent. It raises the question whether, if statute already covers the field, rules of common law on the same subject can still be applicable. This question has arisen in other areas of law, for example, in respect of the interaction between the royal prerogative and statute. In that context, the principle is that, where

---

[98]   For example, in *Fitzwilliam v IRC* [1993] BTC 8003 at 8037, Lord Browne-Wilkinson said that the *Ramsay* principle is essentially based on the construction of statutory taxing provisions.
[99]   At 772.
[100]   [1993] BTC at 8037.
[101]   Ibid.

Parliament legislates in an area previously covered by prerogative powers, the prerogative powers will for the time being be superceded by the statute.[102] Perhaps this is the analogy being drawn here by Lord Browne-Wilkinson. With respect to statutory anti-avoidance rules, the same approach was adopted in Australia, where the the High Court of Australia rejected the *Ramsay* principle on the basis that the statutory rule already covers the field.[103]

One might approach this question in the same way, and say that once Parliament has legislated in an area formerly covered by judicial doctrines, those judicial doctrines will be taken to have been superceded by statute and will become inapplicable *in toto*. Another approach would be that the judicial doctrines would give way to statute, but can lurk in the background as a residual force to be brought into effect if the statutory provision is later found to have gaps. A third approach would be that both the statutory scheme and the judicial doctrines would exist and apply side-by-side.[104]

The last two approaches would be problematic in that two different sets of rules may then potentially or actually govern the same situation. The first approach would seem preferable, not least because it is an approach which has already been adopted by the House of Lords in respect of a similar question (prerogatives versus statute), and by Commonwealth courts in respect of the same question (*Ramsay* versus statutory anti-avoidance rules). It would also be preferable because only one set of rules (the statutory scheme) would cover the situation, leading to certainty. Furthermore, this would be in line with two fundamental principles: the supremacy of Parliament; and the fact that taxation and taxation policy are a matter for Parliament, not the courts.

Tax Mitigation

In some jurisdictions the concept of 'tax mitigation' has been developed. The development in those jurisdictions is often explicit, entitling taxpayers to the tax benefits of their transactions only if those transactions are genuine, in the sense that the taxpayer has actually suffered the loss which entitles him or her to the tax benefits. In those circumstances the taxpayer would deserve, or would have earned, the tax benefits. In an appeal from one such jurisdiction (New Zealand) the Privy Council had the opportunity to consider

---

[102] See *A-G v De Keyser's Royal Hotel* [1920] AC 508; generally, A.W. Bradley and K.D. Ewing, Constitutional and Administrative Law, 12th edn., pages 281-282 (Addison Wesley Longman, 1997).

[103] See *John v FCT* (1989) 166 CLR 417, esp. at 434-435. For comment, see P Harris (1998) BTR 124; compare the Canadian Supreme Court in *Stubart Investments Ltd v The Queen* [1948] CTC 294 (see Estey J at 305).

[104] Lord Cooke in *IRC v McGuckian* ([1997] 3 All ER at 830) said that the *Ramsay* approach does not depend on the type of general anti-avoidance provisions found in Australasia, but is 'antecedent to or collateral with them'. (For a critical view of this statement, see H. Appleton (1999) BTR 86 at 90-91).

this term. In *Commissioner of Inland Revenue v Challenge Corporation Ltd*[105] Lord Templeman said that tax mitigation occurs when a tax payer:

> reduces his income or incurs expenditure in circumstances which reduce his assessable income or entitle him to reduction in his tax liability ... the taxpayers advantage is not derived from an 'arrangement' but from the reduction of income which he accepts or the expenditure which he incurs.

Increasingly, this concept has crept into United Kingdom tax law. In *Ensign Tankers (Leasing) Ltd v Stokes*, Lord Templeman, who often appears to have a crusade against tax avoidance, seemed to be better disposed to tax mitigation. He took the view that there was 'nothing magical about tax mitigation whereby a taxpayer suffers a loss or incurs expenditure in fact as well as in appearance'.[106] He gave the example of 'bed and breakfast' transactions of selling and repurchasing shares, and said that a taxpayer who carries out such a transaction establishes a loss for Capital Gains Tax 'because he has actually suffered that loss at the date of the transaction'. The idea is that tax mitigation is good and acceptable (and perhaps always so), because there is nothing artificial about it. This means, according to Lord Goff in *Ensign*[107], that 'there is a fundamental difference between tax mitigation and unacceptable tax avoidance', because tax avoidance involves a great degree of artificiality, and is no more than a raid on public funds at the expense of the general body of taxpayers. On the other hand, tax mitigation involves a loss to the pocket of the individual taxpayer, who then is entitled to claim relief for that loss.

It is interesting that no distinction is made (if one exists) between 'acceptable tax avoidance' and tax mitigation. The key to tax mitigation obviously lies in its genuine, non-artificial nature, and it would seem that Lord Templeman and Lord Goff equate it with a permitted planning or ordering of one's affairs. This ordering of one's affairs may at first appear to be similar to that referred to in Lord Tomlin's *dictum* in the *Westminster* case. However, the 'ordering of affairs' that Lord Tomlin was referring to was a description of acceptable tax avoidance. Logically this invites a conclusion that acceptable tax avoidance and tax mitigation are the same and are to be distinguished from tax evasion, and unacceptable (artificial) tax avoidance. This 'logic' might, for the moment, be disturbed by suggesting that 'acceptable' tax avoidance and tax mitigation are distinct and separate concepts because of the latter's insistence that the taxpayer 'suffers' in fact as well as in appearance. However, if one points to the decision at the very

---

[105]   [1987] 1 AC 155 at 167. For comment see D. Nicoll (1987) BTR 134.
[106]   [1992] BTC at 124.
[107]   At 128.

heart of acceptable tax avoidance (the *Westminster* case), one can see that the taxpayer did 'suffer' in fact and in appearance. The covenant was for seven years, irrespective of the length of employment of the gardener. Thus, the gardener was entitled to receive the covenanted sum for the covenanted period, even if his employment had terminated within that period. The Duke had, in fact, 'suffered' this obligation to pay the covenanted amount. He might be regarded, therefore, as having earned his tax benefit. This is perhaps what led Lord Templeman to say in *Ensign Tankers (Leasing) Ltd v Stokes*[108] that subsequent events have shown that although Lord Tomlin's dictum in the *Westminster* case 'is accurate so far as tax mitigation is concerned it does not apply to tax avoidance.'

McGuckian

The statement of Lord Templeman that was just referred to indicates that the *Westminster* case can still be considered a good starting point for any debate on tax planning. Whether *Westminster* is actually an example of tax mitigation or of 'acceptable' tax avoidance is a matter for debate. Possibly, it is an example of both. A more thorny question concerns the proper resting point for a discussion on tax planning. As far as the judicial anti-avoidance doctrines are concerned, a strong temptation, which we have succumbed to, is to rest the discussion at the point of the latest leaders from the House of Lords.

IRC v McGuckian[109] is the most recent leading case decided on the subject by the Lords. In this case the taxpayers (Mr and Mrs McGuckian) were resident and domiciled in the United Kingdom, and owned all the shares in an Irish company, B Ltd. The Irish company had reserves of profits, amounting to Ir£400,055, which were available for distribution as dividends. Payment of such dividends directly to the taxpayers would have attracted an immediate charge to income tax. They thus took the advice of a tax consultant and embarked on a scheme to avoid tax on the dividends. The first step was to settle all the shares of B Ltd on trust for Mrs McGuckian as the sole income beneficiary. The trustee of the settlement was a Guernsey company, S Ltd. A direct payment of dividends by B Ltd to S Ltd (as trustee and the legal owner of the shares) would have still attracted tax, because the income would have been that of Mrs McGuckian, as a beneficiary who had a vested interest in the trust income. Thus, in furtherance of the scheme, S Ltd assigned its right to receive the dividends from B Ltd to M Ltd, a United Kingdom company associated with the tax consultant, in consideration of a

[108] [1992] BTC at 124.
[109] [1997] 3 All ER 817.

payment of Ir£396,054. B Ltd then declared a dividend of Ir£400,055, and paid it to M Ltd as assignee of the right to receive it. M Ltd, in accordance with the assignment deal, paid Ir£396,054 to S Ltd, which then kept it. The difference between the two amounts was one per cent, and represented fees and commission. The point of the whole scheme was to establish that the payment of Ir£396,054 to S Ltd was a capital sum - the price for the assignment of the right to receive dividends - and so was not chargeable to income tax.

Two weeks before the expiry of the six-year period for raising the necessary assessments, the Revenue raised an assessment under section 478 TA 1970 - an anti-avoidance provision covering situations whereby a transfer of assets by a person ordinarily resident in the United Kingdom results in income being payable to a person resident or domiciled outside the United Kingdom. The Revenue argued that the assignment by S Ltd of its rights to receive the dividends was a step inserted solely for the purpose of gaining a tax advantage, and that it fell to be disregarded under the *Ramsay* principle. According to that argument, the result was that the payment of Ir£396,054 that S Ltd. received was a dividend from B Ltd and it was therefore income. Being income and not capital, received by a person not resident or domiciled in the United Kingdom (S Ltd), it fell to be assessed as the income of the taxpayers under section 478 TA 1970. Both the Special Commissioner and the Court of Appeal in Northern Ireland decided in favour of the taxpayers, but the House of Lords decided in favour of the Revenue.

A number of approaches are discernible from the speeches. Lord Browne-Wilkinson was content to simply apply the *Ramsay/Dawson* principles, which he felt were clearly applicable. According to him[110] the artificial step inserted was the assignment by S Ltd to M Ltd, and that step fell 'to be disregarded in construing the relevant taxing provisions'. His understanding of the *Ramsay* principle was to the effect that statutory provisions had to be applied to 'the substance' of the transaction.[111] Lord Clyde simply applied the provisions of section 478 of TA 1970 (s.739 TA 1988) to the 'substance of the whole transaction'.[112] Here, the effect of the whole transaction was to carry 99 per cent of the dividend to S Ltd, but by a circuitous route. Thus the assessment was correct.

The speeches of Lord Steyn and Lord Cooke were more far reaching. Lord Steyn took on the whole question of the proper approach to the construction of tax statutes. The proper approach was to reject 'pure literalism'.[113] According to him, the *Ramsay* principle was not invented on a juristic basis

110   At 822.
111   At 823.
112   At 831-832.
113   At 824.
114   At 825.

independent of statute, but was rather developed as a matter of statutory construction.[114]

Even in this context, it was not based on 'a linguistic analysis of the meaning of particular words in a statute', but on a 'broad purposive interpretation, giving effect to the intention of Parliament'. Therefore, the *Ramsay* principle was based on an 'orthodox form of statutory interpretation'. Lord Steyn said that in asserting the power to examine 'the substance' of a composite transaction, the House was simply rejecting formalism and choosing 'a more realistic analysis'.

As to the current state of the law, there were two points to be made. First, Lord Tomlin's observations in the *Westminster* case still point to 'a material consideration' - the liberty of the citizen to arrange his financial affairs as he thinks fit.[115] However, 'they have ceased to be canonical as to the consequence of a tax avoidance scheme'. Thus, Lord Tomlin's observations might be a good starting point, but they do not tell us much about what would be acceptable. Not only that, all the later decisions on the matter do not tell us the whole story either - thus the issue is still, as it were, 'up for grabs'. This is evident in the statement of Lord Steyn that, in the light of 'the reasoning underlying the new approach it is wrong to regard the decisions of the House of Lords since the *Ramsay* case as necessarily marking the limit of the law on tax avoidance schemes'.[116]

With regard to the present case itself, Lord Steyn said[117] that, while the declaration of the dividend by B Ltd was an ordinary commercial decision, the other steps (the assignment to M Ltd, the payment to M Ltd, and the payment by M Ltd to S Ltd) were not taken for any business or commercial reason, and tax avoidance was the sole reason for those steps. He said that a formalistic view of the individual tax avoidance steps and a literal interpretation of the statute in the spirit of the *Westminster* case could possibly lead to the conclusion that the money that reached S Ltd was capital. However, the court was no longer compelled to look at transactions in blinkers, and literalism had given way to purposive interpretation.[118] In the present case, he felt that the objective of the composite transaction was that S Ltd should receive the dividend. It was a classic case for the *Ramsay* principle, and the steps involving M Ltd should be disregarded for fiscal purposes. Accordingly, the 'end result' was the receipt by S Ltd of 99 per cent of the dividend as income.

For Lord Cooke of Thorndon the matter was quite straightforward. He said that one only had to recount the facts to see that what was received by S

[114]   At 825.
[115]   Compare Neuberger J in *Girvan v Orange Personal Communications Services Ltd.* [1998] BTC 181 at 201.
[116]   Ibid.
[117]   At 826.
[118]   At 827.
[119]   At 828.

Ltd. was essentially income. According to him the dividend was intended to be for the benefit of S Ltd., the 'circular route' whereby the payment was made was merely 'machinery' for giving effect to that intention, the assignment was created as a bridge or vehicle for attaining that end, and the money was unmistakably traceable through a single link.[119]

Lord Cooke, like Lord Steyn, felt that the principle of looking at a planned series of steps as one whole transaction was perfectly natural and orthodox - and it was 'decidedly more natural and less extreme than the decision which in 1935 a majority of their Lordships felt forced to reach in the Duke of Westminster's case'.[120]

Thus he could understand why the House was unwilling to carry the *Westminster* decision any further in *Ramsay*. The *Ramsay* principle was interpreted by him to be an application to taxing statutes of the general approach to statutory interpretation whereby, in determining the natural meaning of particular expressions in their context, weight is to be given to the purpose and spirit of of the legislation.[121] Lord Cooke took the view that the present case fell within the 'limitations' specified by Lord Brightman in *Furniss v Dawson*, but added that, if the ultimate question is always the true bearing of a particular provision on a particular set of facts, then those limitations cannot be universal, and one must always go back to 'the discernible intent of the taxing Act'.[122] Thus, as far as the judicial responses to tax avoidance were concerned, 'the journey's end may not yet have been found'.

Looking at these speeches, the following emerge. The court is entitled to look to the 'substance' of a composite transaction[123] and to disregard any artificial steps inserted for no commercial purpose other than tax avoidance.[124] The court is entitled to adopt a 'purposive' interpretation - meaning that it is entitled to examine the purpose and intention of the relevant legislation.[125] And, the answer to the question 'where will it all end?' is very much open[126] - leaving the courts plenty of room to take their anti-avoidance doctrines as far as they wish. This is regrettable, as it is arguable that they have already taken it much too far.

The issue of disregarding certain transactions emerges here again with all its problems. As applied in this case, it raises as many questions as it answers. For example, their Lordships all concentrated on the assignment by S Ltd to M Ltd of its rights to receive dividends as being the artificial step inserted for no commercial purpose which should therefore be disregarded. This is rather odd. In a straightforward transaction without any fiscal

---

[119]   At 828.
[120]   At 829.
[121]   At 829-830.
[122]   At 830.
[123]   Lord Browne-Wilkinson at 823; Lord Steyn at 825; Lord Clyde at 832.
[124]   Lord Browne-Wilkinson at 822 and 823; Lord Steyn at 827.
[125]   Lord Steyn at 825; Lord Cooke at 830.
[126]   Lord Steyn at 825; Lord Cooke at 830.

considerations, B Ltd would simply have paid the dividends that it was waiting to declare directly to Mr and Mrs McGuckian. The whole point of every single step that transpired as an alternative to this straightforward payment was to convert any dividend into capital. The first step in this process was to settle the shares of B Ltd in a Guernsey trust of which S Ltd was trustee. There was no commercial purpose for that first step, or indeed, any of the other steps that followed. The step of creating the Guernsey settlement was no less artificial than the step of assigning the right to receive the dividends. On this analysis, the whole scheme from the beginning to the end should have been disregarded, leaving us with an 'end result' which is a straightforward payment of a dividend by B Ltd to Mr and Mrs McGuckian. Now, this is of course not what happened in the real world - but neither is the 'end result' reached by the House of Lords. What the House of Lords did was a selective disregarding of transactions - but the analysis being put forward now has the virtue of actually looking at the whole scheme (from the first to the last step), as opposed to only a part or subset of the whole scheme (from the assignment of the right to the dividends to the last   step).

The fallacy of fixating on a subset only of the whole scheme had been pointed out by Lord Browne-Wilkinson himself in *Fitzwilliam v IRC*.[128] That case involved a five-step scheme. Clearly, steps two to five were 'pre-ordained', but only after step one had been taken. Thus the Revenue sought to claim tax under what Lord Browne-Wilkinson described as a 'mini-Ramsay', i.e., that steps two to five (leaving out step one) formed a pre-ordained series of transactions. According to Lord Browne-Wilkinson, the Revenue by seeking to set up a 'mini-Ramsay' were attempting to attach fiscal consequences to all or some of the steps two to five, but his view that it was not legitimate to attach fiscal consequences to artificial transactions designed to carry out the real transaction in question just because an attempt to demonstrate that steps one to five constituted one transaction failed for some extraneous reason i.e. that they were not pre-ordained prior to step one.

Yet, what the House of Lords, including Lord Browne-Wilkinson himself, have done and have allowed the Revenue to do in *IRC v McGuckian* is to create a 'mini-Ramsay', also by leaving the first step out of consideration when examining the whole scheme. Thus the Revenue were able to attach fiscal consequences to one of the artificial transactions (the transfer of the shares in B Ltd. into the Guernsey settlement with S Ltd. as trustee) while treating as a fiscal nullity one of the artificial transactions (the assignment,

[128]   [1993] BTC 8003 at 8036.

by S Ltd, of the right to receive dividends, to M Ltd), while also miraculously omitting to treat, for the purposes of the application of the *Ramsay* principle, the transfer of the shares to S Ltd as part of the whole scheme. This rather odd result has of course just set a precedent for the Revenue brazenly to apply 'mini-*Ramsays*' whenever it suits them.

The question might be asked what the difference would be if the analysis had been adopted that, if anything was to be disregarded in this case, it had to be every step, starting from the transfer of the shares into the settlement, and ending with the receipt by S Ltd of payment from M Ltd. The simple answer is that the assessment under section 478 TA 1970 would then not have been valid. That section depends on there having been a transfer of assets, the result of which is that income becomes payable to a non-resident or non-domiciled person. If all the artificial steps in the case were disregarded for tax purposes, then no transfer of assets (shares to the Guernsey trustee, S Ltd) would be deemed to have taken place, and no income would be deemed to have become payable to an overseas person. This would leave the Revenue with an assessment which could not be upheld, and (in the absence of fraud or negligence on the taxpayer's part[127]) with no further recourse. Any new assessment would have been out of time, seeing that the original assessment under section 478 TA 1970 had been raised just in the nick of time. It is unlikely that this analysis would have escaped their Lordships, and so one can only speculate as to why they opted for a 'mini-Ramsay' and the selective disregarding of part of a subset of a partitioned scheme.

A General Anti-avoidance Rule?

The United Kingdom's judicial anti-avoidance doctrines are the direct result of the absence of a general anti-avoidance rule in the United Kingdom.[128] This type of rule exists in New Zealand, and was referred to briefly by Lord Cooke in *IRC v McGuckian*.[129] It also exists in Australia,[130] Canada,[131] and Holland.[132]

Judicial anti-avoidance doctrines of the type now being applied in the United Kingdom are objectionable[133] for four reasons:

---

[127]   See s.36 TMA 1970; *Re McGuckian* [1999] BTC 152.
[128]   See generally, Ward et. al. 'The Business Purpose Test and Abuse of Rights' (1985) BTR 68.
[129]   [1997] 3 All ER at 830.
[130]   See generally, P Harris (1998) BTR 124.
[131]   See generally, I Roxam (1998) BTR 140; B J Arnold (1995) BTR 541.
[132]   See generally, E van Der Stok (1998) BTR 150.
[133]   Contrast P. Gillett, 'The consultative document on a general anti-avoidance rule for direct taxes - a view from business' (1999) BTR 1 at 5: 'What constitutes acceptable and unacceptable tax planning is in my view a matter for the courts to determine, in accordance with the social and political mores of the time. It is far too complex and judgmental an area for it to be established with any degree of certainty by statute'; compare I. Roxam (1998) BTR

(a) The courts are now purporting (with their 'purposive' interpretations) to be seeking to apply the intention or purposes of legislation - however, Parliament has not shown the tendency towards a general anti-avoidance rule - which is arguably what the *Ramsay* principle, especially as construed in *IRC v McGuckian* amounts to.[134]

(b) The question of the proper response of a jurisdiction to tax avoidance is a matter of taxation policy, for the Treasury and the tax authorities, and, ultimately, Parliament[135] - not a matter for the judiciary, which is not subject to any political control, and which is not accountable to the taxpayers or the electorate for its policy choices.

(c) Issues of tax policy are not the types of issues that should be developed on an *ad hoc* or case-by-case basis, subject to conflicting formulations by different judges, as judicially developed policy is bound to be.

(d) The judiciary has no mandate to develop this type of policy and the forensic process whereby it is developed does not allow for the fullest range of consultation to be carried out, or for the fullest range of relevant information to be admitted.[136]

Obviously, tax avoidance is a matter of concern to the Revenue, but while the judicial anti-avoidance doctrines have continued to favour them, they have not always had the incentive to press for a general anti-avoidance legislation. To its credit, the current Labour Government has indicated a desire to introduce wide legislative provisions in this area following a period of consultation.[137] Such legislation would arguably be preferable to the kind of judicial activism that has been seen on the issue in recent times. The Tax Law Review Committee in its Report on Tax Avoidance favoured such a rule.[138] However, others are not convinced, taking the view that a general anti-avoidance rule is likely to introduce uncertainty into the law.[139]

The Labour Government has in accordance with its earlier promise published a consultative document on a general anti-avoidance direct taxes, but initial reactions have not been very positive.[140]

Although the United Kingdom does not currently have any general anti-avoidance provision, the legislature has at times recognised potential planning and avoidance 'loopholes' in statutory provisions and has sought

---

[134]   For a debate about the constitutionality of the *Ramsay* principle, see R. T. Bartlett (1985) BTR 338. 140 at 148.

[135]   For some interesting implications of this, see D. Wilde (1995) BTR 137.

[136]   For an analysis of the types of issues involved in the development and implementation of tax policy, thereby arguably making it an inappropriate task for the courts, see S. James and C. Nobes, 'The Economics of Taxation', pages 115-120.

[137]   For comment, see 'Tax ploy warning', Accountancy Age (1997) 4 July, p5.

[138]   For comment see H. McKay (1998) BTR 86.

[139]   See for example C. Masters (1994) BTR 647.

[140]   See for example, P. Gillett (1999) BTR 1; E Troup (1999) BTR 5.

to take anti-avoidance measures in relation to those, actual or potential, loopholes[141].

These anti-avoidance measures are limited in their application and they are broadly of two types. The first type applies irrespective of the intentions or motives of the taxpayer, while the second type only applies when it is shown that there exists a tax avoidance motive behind the transaction. Included in the first type of provision are those contained in the Taxes Act 1988, Part XV (ss.660A-694). These apply to 'settlements' and are discussed in the chapter on Trusts and Settlements. Examples of the second type of provision can be found in Part XVII of the Taxes Act 1988. These include the provisions in Sections 703-709 which are designed to counteract tax avoidance schemes in relation to certain transactions in securities. Sections 703-709 recognise the tax benefits and potential in relation to activities relating to the distributable assets of a company, but declare that those benefits cannot be enjoyed unless the person concerned can show that the transaction was carried out for either *bona fide* commercial reasons or in the ordinary course of making or managing investments and obtaining a tax advantage was not one of the main objects of the transactions (s.703(1)). Another example of the second type is section 739 TA 1988 (s.478 TA 1970), the effect of which we have already seen in *IRC v McGuckian*.[142]

---

[141]   An example of this process can be found in the March Budget, 1993, when the Chancellor announced that he intended to '... close a number of loopholes which have been exploited to avoid tax.' Those loopholes related to the Business Expansion Scheme and to some Corporation Tax matters.

[142]   See also R. K. Ashton (1990) BTR 251.

Index

short term political 16

social and economic
views 15-6

special interest groups 15

deductible expenses 102-6

deduction at source 281-6

failure to deduct 289-91

anti-avoidance provisions 291

Finance Act 1988 290-1

parties and revenue 289

payer and recipient 289

non-deduction 286 *et seq*

agreements 287

formulae 287

'free of tax' 288

section 348 285-6

section 349 286

discounts 262-3

domestic expenditure 214-6

food 217-8

medical expenses 218-21

travelling expenses 221

duality of purpose 209-14

employment income Ch 4 *passim*

emoluments 81-90

inducements 84-6

restrictive covenants 88

rewards and gifts 86-8

variation/termination of
employment 88-90

fringe benefits 90-102

office or employment 78-81

European Union 18-20

expenses 102 *et seq*

concessions 109

deductible 102-6

domestic expenditure 214 *et seq*

entertainment 108

other 106-8

necessarily incurred 107

performance duties 106-7

'wholly and exclusively' 107-8

Finance Bill 1992 20

fringe benefits 90-102

beneficial loans 99

cars and fuel 100-1

convertibility 91-3

'higher paid employees' 95-101

benefits 96-9

expenses 96

living accommodation 99

scholarships 101

living accommodation 93-4

mobile phones 101

shareholdings 101-2

vouchers and tokens 94-5